VERSE DRAMA I
1900–2015

Irene Morra is Reader in English Literature at Cardiff University, UK. She has published widely in literature, music, drama and cultural history and is the author of *Twentieth-century British Writers and the Rise of Opera in Britain* (2007); *Britishness, Popular Music, and National Identity: The Making of Modern Britain* (2014); and editor, with Rob Gossedge, of *The New Elizabethan Age: Culture, Society and National Identity after World War II* (2016).

VERSE DRAMA IN ENGLAND, 1900–2015

ART, MODERNITY AND THE NATIONAL STAGE

Irene Morra

Series Editors: Patrick Lonergan and Kevin J. Wetmore, Jr

Bloomsbury Methuen Drama
An imprint of Bloomsbury Publishing Plc

B L O O M S B U R Y
LONDON • OXFORD • NEW YORK • NEW DELHI • SYDNEY

Bloomsbury Methuen Drama

An imprint of Bloomsbury Publishing Plc

Imprint previously known as Methuen Drama

50 Bedford Square   1385 Broadway
London   New York
WC1B 3DP   NY 10018
UK   USA

www.bloomsbury.com

**BLOOMSBURY, METHUEN DRAMA and the Diana logo are trademarks of
Bloomsbury Publishing Plc**

First published 2016

© Irene Morra, 2016

British Library Cataloguing-in-Publication Data
A catalogue record for this book is available from the British Library.

ISBN: HB: 978-1-4725-8014-6
        PB: 978-1-4725-8013-9
        ePDF: 978-1-4725-8016-0
        ePub: 978-1-4725-8015-3

Library of Congress Cataloging-in-Publication Data
A catalog record for this book is available from the Library of Congress.

Series: Critical Companions

Cover photo: *King Charles III* by Bartlett; (l–r) Adam James;
Oliver Chris; Richard Goulding; Directed by Rupert Goold;
London UK; 2014 © Johan Persson/Arena PAL

Typeset by RefineCatch Limited, Bungay, Suffolk

To my peeps

CONTENTS

ACKNOWLEDGEMENTS

I am very grateful to those who have supported this project in its various stages. Particular thanks to the Ronald Duncan Literary Foundation, for their enthusiasm, helpfulness and financial support of a much-needed period of intensive research. The Institute of English Studies and the University of Toronto were both very generous in enriching that period of research with visiting fellowships. And a most heartfelt thank-you, as ever, to my family – for their patience, their humour, and their unlimited supply of sustenance in every way.

INTRODUCTION
MODERN VERSE DRAMA IN ENGLAND: THE FORGOTTEN TRADITION

Let's be honest, neither 'verse-drama' nor 'poetic theatre' has an alluring ring, does it? . . . I refuse to believe it's just me who hears the words 'poetic drama' and first imagines something slowly woven from pastel shades of twee. It has an identity problem.[1]

Drama in verse occupies a vexed position in contemporary England, both on the mainstream national stage and in the historiography of modern British theatre. In 2003, Charles Spencer derided Joanna Laurens's *Five Gold Rings* in *The Daily Telegraph* for having 'set off down the same blind alley that lured T.S. Eliot and Christopher Fry'.[2] Three years later, he lamented of Michael Frayn's *Afterlife*, 'Oh God, can things get any worse? / Another play in needless verse'.[3] The National Theatre had made the relatively unprecedented decision to stage two verse dramas within one year; Tony Harrison's *Fram* also received scathing reviews that apportioned primary blame to the poet's decision to write in rhyming verse. Later that year, Glyn Maxwell's *Liberty* opened at Shakespeare's Globe to a similar reception. As *Guardian* writer Lyn Gardner has observed, today, 'verse drama, even in the broad church of theatre, is vilified': 'although audiences like theatre that is poetic, we prefer it if it isn't actually written in verse – unless, of course, it's by Shakespeare. One poet in the national drama is, it seems, quite enough.'[4] The strength of this pervading conviction is such that when London's Almeida Theatre staged Mike Bartlett's *King Charles III* in 2014, advance publicity made no mention of its having been written in blank verse.

As these receptions only begin to suggest, verse drama is today seen at best as an anomaly, as an amusing embrace of anachronistic whimsy – and at worst as a regressive self-indulgence fundamentally opposed both to the essential demands of theatre and to the contemporary reality of the modern audience. Such perceptions are not new: in 1919, poet Wilfred Wilson Gibson acknowledged 'a commonplace of newspaper criticism' that 'poetic-drama has a past – a superb and unsurpassable past – but no possible future'.[5] In 1924, Halcott Glover's ambitiously titled *Drama and Mankind: A Vindication and a Challenge* confidently assumed that verse drama 'connote[s] to many a succession of dreary exercises in blank verse.'[6] In 1932, the literary critic Desmond MacCarthy adopted an extended tone of exasperation:

> Yet of living poets, how many either have spent, are spending, or hope to spend their time, gifts and emotions on this thankless form? ... All I wish to do is ask the question: 'Why choose as the repository of your ideas and fine emotion a form for which the great majority of literary people, and all unliterary people, many of whom are, as we know, capable of being moved by poetry, have an almost invincible distaste?'[7]

The critical, popular and commercial success of T.S. Eliot and Christopher Fry in the 1940s may well be assumed to have quelled such assumptions. Nonetheless, in 1955, Fry himself was to observe that 'there are many people to whom verse in the theatre is an irritating, or boring, or distracting, or pretentious flight of fashion ... This point is not held so strongly about literature in general.'[8]

The validity of Fry's observation is today reflected in the relatively marginal treatment of verse drama in mainstream critical and academic studies, which in the main confine any discussion of a modern verse drama to the works of Eliot, Fry and occasionally W.H. Auden. Typically disregarding the verse drama of the first decades of the century entirely, most see Eliot and Fry as emblematic of 'a relatively short-lived trend ... which flourished for a time in the late 1940s and early 1950s'.[9] This trend 'never *threatened* to become a dominant theatrical form' [italics mine].[10] According to Arnold P. Hinchliffe, 'if it were not for Eliot's "success" in the commercial theatre it would not be necessary to treat the subject of verse drama in our modern period seriously'.[11] Such serious treatments, however, are limited by a tendency to associate that moment of success with what Simon Trussler identifies as 'the false dawn of poetic drama'.[12] A.T. Tolley identifies an 'apparently impressive achievement' in the 'revival of verse drama' in the 1940s, only to conclude that it 'seems now a misdirection rather than a new start'.[13] In his history of the modern British stage, Christopher Innes goes further: verse drama 'has found little resonance ... since the 1890s'; it had become 'recognizably artificial by the mid-Nineteenth Century'.[14] Acknowledging an exception in the dramas of W.B. Yeats, Fry and Eliot, he differentiates between drama in verse and poetic drama to conclude that the modern 'language of "poetic drama" has not been verbal': 'poetry OF the theatre replaced poetry IN the theatre (Cocteau)'.[15]

This differentiation is not new. In 1924, Glover had argued that all true drama is 'poetic', defining poetry as 'that vision which in more or less degree embraces mankind as a whole'.[16] In *On Poetry and Drama* (1937), Harley Granville Barker writes from the perspective of an actor, director and playwright open to contemporary explorations. Recognizing the challenge faced by poet-dramatists in England, he identifies a new tradition of verse drama, 'freed' from the 'mere formula' implicit in Glover's assessment of contemporary blank verse, now 'equally and integrally valid both as drama and as poetry'.[17] He also, however, asserts that the exemplary 'Poetic Drama' is 'not simply drama written in verse'.[18] While 'drama' itself is relatively easy to define, '"Poetry" is treacherous ground. I mean by it, of course, far more than verse, which, admittedly, is only one of the garments in which poetry is clothed'.[19] Both Glover and Barker (like many others) use 'poetry' as a term through which to define an ideal of drama that can exist independently from dramatic expression in verse. Barker saw the potential of verse drama to act within that ideal. Glover, however, identified only a regressive attempt to replicate the achievements of an Elizabethan theatre distinct from contemporary sensibilities. The contemporary age is one of prose, and prose is thus 'the proper medium for the theatre': 'if the day should come when in our streets and taverns we think poetically, a verse will return to our theatres in the genius of the language then current.'[20]

In the first half of the century, the term 'poetic drama' could often signify a theatre whose profound treatment of dramatic subject and character contested the superficial, commercial interests of the mainstream stage. For Barker, for example, that definition of stage poetry can be applied equally to the works of Maurice Maeterlinck, Henrik Ibsen and J. M. Barrie; *Peter Pan*, he declared, 'will take its place in the history of that period of our drama as the pre-eminent poetic play'.[21] In subsequent decades, the term has often connoted a drama that defies – usually through symbolism, mythical subject, or a self-conscious theatricality – an association of realist staging and contemporary social argumentation with the dramatization of human experience and reality. For many, this aesthetic is not dependent on the use of verse. Indeed, in one of the first major academic studies of verse drama (1959), Denis Donoghue concluded that a play is poetic 'when its concrete elements (plot, agency, scene, speech, gesture) continuously exhibit in their internal relationships those qualities of mutual coherence and illumination required of the words of a poem'.[22] In the most recent full-length study (1989), Glenda Leeming argues that poetic drama has evolved to accommodate various non-representational techniques hitherto signified by the use of verse alone:

> a dramatist writing now is free to choose from among these techniques without fear of limiting himself to the avant-garde or festival audience; and one of the techniques he can – but need not – choose is verse dialogue.[23]

In implicit support, Innes subtitles his section on poetic drama as 'verse, fantasy, and symbolic images': he includes within his discussion such prose dramatists as John Whiting, Peter Shaffer and Sarah Kane.

Such assessments do much to expand the definition of poetic drama and poetry more generally. So, too, do those readings of plays whose enigmatic, carefully structured, or rhythmic prose can apparently be likened to verse itself. In 1975, director Peter Hall perceived a poetic rhythm and pattern in the work of Samuel Beckett and Harold Pinter:

> I actually believe that [they] are poetic dramatists in the proper sense of the word: they have a linear structure and a formal structure which you'd better just observe – don't learn it wrong, don't speak it wrong, you can't, you mustn't.[24]

While Hall identifies a dramatic poetry akin to free verse, others have deemed any deliberate affinity with verse to be marginal, if not irrelevant, to the definition of poetic drama itself. As Hinchcliffe asserts in *Modern Verse Drama*, 'Eliot's belief that a craving for poetic drama is permanent in human nature is probably true. But only a poet would have assumed that such drama must be in verse.'[25] Beckett, Edward Bond, Pinter and Kane are now often associated with a 'poetic' drama marked by situations and dialogue that seem simultaneously to represent and figuratively transform a vaguely familiar reality: Tolley concludes that 'the forties produced nothing so intrinsically or cohesively poetic as Samuel Beckett's *Endgame* (1958), a work of prose.'[26] Bond himself argues that the 'grammar of poetry' derives not from syntax but from metaphor, from the need of the 'inner person' to articulate that self against an imposed, repressive, reality: 'the problem of poetry in drama is to find a context (event, situation etc.) in which the characters need poetry', where 'the psyche must re-express itself in new language.'[27] This new language is poetic in its expression of the contemporary self independently of received and inauthentic modes of representation: thus, 'the poetry of the past cant [sic] be imitated – as in pseudo-poetic drama'.[28]

These expansive readings of 'poetry', 'poetry in the theatre' and 'poetic drama' implicitly recuperate what is otherwise critically dismissed as an antiquated, 'twee' and slightly embarrassing tradition with 'an identity problem'. In so doing, however, they also risk overlooking the aesthetic and historical significance of the much more self-conscious emphasis on drama *in verse* that has characterized the work of poet-dramatists from the turn of the twentieth century into the present day. In many respects, in its use of ballad, vaudeville traditions, and popular song, the experimental, post-war political theatre epitomized by the Joan Littlewood Workshop at Stratford East worked to redefine conventional ideas of verse itself – and thus challenge any association of verse drama with 'the deadliest of dead ends'. That challenge has always been somewhat coincidental, however, originating from a theatre more immediately rooted in popular oral traditions than established traditions of versification and poetic drama. In that context, the likelihood of Littlewood's productions, John Arden's *The Workhouse Donkey* (1963), Charles Wood's *H, Being Monologues at Front of Burning Cities* (1969) or debbie tucker green's *random* (2008) being compared to – or comparing themselves to – Fry's *Venus Observed* (1950) or Eliot's *The Cocktail Party* (1949) is somewhat slim.

As the director E. Martin Browne asked in 1947, 'what we really want to know is: can a practising poet, whose usual medium of creative expression is verse, become a successful dramatist in that medium, in our theatre to-day?'[29] Today, the implicit response is that drama in verse is in fact Bond's 'poetry of the past', the 'pseudo-poetic drama' that chooses wilfully to ignore the apparent fact that prose is 'the most flexible weapon the stage has ever had, and still shining new'.[30] To some extent, that assumption is supported by a perception that poetry itself no longer occupies a central position within contemporary valuations of representative national expression and art. It is even further bolstered by the incontrovertible fact that very few dramatists today write exclusively in verse; Maxwell, Harrison, and Peter Oswald are relatively unique in identifying verse *alone* as the primary medium of contemporary theatrical expression. They are also among the few dramatists whose work remains aligned with the more literary origins of an earlier moment, with an instinct towards the development of modern verse itself through theatre.

In the majority of contemporary appraisals, therefore, 'verse drama' has come to connote a literary culture of poetic drama that is essentially distinct from the received trajectory of the modern, post-war stage. Characteristically associated with a willed distance from contemporary realities, with the self-indulgent instincts of published poets, or with interminable attempts to develop a contemporary equivalent to Elizabethan blank verse, it now tends to be dismissed as a marginal, fundamentally outdated curiosity. As this book will argue, however, that assumption overlooks the extent to which the diverse tradition of modern verse drama in England has attempted variously to expand upon, revitalize and redefine the contemporary stage. It also risks overlooking the extent to which the very critical marginalization of that tradition might itself point to an essential conservatism.

The origins of modern verse drama

Any attempt to locate the origins of modern verse drama is immediately confronted with the very diffuse nature of those origins and a diversity of informing aesthetic instincts. It must also contend with the fact that many poet-dramatists had very different appreciations of the practical reality of the stage itself. Indeed, broadly speaking, the beginnings of modern verse drama can be traced to two aesthetic movements, at times distinct from each other and at times complementary. Where some verse drama was bent primarily upon the reform of the contemporary stage, other manifestations were much more focused on the revitalization of contemporary poetry through an essentially literary dramatic form.

As Donoghue observes, no discussion of modern verse drama can '[evade] the nineteenth century. Whether one uses it, as Gordon Bottomley used it, in a pious endeavour to go through it ... or as Mr. Eliot uses it, as something to react against – the thing is still *there*.'[31] For the majority of modern verse dramatists, however, that Victorian 'thing', or spectre, was not manifest in drama, but in poetry. John Masefield's observation that young late Victorians saw themselves as being 'in rebellion against the dominance of Tennyson'[32] addresses Tennyson's poetry rather than his plays. Eliot's essays on poetic drama acknowledge neither Romantic nor Victorian drama; his essay on Swinburne focuses on the verse rather than its relationship to drama.

To the extent that it can be located within this literary poetic movement, the initial flowering of a modern English tradition of verse drama can be traced to the success of the first *Georgian Poetry* anthologies. In 1912, Edward Marsh – civil servant, patron of the arts, translator and all-round polymath – published his first of five such anthologies. Grouping together such writers as Lascelles Abercrombie, Bottomley, W.H. Davies, G.K. Chesterton, Thomas Sturge Moore and D.H. Lawrence, the collection did not make any claims to have identified a coherent aesthetic. Instead, its aim was to create a public audience for a more general spirit of modern poetic creativity. Nonetheless, as Robert H. Ross observes, Marsh 'succeeded, though unwittingly and perhaps unwillingly, in founding a poetic school'.[33] While none of the Georgians were under the illusion of having amongst their number a poet comparable to Dryden, Coleridge or Tennyson, most of them, 'critics and poets alike, agreed in the main with one of their number who claimed that "for mass of good work fit for the anthologies and produced by many hands I do not see any age since the Elizabethan which can compare with ours."'[34] As John Drinkwater – poet, dramatist and the first manager of the Birmingham Repertory Theatre – observed, 'I don't suppose that any new book of verse had created such excitement since the days of Tennyson.'[35] The influence of the anthologies waned over the next decades: in the wake of Eliot and Ezra Pound, the poetry of the Georgians came to be associated with a conservatism and simplistic naïveté in both style and subject. At the time, however, it marked an extremely influential break from the apparent spectre of late Victorianism.

Many of these poets were, as Ross observes, 'intent upon restoring drama to poetry',[36] but not all of them envisioned that restoration in terms of drama itself. The Georgians may have condemned the late Victorians for writing 'exclusively for the study',[37] but many, informed by a strong anti-elitist sensibility, looked to a larger reading public rather than the contemporary stage. It was only with the second *Georgian Poetry* anthology (1915) that the relationship between drama and poetry became tied much more emphatically to dramatic form: the volume saw the publication of Abercrombie's play *The End of the World* (previously published in *New Numbers*, 1914) and Bottomley's *King Lear's Wife*, both of which garnered considerable critical attention. In a letter to Rupert Brooke, Marsh proclaimed *King Lear's Wife* as the 'only one really great literary event' of the year: 'The poetic drama is born again, of that there is no doubt.'[38] In the same year that that 'literary event' was enshrined in the Marsh anthology, the Birmingham Repertory Theatre staged the first production of *King Lear's Wife*. On 19 May 1916, the play was performed at His Majesty's Theatre in London, as part of a fund-raising matinee of 'Georgian plays': the event was attended by various cultural figures and worthies, and Ivor Novello (a friend of Marsh) composed musical settings for two of the songs. In 1926, the play helped to inaugurate the first season of Terence Gray's Festival Theatre in Cambridge. In 1922, the artist

Paul Nash featured his speculative designs and model for *King Lear's Wife* at both the Amsterdam Exhibition of Theatre Arts and Crafts and the International Theatre Exhibition of Designs and Models for the Modern Stage at the Victoria and Albert Museum. The model received acclaim from no less a quarter than the director and designer Edward Gordon Craig, whose review in *The Times* proclaimed it to have been the best at the Amsterdam exhibition.

Nonetheless, *King Lear's Wife* – either as literary event, staged production, or theatrical model – did little to establish a permanent, confident place for verse drama (or Bottomley) on the contemporary stage. It also did little to suggest a coherent movement akin to that which had been signalled for poetry in the publication of *Georgian Poetry*. It did, however, help to translate a modern break from the Victorian poetic legacy into explicitly dramatic terms. Amongst the Georgians, that development continued to be enforced most consistently by Bottomley, who went on to publish numerous plays; most were written specifically for performance. Bottomley's work originated from a strong sense of creative community with his fellow Georgians, particularly with Masefield, Abercrombie and Laurence Binyon, all of whom contributed significantly to the theorisation of drama in verse, both in published plays and in essays.[39] These energies were variously enhanced and complicated by the creative explorations of such poets as Arthur Symons, Clifford Bax and Laurence Housman. Ultimately, the cumulative effect of such activities was to suggest a relatively cohesive, developing instinct amongst poets to realize their literary interest in dramatic structure and form within a nascent tradition of modern drama in verse.

Nonetheless, any attempt to identify in the *Georgian Poetry* anthologies the first evidence of a modern movement in verse drama risks imposing an excessively literary and exclusively national reading onto the historiography of the English stage. It also overlooks one of the most popular and critically-acclaimed poetic dramatists of the twentieth century, now erroneously consigned to an ignominious association with Victorian theatre. Ten years before *King Lear's Wife* was hailed as having initiated the rebirth of an English poetic drama, the commercial plays of Stephen Phillips had been associated with a similar rebirth. Furthermore, the poetic and dramatic impetus for the Georgians had strong roots in the nineteenth-century drama, poetry and theories of Yeats, not to mention the received achievement of the Irish national theatre. Complementing these energies was an established movement, amongst many directors and designers, to revisit and revitalize a larger tradition of poetic drama through the reform of the stage itself. That spirit of reform extended far beyond the writing or staging of poetic drama: the final years of the nineteenth century and the first half of the next saw the publication, production and theorisation of verse drama emerging within a climate dominated by discussions about the New Drama, community and amateur drama, a national theatre and contemporary staging practices. Any attempt to isolate the origins of modern verse drama from that larger context assumes an essentially artificial divide.

Culture of reform

Unsurprisingly, therefore, the diffuse origins of modern verse drama are reflected in works that could often embrace very different ideas of theatre and of the authoring role of the contemporary poet-dramatist. Equally diverse were the ideological assumptions that informed various formulations of an ideal art, poetry and audience. Rather than representing a school of dramatic composition or a coherent genre, the early exponents of a modern drama thus typically reflected a diversity of influences and aesthetic instincts. These instincts ranged from the classically inflected structures and naturalist settings of Gibson and Abercrombie to the increasingly intermedial and symbolist explorations of Yeats, Gray and Bottomley, both in theory and (occasionally limited) practice. Those first years were also marked by an intensive interest in classical Japanese drama: prominent engagements include the experimentations of Yeats and Bottomley with Noh traditions, Binyon's independent interpretation of Noh in the plot and style of the unproduced *Ayuli* (1911) and Masefield's reinvention of *Kanadehon Chūshingura* as a seventeenth-century revenge-tragedy in *The Faithful* (1915).[40] These various enthusiasms existed alongside and occasionally complemented the writing and production of religious drama, the evolution of a socially engaged ideal of community and amateur drama, collaborations between verse dramatists and composers in ballet and music-drama[41] and numerous experimentations in staging and performance.

In the first half of the twentieth century, this creative variety was recognized in relatively mainstream channels, not least in a reviewing culture that engaged with cathedral plays and festivals; stage societies; public lectures and demonstrations of acting and chanting technique; and the various productions of the Mercury Theatre, the Group Theatre, the Liverpool Repertory and the Birmingham Repertory. As Paul Cornwall notes, the coverage of the opening of Gray's Festival Theatre 'was without exaggeration staggering. It seems amazing today that this re-opening of a converted, provincial theatre by two dedicated inexperienced amateurs ... would so excite the theatrical press in London and throughout the land.'[42] In their project to establish a 'national theatre of the air',[43] the BBC commissioned radio dramas in verse by prominent poets. It also televised a production of Eliot's *Murder in the Cathedral* (1935) and of Auden and Christopher Isherwood's *The Ascent of F6* (1938). As further reinforced by the investment of leading directors (Herbert Beerbohm Tree, Barker, Edith Craig), composers (Rutland Boughton, Frederick Delius, Gustav Holst, Benjamin Britten), artists (Charles Ricketts, Charles Shannon, Nash), choreographers (Rupert Doone, Ninette de Valois) and theatre-managers (Barry Jackson, Annie Horniman, Ashley Dukes), drama in verse – both old and new – was recognized as a potential means through which to articulate and develop a much-needed and frequently experimental mode of contemporary theatrical expression.

The very modernity of this 'new' tradition was further suggested by its apparent independence from what, at the turn of the century, was already a barely remembered, rarely acknowledged nineteenth-century heritage of drama in verse. The creative involvement of many well-known Romantic and Victorian literary figures had done very little to promote, reinforce, or establish a prominent tradition of verse drama – either on stage or within the literary culture through which much significant drama continued to be read. Instead, it had done much to establish an often unshakeable association of verse drama with the sensibilities of a literary closet drama and, conversely, with the interests of a spectacle-oriented commercial stage in thrall to a superficial ideal of Shakespearean performance. Noting the creative energies of writers as renowned as Percy Shelley, Lord Byron, William Wordsworth and Charles Lamb in the writing of verse plays, MacCarthy could only conclude:

> Who, except men whose profession it is to know such things, can even tell you the author of the poetic plays, *Halidon Hill* and *The Doom of Devorgoil*? Yet he is not an obscure writer; his name is Walter Scott.[44]

Subsequent appraisals have rarely wavered, and nineteenth-century literary forays by major authors into verse drama continue to languish, relatively forgotten both by theatrical history and literary criticism. As this project contends, however, a similar fate now seems to threaten many of those verse dramatists who, while rarely achieving what might be termed a prominent mainstream status, emerged in the first decades of the twentieth century as active participants within a broader climate of dramatic creativity and reform.

Into oblivion

The contemporary critical fate of verse drama in England can be attributed in no small part to the association of its very renaissance or dawn with Christian drama. By the middle of the century, in large part thanks to Eliot's *Murder in the Cathedral*, verse drama had achieved a prominent mainstream status: as Lambert wryly observes, the play '[broke] out of its Canterbury framework into the world at large, and set many a pen scratching'.[45] It also gave particular strength to an established trend of verse dramatists writing plays on a religious and spiritual theme: works such as Dorothy L. Sayers's *The Zeal of Thy House* (1937), Fry's *The Boy with a Cart* (1938), Charles Williams's *Thomas Cranmer of Canterbury* (1936) and Anne Ridler's *Cain* (1943) engaged explicitly with Christianity in terms that differed from the more individualist, historicizing and social focus that characterized Shaw's *Saint Joan* (1923) or Robert Bolt's *A Man for All Seasons* (1954, rev. 1960). The popularity of these plays encouraged the commissioning of religious drama for broadcast by the BBC, for staging at the Mercury Theatre and for performance at smaller theatres throughout the country. Ultimately, it was through religious drama that the otherwise diffuse movement of poet-dramatists in the first half of the century seemed to achieve an immediately recognizable coherence.

In the 1930s and 1940s, these dramatists could also assume a relationship between content, audience and performance that transferred easily beyond the space of the church or cathedral. That assumption had marked the state support and wartime formation, by E. Martin Browne and Henzie Browne, of the touring company the Pilgrim Players. Necessitated in part by the wartime closing of the theatres and inspired by a recognized need to promote communal morale, the Players were committed to fostering and developing art and a collective sense of identity through theatre. According to Henzie Browne, while some did not always approve of religious plays, their criticism was always superseded by an appreciation of aesthetic diversity and of the larger, collective project:

> We would do religious plays. ... They could and should include comedy and farce, as well as suitable plays from the old mysteries and

their modern counterparts: even liturgical plays to be done in church. Thus every type of audience could share in the repertory.[46]

This presumption that religious drama could appeal to 'every type of audience' barely lasted to the middle of the century: by the end of the 1950s, the majority of aspirational poet-dramatists – including those whose pens may have been 'set scratching' by *Murder in the Cathedral* – had long given up on either a stage or a page for modern verse drama as a whole.

Many who composed religious dramas had in fact been less invested in Christian themes than in the theatrical possibilities that that tradition afforded. The director William Poel, for example, was adamant that his 1901 production of *Everyman* had not seen the play as religious, but 'as a piece of art; if offers a hundred opportunities from the point of view of beauty'.[47] Many were drawn by the creative opportunities of the performance space and definition of audience provided by productions in churches, cathedrals and chapter-houses. Others now critically 'tarnished' with the brush of Anglo-Catholicism or reputed Quakerism (most notably Ronald Duncan and Fry) wrote plays on a diversity of themes and subjects. By the late 1950s, however, the critical climate was such that all verse drama seemed to become associated with Christian themes and consequently with the moralizing tendency of a self-righteous few. Looking back at the brief success and subsequent fate of religious verse drama, theatre critic Harold Hobson concludes: 'the stage is mainly a pagan place . . . in general what [those who are there] embrace is not Christian religion. Politics, certainly; pleasure – perhaps; but religion, no.'[48] By 1977, Hinchliffe would assert with confidence: 'religious verse drama is a coterie theatre and basically irrelevant to the problem of verse in the theatre of our time.'[49]

It was in the 1950s that modern verse drama became rapidly and apparently irredeemably associated with an outdated, exclusionary emphasis on religion. Further enabling that marginalization was the perceived resistance of verse dramatists to the development of the modern national stage – 'the theatre of our time' as increasingly defined within national institutions and critical discourse. As early as 1947, E. Martin Browne had concluded that the success of *Murder in the Cathedral* 'does not prove that verse-drama has regained a place in our theatre; and the few other excursions made with such plays have provided quite insufficient evidence on which to base a conclusion.'[50] As explored in Chapter 7, that perception was effectively solidified in the 1950s and 1960s through the foundation of the National Theatre, the formal establishment of the Royal Shakespeare Company and the received emergence of the English Stage Company at the Royal Court Theatre as the primary site for contemporary, challenging drama. As the actor and director Robert Speaight, well-known for his role as Becket in *Murder in the Cathedral*, observes, 'poetic drama suffered from a very violent change in the public taste—a change which [can be dated] from Osborne's *Look Back in Anger*, in 1956'.[51] In a 1976 interview, Browne conceded that 'the whole verse-drama movement, as we spent our lives on it, has come to an end'.[52] The lasting influence of this moment was such that modern drama in verse now holds little to no quarter within prevailing discussions of a vital national tradition. It has also ensured that subsequent attempts are often assessed as antiquated, old-fashioned anomalies.

National Theatre as English theatre

Notwithstanding the occasional slippage in theatre histories between 'Britain' and 'England', this vexed position is relatively unique to verse drama in England.[53] In Scotland, the negative social and cultural connotations of verse drama never took root, and the development of its modern theatre has been fundamentally independent of the English, London-based ideal now centred around the history of the Royal Court, the National Theatre and the Royal Shakespeare Company. Indeed, Bottomley found the direction of Scottish drama and verse-speaking so much more conducive to his aspirations for poetic drama that he would eventually declare (following a Glasgow production of his play *Gruach*), 'This is my place: I am part of it and belong to it'.[54] As Claude Colleer Abbot notes, in the first decades of the century, Scotland seemed to 'welcome a verse drama when England, as yet, had no room for it'.[55] Those years also saw Marjorie Gullan encouraging the revival of verse-speaking in theatres and schools; Gullan became one of the most influential teachers of choral speaking (in England and Scotland), the author of eight textbooks, a popular reader and lecturer, and co-founder of the Speech Fellowship.[56] The development of Scottish theatre (and the Edinburgh Festival)[57] has characteristically continued to accommodate and encourage a variety of expressive idioms – and the continuous, contemporary vitality of verse drama is today clearly evident in performance and in the works of such dramatists as Liz Lochhead, Edwin Morgan, Douglas Maxwell and David Greig.

Verse drama has also found prominent and extensive support in Wales, particularly in the Welsh language, where the relative dominance of verse in modern dramatic expression has never been challenged. The prolific and influential creativity of Saunders Lewis, George Fisher and Gwenlyn Parry attests to a vibrant, living tradition that has been perpetually encouraged in both publication and production. Outside of Wales, that tradition has been only passingly and inaccurately acknowledged in relation to Dylan Thomas's now-ubiquitous English-language radio-play (only partially written in verse), *Under Milk Wood* (1954). More recently, the productions of the English-language National Theatre Wales, founded in 2009, have been characterized by interpretative verse translations of classical drama and site-specific performances of new verse plays. In 2011, Kaite O'Reilly's contemporary translation of Aeschylus' *The Persians* was awarded the Ted Hughes Award for new poetry; in 2014, the Owen Sheers BBC-commissioned verse play, *Pink Mist* (2013), was awarded Wales Book of the Year. Sheers's poem *Mametz Wood* (2005) provided the inspiration for a 2014 stage production by National Theatre Wales; scripted by Sheers, the production also invoked the war experience and literary legacy of David Jones and Llewelyn Wyn Griffith. In a disarmingly condescending revelation of the fact of 'a great Welsh literary tradition', a *Daily Telegraph* column that year identified Sheers as 'the natural heir to Dylan Thomas's crown'.[58]

This is not to say that English verse dramatists have seen themselves as working within an exclusively national or nationalist framework. The first decades of the century saw a particular enthusiasm for evolving traditions in Ireland and Scotland; as particularly manifest in the dramas of Yeats, those traditions could themselves embrace influences as diverse as the Japanese Noh and the illustrations of Edmund Dulac. The increasing engagement of many English verse dramatists in the middle of the century with developments on the Continent would eventually conflict with an increasingly intransigent, nationalized stage. With the notable exception of contemporary verse translations of Greek and classical French drama, that stage has made very little space for the non-realist, illusionist drama in verse that continues to be promoted from the margins by contemporary poets.

Modern verse drama in England can be no more identified as a coherent tradition than the many disparate and diverse manifestations of prose drama that dominate the contemporary stage. With a few prominent exceptions, however, it tends to be differentiated and dismissed as such, associated as much with consistent ideological assumptions as with an aesthetic adherence to the promotion of poetic verse on the stage. Within that prevailing appraisal, verse drama is marked by a literary tendency towards poetic self-indulgence and an indifference to the very fact of the theatrical stage itself. It is also now associated with an elitism inherently at odds with a modern English national drama that is socially progressive, bent both upon the authentic representation of contemporary society and the perpetuation of its own excellence through a consistent, primarily realist tradition.

This book aims to uncover many of the now-overlooked contributions of many poets to a larger modern history of dramatic writing, production, and theorization in England. In so doing, it inevitably interrogates many of the social and aesthetic presumptions that have come to inform prominent appraisals of the development of the modern English stage. With its origins in a larger movement once acknowledged equally by poets, directors, designers and musicians, twentieth-century verse drama has now been essentially excised from the contemporary historiography of that modern stage. In its exploration of the evolving manifestations and theorizations of modern verse drama in England, in its simultaneous examination of the critical and cultural reception of that drama, this book advocates for a scholarly revaluation of what must be identified as an influential and overlooked tradition of aesthetic challenge and creativity.

This study is divided into eight chapters. The first chapter examines the lingering legacy of the Victorian poetic stage and its presumed influence on the 'smash-hit' plays of Stephen Phillips and James Elroy Flecker's *Hassan* (1922). Phillips, one of the most popular verse dramatists of the early twentieth century, was swiftly and inaccurately consigned thereafter to an ignominious association with melodramatic Elizabethan pastiche. *Hassan* is now associated with the last gasp of the Victorian and Edwardian spectacular. Ultimately, however, both Phillips and Flecker represent two notable, if relatively rare, attempts to modernize verse drama within the mainstream traditions of the commercial stage. In so doing, they contest any simple definition of modern verse drama as a poetic tradition originating exclusively with the Georgians.

The second chapter explores the position of that primarily Georgian movement in relation to a larger climate of dramatic and social reform. In its overview of some key tensions, creative instincts and influential voices within that environment, it also establishes a historical and argumentative context through which to develop the consideration of dominant trends, dramas and dramatists in the chapters that follow. Central to this discussion is the fraught relationship of many verse dramatists with a New Drama often defined by an emphasis on realist staging and social argumentation – and by a much more complementary emphasis on theatrical reform more generally.

The third chapter focuses on some key Georgian dramatists. It begins with an overview of some of the plays and theories of Abercrombie and Drinkwater, then turns to a discussion of the many, seminal projects of Masefield and of their aesthetic relationship with a prevailing social politics focused on 'the people', rooted in ritualistic theatre and oral tradition. It also discusses the frequently vexed relationship between these promoters of a self-consciously modern verse drama and the literary and poetic legacy of Shakespeare – a concern that runs throughout the modern history of English drama in verse. The remainder of the chapter provides a substantial close reading of Bottomley's *King Lear's Wife* in relation to that Shakespearean legacy and to its received position as the first major drama in verse to emerge after Phillips's *Paolo and Francesca* (1900).

The fourth chapter is devoted to a study of the emergence and development of religious verse drama in the church and cathedral. Where *Murder in the Cathedral* is the most well-known of the cathedral plays, Masefield's *The Coming of Christ* (1928) provides an early, important example of an attempt to promote various dramatic and social instincts within what had emerged as a distinct form and theatre-space. As recognized by early exponents of religious drama, as manifest in Masefield's play, that form could be far from conservative in its sense of theatricality and in its promotion of an ideal of communal values and sensibilities. As exemplified by Williams's *The Seed of Adam* (1936) and Sayers's *The Zeal of Thy House*, it could also accommodate very different ideas about verse drama and dramatic tradition more generally in terms of its informing values, its essential origins and its contemporary imperative.

Chapter Five turns to the drama of the 1930s, focusing on the evolution of Eliot's pre-war aesthetic and the diverse theatrical career of Auden. Eliot's drama is often assessed in relation to *Murder in the Cathedral* and the post-war plays. This chapter argues, however, that those works were informed by Eliot's experience with the experimental, often political theatre of the 1930s, particularly the intermedial productions of the Group Theatre. This chapter focuses on the evolution of Eliot's dramatic sensibility in relation to that experience, and particularly in relation to his growing recognition of the musical effect of verse when spoken on stage. The dramas of Auden superficially bear little resemblance to those of Eliot. They were much more open to the political emphasis and collaborative intermediality of the Group Theatre, and the Auden-Isherwood plays in many respects anticipate the experimental initiatives of much post-war political theatre. Nonetheless, the creative trajectory of both poets points to a similar recognition of – and very different response to – the ideological and aesthetic implications of the form.

The following three chapters are focused on the fate of verse drama after the war and on its individual re-inventions in the wake of its changing critical fortunes. Chapter Six is focused on the brief emergence of modern verse drama into the contemporary mainstream. In its close readings of dramas by Anne Ridler and Norman Nicholson alongside those of Eliot and Fry, it exposes the creative diversity and social engagement of that moment. It also advocates for a much closer critical attention to the career of Duncan, whose promotion of Continental theatre and intermedial drama may have fallen on primarily deaf ears – but whose seminal role in the formation of the English Stage Company reacted against what was becoming an increasingly centralized definition of the modern national stage. Ironically, that initiative – soon taken over by the Artistic Directorship of George Devine – was to prove one of the most influential forces in the eradication of verse drama from the mainstream stage and from the contemporary historiography of modern drama.

The final two chapters examine some of the self-consciously resistant attempts that emerged in the wake of that moment. Chapter Seven begins with a consideration of the social and cultural factors that effected a swift change in critical, if not public, taste at the end of the 1950s. It then examines the anti-realistic, collaborative political theatre of John Arden and Margaretta D'Arcy. In its invocation of popular forms, in its containment of the individual poetic voice within that of the authoring collective, that theatre resonates with the earlier ideology of Auden and Isherwood. A very different manifestation of aesthetic continuity is suggested by the opera libretti of Michael Tippett. Ultimately, however, neither 'tradition', thus individually represented, has succeeded either in entrenching a consistent lineage or establishing a distinctive post-1950s tradition.

As explored in Chapter Eight, the much more personal, emotional and openly expressive theatre of Steven Berkoff has aligned verse drama with a self-consciously resistant, ostracized ideal of theatre as ritual. In its invocation of classical forms, it has also translated the aims of many earlier verse dramatists into a self-conscious dramatization of social anger and working-class empowerment. Rather than articulating those themes as argument, Berkoff's drama – like the many classically informed, formally developed verse plays of Harrison – manifests those themes in theatrical idiom itself. These later chapters identify some of the diverse manifestations and definitions of verse drama that have emerged in the wake of the late 1950s. While some dramas embraced an explicitly political imperative through non-realist forms, others have persisted in promoting an implicitly more universalizing ideal of ritual and art in the theatre.

In its consideration of Caryl Churchill's *Serious Money* alongside the theatre of Berkoff and Harrison, Chapter Eight explores the renewed role of earlier traditions of drama in verse in informing the themes and aesthetic of contemporary theatre. That theme is continued in the conclusion, which turns its analysis to the recent success of Bartlett's *King Charles III*. Bartlett's play calls overt attention to what many twentieth-century verse dramatists had worked to overcome: the continuous cultural prominence and aesthetic centrality of Shakespeare as the 'one poet in the national drama'. In so doing, it does not so much signal the revival of that Shakespearean tradition as dramatize a certain resigned if critical capitulation.

Verse Drama in England explores a vital and often overlooked tradition of modern dramatic creativity. It cannot hope to do full justice to the individual plays and careers contained within that tradition, and unfortunately the study of early twentieth-century closet drama and of radio drama – itself in many ways a discrete mid-century tradition – must be left for future examinations. While the dramatic explorations of Yeats and Eliot have been relatively well-served by scholars, the equally significant and influential work of many others has been strikingly neglected. So too has been the interaction of many of these poet-dramatists with larger and more interdisciplinary definitions of drama. This study hopes to promote a less discipline-specific approach to dramatic historiography more generally. Even more urgently, it aims to inspire further critical attention to the complexity and significance of what is fast becoming an almost forgotten tradition of dramatic creativity in modern England.

CHAPTER 1
NINETEENTH-CENTURY LEGACIES: SPECTACLE, SONORITY AND ROMANTIC REFORM IN THE THEATRE OF STEPHEN PHILLIPS AND JAMES ELROY FLECKER

In 1937, Barker identified an established historical divide between poetry and theatre. In the eighteenth century, the influential, discursive interventions of 'Dryden and his school' had ensured a primarily literary formulation of an ideal of dramatic poetry, an emphasis on 'reform from without, not from within'.[1] The consequent rift between poetic drama and the stage had developed and widened in the following decades, 'disastrously separating literature from the theatre'.[2] For many twentieth-century stage reformers, that separation was no more evident than in the fact that many Romantic and Victorian verse dramas had been composed by writers with little to no intention of staging their work.

The plays of John Keats, Robert Browning, Thomas Hardy and Algernon Swinburne attest to the self-conscious development of a poetic idiom within what had become a minor tradition of literary closet drama.[3] Others wrote dramas for a stage of whose quality they were (often justifiably) suspicious and of whose practical nature they professed themselves to be either ignorant or indifferent. In the first part of *Nero* (1885), future poet laureate Robert Bridges has the character of Lucan declare – on stage – the fundamental autonomy of dramatic poetry from the 'gross material' of theatrical presentation:

[Poetry] needs not tools nor gross material,
And hath twin doors to the mind, both eye and ear.
Nay, even of drama Aristotle held,
Though a good play must act well, that 'tis perfect
Without the stage; which shows that poetry
Stains not her excellence by being kind
To those encumbrances, which, in my judgment,
Are pushed to fetter fancy . . .[4]

Hallam Tennyson observes that his father wrote 'with the intention that actors should edit [his plays] for the stage, keeping them at the high poetic level'.[5] Indeed, as the actor-manager Henry Irving remarked of their collaborations, 'like many great poets [Tennyson] knew nothing of the regular requirements of the commercial stage and had little aptitude for dramatic construction'.[6] He was nonetheless sufficiently invested as to be disappointed in the staging of his plays; according to his son, Tennyson concluded that 'this might be theatrical art, but is entirely opposed to the canons of true dramatic art'.[7]

Barker identifies a nineteenth-century 'divorce' between poetry and the theatre despite 'the efforts of the well-wishers of both parties to bring them together.'[8] As the assumptions of both Tennyson and Bridges suggest, however, those efforts were not always immediately apparent. By the end of the nineteenth century, Romantic and Victorian drama – particularly verse drama – had become associated by many with an emphasis on static oratory over drama, imitation over innovation, sentimental effusion over 'spiritual' expression, and some of the very worst excesses of the commercial theatre. Looking back, Barker condemns a poetic theatre traduced by the indifference of its dramatists to the realities of stage and audience:

> Small wonder if by then the English poetic drama was at its nadir! How should the theatre not be barren, when the two parties to the union were thus estranged? ... The poets ... wrote blank verse as if it were a sort of magic formula, and were surprised when the formula did not work.[9]

Such perceptions could only strengthen efforts to restore verse drama to a central position after years of apparent neglect. They also ensured a relative creative freedom: for some, it encouraged the formation of a tradition entirely new, while for many others it acted as an incentive to return, re-examine and revitalize the poetic example of earlier dramatic traditions. When early twentieth-century poets turned to the contemplation of drama, they tended to respond to more established, implicitly more authentic models of poetic drama – Greek, medieval, Elizabethan and French – than the vexed Romantic and Victorian traditions of the previous century. In so doing, they did not just evade the poetic legacy of those traditions; they distanced themselves from the recent evolution of the poetic stage itself.

Romantics and Victorians: the Shakespearean ideal

In 1951, the poet, dramatist and critic Clifford Bax reflected on a long-standing presumption, on the part of poets, that 'they ought to be writing plays, probably because of Shakespeare's double triumph'.[10] As manifest in the majority of Romantic and Victorian verse dramas, however, that assumption often ignored the distinct demands of the dramatic stage, not to mention the two-fold nature of Shakespeare's triumph. Many of the Romantics read Shakespearean and Jacobean drama in a creative climate marked by German Romanticism and by a poetic embrace of subjective, interior extremes of passion and experience more suited to the page than the stage. The truth of Barker's assertion, that 'playwriting is a craft as well as an art, and a craft must be learnt',[11] is now an accepted commonplace. The nineteenth century, however, saw a proliferation of blank-verse closet dramas that seemed implicitly to endorse the well-known (if often misread) assessment of Charles Lamb that Shakespeare's plays were 'less calculated for performance on a stage, than those of any other dramatist whatsoever'.[12] As George Rowell observes, 'To Schiller or Hugo the theatre offered a challenge which they rejoiced to accept. To the English Romantic poets it was something which they mostly preferred to ignore.'[13]

The 'challenge' of theatre itself was not ignored entirely by poets, however, and on stage the Shakespearean legacy was equally strong: more often than not, it elicited stylistic imitation. Reflecting upon Keats's *Otho the Great* (1819), Trewin identifies 'a volley of echoes', 'a portentous melodrama that sounds like mock-Shakespearean pastiche'.[14] Victorian verse dramas placed a similar emphasis on poetic sonority, and tended to be characterized by lengthy set-pieces in blank verse and developed figurative constructions. Edward Bulwer-Lytton's highly successful *Richelieu* (1839) provides a representative (and well-known) example:

> Beneath the rule of men entirely great
> The pen is mightier than the sword. Behold
> The arch-enchanter's wand! – itself a nothing! –
> But taking sorcery from the master-hand
> To paralyse the Caesars – and to strike
> The loud earth breathless![15]

Forty years later, in *Becket* (1884), Tennyson's King would muse on his relationship with the Archbishop in similarly rhetorical and figurative, if slightly less excited, terms:

[I] [h]oped, were he chosen archbishop, Church and Crown,
Two sisters gliding in an equal dance,
Two rivers gently flowing side by side—
But no!
The bird that moults sings the same song again,
The snake that sloughs comes out a snake again.
Snake – ay, but he that lookt a fangless one,
Issues a venomous adder.[16]

The very static, lengthy nature of such pronouncements suggests a reading of the Shakespearean tradition for moments of heightened poetry independent of a larger, containing theatrical action. Indeed, as Donoghue contends, 'Tennyson and Swinburne dissipated the Shakespearean tragic form by retaining its mechanical semblance and turning it into a series of interrupted monologues.'[17]

Such structures nonetheless conformed to the rhetorical expectations of the contemporary Shakespearean actor. In 1934, Priscilla Thouless reflected that English audiences 'have always loved the melodramatic, the startling, accompanied by highly coloured language.'[18] In the nineteenth century, these tastes were actively encouraged in a commercial theatre dominated by actor-managers such as Charles Kean, Henry Irving and Herbert Beerbohm Tree. Central to the popularity of that theatre was its simultaneous promotion of popular melodrama, well-made plays, musical theatre – and Shakespeare. The most successful Victorian productions of Shakespeare plays were characterized by their emphasis on the actor as celebrity, on stage spectacular, and on what Ernest Reynolds identifies as 'full-blooded picturesque acting': 'significant dramatic gesture, the playing on the human voice as on the stops of an organ, the fine wearing of a splendid costume, the cultivation of a distinctive stage presence, well-modulated stage movement.'[19] These expectations left very little room for a Shakespeare unenhanced by costume, elaborate set design, music and 'judicious' rewritings that foregrounded the rhetorical performance of the star actor. They also encouraged a perpetuation of that large-scale, historical and histrionic tradition within the contemporary poetic theatre itself.

Trewin identifies a consequent phenomenon of 'all revival; no begetting'[20] in poetic drama: plays so 'echoed with Elizabethan and Jacobean tags and rhythms' that the nineteenth-century drama became a 'haunted ruin, haunted by the iambic pentameter'.[21] Terry Otten offers a typical, if particularly scathing, critical summation:

Never have so many major authors contributed so very little to English drama. Despite the fact that every major nineteenth-century author wrote dramas and almost all of them condemned the current stage, not one could rescue the theatre from senile plots, pseudo-Elizabethan techniques, melodramatic claptrap, stock characterizations, and bombastic language.[22]

Rather than contesting that 'pseudo-Elizabethan' instinct, some of these writers participated actively in its perpetuation. In its versification and structure, in its thematic resonance with received Shakespearean themes and dramatic conventions, the conclusion of Augusta Webster's *Disguises* (1879) provides an indicative example:

> Hush! We'll feign no more.
> We have, in turns, all played disguiseful parts
> Been life's forced actors, puppets to ourselves:
> The masque is ended.[23]

Such imitative, allusive instincts were not restricted to the use of blank verse, epigrams or oblique references to the world as a stage. Where modern prose drama was becoming increasingly defined by its engagement with contemporary social realities and concerns, the majority of Victorian verse plays were historical romances centred on the tensions between kings, queens and rulers: Browning's *Strafford* (1837), Swinburne's *Bothwell* (1874) and *Mary Stuart* (1881) and Tennyson's *Becket* (1884) are prominent examples. In 1901, Stephen Phillips contemplated writing a verse drama on a contemporary theme ('the Tragedy of Wealth'). Asked if 'blank verse is compatible with modern costume', he replied: 'I don't see why it shouldn't be. But I might write the play in prose ...'[24] Phillips never wrote that drama, either in verse or prose; his next major plays were *The Sin of David* (1904), *Nero* (1906) and *Pietro of Siena* (1910).

By the turn of the century, many critics and self-conscious reformers had come to associate the very use of blank verse, particularly in conjunction with historical subject-matter, with a fundamental indifference both to the dramatic qualities of Shakespeare and to the urgent imperative of the contemporary stage. In his late-Victorian assessment of the nineteenth-century stage, the influential critic William Archer was unambiguous:

> The ghost of Romantic drama stalked the stage, decked out in ...
> gibbering blank verse. ... Whatever was least essential to Shakespeare's

greatness was conscientiously imitated; his ease and flexibility of diction, his subtle characterisation, and his occasional mastery of construction were all ignored. Laboured rhetoric, whether serious or comic, was held to be the only legitimate form of dramatic utterance.[25]

Reynolds similarly aligns blank verse with empty imitation: 'the Shakespearean cult of the nineteenth century was disastrous and led only into a blind alley'.[26] Glover identifies 'all that is associated with the term "blank verse" [as] an anachronism'.[27] For Trewin, it could only serve a theatrical climate in which 'tushery ruled': it 'was made for the chlamys, the toga, or plate-armour, or what a writer of the time called doublet-work'.[28] In Barker's influential assessment, 'It was no paradox, but a matter of direct significance, that when the revival of poetic drama did come, it came, seemingly, in prose.'[29] This revival entailed the return of 'poetry' – as *prose* – to a rightful interaction with the art of theatre itself. It also entailed an association of that prose idiom with a much-needed contemporary vitality hitherto traduced by a poetic theatre in thrall to an empty, undramatic ideal of aesthetic imitation.

The influence of such assessments was such that by the first half of the twentieth century, modern drama in verse was already seen by many reformers as a niche and outmoded interest, the manifestation of a naïve literary nostalgia rather than a contemporary creative vitality, let alone theatrical viability. Verse drama today continues to be relegated to the margins (if not the outer reaches) of contemporary appraisals of a modern national tradition, its detractors implying if not explicitly identifying the same divisions between theatre craft and poetry, literary pastiche and poetic expression critiqued at the turn of the century. As Barker himself observed, however, many twentieth-century poets themselves addressed and worked to rectify the unnatural 'breach' established between the exemplary poetic drama manifest in Shakespeare's plays and its misrepresentation in recent poetry and practice.[30] For many of those poet-dramatists, that breach could only be repaired with a deliberate movement away from the received idiom of Shakespeare and his Romantic and Victorian imitators, through the development of a more self-consciously contemporary drama in form, structure and subject.

Stephen Phillips

One of the first attempts at such reform was made at the turn of the century by Stephen Phillips (1864–1915), whose first five plays (staged in London

1900–8) were 'so successful, both with audiences fashionable and popular and with critics, that he was for some years one of the best known figures of the theatrical world'.[31] In Trewin's memorable account, 'the comet of Stephen Phillips fired the sky' in that moment, only to '[hurtle] to its doom' soon thereafter: 'there had been no true dramatic poet in the theatre for so long that … there was a frenzied rush to greet [Phillips] as the genius for whom the stage had waited'.[32] Reynolds adopts a similar tone: the 'extraordinary successes' of Phillips opened the twentieth century: 'Critics, eminent and obscure, alike lost their heads and proclaimed [him] as the Messiah of the poetic stage. Glittering rivers of encomium flowed as *Paolo and Francesca*, *Herod*, and *Ulysses* appeared.'[33] Furthermore, as Bax observes, 'it was almost a miracle for a poet at the beginning of our century to capture the West End Theatre'.[34]

As such assessments suggest, the success of Phillips can be attributed in no small part to a recognized need – on the part of the popular, commercial stage as much as contemporary critics – for a 'Messiah' who would rescue the poetic stage from the attenuated legacy of Bulwer-Lytton and the resilient tenacity of Swinburne. Most accounts of modern verse drama now tend to associate Phillips with the preposterous reaches of Victorian and Edwardian spectacular, with the expressive, glorious finale to the misguided rhetorical Elizabethanism of the nineteenth century. For Reynolds, he was but 'the last of a rather sorry line', 'the last flicker of the dying Victorian candle of Elizabethan-style drama'.[35] That reading, however, fails to acknowledge the extent to which Phillips himself positioned his plays at the solitary vanguard of the contemporary restoration of poetic drama. He also – unlike many of his immediate successors – emphatically positioned that restoration in relation to an existing commercial stage.

Phillips, unlike many of his predecessors, had considerable practical experience in that theatre: he had been an actor for six years, primarily in the company managed by his cousin Frank Benson, who was to become an increasingly influential director. Shortly after leaving the company, Phillips established his name as a contemporary poet: in 1897, his first collection, *Poems*, garnered considerable critical and popular acclaim. Following the success of *Poems*, Phillips was commissioned by the actor-manager George Alexander to write a play: the publication of *Paolo and Francesca* in 1900 elicited immediate outpourings of critical praise. As dutifully republished by John Lane in one of the play's many editions, reviews hailed 'a noble poem [that] is so, largely, for the reason that it is noble drama as well'.[36] Owen Seaman of the *Morning Post* praised 'a great dramatic poem which happens also to be a great poetic drama'.[37] The *Spectator* acclaimed in Phillips a poet who 'will go on to give us plays that are both plays and poems, and so to enrich what is, after all, the most glorious dramatic literature in the world'.[38] According to *Punch*, the play 'fulfils, as no great poem of our day has yet fulfilled, the primary demands of a stage play', while Churton Collins in the *Saturday Review* identified a kinship between Phillips and 'the aristocrats of his art: with Sophocles and with Dante'.[39]

Such responses underline the extent to which both poetic drama and the poetic stage were presumed to be in a state of crisis. They also enforce the extent to which literary ideals could prevail in contemporary discussions of a revitalized stage. The hyperbolic comparisons of Phillips to Sophocles, Dante and Milton tended to locate an ideal of dramatic poetry, Le Gallienne's 'noble drama', independently of its realization on the stage. *Paolo and Francesca* was not produced until 1902, when *The Times* was able to reassure its readers, 'those who care for the stage at all will rejoice to find that this work is essentially a stage-work'; the public 'are delighted with Mr. Phillips because – not a little to their surprise – they find that he does not bore them. . . . is it then possible in the twentieth century to wed blank verse to really human passions, to beings like ourselves, of flesh and blood?'[40] As Thouless suggests, 'after the torturous language of Browning's plays, the formal expression of Tennyson's *Queen Mary*, the ease and flow, the spontaneity of the verse of Phillips was a new discovery'.[41] She also, however, identifies *Paolo and Francesca* as Phillips's best play precisely because it is 'the play in which the theatrical is subordinated to some extent to the poetic':

> Much more consciously than in his other plays, he is writing in the literary traditions of the past, and from these traditions trying to evolve a new form of poetic drama which should satisfy the feelings of the people of his time.[42]

Thouless reinforces a prevailing tendency to identify the strength of poetic drama in its engagement with literary definitions of poetic drama. In so doing, she also suggests a certain critical distrust of 'the theatrical' itself.

Paolo and Francesca is by no means purely dependent upon 'literary traditions of the past'. In comparison to the vast majority of Victorian poetic dramas, its action is emphatically dramatic, its poetic set-pieces punctuated by prescribed theatrical effects and actions ('a noise of falling chains is heard'; 'Giovanni bows to her'; 'a drum is heard'; 'seizing her arm'; 'drooping towards him'). The play differentiates itself from melodrama in the very integrity of its verse, in the careful delineation of passion, conflict and motive rather than empty expostulations or violent extremes of action. In one early scene, for example, Lucrezia, cousin to Giovanni ('Tyrant of Rimini') expresses her bitterness at having been left a childless widow:

> My thwarted woman-thoughts have inward turned,
> And that vain milk like acid in me eats.
> Have I not in my thought trained little feet
> To venture, and taught little lips to move
> Until they shaped the wonder of a word?
> I am long practised.[43]

The verse of Phillips is markedly different from that of Swinburne or Tennyson in its relative directness, in its preference of simplicity over ornate figurations and in its development of thought or action rather than elaboration of conceit. An indicative passage from Tennyson's *Queen Mary* (1875), in which the Tudor Queen anticipates the arrival of Philip of Spain, underlines an immediate distinction:

> God change the pebble which his kingly foot
> First presses into some more costly stone
> Than ever blinded eye. I'll have one mark it
> And bring it me. I'll have it burnishd firelike;
> I'll set it round with gold, with pearl, with diamond.
> Let the great angel of the church come with him;
> Stand on the deck and spread his wings for sail![44]

In this speech, Tennyson invokes a single emotion (Mary's passion for Philip) and decorates it with poetry. Lucrezia's outburst, however, is considerably more focused on the exposition and development of emotional character.

Unlike many of his immediate predecessors, Phillips characteristically focuses on the sustainment of such emotional development throughout a scene. Tennyson's Renard acknowledges the speech of Queen Mary with, 'O Madam, you fly your thoughts like kites' before moving on to give her political counsel in similarly figurative tones. In contrast, Giovanni's response to his cousin in *Paolo and Francesca* is invested in her emotional revelation; he urges her to recognize the pain that children can 'wring'. His interjection elicits a lengthy set-piece from Lucrezia. Rather than developing poetic imagery or conceits, rather than simply reinforcing a single emotional state, the speech dramatizes the conflicting passions of its heroine in such a way as to establish her complexity – and a dramatic suspense as to her future actions:

> I am a woman, and this very flesh
> Demands its natural pangs, its rightful throes,
> And I implore with vehemence these pains.
> . . .
> I am become a danger and a menace,
> A wandering fire, a disappointed force,
> A peril – do you hear, Giovani? – O!
> It is such souls as mine that go to swell
> The childless cavern cry of the barren sea,
> Or make that human ending to night-wind.[45]

Lucrezia halts her speech, wondering why she has thus 'bared' herself to her cousin, only to conclude:

> Unless, indeed, this marriage – yes this marriage –
> Near now, is't not? – So near made me cry out.
> Ah! She will bring a sound of pattering feet![46]

The movement of the speech points to a continuous awareness, on the part of Phillips, of narrative and dramatic development. Lucrezia expresses both a wistful tenderness towards the children she does not have and a yearning bitterness and disappointment. It is not until the end of the play that these various, potentially conflicting emotions are resolved in her final actions on behalf of the young lovers.

The dramas of Phillips also differ from those of many Victorians in their particular emphasis on emotional expression and experience over political intrigue and proliferating subplots. *Herod* (1902), for example, focuses almost exclusively on the emotional consequences of Herod's decision to have his wife's brother killed. Distraught, Mariamne dies, and the play concludes with Herod defying the attempts of his courtiers to distract him from realizing that his wife is dead. *Paolo and Francesca* takes its inspiration from an episode in Dante's *Inferno*, dramatizing the arrival of Francesca as young bride to Giovanni, the revelation of the love between Francesca and

Giovanni's beloved brother Paolo, and the eventual, inevitable tragic death of both. Its dramatic focus is the developed, emotional response of each of its protagonists to the romantic tension and to the betrayals that it perpetuates. It also, however, seems to be the deliberate invocation and complication of the Elizabethan and Jacobean models that had so dominated the Victorian poetic stage and its critics.

Paolo and Francesca echoes Romeo and Juliet in its tale of relatively star-crossed young lovers (who also visit an apothecary-shop and wonder at the dawn). Unlike Romeo and Juliet, however, it does not focus on idealizing that relationship, but rather dramatizes the conflicting emotional responses and loyalties of various characters – including those of the guilt-ridden protagonists themselves. In its Italian setting – 'a gloomy Hall in the Malatesta Castle at Rimini, hung with weapons and instruments of the Chase' – in its dramatization of illicit love and familial betrayal, the play resonates comfortably with Elizabethan and Jacobean revenge-tragedy. Indeed, the play ends with an echo of John Webster's The Duchess of Malfi: as Giovanni looks at the bodies of Paolo and Francesca, he reflects, 'Unwillingly / They loved, unwillingly I slew them'. Kissing them on the forehead, he concludes: 'I did not know the dead could have such hair. / Hide them. They look like children fast asleep!'[47] The remarks resemble those of Ferdinand in IV, ii of Webster's drama: 'Cover her face; mine eyes dazzle: she died young.' In the context of a play that seems overtly to defy the revenge-motifs, political contextualization and subplots of Jacobean drama, however, that reference hints less at an indebtedness than a certain refutation of its defining characteristics.

Phillips himself was adamant about his break with established, nineteenth-century definitions of poetic drama. In an early letter to his cousin Binyon, Phillips urged him (as a poet) not to 'look at Shelley, Keats, Tennyson and Browning, all of whom had formed themselves on great models'.[48] Instead, 'We must go to the fountainhead for style. Write out your own ideas in good strong style, if possible of your own … style seems almost to have stopped with the Greeks and our best stylists have merely been haunted with echoes from the "isles of Greece"'.[49] Phillips identifies the primary weaknesses of his Romantic and Victorian predecessors in the method, rather than the fact, of their imitative tendencies. In insisting that his cousin 'go to the fountainhead', in identifying style 'with the Greeks', he advocates a break from those later poets through the development of a unique, strong and more authentic style that nonetheless turns to established models.

A similar instinct seems to have informed his approach to poetic drama. In a published 'real conversation' with Archer in 1904, Phillips acknowledges the limitations of a critical and cultural climate that consistently evaluates poetic drama against an Elizabethan ideal. He recognizes the influence of Shakespeare on critical expectations of verse drama and invokes earlier models as a means to escape that legacy. According to Phillips, the 'best hope for English poetic drama' lies in 'a deliberate rebellion against the Elizabethan tradition'.[50] He finds that his audience (and readers), however, are incapable of recognizing his own attempts at such rebellion:

> They assume as a matter of course that I am imitating Shakespeare and imitating him badly. All they know about the poetic drama being gathered from Shakespeare, they think every drama that is written in verse must be judged by Shakespearean canons and no other.[51]

Phillips identifies his divergence from the 'beaten track of Shakespeare' in his adherence to a Greek and French ideal of unity and simplicity. He does not expand further upon his reading of classical tragedy, although the emphasis in his plays on discrete moments of emotional experience, a relatively simple plot and a directness of poetic expression seems to endorse the speculation of Thouless that 'he saw in the classical form an opportunity for expressing in a simple medium lyrical emotions'.[52]

Rather than reacting against (or indeed recognizing) this apparent embrace of 'alternative' dramatic traditions, the majority of his contemporaries acclaimed in Phillips the long-awaited restoration of a powerful dramatic voice. This rhetoric of restoration alone could invoke the legacy of Shakespeare: actor and director Hesketh Pearson praises Phillips as 'the only English poet since Shakespeare who has written highly successful and dramatically effective blank verse plays'.[53] Where some reviews cited his excellence in 'the bravest and most beautiful vehicle in literary art, the supreme accomplishment for poets at any time',[54] Pearson emphasizes 'success' and 'effect' on the stage itself.

Ultimately, these distinctions expose the very different expectations upon which such invocations of Shakespearean accomplishment can be founded. In a discussion at the Manchester Literary Club in 1901, Tinsley Pratt noted that where one critic had claimed Phillips 'a disciple of the Elizabethans', another contended that he 'has broken absolutely with the Elizabethan models'.[55] For some, the work of Phillips signified a uniquely *dramatic* contribution to contemporary theatre – and thus a vital break from the rhetorical imitation that had sullied and stifled the Victorian poetic stage.[56] Many others, however, saw in the expressive blank verse, passionate conflict and historical settings of his plays a spectacular realization of the Shakespeareanism to which the Victorian commercial stage had consistently aspired: a contemporary review hails 'blank verse abounding in at once sonorous and deeply pregnant lines and passages that have the real Elizabethan ring about them'.[57] Where the poet Harold Monro dismissed the dramas of Phillips as a 'mere echo of the Victorian manner',[58] Bax tellingly defends them by invoking a prevailing, if perpetually malleable standard of dramatic excellence: 'any Elizabethan playwright would have given his best doublet or his second-best bed to have conceived the final picture of *Herod*'.[59]

The success of Phillips was not long-lived, and much of his 'meteoric' fall can be traced as much to his personality and financial difficulties as to a sudden dissipation of talent. It can also be attributed to a changing critical climate in relation to both the theatre and modern poetic expression. In assessing the apparent capitulation of Phillips to the theatrical over the poetic, Thouless implies his deliberate appeasement of a public taste for event, spectacle and the melodramatic sonority of the star actor. Indeed, notwithstanding his own professed advocacy of a simplicity of plot and directness of expression, the success of Phillips can be associated with his keen understanding of the conventional, commercial theatre of his day. The final scene of *Herod* concludes with the following stage directions:

> Herod is left alone by the litter . . . The curtain descends: then rises, and it is night, with a few stars. It descends, and again rises, and now it is the glimmer of dawn . . . [Herod is] still standing rigid and with fixed stare in the cataleptic trance.[60]

At the time, the *Morning Leader* was unambiguous in aligning the poetry of the play with its imagination of spectacle: *Herod* was 'splendidly opulent in conception'.[61] *The Times* similarly acclaimed 'the bold, visualizing imagination of the dramatist'.[62] Pearson sees Phillips as having bettered Shakespeare himself in writing dramas that both invited and accommodated such scenic and musical embellishment:

> Shakespeare might have objected to the sacrifice of his poetry for scenery; but Stephen Phillips ... allowed for all the pageantry imaginable. The profusion on the stage matched the grandiloquence of the verse, and there never was such a theatrical spectacle as *Nero*, which included the triumphant entry of the emperor into Rome ... driving in a chariot drawn by two milk-white steeds with distinguished

stage careers – and the burning of the city, when houses crumpled, temples crashed, arches swayed, and flames shot up, the whole being realistic enough to make the more nervous among the audience look for the exit doors or rise from their seats.[63]

By the turn of the century, however, this appreciation of theatre as sonorous spectacle had become anathema to some of the most vocal proponents of a modern theatre and dramatic reform.

The essays of Arthur Symons on poetic drama remain curiously underexplored by contemporary scholars, and provide acute theorizations of the relationship between drama and the stage, poetry and poetic drama. In his contemporaneous assessment of Phillips's *Ulysses* (1902), Symons admires 'an action that moves' and 'plausible characters, who speak in clear and elegant verse'.[64] He declares, however, that 'we want something more': 'Poetry is one thing, stagecraft is another; and there are different kinds of poetry as there are different kinds of stagecraft'.[65] For Symons, the essential difficulty of *Ulysses* lies in the tension between its 'idyllic' poetic idiom and its 'theatrical' dramatic action. Where 'true dramatic poetry [should be] an integral part of the dramatic framework, which, indeed, at its best, it makes', *Ulysses* is ultimately 'a spectacle-drama, with a commentary in verse'.[66] Rather than advocating a poetic idiom to serve that spectacle, Symons echoes the sentiments of many of his contemporaries – and anticipates the later assertions of Eliot – when he demands a poetic drama whose 'verse must speak as straight as prose, but with a more beautiful voice. . . . It must not "make poetry," however good in its way'.[67]

For Symons (and many others), this new poetic drama 'must hold us, as a play of Ibsen's holds us, by the sheer interest of its representation of life'.[68] As such, it will demand nothing less than the reform of the stage itself:

> between declamation and dramatic poetry there is a great gulf. The actor loves declamation, because it gives him an opportunity to recite, and every actor loves to recite poetry. It provides him with a pulpit. He does not like to realise, any more than his author likes to realise, that every line of poetry which is not speech is bad dramatic poetry.[69]

Symons writes of a poetic drama that has not yet emerged, one that will depend as much on the reform of the actor and the contemporary audience as on a dramatist more attuned to 'reality' and the 'representation of life'. For Symons (a prominent member of both the Rhymers' Club and the

Independent Theatre Society) and many of his contemporaries, that drama could only come into being with a rejection of the very stage that Phillips had set out to reform from within.

James Elroy Flecker's *Hassan*

As we shall see, the various and varying preferences of many subsequent poet-dramatists for closet drama, amateur theatre, small-scale production and theatre reform suggests an overarching tendency to reject the large-scale pictorial productions of the Victorian and Edwardian actor-managers. It also, of course, suggests the unsuitability of their works for that larger stage. Notwithstanding the critical fall of Phillips, however, not all poets rejected his legacy; Bax, a prolific and successful writer of light, rhyming verse comedies, was a stalwart defender. Bottomley saw himself initially as working within the same tradition.[70] Furthermore, any assumption that verse drama retreated immediately to a humbled stage position risks overlooking one of the most popular, critically acclaimed and culturally referenced poetic dramas of the first half of the century. Composed between 1913 and 1914, published in 1922 and spectacularly produced at His Majesty's Theatre in London in 1923 under the direction of George Grossmith and J.A.E. Malone, James Elroy Flecker's *Hassan* was to prove, in the words of Reynolds, 'the *Götterdammerung* of large-scale poetic drama in England'.[71]

Unlike Phillips, Flecker (1884–1914) had no experience in the theatre. He also gained no experience in the theatre: he died of tuberculosis at the age of thirty, and neither *Hassan* nor his much more Shavian drama, *Don Juan* (1925), was produced or published in his lifetime.[72] After studying at Oxford, Flecker studied Oriental Languages for two years at Cambridge; in 1910, he was posted to Istanbul with the Consular Service, and he later served in Smyrna and Beirut. During that time, he published several volumes of poetry and saw some of his poems enshrined in the first *Georgian Poetry* anthology. While it is difficult to identify a coherent, consistent Georgian aesthetic, it is safe to say that Flecker differed from many of his peers in that anthology in his embrace of a more languid romanticism, in his enthusiasm for an orientalism not overly distanced from that of Edward Fitzgerald, and in his greater stylistic and thematic affiliation with the French Parnassian school. Reflecting on Flecker's early death, Alec Macdonald in the *Fortnightly Review* bemoaned 'unquestionably the greatest premature loss that English literature has suffered since the death of Keats'.[73]

As recounted by the theatre (and later film) producer Basil Dean, Flecker consistently envisioned his play in relation to the spectacular stagings at His Majesty's Theatre, then managed by Tree. Flecker submitted *Hassan* initially for consideration in 1913, but Tree was reportedly too overwhelmed by its length to read it.[74] Instead, that task was left to Dean, who enlisted the help of Marsh in convincing Tree to reconsider the play 'when it had been brought into shape'.[75] Both Dean and Flecker set about revising (and primarily cutting) the play, often independently of each other; they never met, but corresponded by post – Dean from infantry training camp, and Flecker from a sanatorium in Switzerland. As republished by Dean, the correspondence reveals Flecker's constant willingness to render the play 'more actable': 'Please never think that I want to institute a sort of Literature *v* Drama quarrel!'[76] It also reveals a conviction of the play's worth as mainstage, commercial spectacle: 'Can we have *real camels* for the final scene?'[77] According to Dean, the popularity of the published play, the untimely death of Flecker and the long delay in production ensured that by 1923, public anticipation had risen 'like a fever. Indeed, old playgoers remarked that nothing comparable had occurred since the great days of Irving and Tree.'[78] The production was unquestionably 'one of the most eagerly awaited events of the London stage in the years after the Great War',[79] and the opulent, elaborate production – replete with camels, falling sheets of iron, fountains running with blood and elaborately choreographed ballet – was an unprecedented success, running for 281 performances.

Like the plays of Phillips, the critical and creative legacy of *Hassan* has been less enduring. Reynolds defines the play's success as both 'ephemeral' and 'accidental': the crowds 'were attracted as much by the glamour of the production . . . as by the emotional experience of listening to its fine language', and *Hassan* only fulfilled the gap left by the departure (after a five-year run) of 'the scenic glories of *Chu Chin Chow*'.[80] Flecker now figures rarely, if at all, in discussions of poetic drama, despite the fact that at the time 'We lacked a bold, trampling fellow to revitalise dramatic poetry' and 'everyone expected as much from [the play] as a previous generation from Phillips'.[81] E.R. Wood similarly notes that *Hassan* was initially (like *Paolo and Francesca*) 'hailed as a forerunner of a new Poetic Drama'.[82] In his 1937 assessment, Barker mourns 'a true poet, cruelly robbed of his chance to learn his dramatist's craft'.[83] The production of *Hassan* was also, as Reynolds observes, 'the last full-scale West End performance of a new English poetic drama' before *Murder in the Cathedral*, which was the first play since Flecker's 'to be an outstanding success both as a book of verse and as a stage work'.[84]

Ultimately, the critical fate of both Phillips and *Hassan* point to an increasing dissociation of any 'new Poetic Drama' from a stage characterized by spectacle, grandiloquent language and grand acting, no matter the perceived quality of the verse.

To some extent, that shift can be attributed as much to the financial state of the theatre after the war as to any immediate change in public tastes. It can also be attributed to an increasing perception, on the part of dramatists and critics alike, that modern poetic drama should reflect a sensibility more akin to that being promoted in the 'progressive' theatre of such contemporary prose dramatists as George Bernard Shaw, Barker and John Galsworthy. The definition of that sensibility could vary considerably; some advocated a more emphatically modern theme or subject, and some looked for a more 'natural', less overtly literary poetic idiom. Most, however, seemed to agree that the poetic drama could not be reborn through the popular stage traditions established by Victorian and Edwardian actor-managers. Indeed, according to the poet and theatre manager Ashley Dukes, Flecker had already recognized a divorce between the commercial stage and the poetic drama: he 'was so far imposed upon by the conventions of the modern theatre that he composed all his dialogue in prose, leaving the dominant lyrical element to the chorus alone'.[85] *Hassan* is written primarily in what Trewin describes as 'Turkish-delight poetic prose', with interspersed songs and choruses.[86] That it was received as a poetic drama to follow that of Phillips (and thus revive poetic drama as a whole) nonetheless suggests that that poetic prose was – and can be – read essentially as free verse, and the play itself as a prominent intervention within an established tradition.

According to Wood, the subject for *Hassan* had been originally inspired by an old Turkish farce.[87] The play eventually evolved from a three-act comedy into a tragedy whose tone slowly and forcibly changes from one of gentle and often witty comedy to heavily romanticized horror. The play begins with the plot of the comic, overweight character of Hassan the confectioner: he is in love with Yasmin, a selfish and fickle young maiden, and he unwisely confesses his love to his friend Selim. Hassan is betrayed and humiliated by both, and as he collapses in a fit of fury, the play introduces the character of the tyrannical Caliph and his retinue, amongst whom is the disillusioned poet Ishak. Caliph is captured by Rafi, bent upon brutal revenge for the Caliph's capture of his beloved Pervaneh. He also styles himself the King of the Beggars, declaring vengeance not only for himself, but for a wronged underclass: 'When high office is polluted, when the holy is unholy, when justice is a lie, when the people are starved, and the great fools of the world in high office, then dares a man so talk' of filling his 'bowl of oblivion with the blood of the Caliph of Baghdad'.[88] The Caliph is rescued by the awakened Hassan, who is rewarded with a position at the royal court. From that position, Hassan bears witness to the renewed ambitions of Yasmin, the cynical sorrow of the poet, the vexed love of Rafi and Pervaneh, and the brutal actions of the Caliph.

The Caliph gives Rafi and Pervaneh a choice: they can submit to separation and Pervaneh's perpetual servitude within his harem, or they can be granted one day and one night of bliss before suffering a lingering and torturous death. Unlike more conventional romantic protagonists, Rafi is not immediately tempted towards the latter option. Instead, he reasons:

> I am young. . . . There in the clouds I shall see your face, and remember you with a wistful remembrance as if you had always been a dream and the silver torment of your arms had never been more than the white mists circling round the mountain snows.[89]

Rebuked angrily by Pervaneh, who reminds him of her impending humiliation and slavery, Rafi bemoans 'a woman's vanity: am I to be tortured to death for this?': 'By Allah, I am afraid of death, and the man who fears not death is a dullard and a fool!'[90] Soon, however, he entreats his beloved not to choose death for herself; he alone has witnessed the brutality of torture, and her speech of enduring love and willed suffering 'is metaphor'.[91] When Pervaneh asks him to recount what he has seen, 'clear and plain',[92] Rafi does so – in her ear.

The play thus constantly – and increasingly – calls attention to the tension between the aestheticization of torment and death and the stark reality of that experience. It does so, however, within an idiom that itself remains at the level of romanticized 'metaphor'. Alone in a state of 'ecstasy', Pervaneh chooses 'Death with thee, death for thee, death to attain thee, O lover', invoking imminent immortalization in death.[93] The romanticism of that aspiration is immediately qualified, however, by the resigned submission of Rafi: 'Die then, Pervaneh, for thy great reasons. Me no ecstasy can help through the hours of pain. I die for love alone.'[94] Horrified at being forced by the Caliph to watch the torture and execution, Hassan appeals to the palace guards, only to discover that their tongues have been cut out so as not to betray the brutal reality of this 'Master of the World'. The penultimate set-piece of the play consists of a large-scale Procession of Protracted Death, involving a variety of several torturers. While Hassan looks on in horror,

Yasmin, gleefully assimilated into the realities of the court, hurries forward to watch; afterwards, she declares that she had 'laughed to see them writhe'.[95]

This tension between exotic language, spectacular staging and the grotesque horror of the play's events – what Reynolds identifies as a 'sordid and sadistic story' – comes to a height towards the end of the play. The Procession of Protracted Death, along with Hassan and the doomed lovers, moves into an onstage pavilion:

> The stage grows dark … In the silence rises the splashing of the fountain and the whirring and whirling of a wheel. The sounds blend and grow unendurably insistent, and with them music begins to play softly. A cry of pain is half smothered by the violins. … Hassan, thrust forward by his Guards, appears at the door of the pavilion. … he totters a few steps and finally falls in a faint in the shadow of the fountain.[96]

Hassan is eventually found by Ishak, who twice repeats that he has 'broken [his] lute' and will no longer perform for kings.[97] Instead, he urges Hassan to return to his simple roots; rather than returning as a poor man to work within a society ruled by the Caliph, he advocates flight from Baghdad: 'I will try the barren road, and listen for the voice of the emptiness of earth. And you shall walk beside me.'[98] The lyricism of the scene is soon interrupted; the fountain of the palace runs red, and the two flee to follow the gathering caravan to 'happy Samarkand'.[99] The play ends with Hassan and Ishak, robed as pilgrims, joining a spectacular scene of pilgrimage amidst 'blazing moonlight', with 'Merchants, Camel-Drivers and their beasts, Pilgrims, Jews, Women, all manner of people' as they collectively recite, in choral exchanges, Flecker's 'Golden Road to Samarkand' – originally written independently of the play, and soon to become an oft-quoted poem.[100]

Before that final scene, however, the Ghost of the Artist of the Fountain emerges, 'in pale Byzantine robes', to call forth the ghosts of Rafi and Pervaneh. The appearance had been anticipated by Pervaneh earlier in the play, when she envisioned 'walking side by side' by the fountain with her lover, in immortality. The play invokes this romantic apotheosis, however, only to stage its grim impossibility. The fountain ghost is unable to answer the questions of Pervaneh – 'what of Paradise, what of Infinity – what of the stars, and what of us?': he replies, 'Why should the dead be wiser than the living? The dead know only this – that it was better to be alive.'[101] The scene proceeds to deconstruct conventional figurations of eternal love in death: Pervaneh might feel 'no more pain' in death, but she 'will feel so cold'. When Pervaneh invokes 'the fire of love', the ghost affirms that she 'will forget when the wind blows'.[102] As Pervaneh becomes increasingly more distraught, she calls out to Rafi, who 'in a thin voice like an echo' can only repeat fragments: 'Forget ... Rafi ...', 'Cold ... cold ... cold ...' and an essential, culminating question: 'Rafi – Rafi – who was Rafi?'[103]

In its dramatization of the disillusionment of the poet, the horrors of the exotic court, the moral corruptibility of Yasmin, the fleetingness of romantic happiness in the face of extended brutality and the futility of romantic death, Flecker's play is emphatically anti-romantic. That tone is in fact immediately signalled at the start of the play, in its consistent invocation and deflation of exoticized language and poetic speech. Hassan is initially presented as a comic and foolish character, easily duped into thinking that he can purchase a magic elixir that will enchant his beloved into falling for him. Rather than emphasizing the farcical element of this situation with the 'low' dialogue or wit often characteristic of such plots, Flecker underscores its humour with deliberately excessive, florid language. Selim remarks, for example, that 'it would be better to cut the knot of reluctance and uncord the casket of explanation'.[104] When Hassan questions the presence of Selim in the boudoir of Yazim, he is told, 'Plunge not the finger of enquiry into the pie of impertinence, O my uncle'.[105] Later, Ishak entreats the overly deferential chief of police to 'brush away, I implore you, the cobwebs of ceremony with the broom of expedition'.[106] The effect of such exchanges is to undercut rather than promote any reading of these initial scenes as a thoroughly romanticised representation of exotic fable.

It is also, in the larger context of the play, to invite a more immediately cynical reading of the similar effusions that characterize the exchanges between Rafi and Pervaneh, the proclamations of the Caliph – and the poetry of the poet himself. As Selim buries his face mockingly in the bosom of Yasmin, he declares:

> Could'st thou but see, O my Uncle, the silver hills with their pomegranate groves; or the deep fountain in the swelling plain, or the Ethiopian who waters the roses in the garden, or the great lamp between the columns where the incense of love is burned.[107]

After Hassan has collapsed, insensible, the poet enters with the Caliph, who seeks out entertainment for his 'heavy heart'. Ishak declares, 'is there not vast entertainment for the wise in the shining of the moon, in the dripping of that fountain, and in the shape of that tall cypress that has leapt the wall to shoot her arrows at the stars?'[108] Rather than encouraging a recognition of the poet's greater sensitivity, this declaration is presented in such a way as to suggest an essential similarity between the idiom of the poet and that of the treacherous, lower-class Selim. The language of *everyone* in the play is characterized by its floridity, extended constructions and emotional, romantic effusions. Rather than aligning the beauty of such expressiveness with a more poetic reality or sensibility, the play increasingly suggests the extent to which that language only masks a more cynical, brutal truth.

That truth is, of course, the savagery and finality of death. It is also the political ruthlessness of rulers. At the beginning of the play, Hassan muses, 'Had I been rich, ah me! How deep had been my delight in matters of the soul, in poetry and music and pictures.'[109] When he is first appointed to the court, he explains to the Caliph that his primary ambition is to 'hear Ishak play and ... hear Ishak sing': 'till you forget that you are Lord of the World, and I forget that I am a baseborn tradesman.'[110] While poetry is a 'princely diversion' for the Caliph, 'for us it is a deliverance from Hell. ... Men who work hard have special need of dreams. All the town of Bagdad is passionate for poetry, O Master.'[111] For Hassan, therefore, poetry and art, promoted to their height at the court, enable a temporary liberation of the soul from the realities of social hierarchy. Throughout, Flecker emphasizes the irony of this conviction. At the start of the play, the disillusioned Ishak muses to himself:

> for you [the Caliph] I have strung glittering, fulsome verses, a hundred rhyming to one rhyme, ingeniously woven, my disgrace as a poet, my dishonour as a man. And I have forgotten that there are men who dig and sow, and a hut on the hills where I was born.[112]

By the end of the play, the poet has broken his lute, and Hassan has come to recognize that the 'poetry and music and pictures' of the court do not express higher matters of the soul, but only mask the sadistic brutality of the powerful.

While *Hassan* can certainly never be read as a socialist propaganda play, its theme of the injustice of the powerful and the disillusionment of the appeased lower classes may well have resonated strongly at the time of its conception and in the post-war era of its production. Even more immediately resonant, perhaps, is the play's engagement with the very role and idiom of art itself. *Hassan* deflates conventional romance in a language whose comical sections suggest self-parody, and in a primary plot whose grim cynicism condemns the conventional actions of lovers separated by tragic circumstance. In so doing, it essentially undercuts the legitimacy of its own poetic idiom as anything other than willed, aesthetic escapism. As Wood notes, the prose dialogue 'sounds at times too poetic for ordinary mortals': the language 'is suitable only for this kind of play; it would be inappropriate to express the predicaments and preoccupations of our times'.[113] Towards the end of the play, 'the language is perhaps too beautiful for the ugly situation'.[114] Ultimately, however, the dialogue and themes of the play suggest that that 'excess' of beauty is deliberate, and that Flecker is calling attention to a fundamental tension between escape through art and stark reality.

As most retrospective assessments have indicated, that escapism was more than provided by the spectacle of the production itself, with its comfortable invocation of the glory years of Irving and Tree. It was also, however, slightly problematized by the very modernity of the dance and music traditions that it helped to promote. The revised play called for numerous occasions for incidental music; it also allowed for extended scenes of choreography. The play was staged at a time when the popularity of the Ballets Russes as a contemporary artistic voice had been well-established, and Dean hired as a choreographer one of the earliest, most well-known (former) representatives of that company, Michel Folkine. He also enlisted Frederick Delius to write the score. The score proved immensely successful both with critics and with audiences – and not as a comfortable reinforcement of the simplicity of *Chu Chin Chow*, but rather as an artistic and contemporary accomplishment in its own right. As Martin Lee-Browne and Mark Elder observe, the music to the scene in which the ghosts of Pervaneh and Raffi meet at the fountain constitutes 'the closest Delius ever came to sounding like Schoenberg', while 'the masterly final scene' is essentially 'operatic in scope'.[115]

Much of the play calls for such operatic treatment, invoking its possibility both in structural set-pieces and in the overt musicality of its poetic language. As Flecker himself seems deliberately to reinforce, that language is fundamentally rooted in inauthentic, if not tired, literary conventions of romantic escapism. As translated into modern dance and modern orchestration, however, it nonetheless enabled the contemporary development of those other arts on the same dramatic stage. In that context, Reynolds's identification of Hassan as a '*Götterdammerung*' takes on added meaning: the event may well have staged the final collapse of 'large-scale poetic drama', but it can also be seen as having contributed to the perpetuation and development of a self-consciously modern – and dramatic – tradition in music and dance.

CHAPTER 2
THE NEW DRAMA: SOCIAL CHALLENGE AND POETIC THEATRE FROM W.B. YEATS TO TERENCE GRAY

The brief critical and mainstream success of the early dramas of Stephen Phillips and of *Hassan* did very little to establish verse drama as a continuous or contemporary tradition on the twentieth-century commercial stage. Nonetheless, the first decades of the century did see verse drama emerge as a lively site for creative and theatrical exploration; as Leeming suggests, verse drama can be seen as having constituted the first 'major movement' in British theatre 'since Shaw or the Manchester School'.[1] The nature of that movement varied considerably, reflecting disparate and often divergent creative sensibilities and ideological instincts. It was typically united, however, in its very self-consciousness, in its recognition of an imperative to break with or challenge recent, established traditions. The definition of those traditions differed both in terms of aesthetic and form: some actively redressed Victorian poetry through drama; others challenged stage traditions. Some continued to envision a new poetic drama primarily in literary terms, content to publish their dramas and theories of drama with little thought of the stage itself. Others focused on rediscovering earlier traditions of verse drama through a renewed attention to versification and staging practice. The vast majority, however, were united in their rejection of the very contemporary commercial stage to which Phillips and Flecker had aspired.

With varying levels of enthusiasm, many of these verse dramatists consequently found themselves in an unprecedented engagement with the realities of an innovative, progressive culture of theatrical reform. As theatre director and manager Norman Marshall was to observe, those first decades were marked by a 'state of affairs in which a timid and reactionary commercial theatre existed side by side with an immensely vital and progressive group of rebel theatres and play-producing societies'.[2] Trewin is similarly emphatic: 'The commercial theatre ... was environed by rebels ... beyond the lights of the late Edwardian drawing-room there lurked the dangerous footpads of the new drama, their knives raised'.[3] This atmosphere of subversive challenge was not exclusive to dramatists, but was adopted and promoted by actors, directors, managers and designers alike to ensure an energetic creative environment focused on the very redefinition of the contemporary theatre.

While many verse dramatists participated actively within this environment, many were also seen – by themselves and by others – to be at increasing odds with its prevailing aesthetic and social values. The result, to some extent, was the simultaneous emergence of two distinct definitions of the 'new' drama. One insisted on the inseparability of social argumentation from theatrical reform. The other often looked to verse drama as a ritualistic 'Theatre of Beauty', as a means through which to effect a more profound spiritual and social transformation – and often through an emphatically anti-realist and intermedial aesthetic.

Verse drama and the theatre of reform at the beginning of the century

From the turn of the century and well into the next, such determined progressives as Shaw, Archer and Barker busily advocated an ideal of the new drama. In published plays, prefaces and reviews, in their association with various Sunday stage societies and repertory theatres, these reformers insisted that the vitality of that drama could only be ensured by liberating the theatre of the censor, of the artificial expectations engendered by a mainstream commercial theatre, and of a lingering indebtedness to outdated (and often misunderstood) traditions in drama and literature. Shaw in particular saw in drama (or the dramatic preface) the potential to instigate social reform, primarily by addressing and exposing the absurdity of social hypocrisy, complacency and entrenched institutions. While Barker embraced many of these sentiments, he also shared with such directors as Poel, Craig, and Nugent Monck an acute interest in addressing similarly entrenched approaches towards the stage, the actor, theatre design and dramatic tradition itself.

Many of these reformist voices identified a blinkered resistance to developments on the Continent in the staging, acting and theorization of a modern drama. Many also advocated the revitalization of a larger dramatic tradition hitherto rendered staid, conventional and inauthentic by mainstream practice. The effect was to establish a vital space through which to develop drama in verse as both a contemporary form and as an established but long-forgotten tradition whose rediscovered conventions might revivify and inspire. These instincts were at the fore of Barker's three-year management at the Court Theatre with J.E. Vedrenne (1904–7), which introduced an unprecedented number of Shaw plays to English audiences along with a diverse programme marked by the works of Maeterlinck, Euripides, Yeats, Arthur Schnitzler, Ibsen, Elizabeth Robins and Masefield. They also informed the 1907 founding of the amateur Pilgrim Players by Barry Jackson, who would eventually establish the Birmingham Repertory Theatre as one of the most innovative, eclectic and ambitious theatres for the staging of Shakespeare, Anton Chekhov, Shaw and other contemporary (and verse) dramatists such as Drinkwater and Bottomley. Similar energies were manifest in the management of the Manchester Gaiety Theatre by Annie Horniman, the 1911 establishment of the Liverpool Repertory Theatre and the foundation of the short-lived and overtly experimental Cambridge Festival Theatre under Terence Gray.

Under Poel and the Elizabethan Stage Society, under the directorial and (later) critical influence of Barker, the production of Shakespeare in these first decades became a dominant focus of theatrical reform. These productions encouraged an emphatic break from Victorian staging practices – and thus a determined re-imagining of the staging, poetry and performance both of Shakespearean drama and of verse drama more generally. The productions of Poel and Barker are known in particular for their challenge to the spectacular, pictorial stagings promoted by such actor-managers as Kean and Tree. Trewin describes a typical Tree approach to *A Midsummer Night's Dream* in 1900: the production was 'densely arboreal, its woods well-rabbited, and the play fortified by every available atom of Mendelssohn's entrancing sounds'.[4] In contrast, Poel established a reputation as 'the Father of the Puritan Revolution in the theatre'[5] with his minimalist sets, archaeological emphasis and productions designed for a spare platform stage. He was equally influential in challenging the conventional performance of dramatic verse on the stage. As Barker noted admiringly, Poel insisted on doing away with empty rhetorical recitations, on recognizing instead 'the whole merit of Elizabethan verse with its consonantal swiftness, its gradations sudden or slow, into vowelled liquidity, its comic rushes and stops, with, above all, the peculiar beauty of its rhymes'.[6]

Equally essential to this moment – and particularly to those bent on a contemporary drama in verse – was the rediscovery of other traditions of verse drama beyond that of the Elizabethans. The founding of the Phoenix Society in 1919 explored a larger, hitherto-neglected heritage of drama in verse: both the Stage Society and the Phoenix were influential in renewing and staging the works of Francis Beaumont, John Fletcher, William Congreve,

Richard Sheridan, Dryden, Thomas Otway, George Farquhar and John Vanbrugh. In 1896 and 1900 respectively, Poel had produced the first modern performances of Marlowe's *Doctor Faustus* and Milton's *Samson Agonistes*. Most significant, perhaps, was his 1901 production of *Everyman* in the Master's Courtyard of the London Charterhouse. The success of that production, soon followed by *The Sacrifice of Isaac* from the Chester Cycle, was such that *Everyman* was rapidly 'established as a stage classic'.[7] In its open-air staging and redefinition of the traditional theatre space, in its formalist structure, in its use of a verse form very different from that of Shakespeare – and in its initial casting of a woman to play the role of Everyman – the play seemed overtly new.

Poel's production did not just reveal a tradition that had been forgotten for centuries; it saw the received conventions and connotations of that tradition (anti-naturalist, colloquial, undecorative, religious) find vocal and varied proponents in such reforming directors as Max Reinhardt, Philip Ben Greet and Gray. It would also find enthusiastic support in the proliferation of verse dramas that looked to medieval drama as an alternative model to that of the Elizabethans. Reinhardt made annual performances of Hugo von Hofmannsthal's adaptation *Jedermann* (1911) central to his Salzburg Festival, itself a prominent influence on drama and music festivals in Britain. Monck, a former actor in Poel's Society, went on to found the Norwich Players, whose productions at the Maddermarket Theatre specialized in medieval religious drama. As Speaight asserts, the dramatic effect and novelty of *Everyman* 'attracted a public which would never have been touched by [Poel's] Elizabethan revivals'.[8] It also brought the medieval drama back 'into limited circulation, so that we can trace a whole cycle of public taste from the rediscovery of *Everyman* . . . to the revival of the York Mystery plays by Martin Browne fifty years later'[9] – and, arguably, to the staging of Tony Harrison's *The Mysteries* at the National Theatre in 1977.

Equally revelatory, for many, were the possibilities of a revitalized Greek drama, freed of decorative trappings and intensely experimental in its defiance of a naturalist model. Yeats, Craig and Gray are among the most notable directors and drama theorists who recognized in classical conventions a means through which to transform the modern stage and modern drama. Playwrights from Phillips through to Masefield and Eliot were quick to exploit the formal structures of a drama that – like medieval drama – differed intensely both from the contemporary realist drama and from the Shakespearean poetic heritage through which so much Victorian drama had been developed. Undoubtedly one of the most influential figures in this moment was Gilbert Murray, a prominent scholar of ancient Greece, a friend of such literary figures as Shaw, Masefield and H.G. Wells, and a leading translator of Greek plays for reading and performance. According to Masefield, Murray wrote with an acute awareness of the contemporary possibilities of those translations: 'about his translation of *Oedipus* he wrote to me: "I would very much sooner have the opinion of a poet without Greek than that of a scholar without the other requisites: in fact, I am not sure whether the poet without Greek is not exactly the reader that I am seeking".[10] Murray also recognized the extent to which Greek verse differed from conventional understandings of verse on the English stage:

> [it is] not at all like the loose go-as-you-please Elizabethan verse, which ... makes up for its lack of strict form by extreme verbal ornamentation. In Greek tragic dialogue the metrical form is stiff and clear; hardly ever could a tragic line by any mistake be taken for prose; the only normal variation is not towards prose but towards a still more highly wrought musical lyric. Yet inside the stiff metrical form the language is clear, simple, and direct. A similar effect can, in my opinion, only be attained in English by the use of rhyme.[11]

In his emphasis on re-visitation rather than re-creation, in his comparative appreciation of different techniques and dramatic forms, Murray spoke directly to a creative environment marked by its exploration of diverse traditions of dramatic expression and production.

For many, this exploration was motivated as much by an appreciation of the social role of drama as it was by aesthetics alone. In the first decades of the century, the prominent, politicized debates around theatre censorship crystallized equally around Barker's *Waste* (1906) and Sophocles' *Oedipus Rex*, with all the contemporary defenders of the modern theatre – Barrie, Galsworthy, Shaw, Barker, Housman and Murray himself – united in righteous protest. Even more influential to the development of much modern verse drama in this period was the recognized ideal of Greek drama as festival, as a ritualistic people's theatre that could challenge the relationships embodied by the aesthetic and commercial practices of the mainstream stage. In 1926, Gray lamented the apparent fact that '[t]he instinctive and natural appreciation of drama which must have underlain the popularity of the Greek plays and the mediaeval mysteries appears to be entirely lacking in the general Anglo-Saxon popularity of to-day'.[12] Rather than merely mourning the loss of that ideal, many directors and playwrights looked to encourage a return to the amateur, popular roots of theatre in subject, staging and practice. This return emphasized the spiritual revivification of the communal audience and a renewed appreciation of the intermedial nature of an originating poetic and ritual theatre. As Dukes declared in 1928: 'One fine spring day on a Greek hillside [theatre] produced itself out of a festival chorus and dance. Then, having first created drama, it gave the dramatists the forms in which they should express themselves. Is not that the sequence of dramatic history?'[13]

Amateur drama

This larger enthusiasm for the social origins and aesthetic practices of Greek and medieval drama, for earlier performing conventions and conditions, and for the spiritual significance of drama as a whole gave significant incentive to creative explorations. It also ensured a particular appreciation for what had become a flourishing culture of amateur drama in diverse forms and contexts. Much amateur drama has been associated with an instrumental and political definition of theatre, particularly due to the proliferation of workers' theatre in the first half of the decade and its emphasis on access and communal participation. Other amateur productions, particularly those that built upon a burgeoning taste for local patriotic pageants, have been associated with a more conservative social politics. In the cultural climate of the early twentieth century, however, the very rootedness of that theatre in a communal and local creative environment also ensured the embrace of the amateur by those eager to seek out and build upon an 'instinctive and natural appreciation of drama' in the much-idealized people.

In 1923, Archer's influential re-valuation of 'The Old Drama and the New' provided a useful summation of some of the values – social and aesthetic – associated with amateur theatre:

Village players and community players sprang upon every hand. Folk-dancing was revived along with folk-song. And in these little local enterprises there was a strong tendency to include all the arts of the theatre. . . . in the base camps and rest camps semi-amateur companies acted before appreciative audiences plays of a higher class than any that were to be seen on the London stage of thirty years earlier.

It was by no mere chance, we may be sure, that the pageant movement and the Repertory Theatre movement came into being almost simultaneously. They were concurrent results of one and the same impulse towards dramatic expression; and in each case the desire to make money, if it existed at all, played a quite secondary part.[14]

In this characteristic assessment, amateur drama both identified and perpetuated a hitherto-forgotten manifestation of indigenous, communal expression. In its celebration of 'all the arts of the theatre', it invited comparison with the ritual origins of theatre; in its creative inclusiveness, it manifested an ideal of social community. For some, that non-commercial emphasis was political; it could suggest a communal resistance to centralized structures. For others less invested in social or political reform, that freedom from commercial concerns nonetheless encouraged a greater artistic, exploratory freedom. Such assessments were not left in the hands of outside commentators, but were rapidly promoted in the formation of amateur theatre companies and community associations across the country.

Common to many of these aesthetically minded reformers was a tendency to excoriate the complacent status of British theatre, its promotion of what Geoffrey Whitworth, founder of the British Drama League, condemned 'as entertainment pure and simple – "a night out"'.[15] Equally crucial was an attempt to counter exclusively literary approaches to the appraisal and creation of drama, the 'Puritan fear of the theatre [that] still lingered in some scholastic minds, and [that] made grease paint smell a little like brimstone'.[16] Furthermore, as Claire Cochrane notes, the 'experimental' plays of nineteenth-century Europe had only 'infiltrated British theatre' through the 'independent, unpaid initiatives' of stage societies. The result was to ensure a certain 'intellectual kudos' to the amateur, whose 'ultimate objective . . . was to change the ideological and aesthetic basis of professional theatre'.[17] In this context, it is unsurprising that such self-conscious reformers of the modern theatre as Barker, Archer, Shaw and Bottomley were heavily involved in the support and patronage of amateur theatre production. Indeed, the established divide between the evaluation (and production) of amateur and professional drama is relatively recent, the result of a mid-century professionalization of specialist occupations within the theatre.[18] In the first half of the century, many professional actors honed their skills in amateur theatre and occasionally returned to that environment in recognition of its creative vitality.

An equally strong – and more frequently overlooked – manifestation of the non-commercial, ideological and aesthetic challenge epitomized by much amateur theatre was found in the proliferation of cathedral plays and religious drama. In 1913, the Lord Chamberlain reversed the blanket ban on all stage plays that dealt with biblical subjects. Unlike the plays subsequently written for the commercial stage, those written for amateur performance and for performance in church spaces tended to be more experimental, freed both of the traditional dynamic between paying audience, professional actor and commercial playwright – and of the conventional staging limitations of the theatre space itself. As Kenneth Pickering notes, the result was a drama relatively 'free to evolve along experimental or commercially less popular lines'.[19] That evolution was encouraged by churchmen such as George Bell, who, upon becoming Dean of Canterbury in 1924, acted upon an apparent conviction that 'the Church was above all things a creative body'.[20] Bell immediately set about sponsoring play readings, the staging of new Christian drama for performance within the cathedral and, in 1929, the institution of the Canterbury Festival.

This association of the Church and the church space with a vital creative energy was embraced by many voices bent upon the reform of the theatre, who saw in the writing of drama for church performance an incentive both to develop and to revivify diverse modes and traditions of dramatic expression. As explored in Chapter 4, it was also embraced by many established dramatists, poets, theatre designers and actors eager to attempt a distinct genre, to build implicitly upon the traditions excavated by Poel and his followers. For some, that genre was exclusively religious; for many others, it was first and foremost poetic. The success of *Murder in the Cathedral* did much both to popularize religious drama and to promote an assumption that 'religious drama was a non-realistic branch of theatre for which non-realistic dialogue was appropriate'.[21] By the time of that play, however, religious drama had already been established as a new theatrical genre, drawing to it such prominent names in music, art, and theatre as Holst, Ricketts, Laurence Irving, Eileen Thorndike – not to mention Masefield, Housman, Binyon and Charles Williams.

Counter-revolution: the fight against social realism

The first decades of the twentieth century thus saw a clear resonance between the aesthetic interests of verse dramatists and larger reforms in staging, in the revival of earlier dramatic traditions, in the exploration of Continental forms and in the promotion of amateur theatre. Notwithstanding this clear affinity, however, many verse dramatists also adopted an early attitude of defensiveness and willed resignation, if not self-conscious failure, against that larger environment. Informing that attitude was a perception of their divergence not only from the dominant trends of the commercial stage, but also from a more self-consciously progressive drama bent primarily upon the realist dramatization of contemporary society and socially-argumentative themes. For poet-dramatists, only verse drama provided an authentic expression if not manifestation of essential human experience, and its inherent anti-realism rendered it fundamentally opposed to the New Drama.

As many of these poet-dramatists were also acutely aware, however, this 'higher' ideal and anti-realist aesthetic did not ensure a receptive audience. The most oft-cited poet-dramatist in this regard is undoubtedly Yeats. With the opening of the Abbey Theatre he had publicly envisioned a drama that might restore 'a way of life in which the common man has some share in imaginative art'.[22] That ideal had its roots in the natural lyricism, oral traditions and folk identity of the Irish people: his poetic drama would simultaneously resurrect and represent the 'living voice' of its national audience as a whole.[23] In 1919, however, after years of practical experience with theatre audiences (and critics), Yeats redressed these sentiments in an open letter to Lady Gregory. He could now only advocate artistic retreat with select, like minds into an increasingly more experimental theatre: 'I want to create for myself an unpopular theatre and audience like a secret society where admission is by favour and never to many'.[24] This theatre would ideally be open to 'an audience of fifty' in 'a room worthy of it (some great dining-room or drawing-room)'[25]: 'who but the leisured will welcome an elaborate art or pay for its first experiments? . . . I want to make, or to help some many some day to make, a feeling of exclusiveness, a bond among chosen spirits, a mystery almost for leisured and lettered people.'[26]

Most of the Georgians seemed to share this assumption of the limited understanding of the larger audience; indeed, for many, 'commercial failure' seemed to become 'virtually prima facie evidence of artistic success'.[27] Although Abercrombie noted his own 'failure to make poetic conquest of the stage', he also contested any consequent assumption 'that to write a play in verse is thereby to render it unstage-worthy'.[28] Writing of the hostile reception of King Lear's Wife in Birmingham in 1915, Drinkwater professed himself unsurprised: 'A "fit audience find though few" – to do this is all the poets can yet hope to do in the theatre, but it doesn't matter. Those who do care, care very much.'[29] Like Yeats, Bottomley identified a theatrical environment innately hostile to poetic drama, a culture that 'had never understood or conceived that poetry could have a relationship to drama at all – or that there is a heightening power in it which the poet and the actor can share between them in delighted partnership'.[30] In the 1932 preface to his *Lyric Plays*, he praises Yeats as the last exemplar of a theatre nobly impervious both to the realist stage and to the dehumanizing forces through which its audience has been shaped:

> That time has ended, as in Athens once
> And Florence and Shakespeare's London a great age
> Ended: we survive into a time
> Of shortened vision, disharmony, distrust,
> That will not let the immortals work with us.[31]

Such defensive, if not elegiac, responses do much to reinforce Allardyce Nicoll's assessment that many of these early dramatists adopted a 'trend towards increasing exclusiveness'.[32]

This instinct was unquestionably encouraged by a dominant critical climate that insisted on defining modern drama in relation to its authentic representation of contemporary life. In this environment, verse suggested a willed artificiality and social irrelevance. In 1919, a piece by Chaman Lall in *Coterie* condemned verse drama as 'a dead thing': 'our ears ... no longer strain to familiarity with the sustained diction of uttered verse'.[33] Furthermore, verse in theatre renders drama 'the pastime of the esoteric few': the appeal of 'theatrical art' must be 'to the wide, indiscriminate, uninitiated masses' and 'for this reason alone the days of Verse-Drama are extinct'.[34] In 1924, Glover reiterated this critical (and now long-standing) perception that verse drama could not – and did not attempt to – speak to a larger social community: 'ours being an age of prose, prose is the proper medium for the theatre'.[35] Furthermore, contemporary poetry itself had so moved away from making humanity its theme that the dominant 'theme of the modern poet is himself':

> Until the poet can forget himself and remember men, until the urgency
> of his matter transforms the pettiness of his manner, there will be no
> more grand poetry. In the theatre especially there will be no poetry.
> For there an egotistical bleat appears crudely for what it is.[36]

Glover's assertions suggest a yearning for the 'grand poetry' that had characterized earlier decades and that had been actively challenged by much modern poetry thereafter. He also, contradictorily, demands that poetic drama engage more closely with the everyday idiom and social reality of 'the age' itself, 'an age of prose'.[37]

Lall and Glover thus assume in verse drama a deliberate distancing of both poet and play from the realities and experience of the contemporary audience. The very redress of any artificial distance between poet and reader, however, was one of the primary concerns of the Georgian poets. They also promoted that emphasis in relation to their idealization of verse drama, where they identified an imperative (and opportunity) to articulate an urgent theme of 'humanity'. For the Georgians, only a more natural verse idiom would move poetry in theatre away from artificial decoration, static declamation, or the solipsistic introversion identified (by some) in modern poetry itself. As early as 1903, Symons had declared:

> The poetic drama ... must live, and it must live in poetry, as in its natural atmosphere. The verse must speak as straight as prose, but with a more beautiful voice. It must avoid rhetoric as scrupulously as Ibsen avoids rhetoric. It must not 'make poetry', however good in its way.[38]

For many, this 'beautiful voice', liberated of literary ornament, would ensure the development of a *more* realist drama, a theatre that transcended the surface details of quotidian life and social argumentation by expressing – as only verse can – the innate human realities beneath that surface. In 1912, Abercrombie asserted that 'in a perfectly successful poetic play the whole of the talking *can* be done naturally in poetry; and we must always feel it to be natural'.[39] Through a felicitous combination of dramatic situation, character and verse, 'the ultimate end of drama [should be] the excitation of self-consciousness, of a state of being in which we find it something of an exultation to know that we are ourselves'.[40] This emphasis was echoed by Drinkwater, who saw in verse drama the potential to re-awaken an innately human sensibility to essential realities, 'the poignant significance at the heart of the matter'.[41]

For the first modern verse dramatists, that focus differed fundamentally from a more prominent reforming theatre whose emphasis on stage realism and social argumentation rendered it essentially indifferent to 'the heart of the matter'. In 1928, Dukes – a keen promoter of verse drama in these decades – identified a new hope for modern drama in the fact that 'The age of the study-plays – the dull Ibsenite age – is quickly passing. The dramatists of the future will be more and more theatre men and less and less men with messages.'[42] Shaw's *Quintessence of Ibsenism* (1891) had done much to encourage this misperception of Ibsen, invoking his dramas in order to argue for a theatre and society that would question and challenge. As Eric Bentley notes, Yeats rejected Ibsen precisely because 'he ignorantly believed him to be dull and chiefly sociological'.[43] For some, that social emphasis had been essential to the reform of the stage; James Agate identifies 1893 as 'the year when drama, taking a dive in Norwegian waters, suffered a permanent sea-change': 'before the 'nineties it had never entered the heads of playgoers that they might be called upon to use them'.[44] In contrast, Donoghue contends that the English reception of Ibsen's plays ensured 'the most serious disaster in the modern English theatre': it had 'stopped with the mere recognition of *theme* and *argument*'.[45] Ironically, that reductive reading of both Ibsen and 'the age of the study-plays' was challenged by such exemplars of the New Drama as Barker and Shaw himself. Its influence, however, was such as to ensure that many verse dramatists would position themselves as uniquely resistant to a prevailing, misguided trend. As Katharine J. Worth observes, 'the line stretching from Yeats through Eliot … to Auden and Isherwood is the line of the new age, the counter-revolution'.[46]

That resistance was informed by much more than a taste for verse expression. In 1920, Monro, founder of the Poetry Bookshop, editor of the *Poetry Review* and publisher of *Georgian Poetry*, exhorted 'poets of the modern world' to write 'plays, simple, direct, dependent, for their beauty, not on outward decoration, but on the inward force of the spirit that conceives them'.[47] For many, the poetic manifestation of this 'inward force' was vital in a contemporary era fast losing its appreciation for the spiritual importance of art itself. According to Abercrombie, 'The preference for prose plays over poetic plays is … a preference for ordinary appearance over spiritual reality: it is, in fact, a form of materialism.'[48] Only the true art represented by poetic drama can reach towards 'the significant world', that which 'was given to us in the first instance', 'the world of actual aesthetic experience … [and] a world we have *destroyed*'.[49] Abercrombie echoes the words of Yeats, twenty years earlier. Responding to the perception of George Moore and Edward Martyn that the decline of England could be seen in the decline of her drama, Yeats had concluded:

> It is indisputable that the highest perfection of human society has ever corresponded with the highest dramatic excellence; and that the

corruption or the extinction of the drama in a nation, where it has once flourished, is a mark of the corruption of manners and an extinction of the energies which sustain the soul of social life. I myself throw the blame for that decline ... upon that commercialism and materialism on which these men warred; and not upon race as do certain of my countrymen.[50]

Drinkwater was only slightly less emphatic: the role of verse in drama is to reawaken the intuitive 'passionate life' against which is 'arrayed' 'the condition of our civilisation, a strongly organised and capitalised industry' that is the commercial theatre and capitalist society more generally.[51] Binyon adopts a similar argument: 'Prose accepts, poetry rebels. In the prose view of the world all is fixed ... in the poetic view, all is energy, relation, change.'[52] For Bottomley, 'fact has a deeper function than it has in the presentation of the realistic drama; for, where that has just realism for its object, poetry can use stylisation to further its penetration to reality'.[53] In prescient anticipation of the reputational fate of later verse dramatists, Abercrombie terms that 'innermost reality, the one with which art is most dearly concerned' 'emotional': 'it is what is commonly called the spiritual reality' but can 'be more easily handled' with a comparatively neutral appellation.[54]

Many early dramatists were relatively sanguine in accepting that this appeal to 'the general substratum to all existence'[55] through verse drama could not find a contemporary audience or stage. In a correspondence with Drinkwater, Gibson was 'confident that poetic drama is *the* art of the future'.[56] He also, however, felt that that appeal was impossible to realize on the stage itself: he was 'not much drawn to the theatre as a medium of expression', wanting in his plays 'to make a much more intimate appeal than is possible from the stage'.[57] The majority of poet-dramatists, however, were committed to an ideal of the stage that demanded restoration and reform in equal measure. While the plays of Abercrombie, Sturge Moore and Symons were rarely produced outside of stage societies or small theatres, they were nonetheless written in the conviction that poetic drama was an 'art of the future'. Central to these poets was an emphasis on drama as a neglected *art* and as a form whose traditional spiritual role had been forgotten in the face of an inauthentic redefinition of theatre as social propaganda and mundane, realist portraiture.

This emphasis overtly contradicted some of the most prominent voices of dramatic reform, who associated that ideal of beauty in theatre with an unnecessary extravagance better left to more emotional forms of dramatic art. In his preface to *Mrs Warren's Profession* (1893), Shaw had asserted: 'The drama of pure feeling is no longer in the hands of the playwright: it has been conquered by the musician ... there is, flatly, no future now for any drama without music except the drama of thought.'[58] His sentiments were echoed by Archer in 1923:

> The two elements of the old drama, imitation and lyrical passion, have at last consummated their divorce. For lyrical passion we go to opera and music drama, for interpretation through imitation we go to the modern realistic play. And surely we ought to recognise that this divorce, so obviously inevitable, is a good and not a bad thing – a sign of health and not of degeneracy.[59]

As Ronald Schuchard notes, 'England did not dislike poetic drama, but ... poetic drama could not thrive or survive there alone.'[60]

To some extent, this condition was exacerbated by the fact that not all poets embraced the reality (rather than the idea) of the stage in equal measure. Abercrombie's publications and his public talk on 'The Function of the Poetry in the Drama' attest to his investment in a new poetic drama for the stage. He was ultimately fated to publish that drama for his fellow poets, however, a fate that Drinkwater attributes to his refusal to engage with the expectations of the modern stage and play-goer:

> he refused to become a dilettante in a medium for which he had a profound respect ... The heady texture of his poetry asked too much of audiences that had forgotten how to listen to poetry at all, but the fault would have been cured by the experience of regular work in a theatre.[61]

For Drinkwater, whose focus was the reform of the theatre itself, the inevitable recourse was instead to move away from the writing of drama in verse:

> if I had been born into a theatre that took kindly to verse as a medium I believe that interesting things might have been done in its development. ... if I was to take any effective part in the practical theatre of my time, I should have to abandon verse for prose. Full of reforming ideas as we all were, I soon began to realise that in this fundamental matter of expression it would be futile, and indeed pointless, to try to alter the habit of an age.[62]

Ultimately, the different careers of all of these poet-dramatists underline a prevailing acceptance of the inevitable isolation of modern verse drama from the dominant tastes and expectations of the contemporary stage.

Celtic Twilight and Yeats

This sense of isolation was to some extent informed by a distinct perception that the loss of a communal, ritual art and that the marginal status of verse drama were relatively unique to England. English verse dramatists in the first half of the century often found occasion to look wistfully to the contemporary drama of Ireland, to the dramatic culture of Scotland and to what was seen as the inherently mythical, poetic identity of a mist-enshrouded Wales. Much of that initial interest can be traced to the Pre-Raphaelite enthusiasm for Arthurian romance and its varied dissemination into late nineteenth-century explorations of British origin myths and celebrations of a 'Celtic Twilight'. It can also be traced to the socialist aestheticism of the designer, writer and activist William Morris, whose emphasis on the natural, poetic beauty of rural folk traditions unsullied by industrialization could often provoke wistful romanticizations of England's Celtic neighbours. Masefield, for example, recalls his ambition to reawaken and cultivate a natural, popular 'feeling for poetry' in England by writing plays for 'little groups like the Guild of Handicraft': 'This thought, or something like it, was in many minds at the time ... as the direct result of the words and practice of William Morris.'[63] It also took strength from the vital example of Ireland, where 'the nation's imagination ... [was] burning brightly.'[64]

The first self-conscious promoters of a modern English verse drama often contemplated Ireland, Scotland and Wales as living cultures from which myth – the origins of drama – had never vanished. Gray (himself of established Anglo-Irish stock) provided a characteristic assessment in 1926: 'save in Gaelic Ireland, in Gaelic Scotland, and in British Wales, no figures of popular tradition, no gods and heroes survive in the public imagination, there no longer exists in the thoughts or the memory of the people any trace of a folk-history or mythology as a basis for imaginative thought.'[65] In England, this memory 'died out with the Arthurian cycle in the Middle-ages'; it now had no natural 'appreciation of great drama.'[66] In an apparent attempt to redress this vital lack of national – and dramatic – mythical expression, the nineteenth and early twentieth centuries saw a proliferation of English verse dramas and music dramas on Arthurian themes. Prominent examples include Rutland Boughton's *The Immortal Hour* (1914), Symons's *Tristan and Iseult* (1917), Binyon's *Arthur: A Tragedy* (1923) and Masefield's *Tristan and Isolt* (1927). Those years also, unsurprisingly, saw a particularly enthusiastic (if inaccurate) invocation of the culture and history of those nearby lands whose oral traditions and customs had ensured the perpetual 'brightness' of their imagination.

Equally central was the perception of an unforced, naturally poetic idiom that tied living expression to living myth (and thus drama). In 1910, Drinkwater observed that London audiences had been 'enraptured' by Ireland's Abbey Players, and particularly 'by the novelty of their methods and cadences. An English company, good or bad, had no chance . . . in rivalry on the stage with these newcomers.'[67] This appreciation often saw (and occasionally still sees) the association of all Irish expression – dramatic or otherwise – with an inherent poeticism. As Masefield recounted in 1951, 'Yeats once said to me: "The English do not talk." Certainly, the English of that time could not and did not talk like Yeats.'[68] In 1931, Martin Ellehague located the origins of the local dialect in John Millington Synge's plays to 'a time not far removed from the period of biblical English.'[69] Thus, the poetic 'Elisabethan and biblical rhythms in Synge' derive from 'actual speech', offering a stark contrast to the 'bookishness and artificiality' that characterizes the efforts of English verse dramatists deprived of such primary material.[70] Some twenty years later, Eliot would agree: critiquing a frequent slippage between identifications of verse in drama and poetic prose, Eliot concedes an exception in Synge, whose plays 'are based upon the idiom of a rural people whose speech is naturally poetic, both in imagery and in rhythm'.[71] Eliot's aim was to formulate a tradition of verse drama that would develop such a natural poetic idiom in England. He was relatively alone in that larger ambition, however, and many of his immediate predecessors and contemporaries only enviously contemplated the 'living poetry' in the speech and traditions of their neighbours.

Many of these poet-dramatists also recognized in Scotland and Ireland a very different culture of dramatic reform and development. The advocates of a modern national theatre in England took considerable inspiration from the foundation of the Irish Literary Theatre and the eventual establishment of the Abbey Theatre, Dublin, in 1904. That enthusiasm, shared by proponents of verse and prose drama alike, focused on the state-sponsored establishment of a national theatre, on the plays of Yeats and Synge, and on the support of that drama by a large national audience. The recognized position of Yeats as poet, poet-dramatist and theorist also ensured a particular interest from those in England determined to establish a contemporary tradition of modern drama in verse. That interest was reciprocal: as Schuchard has detailed, the years between the dissipation of the Irish Literary Theatre and the establishment of the Abbey saw Yeats actively working in London with the actress, activist and director Florence Farr, with Sturge Moore, with Binyon and with other like-minded enthusiasts. Eager to see his plays staged, Yeats joined with Symons, Edith Craig and Murray to affiliate the energies of the Literary Theatre Club with a new society, initially the Theatre of Beauty, soon to become the Masquers. As the fortunes of the Masquers seemed to stall under internal disagreements, Yeats eventually moved his creative energies to Dublin, where he found more financial support. As Schuchard speculates, had the Masquers 'remained cohesive', Annie Horniman, primary financial patron of the Abbey, may well have chosen to support Yeats's Theatre of Beauty in England rather than Ireland.[72]

Despite his nationalist sympathies, Yeats's artistic projects were certainly not exclusive to Ireland, and the reciprocal influence of English directors, designers, poets and actresses proved significant to the practical development of his theatrical aesthetic and to his projects for the Abbey. That collaboration continued after the opening of the Abbey: Ricketts designed costumes for the London visits of the Abbey in productions of *The King's Threshold* and *On Baile's Strand* in 1914 and 1915; Gordon Craig's staging experimentations in lighting and the use of screens were a constant influence on the development of Yeats's dramatic aesthetic; Farr was the primary collaborator with whom he developed and promoted his ideal of verse chanting. In 1934, disillusioned with the realism promoted at the Abbey, Yeats entered into partnership with the choreographer Frederick Ashton, Dukes, Eliot and members of the Group Theatre in a renewed attempt to promote modern verse drama on the London stage. Like the Masquers, the Poets' Theatre eventually failed amidst internal division and indecision; it did much, however, to underline the shared enthusiasms of Yeats and contemporary proponents of verse drama in England.[73]

Towards an English Theatre of Beauty

Rather than spawning overt imitation, the influence of Yeats in England was such as to encourage continuous efforts to establish a contemporary poetic theatre. His attempts to develop a distinctly dramatic metre and verse informed the experiments of his fellow-poets; Eliot, for example, claimed that in *Purgatory* (1938), Yeats had 'solved his problem of speech in verse, and laid all his successors under obligation to him'.[74] The very ideal of a Theatre of Beauty in England was both inspired and developed by Yeats. So, too, was a strengthened enthusiasm for myth and folklore as a foundation for creative experimentation and innovation: Yeats himself had been a frequent visitor at the house of William Morris, where their shared ideals extended beyond a similar appreciation of oral tradition, myth and medievalism to a particular interest in ancient traditions of verse chanting.[75] Many consequently took inspiration from Yeats's return to indigenous myth and folklore as a means to promote a contemporary oral tradition of popular theatre. Where Gray composed dramas based upon Irish heroic themes, Binyon and Sturge Moore attempted to translate Yeats's early dramatic aesthetic into 'poetic dramas based on Greek rather than Irish heroic plays'.[76] Others looked for more indigenous sources; Bottomley turned to ancient Northern and Scottish legends, while Masefield saw both Yeats and Synge as 'the beginners of the movement' that was to follow in both dramatic writing and amateur production:

> Listening to Synge's play ... made me feel what a wealth of fable lay still in the lonely places in England.... We had not become alive to its presence: we were dead to it: and much of the theatre of that time was dead in consequence.... The thought occurred to some of us younger Englishmen that some of us might find, in the English country, subjects as moving, fables as lively: possibly, also, amateur actors as talented.[77]

Equally significant – and perhaps particularly overlooked – was the considerable impact of Yeats's attempts, with Farr and the composer Arnold Dolmetsch, to revivify, restore and establish a bardic tradition of verse speaking and poetic chanting.[78] The realization of these attempts on the stage in either Ireland or England was limited. They did, however, encourage a renewed attention to the performance and musicality of verse that was actively developed and promoted by the Literary Theatre Club, that was a strong influence on the vocal coaching (in England and Scotland) of Marjorie Gullan and Elsie Fogerty, that undeniably informed the poetics of Eliot and Pound, and that gave particular impetus to English verse dramatists bent on establishing poetic drama as a communal ritual with its origins in oral tradition. In 1922, Masefield, an established enthusiast of Yeats's approach to chanting and recitation, was invited to adjudicate a verse-speaking competition at the Edinburgh Musical Festival. Masefield had already established a group of amateur and semi-professional performers (The Hill Players) to stage classic verse dramas. On his visit to Scotland, however, he was overwhelmed by the excellence of the verse-speaking:

> a young woman began in a way that made me hold my breath, with the thought, 'O, if only Yeats could hear this.' ... [Marjorie Gullan] had from Yeats's suggestions devised a method of speech that could delight any poet, or, indeed, the world.[79]

Such was the power of the experience that Masefield and his wife resolved to establish a similar festival in Oxford: 'We did not know what talent England hid, nor what genius directed it. We hoped to find out these matters.'[80] For seven years thereafter, Masefield's annual Oxford Recitations encouraged the advancement of verse speaking and the writing and staging of verse drama. In 1924, Masefield built a private theatre at his home in Boars Hill, Oxford, where the Recitations expanded to feature lectures, readings and private stagings of new verse dramas by poets such as Bottomley, Binyon and Masefield himself.

On 5 November 1930, Masefield held a verse festival at Boars Hill to commemorate the thirtieth anniversary of his meeting with Yeats. In his speech, Masefield declared that when poetry is 'heard upon the modern English stage . . . it is largely due to Mr. Yeats that it is heard with any pleasure.'[81] Despite Masefield's best efforts, despite reviews from local and national papers, the recitations and the verse dramas composed for Boars Hill never established an environment comparable to that which had already been developing in Scotland, let alone in Ireland's national theatre. As Masefield notes, ill-health eventually forced him to '[lay] aside this work, never to resume it.'[82]

Total art: Terence Gray and the Cambridge Festival Theatre

Yeats himself was constantly evolving his own theatrical aesthetic, and his dramas developed increasingly towards a more symbolic and intermedial ideal. That evolution was keenly marked by Bottomley, who saw himself as moving towards 'a similar disturbing and re-balancing of the factors of drama' through the exploration of dance, masks, music, curtains and Noh traditions on the poetic stage.[83] More lastingly significant, perhaps, was the impact of Yeats on Gray, himself an overlooked, seminal influence.

Only a year after the publication of Yeats's *Plays for Dancers*, Gray penned an article in *Dancing Times* that claimed that 'the origins of drama itself was in dancing'.[84] A few years later, he published a cycle of heroic plays on Cuchulainn (never staged) and his own theorization of dance-drama, complete with six plays. In 1926, Gray opened the Festival Theatre in Cambridge: a third of the plays in the first season were Irish, and the productions were self-consciously experimental. Central to that experimentalism was a reiterated ideal of drama as theatre that demanded new definitions of drama, new approaches to the stage and new appreciations of the relationship between the arts themselves on that stage. In one of his (many) contributions to the in-house publication, *Festival Review*, Gray declared: 'In practising the Art of the Theatre we no longer bow down before the shrine of English literature. It has lost its godhead in our eyes and, truth to tell, it is more of a curse than a blessing in the world of acted drama.'[85]

Unlike Yeats, Gray was emphatic in his conviction that the controlling authorship in theatre should be that of the director, rather than the dramatist. Ultimately, the effect was to align his enthusiasm for the drama, poetry and aesthetic ideals of Yeats with many of the theories being promoted on the Continent into an ambitious, mainstage ideal of total art theatre:

> The spoken word is but one element among others, of which the most important are Movement (dancing, expression by gesture, crowd-movement), Lighting (colour expression by atmosphere, scenic and decorative projection), Painting (pictorial and decorative expression by means of pigment), Architecture (form, emotional expression by means of planes and mass), Sculpture (expression outside the limited range attainable by the human face and body, through masks and lay figures), Sound (music, emotional expression by means of audible devices, repetition, recurrence, crescendo of natural and artificial noise formations), and the as yet barely attempted use of the sense of Smell.[86]

This theatre was in many ways mandated by the design of the stage itself, which ensured 'that conventional realistic production was almost impossible'.[87] The experiments of Gray at the Festival Theatre eventually proved to be too much for its audience, burdened equally by the intransigent voices of the local critics and the increasingly resolute and deliberately aggressive position of its director. (One staging of *The Merchant of Venice*, for example, featured actors playing out the director's own boredom with the play, bouncing yo-yos during the court-room scene.) Discouraged, Gray left the Theatre (and the theatre) permanently in 1933, only to re-emerge some many years later as Wei Wu Wei, author of several books of Eastern philosophy and metaphysics.

According to Marshall, who worked briefly at the Festival, Gray's 'seven years of ceaseless experiment ... had in the end little practical effect upon the English theatre.'[88] As Paul Cornwell recounts, however, when Ninette de Valois first saw the new Olivier Theatre at the National Theatre, 'she immediately recognised certain design features, such as the wide stage, the central revolve and the cyclorama; for the Festival theatre, as she remembered it, had been a similar house in miniature.'[89] In its advocacy of a revolutionized staging space and art, the Festival Theatre also provided an early, initial home to many voices that would subsequently influence developments in the larger national theatre. Directors at the Festival included Marshall and Tyrone Guthrie; the architect and designer Hugh Casson (then a student at Cambridge) painted scenery; Dukes delivered regular talks; and the dancer and choreographer Rupert Doone organized a play-reading group. That group evolved soon thereafter into the Group Theatre (formed 1932), which developed and staged verse dramas by Eliot, Auden, Isherwood and Stephen Spender. The incidental music for many of these dramas was provided by the young Benjamin Britten, who would later collaborate with Auden on his first opera, *Paul Bunyan* (1942).

While Yeats can hardly be credited with the design of the Olivier stage, the hiring of Casson, the formation of the Group Theatre, or the beginnings of modern British opera, his very promotion of an ideal of intimate, non-realist and symbolic theatre in verse was a clear influence on these subsequent developments. So too was the sympathy of his aesthetic with the development of other forms of dramatic expression. Such developments were encouraged both by the Cambridge Festival Theatre and the Group Theatre. In 1930, the economist John Maynard Keynes and his wife, dancer Lydia Lopokova, founded the Camargo Society with conductor and composer Constant Lambert, music critic Edwin Evans, ballet critic Arnold Haskell and Philip Richardson, editor of *Dancing Times*. Although the Society disbanded after three years, it proved a formative influence on the development of the Royal Ballet and reflected perpetual attempts within that decade to formulate a more experimental, intermedial form of dramatic art. In 1931, the Society staged the premiere of Ashton's ballet version of William Walton and Edith Sitwell's experimental 1923 'Entertainment', *Façade*. That year also saw the first staged production of *Job*, the first entirely British ballet: it was inspired by the engravings of Blake, choreographed and directed by Ninette de Valois, and featured a score from Ralph Vaughan Williams, with orchestrations by Lambert.

At the Festival Theatre, Gray had implicitly encouraged such developments by bringing the 'modern' (and often modernist) arts more closely together on the spoken stage. In 1926, he had hired de Valois – his cousin and eventual founder of the Royal Ballet – as a choreographer and occasional dancer. In 1927, Yeats attended the Festival Theatre and was reportedly so 'moved' by the choreography that he invited de Valois to the Abbey to assist in his own *Plays for Dancers*.[90] De Valois worked with Yeats and the Abbey Theatre School of Ballet until 1933. As Ernest Reynolds reflected in 1949:

> It is interesting to trace the influence of the new 'dance-dramas' of Yeats on the similar experiments of Terence Gray ... and the subsequent great revival of ballet in England. ... And if modern ballet could somehow link itself with poetry again and re-establish the partnership of dance-drama on a large scale, then the pioneer ideas of Yeats would indeed have a splendid apotheosis on the modern stage.[91]

Reynolds was not alone in this ambition; in 1962, de Valois herself protested against a critical and cultural tendency to enforce a separation between the arts in the formulation of dramatic art.[92] Notwithstanding the limited realization of any ideal of dance-drama in England (or, indeed, in Ireland), the varied influence of both Yeats and Gray on twentieth-century English verse drama and on English attempts to develop and stage a more intermedial ideal, often through verse drama, cannot be underestimated.

As the reviews cited at the beginning of this study only begin to suggest, the dominant critical tendency is now to associate all verse drama with the interests of an 'irrelevant' and 'coterie' theatre. That assumption, however, goes very much against the stated intentions of many of the most prominent representatives of the diffuse movement variously (and sometimes simultaneously) invoked, imagined and mourned by poets, directors and artists in the first decades of the twentieth century. It also overlooks the diverse social values and artistic modes through which the tradition of modern verse drama in England was promoted and developed – not to mention its participation and engagement with the very environment of theatrical reform that also encouraged the realist, socially argumentative play. This dominant critical discourse has effected an incomplete and fundamentally inaccurate reading of the early history of the modern English stage. It has also, ironically, ensured the relative enforcement of the very text-based theatre that some of the earliest, most self-consciously experimental poets set out to challenge. The following chapters look more closely at some of the plays and trends that marked this overlooked and extremely diverse moment of dramatic creativity.

CHAPTER 3
GEORGIAN REVOLT: JOHN MASEFIELD, SHAKESPEARE AND GORDON BOTTOMLEY'S *KING LEAR'S WIFE*

As manifest in the directorial projects of Barker and Craig, the intermedial explorations of de Valois and the theatrical experimentalism of the Cambridge Festival Theatre, the definition and development of verse drama in the twentieth century was never exclusive to writers alone. Amongst poet-dramatists in England, however, that development can be traced through a growing realization and acceptance of the inevitable fact of the stage itself – and to the consequent diminishment of the closet drama as a contemporary literary form. Where poets such as Bridges, Abercrombie and Gibson were relatively content to publish their drama as literature, just decades later such representative voices as Eliot, Auden and Fry were emphatically focused on reconciling poetic drama to the stage and the contemporary audience itself. Those attempts were facilitated in many ways by the preceding, unsung theatrical projects of Bottomley and Masefield and by the directorial innovations of producers as diverse as Craig, Poel, Barker, Jackson and Gray. That very recognition of an inherent inseparability between drama and the stage would slowly emerge as one of the dominant characteristics of a distinctly modern tradition of drama in verse. Equally characteristic would be an emerging conviction of an imperative to reform and redefine the stage itself.

As we have seen, that redefinition was encouraged by the directorial revisitations of Poel and Monck, promoted in the translations of Murray, and bolstered by an environment of theatrical reform bent on the revitalization of earlier traditions of poetic drama. Many of the Georgians eagerly revisited Greek drama and French classical drama, while the rediscovery of mystery and medieval plays constituted a formative influence on the development of a contemporary religious drama. Equally significant, for many, was Japanese Noh drama, with its ritualistic and static conventions unencumbered by a received legacy of poetic, theatrical and scholarly appropriation in England. A considerably more vexing presence, in contrast, was that of Shakespeare (and often, by default, the Elizabethans and Jacobeans as a whole). The literary and cultural position of Shakespeare had never wavered.

His influence both on nineteenth-century traditions of poetic drama and on the commercial stage, however, rendered his legacy problematic for those bent on dramatic reform. For directors such as Barker, that reform could be articulated through the presentation of Shakespearean drama itself: through new staging practices, stage design and approaches to verse-speaking. For many poets, however, it was best articulated independently of the Shakespearean heritage: with the notable exception of Bottomley, the early representatives of a modern verse drama were much more likely to turn to traditions outside of that informing poetic ancestry.

Georgian revolt: Laurence Binyon, John Drinkwater, John Masefield and Lascelles Abercrombie

In his 1912 essay 'The Return to Poetry', Binyon declared a break from the 'passivity' of the previous century: 'Unconsciously enslaved, we were growing benumbed. And now we want to stretch our limbs, to move, to dance, to feel our life-blood running again.'[1] Binyon's assertion is directed at poetry, but his emphasis on action, rhythm and a natural, physical vitality is evident in a characteristic passage from his *Attila: A Tragedy in Four Acts* (1907):

> We rode like the wind, we leapt like rattling hail;
> Danube in flood-time could not race with us.
> But now we must make platters of our shields,
> And see our royal eagle witched and tamed,
> A strutting pigeon in a castle-court
> That coasts about the housetops and alights
> To preen and coo.[2]

Notwithstanding Binyon's assertion of a vital break from the nineteenth century, the historical subjects and four-act structures of his plays tend to betray the lingering influence of his predecessors. *Arthur: A Tragedy* (1923), for example, is characterized by a wistful medievalism only slightly more tempered than that of the Victorians, while the large-scale focus on historical rulers in *Attila* and *Boudicea* (1927), no matter their critical politics, suggests a similar tendency towards epic subjects and characters. In a review of the production of *Attila* at His Majesty's Theatre, *The Spectator* acclaimed a blank verse that is 'more direct and compact than any we can call to mind in recent English poetical drama.'[3] Although it contains 'fine images in it . . .

they are unusually relevant; there are no frillings. It is an unfamiliar experience for a verse-play to set you free as early as most of the plays in other theatres.'[4] As the reviewer also notes, however, as produced by the actor-manager Oscar Asche (writer, performer and director of *Chu Chin Chow*), 'if the verse were bad and the costumes and colours were a little less expensive and beautiful than they are, we should still have in *Attila* something comparable with a "pageant".'[5] As this response suggests, any Georgian 'revolt' in Binyon's plays was relatively exclusive to a verse that emphasized directness, controlled poetic conceits and a more 'naturalistic' focus on elemental imagery.[6]

The majority of Binyon's later plays were written for Masefield's Boars Hill Theatre, and in many respects they betray the primary intention of that theatre: to develop a contemporary drama, dramatic verse and method of verse speaking comparable to that which had animated Greek drama. As promoted by Masefield, Murray and their contemporaries at the Boars Hill Theatre, that ambition was emphatically democratic and anti-elitist, focused on an ideal of drama as communal, oral ritual (and entertainment).[7] To the casual or critical outsider, however, that ideal was not always immediately evident in the subjects chosen for these dramas, nor, indeed, in their promotion of the classical unities and chorus. Furthermore, as E. Martin Browne later observed, the relative exclusivity of that theatre did not always ensure the development of a drama that could be performed anywhere other than at Boars Hill: 'though some of [these poets] were making valuable experiments in poetic form, they could not test these against the reaction of a general public'.[8] When Masefield proposed, in *The Times*, to promote his ideal of community drama by establishing the country public-house as a venue for verse-speaking and drama, the idea was scorned from no more likely a quarter than that of Eliot. Kenneth Muir describes coming across an editorial note in *The Criterion*:

> [Eliot] had always thought of the public-house as one of the few places to be which one could escape from verse speaking, drama and readings of prose. If the public-house is to fall into the hands of the English Association and the British Drama League, where, one must ask bluntly, is a man to go for a drink?[9]

Notwithstanding his occasional excess of idealism, Masefield's contribution to the development of community drama, speech training and drama in education was very influential. By the 1930s, the study of speech and elocution had become key components in educational curricula, and the recitation of choral odes a vital educational tool. As Richard Badenhausen notes, that attention to choral speaking would in turn inform the rebirth of poetic drama through *Murder in the Cathedral*, with its amateur choruses trained by Gwynneth Thurburn and Elsie Fogerty, now at the Central School for Speech and Drama.[10]

Considerably less influential, perhaps, were Masefield's dramas themselves. As Ronald E. Shields contends, the career of Masefield can be divided into three periods: 'his apprentice years as poet and dramatist for the professional stage; his years ... as a promoter of verse drama and verse speaking for amateurs; and, finally, those years following his appointment as the Poet Laureate in 1930.'[11] Masefield's first and only commercially successful dramas were in fact written in prose. *The Campden Wonder* (1907) is a historical melodrama, based on a true story of revenge in the seventeenth-century Cotswolds. The piece is characterized by its dramatization of Gloucestershire dialect and violent, dark deeds – what Dennis Kennedy identifies as 'an attempt at an English *Riders to the Sea*.'[12] The play garnered the praise of both Shaw and Barker, who staged it at the Court with Cyril Harcourt's *The Reformer* (1907), with which it was ill-matched. In Kennedy's assessment, the presentation did not just destroy the chances of the play; it 'damaged the chances for a vigorous poetic drama.'[13] Masefield continued to develop his interest in writing an English *Riders to the Sea* (even if he did not put it that way) in *The Tragedy of Nan* (1908), a forceful rural tragedy that proved a modest popular success and that Bentley later identified as 'one of the best English plays of this century' – a work that 'shows what happens when a man tries to construct a tragedy out of mere knowledge of what poetic tragedy used to be like.'[14]

Ironically, Masefield had considerably less success when he turned to the writing of verse drama; in his autobiography, he confesses to having learnt that 'a writer ... submits his work to the world, and if the world refuse it and trample on his face besides, he must know that there is no appeal'. He regrets that his plays have consequently 'not brought any actor or actress any very happy success; but some of them have had good notices.'[15] As Masefield fostered his emphasis on a communal drama liberated from the commercialism of the popular stage and the elitism of the literary page, he often turned to subjects far removed from that local and populist emphasis. Where *The Campden Wonder* and *The Tragedy of Nan* focused on rural and regional experience, subsequent works included *The Tragedy of Pompey the Great* (1910; staged at the Aldwych Theatre and televised by the BBC in

1950), *Philip the King* (staged by Barker on 5 November 1914, with music by Gustav Holst), adaptations of Racine's *Esther* and *Berenice* (for Boars Hill in 1922) and *A King's Daughter* (a drama about Jezebel, for Boars Hill, 1923).

While these historical subjects suggest an affiliation with the pomposity and spectacle of Edwardian pageant-dramas, the dramas themselves centred on themes characteristically close to Masefield (and many of his peers) – most particularly the injustice and tragedy of war and the levelling experience of human emotion.[16] Central to *A King's Daughter* was an emphasis on the social experience and historical misrepresentation of powerful women. In the three-hour *Tristan and Isolt* (1927, also for Boars Hill), Masefield attempted to extricate the tragedy from its romanticized associations by affiliating both the narrative and the verse much more closely with a medieval 'rusticity' and thus, as Joan Grimbert Tasker observes, returning 'the legend to the rude, barbarous setting from which it sprang.'[17]

Masefield was undoubtedly one of the most consistently experimental of these early verse dramatists. In his autobiography, he reveals that he came to drama initially out of an enthusiasm for Yeats's reform of verse-speaking. For Masefield, the appeal of Yeats's bardic chanting was to be found in its emphasis on rhythm and a poetic musicality far removed from that of the Victorian reciter – and in its consequently greater emphasis on the power of oral story-telling.[18] At the time, however, he knew very little about the theatre, only that he was himself 'a story-teller, fond of reading old poetical plays, and convinced that only William Poel knew how to produce them.'[19] Masefield's enthusiasm for Poel is also telling, given that director's reputation for the prioritization of verse speaking on the stage: as Fogerty observed, Poel 'revolutionise[d] the current idea of speaking Shakespeare – which had alternated between a sonorous rant and a pleasant chattiness not unsuited to comedy, but definitely comic in tragedy.'[20] Ultimately, Masefield developed his own theatrical aesthetic in response to the lectures of Yeats, the dramas of Synge and the Shakespearean stagings of Poel. The result, in his own account, was the realization that his 'love of language, fondness for effects of style, worship of the right word, all the old dear tricks, must be cut': 'a good mime needs no words, and . . . a good playwright can do without them. . . . What a blow to a youth . . . to find that, on the stage, dumb-show may be more telling than eloquence.'[21]

Masefield's dramatic enthusiasms embraced not only an emphasis on simplicity and 'telling' in verse, but also this possibility of dumb-show – the dramatic role of the 'other arts' on the story-telling stage. In so doing, he came close to Yeats and to Gray, whose productions were based essentially upon a conviction that 'there are moments in great drama for which words prove an inadequate medium for the expression of emotion. Always has this been so and always shall it be, and the limitation has never been more satisfactorily circumvented verbally than it was in the beginning by the Greeks.'[22] Asserting that he 'cannot be the only one to have longed for such a mingled art through more than two generations,'[23] Masefield confirms:

> When I come to consider the arts of story-telling that I should like to hear, I think of three types: the one, the poetical epic, such as the Homeric; the second, the kind of story, diversified with music, song, dancing, and impersonation, that was still, in the main, a story, but developed later into the Greek play; and the third, the saga, as it must have been before the age in which it was written down.[24]

Unlike Gray, who was to encourage an increasingly more abstract, symbolic theatre, Masefield never ventured from his emphasis on story (particularly as an inevitably political, democratic ideal). Unlike Yeats, he did not attempt to inscribe this 'mingled art' within his plays themselves; his works contain no moments for musical set-pieces, and his verse tends towards a simplicity of statement centred around the narratives of messengers. His plays also, however, point consistently to the necessary art of verse-speaking itself within a dramatic framework focused on simplicity of situation, setting and structure. Like Yeats, Bottomley and Binyon, Masefield became increasingly more attracted to Japanese Noh drama, less for its emphasis on structured movement than for its alignment of ritual, poetry and musicality with this apparent simplicity and rigidity of aesthetic.

This emphasis on simplicity did not preclude variations and experimentations in verse itself, either between or within plays; in *Philip the King* (1914), for example, Masefield employs prose, various rhyming structures and a controlled, unrhyming verse – often within one scene – to ensure dramatic movement, characterization and a consequent variation of theatrical effect and mood. In one exchange, for example, the King recounts his building of the Armada in rhyming couplets: the effect suggests the origins of his verse in ballad traditions, fitting both for Masefield's emphasis on oral traditions and the Armada subject of the play. It also ensures a consistent dramatic pace:

All the long days of beating down the Turk,
Then when Don John had thrust the Crescent down

(You cannot know) he plotted for the crown;
Don John, my Admiral, plotted against me.
He would have sunk the English in the sea,
But since he plotted, that was ended too.
Then a great world of labour still to do,
The French to check, and then the Portuguese,
Clearing myself a pathway through the seas.
...
Seventeen years of subtleties and crimes.[25]

That reflection causes a shift both in the content and the rhyming structure of the verse, inviting a slower and uneven rhythm – and thus a greater attention to character and his contemplation of the consequence of his actions:

But it is done. I have resolved those years,
Those men, those crimes, those great attempts, those tears,
Sorrows and terrors of a twisted earth,
Into this fleet, this death, this Dragon's birth;
I have who never seen it, nor shall see.[26]

In this moment, Masefield emphasizes the emotion of the King, his reflection both on his own brutality and passing years. By having the Princess complete her father's rhyme in the following line ('I shall thank God that it was shown to me; / I saw it sail'),[27] he also dramatizes the emotional closeness between the characters and their intuitive, rhythmic response to each other's sentiments.

In contrast to Masefield's increasing preference for historical or classically-themed subjects, the primarily one-act works of Abercrombie and Drinkwater formulated an intensive, tragic focus on rural subjects. Clearly inspired by the example of Synge and the precedent of Greek tragedy, plays such as Drinkwater's *The Storm* (1915) and Abercrombie's *The Adder* (1913), *The Staircase* (1922) and *The End of the World* (1922) developed a poetic language and setting that was strongly naturalist in its emphasis on primal experience and a direct but heightened expression. In *The Storm*, Alice, Joan and Sarah sit in a mountain cottage, looking out for the return of Alice's husband. The fatalistic tone is set immediately by Alice:

I have prayed these hours, and now I'm tired of it.
He is caught in some grip of the rocks, and crying out,

And crying and crying, and none can hear him cry,
Because of this great beastliness of noise.[28]

The play concludes with the return of the search party: 'Why have we waited
…all this time…to know…[*Her sorrow breaks over* her].'[29] In the one-act
Cophetua (1911), *Rebellion* (1914), *The God of Quiet* (1916) and *X = O: A
Night of the Trojan War* (1917), Drinkwater turned to more ancient, remote
subjects. All of these plays contain a political undertone, and the fable-like
dramatization of the inevitable violence of humanity in *The God of Quiet*
would have resonated particularly in its wartime context. The tone of the
plays is anti-romantic and almost consistently fatalist, and the verse, like
that of Masefield, is economic and undecorative. It differs from that of
Masefield, however, in its relative consistency, leading one contemporary
towards rather qualified praise: 'His exaggerated solemnity tends to make
him monotonous. And yet in spite of defects he maintains a fair standard.'[30]

The plays of Abercrombie tended to be more ambitious both in their ideas
and language. They also tended to be considerably less successful as stage
productions than as published literature, a fact that Abercrombie himself was
soon to concede. *The Adder* consists primarily of an extended conversation
between two charcoal-burners that focuses on sin and illegitimacy as
metaphysically suggested by an adder. It is also notable for its attempt to
translate colloquial dialect into verse: 'It is main quiet in a copse these days; /
Fall's here and no mistake: do you snuff the mould?'[31] As received by literary
critics, the result was an act of deliberate ugliness and brutal obscurity. As
staged at the Liverpool Repertory Theatre, the play would have appealed to
the Company's increasing attempts to establish a distinct regional identity. In
its implicit acknowledgement of social tensions, it would also have resonated
with the emphasis of both Drinkwater and Masefield on the importance of
theatre as oral tradition rather than a disseminated literary culture. In one
passage, the older man rebukes his younger companion:

We know the woods and understand their folk.
We aren't dazed with grammar. Schools and books
May grind the trade in a man to a Sheffield knife;
But put a scholar in the woods: he'll make
No more of them than a dog would make of a book.[32]

All of these writers characteristically aligned themselves with regional and
community identities, doubtless helping to ensure their later dismissal as

'naïve' or 'unsophisticated' in comparison with many of the university-educated modernists to come.[33]

Despite sharing many aesthetic and social values, the work of these playwrights was diverse and varied, and cannot be said to represent a unified school of dramatic composition. It does, however, point to a collective instinct to explore the precedent of earlier traditions in drama, popular ritual and poetry. That instinct was never purely aesthetic, but rooted in a strong sense of community and egalitarian social politics. It was also informed by a perpetual distrust of the supremacy of the commercialized popular stage and of the realist drama of social argumentation.

The Shakespearean spectre

Many of the self-conscious reformers of the contemporary stage identified the worst excesses of the commercial theatre in its opulent stagings and misrepresentations of Shakespearean drama. Others, most notably Shaw, also associated the popularity of that Elizabethan tradition with a complacency that precluded the development of a new drama and new dramatists. In 1901, Shaw published a short verse drama of his own, *The Admirable Bashville*. Written to protect the American copyright of his novel *Cashel Byron's Profession* (upon which it was loosely based), the play is written in blank verse. In his preface to the play, Shaw declares: 'Blank verse is so childishly easy and expeditious (hence, by the way, Shakespear's copious output), that by adopting it I was enabled to do within the week what would have cost me a month in prose.'[34] Intriguingly, his assessment was echoed by Masefield (more publicly fond of Shakespeare and blank verse) in his 1924 essay, 'Play-Writing', which offers advice to a beginner playwright: 'the play had better be in blank verse as it is so much easier to write than prose, and easier to speak than rhyme.'[35]

Shaw's play is deliberately anachronistic, a work of comic pastiche. His preface is more serious in its attempt to demystify both the value of blank verse in drama and the contemporary cultural position of Shakespeare. Shakespeare himself had seen his style end 'in a chaos of half-shattered old forms, half-emancipated new ones … with, alas! a great deal of filling up with formulary blank verse which had no purpose except to save the author's time and thought.'[36] Contemplating the influence of that tradition on his contemporary dramatists, Shaw can only conclude: 'When a great man destroys an art form in this way, its ruins make palaces for the clever would-be great.'[37] Unsurprisingly, Masefield is much less acerbic or set against blank verse as a whole. It is telling, however, that his example of how to write a contemporary verse play – part formal model, part parody – should effectively satirize the contemporary association of verse drama with Elizabethan and Jacobean conventions of expression and plot. In one exchange, for example, Masefield's Ruffiano exhorts his companions, 'varlets', to go to a nearby inn and poison 'the Duke and good Roberto':

> It is a sleepy drug that in a breath
> Makes the red brain fall drowsy, and doth dull
> The nimblest soul. When thou hast drugged the pair,
> Swift drag them to the cellar and there strip
> Their senseless bodies of their marriage robes
> And the Duke's brow of all its strawberry leaves
> And bring them to me here. About it. Go.[38]

The gentle parody of Masefield and the more concerted satire of Shaw underline the extent to which dramatic attempts to emulate the achievement of the Elizabethans – no matter how nebulously defined – were seen to be at odds with more modern instincts.

They also go some way to explain the prevailing association of Phillips's dramas – with their romantic historical subjects, soliloquies *and* blank verse – less with those modern instincts than with those of the imitative Victorians. According to Thouless, naturalistic drama ensured that by the first decades of the century 'the soliloquy was dead'; it 'killed the old ideal of the poetic dramatist ... that of the pseudo-Elizabethan'.[39] Reynolds characterizes Phillips as having shaken 'the dying bones of pseudo-Elizabethanism into a slightly less hollow rattle than Tennyson had done in *Queen Mary* and Swinburne in that monstrous dramatic dragon *Bothwell*'.[40] Despite this clear association of 'Elizabethanism' with a regressive and outdated definition of poetic drama, however, such comments are considerably less forthcoming as to what must emerge to take its place. Indeed, at second glance, Reynolds's dismissal of Phillips suggests a fundamental uncertainty as to the possibility of a viable verse drama *without* such Elizabethanism, pseudo- or otherwise. Phillips is the last representative of 'the Shakespearean style of writing for the theatre': 'only spasmodically has verse-drama held up its head again since then'.[41] Similarly, according to Thouless, rather than liberating dramatists into new poetic forms, the banishment of 'the pseudo-Elizabethan' had only meant that 'no fitting substitute ... had been found'.[42]

Such valuations underline the extent to which the 'one poet in the national drama', the nature of his defining achievements interpreted differently across the centuries, could cast a shadow over both critical and commercial expectations of poetic drama. As the fate of Phillips suggests, that expectation could persist independently of the best efforts of dramatists to liberate themselves from any such association. Indeed, where Victorian dramatists embraced the Shakespearean 'example', twentieth-century playwrights were increasingly more likely to identify an inhibiting creative legacy. In 1916, Yeats had already concluded, 'if our modern poetical drama has failed, it is mainly because, always dominated by the example of Shakespeare, it would restore an irrevocable past'.[43] (Ronald Peacock sees Yeats's later enthusiasm for Noh drama as 'giving rein to his impulse to keep Shakespeare at the greatest possible distance'.)[44] In 1927, Drinkwater recalled the warning of Galsworthy 'that the shadow of the man Shakespeare was across the path of all who should attempt verse drama in these days'.[45] The next year, Dukes addressed this anxiety about the Elizabethan legacy, particularly in relation to blank verse:

> blank verse as a dramatic instrument died out with the passing of the Elizabethans. The writers who attempted to revive it during the course of three succeeding centuries were consciously using an archaic form, and therein lay their weakness. The theatre has little use of archaeologists; its forms must be alive and spontaneous or they are naught.[46]

The association of verse – and blank verse in particular – with a regressive theatrical instinct would both haunt the reception of poetic drama in subsequent decades and embolden its exemplars to develop new forms of versification. It would inspire some (but certainly not all) to move away from historical narratives whose very subject-matter might inspire comparison with the imitative traditions of 'three succeeding centuries'. It would encourage a revisitation of other forms and traditions of poetic drama through which to formulate and identify an apparently more authentic ideal of contemporary dramatic expression. Central to most of these efforts was a concerted break not from an acceptance of Shakespeare's accomplishment, but from the subsequent traditions (on stage and page) through which his legacy had been traduced, and from the forms and narrative subjects through which it had been assumed that his legacy must be met.

In 1928, Dukes prefaced his essay collection, *The World to Play With*, with a poem that directly addresses the informing presence of Shakespeare within any such ambitions. Rather than promoting a static reliance on empty constructions of heritage and achievement, the very example of Shakespeare should encourage a continuous and diverse mode of creativity. Speaking to 'Sir John Citizen', Shakespeare fears that he is about to die, 'To petrify, and yet be called sublime.' He entreats the contemporary everyman to help him 'hold / To life' and save him from the 'frosty arms' of immortality.[47] In this reading, the most fitting manifestation of a living Shakespearean heritage is the development, through verse drama, of a diverse, contemporary art for a necessarily reformed stage: 'when living words are spoken afresh from our stage, we shall no longer think of actual drama and "poetic" drama as two separate entities. It is our task to make them one and the same'.[48] In 1949, Eliot articulated a similar ideal. He hoped for a verse drama that would match rather than emulate the cultural tradition of Elizabethan drama; he wanted to establish 'a dramatic age which will have as strong an identity as the drama of Elizabethan and Jacobean times, or of seventeenth-century France'.[49] For both Dukes and Eliot, this restoration would reinvigorate a tradition of dramatic writing hitherto appropriated by literary archaeologists and theatrical imitators. In so doing, it would also implicitly repair the historical 'breach' between 'poetic drama' and 'actual drama' lamented by Barker.

Gordon Bottomley's *King Lear's Wife*

One of the earliest, most fleetingly prominent dramatists to attempt such a reconciliation was Gordon Bottomley. In *King Lear's Wife* and *Gruach* (1918), Bottomley embraced and attempted to re-engage with a Shakespearean past rooted in a British past. The success of *King Lear's Wife* (in publication) was extremely modest in comparison to that of Phillips. It was, however, the first relatively major, critically acclaimed attempt in England to follow in the wake of that 'meteor'. Unlike Phillips, Bottomley did not have practical experience in the theatre, and his first dramas originated primarily from an environment of poetic reform. Rather than aspiring towards mainstream success with the London actor-managers, he tended to embrace a communal spirit of artistic exchange and dialogue that earned his association with an exclusive, if relatively humble, coterie. While such associations have plagued the reception of many verse dramatists since, they also underline the extent to which these advocates of a new poetic drama could only envision that drama independently of the mainstream contemporary stage.

In 1912, Monro declared that any poet who 'gets into [the] hands [of actor-managers] may be expected to share the sad fate of Mr Stephen Phillips. That the writer of *Paolo and Francesca* should eventually fall to *Pietro of Siena* may well serve as a caution to aspiring dramatic poets.'[50] For Monro, the only verse drama of worth was that which could exist independently of the 'sad fate' imposed by the commercial stage. This new poetic drama must not return to the tendencies of the Romantics and hide in the literary closet, however; it must instead induce its enthusiasts to 'found a theatre':

> Expenses will be few: scarcely any scenery is required. Let us hear their lines recited merely within crimson or green curtains, and, if they are good enough, they will hold us and stir us, of course, all the deeper for there being no electric moons or sham waterfalls in the background to distract our attention, and, above all, no soft music drowning the beauty of language at moments of high emotion.[51]

Like many of his contemporaries, Monro can only conclude that 'under the present [theatre] regime, the better [the poet-dramatists'] work, the worse their chance'.[52]

King Lear's Wife provides a moderating voice within this debate. It both establishes a divergent aesthetic in the very intimacy of its subject and staging, and it acknowledges a familiar tradition of Romantic Shakespeareanism on the contemporary stage. Bottomley saw himself as writing for 'our contemporary theatre buildings', and in his moderate embrace of recent innovations on the stage does not seem to have contemplated Monro's more absolutist convictions:

> *King Lear's Wife* and *Gruach* were not written with any idea of different production or mounting. They accepted the idea of realistic setting . . . [but trusted] to the element of greater taste and imagination which came from Gordon Craig's stylistic interpretation of realistic factors.[53]

Bottomley's conscious, if gently articulated, divergence from established stage traditions was not confined to staging: he had identified in his composition of *King Lear's Wife* a method more closely attuned to the sound, rather than the independent literary quality, of the verse. For Bottomley, that process did not just enable his own writing, but produced a style of dramatic verse that acted as a vital corrective to that of the Victorians: 'I began to enjoy saying it over to myself . . . at moments I was only a delighted auditor. . . .

Presently I noticed that the verse was vocal in a way that dramatic verse had ceased to be.'[54] Like Phillips, Bottomley articulates his ideal for poetic drama in relation to the stage; unlike Phillips, he would identify that stage less with the spectacular, sonorous productions of the actor-managers than with a more intimate ideal of dramatic art.

The modernity that garnered *King Lear's Wife* pride of place in the Marsh anthology can be most immediately identified in its challenge to the heroic effusiveness, romantic sentimentalism and spectacular opulence through which the Shakespearean legacy had been disseminated and imitated in commercial production. The play is a prelude to *King Lear*: it opens at the sick-bed of Hygd, King Lear's wife. King Lear, 'a great, golden-bearded man in the full maturity of life',[55] is carrying on an affair with the maid-servant Gormflaith (often literally) behind the curtain of his wife's bed chamber. Regan is absent from the play; according to Goneril, she is keeping company with 'the sweaty half-clad cook-maids [who] render lard' after pig-killing, '[sidling] among their greasy skirts, / Smeary and hot as they, for scraps to suck'.[56] Cordelia is an unwanted child, clamouring offstage at the door of the sick-room: she seeks out the father who spoils her, but is dismissed by her mother as her 'little curse', an 'evil child' and an 'ill-comer':

> Cordeil the useless had to be conceived
> (Like an after-thought that deceives nobody)
> To keep her father from another woman.
> And here I lie.[57]

Goneril, in contrast, is 'an almost gleaming presence, a virgin huntress' 'just turning to womanhood'[58] who worships nature 'in cold stern adoration'.[59] Hunting with the spear 'from [her] bed-side' whose 'purity' she claims can be touched by 'none but [she]', Goneril is surprised into a feeling of uncleanliness when she uses that spear in hunting to 'crush delicate things'.[60] She is only restored to her usual 'untroubled mind' when she kills a rabbit by catching it with her hands and 'with this thin knife / [piercing] it from eye to eye': 'untorn, unsullied, and with flawless fur'.[61]

As this language suggests, *King Lear's Wife* is most distinct from its neo-Elizabethan and neo-Jacobean predecessors in its emphatic, if relative, naturalism. That difference is further established by the set, which reinforces Bottomley's declared enthusiasm for Craig's 'stylistic interpretation of realistic factors'. The play opens in a bedchamber whose walls 'consist of a few courses of huge irregular boulders roughly squared and fitted together;

a thatched roof rises steeply from the back wall'.[62] It is decorated simply, with hangings, curtains of different textures and a few props to indicate the royal nature of the room. The play takes place in this single setting; the change of action is effected with the drawing and closing of onstage curtains around the bed. This minimalist presentation immediately signals a difference from popular, commercial stagings of Victorian and Shakespearean verse drama. It also, however, aligns itself with the pictorial enthusiasms of the Pre-Raphaelites. The setting is simple, but it is far from bleak; the language of the stage directions alone invokes Celtic Romanticism and the medievalism of Rossetti and Morris. The Queen is beautiful in her emaciated state, 'her plenteous black hair, veined with silver, spreads over the pillow'.[63] Goneril is 'an almost gleaming presence' with 'her kirtle caught up in her girdle, a light spear over her shoulder'.[64] Gormflaith is 'young and tall and fresh-coloured; her red hair coils and crisps close to her little head'.[65] Her laugh is 'clear, like a bird's sudden song',[66] and her characteristically 'girlish' actions (tip-toeing, dropping handkerchiefs, passively receiving embrace) would not be out of place in either the Arthurian poetry of Tennyson or the paintings of Millais.

The language and themes of the play mark a considerably more noticeable departure. Where Phillips avoided static elaborations of poetic conceit, his verse tended nonetheless towards the consistently beautiful, leading Symons to conclude, 'in all this beautiful talking and moving, in these picturesque scenes which look so well on the stage, there is no real life, no real dramatic life, but always, in the fatal sense, "literature"'.[67] Bottomley is no less conscious of poetic beauty – he confessed in 1927 to having always been 'an ornate Romantic'[68] – but the verse is intent on evoking an ancient, often brutal setting and the themes that that setting invites. He suggests an essential primitivism with the occasional use of archaic vocabulary ('holpen'), but more often with verse that focuses on a single developed image, on the suggestiveness of single colours (red, green, gold), and on the close relationship between humanity and primal, violent nature. In one indicative scene, Lear kisses Gormflaith 'suddenly and vehemently, as if he would grasp her lips with his'.[69] The potential violence of this passion – and the relationship of that passion both to Lear's power as king and to the instincts of wild, untamed nature – is reinforced in his speech:

Goldilocks, when the crown is couching in your hair
And those two mingled golds brighten each other's wonder,
You shall produce a son from flesh unused –
Virgin I chose you for that, first crops are strongest –

A tawny fox with your high-stepping action,

...

To keep my lands from crumbling into mouthfuls
For the short jaws of my three mewling vixens.
Hatch for me such a youngster from my seed,
And I and he shall rein my hot-breathed wenches
To let you grind the edges off their teeth.[70]

Within this one speech, Lear moves from romanticizing the beauty of his 'golden' mistress to articulating the brutal politics of marriage, fatherhood and kingship, aligning his instincts with the coarseness and brutality of nature itself.

To a considerable extent, of course, this suggestion of a violent, primal environment only builds upon the elemental imagery of Shakespeare's play itself. The play's allusions to ancient Christian saints and pagan worship similarly echo the pagan setting and Christian themes of *King Lear*. Equally central is the vexed theme of justice and order. In Bottomley's play, Goneril comes to a slow realization of the potential for kings to be unjust: she accepts that her father has been unkind to her as a daughter (Lear himself refers to having whipped her),[71] but when she sees his infidelity to her mother, she also perceives the sexualized transgression of a king against political order: 'I never thought a king could be untrue, / I never thought my father was unclean.'[72] Goneril's elision of marital fidelity with kingly responsibility resonates immediately (and ironically) with the actions of Shakespeare's Lear, who bewails in his abdication of the crown the 'sudden' loss of both paternal and social authority.

Equally resonant is the language in which Shakespeare's Lear curses Goneril in Act I, scene 4: he famously entreats Nature to 'convey sterility' 'into her womb', to 'Dry up in her the organs of increase'. If she should give birth, he begs that her child be one of spleen, 'and be a thwart disnatured torment to her'. In Bottomley's play, Goneril to some extent anticipates this fate. She also, however, attributes the probable corruption of her 'natural' maternal affection not to a pagan curse or the justice of Nature, but to the harsh upbringing of her father:

[he has] knitted up within my mind
A love of coldness and a love of him
Who makes me firm, wary, swift and secret,
Until I feel if I become a mother

I shall at need be cruel to my children,
And ever cold, to string their natures harder
And make them able to endure men's deeds[73]

Where Shakespeare's Lear speaks from a position of wounded and uncomprehending disempowerment, Goneril speaks from the position of one who 'sees better' the potential consequences of her own father's actions as king, father – and man.

In many respects, Bottomley's play acts as a kind of prequel to Shakespeare's play, providing a more developed explanation for the later actions of Goneril, and reinforcing the emphasis in *King Lear* on the often tenuous bonds of affection, family and patriarchy. It also develops an unambiguously critical reading of Shakespeare's tragic protagonist, whose adultery, whose neglect of his children, and whose fixation with begetting a male heir while satisfying fickle desire creates an atmosphere of bitterness, rejection and competition that also threatens the stability of the realm. In one seminal exchange, Gormflaith demands that she be allowed to wear the Queen's crown: when Lear objects, she steals the crown from the Queen's chamber. Lear asserts that only kings can crown queens; Gormflaith ignores him and crowns herself. Lear yields to her will: 'Girl, you are changed: you yield more beauty so.'[74] While the scene dramatizes the cruelty of Gormflaith towards the Queen (who watches from her chamber), the memory of Shakespeare's play ensures that its primary focus is the weakness of Lear himself, his attempt to assert kingly authority only to cede to manipulative seductions and flattery. In thus emphasizing the malleability of Shakespeare's protagonist, the scene foreshadows the seminal opening scene of *King Lear*.

Nonetheless, the play's Shakespearean allusions are not exclusively focused on *King Lear*. Goneril confronts her father for having left her mother to die alone while he seduced Gormflaith: 'what should be the doom on a seducer / Who drew that sentinel from his fixt watch?'[75] Refusing to accept (or feel) guilt, Lear echoes Macbeth's more existential 'she should have died hereafter': 'She had been long dying, and she would have died / Had all her dutiful daughters tended her bed', and 'I did not know that she could die to-day.'[76] Where Macbeth is motivated by a fatalistic conviction of destiny, Bottomley's Lear is motivated by misplaced desire and a selfish disregard for both family and Queen. In contrast, the grief of Goneril for her mother is likened to the longing of Ophelia for her dead father: where Ophelia sings, 'And will 'a not come again? / No, no, he is dead; / Go to thy deathbed, / He never will come again,' Goneril is rebuked by the waiting-woman Merryn:

'Child, she is gone and will not come again / However we cover our faces and pretend / She will be there if we uncover them.'[77] Where Ophelia suffers a much-romanticized death soon thereafter, Goneril is left to confront inevitable realities, not least the fact that should Merryn not prepare the body of Hygd in a timely fashion, the body will 'be as stiff / As a straw mattress is'.

These allusions do much more than draw attention to the play's Shakespearean inspiration: they offer an implicit rebuke to the picturesque sentimentalism through which many of Shakespeare's plays had been typically idealized in the preceding century. They most especially effect a juxtaposition between the primitive setting and violence of *King Lear* (and of *Macbeth*, the inspiration for Bottomley's next Shakespeare-themed play, *Gruach*) and the considerably more popular, romanticized *Hamlet* that had so enthralled the Romantics and Victorians (not least the Pre-Raphaelites). In *Hamlet*, the assembled characters grieve for Ophelia – beautiful both in her own flower-strewn melodies and in the poetic remembrances and tributes of the Queen. They do so in the graveyard, following Hamlet's famous ponderings over the skull of Yorick. Eventually, however, Hamlet moves from these philosophical contemplations to enact revenge; the play itself resolves in the restoration of political order and the imagined rest of its protagonist amongst angels. In *King Lear's Wife*, however, the levelling reality of death is at the staged forefront of both the opening and conclusion of the play. Equally central is the experience of the female protagonists: where Ophelia and Gertrude are prominent accessories to a larger drama of kingship and filial revenge, Bottomley's female characters dominate the stage.

The selfish and inconsistent actions of Bottomley's Lear threaten the stability of his kingdom and the filial love upon which he later attempts to depend. The primary dramatic focus, however, is the motivation of the female characters; indeed, for Ruby Cohn, the play's very thoroughness in that regard is 'neat, comprehensible, and too simply credible'.[78] Cohn's assessment reads Bottomley's play as an excessively explanatory prequel to *King Lear*. In so doing, however, it undervalues the extent to which that play is independently engaging with and contesting the truth of received female types. *King Lear's Wife* dramatizes the consistently unhappy plight of its female characters – the rejected wife, the unloved daughter, the abandoned child and the ambitious, socially inhibited mistress – all in an environment controlled by men. To a certain extent, the characters conform to conventional types: the wife dies in bitterness and despair, the daughter awaits marriage, the abandoned child remains offstage and the ambitious mistress is rightly killed. The play provides a detailed exploration of the motivation and limited agency of these women, however, an unsentimental examination of their position within an overarching patriarchal structure. The effect is a critical tone that would have resonated with many of the themes that preoccupied much of the 'new drama' at the time.

The women in *King Lear's Wife* are bound to prescribed social and sexual roles, vulnerable to the injustice and violence of the men upon whom they are forced to depend. This theme is emphasized in the play's juxtaposition of the willed death of the rejected wife – and queen – with the actions of the ambitious mistress whose only opportunity for social advancement is to seduce the king. Neither woman is motivated by love nor by desire; both are dominated by an awareness of their limited role and power – as women – within a social hierarchy. This awareness does not just influence their behaviour towards men; it sullies their emotional kinship with other women. In revenging her mother's death, Goneril asserts the return of her crown, now 'sullied' with the 'menial warmth' of Gormflaith's head.[79] It is only after she has restored this social order that Goneril can acknowledge the emotional motivation behind her actions: 'A broken body for a broken heart.'[80]

Bottomley develops the implications of this idea of brokenness most extensively in his characterization of Goneril. Indeed, in its dramatization of a virginal huntress not yet aware of the 'natural' taint of womanhood, the play is not entirely dissimilar from Strindberg's considerably more controversial *Miss Julie* (1888). Goneril is initially unwilling to use the hunting spear that she keeps in her bedchamber, filled with 'shame' 'and loathing and contempt' at its 'unclean coarse blows'.[81] After she kills Gormflaith, however, she discovers cause in killing. In language that echoes her earlier account, she reflects that 'this striking without thought is better than hunting'.[82] It is also more ruthless: Gormflaith 'showed more terror than an animal'.[83] Whereas Goneril had earlier been appalled by the brutal ugliness of nature 'blemish[ed]' and 'crush[ed]', she now concludes:

A little blood is lightly washed away,
A common stain that need not be remembered;
And a hot spasm of rightness quickly born
Can guide me to kill justly and shall guide.[84]

Goneril has experienced much more than righteous anger: her language aligns her experience with the loss of virginity, and thus her assimilation within a more violent, ugly reality. That reading is enforced by Lear himself, who sees her actions as evidence of the influence of men, of her absorption within the reality from which, in her 'blind virgin power' she had 'stood apart / In an unused, unviolated life.'[85] In thus 'mingling in mortality' rather than judging from a distanced position, Goneril has 'violently begun the common life.'[86] As Goneril reinforces, however, she is 'not woman yet'; she has begun to learn of the deceitfulness of women 'and how some men desire deceit from us,'[87] and that knowledge is empowering. Lear sees this power as unnatural and dangerous. His final words in the play recognize the need to contain and break his daughter's agency within a social, sexual structure: 'She must be wedded and broken, I cannot do it.'[88]

This final invocation of violent patriarchy, marriage and broken nature resonates with the later events of Shakespeare's play. It also enforces the over-ridingly fatalistic tone of the play as a whole. *King Lear's Wife* opens with the waiting-woman Merryn, 'middle-aged and hard featured', ruminating over the ailing queen: 'Many, many must die who long to live, / Yet this one cannot die who longs to die.'[89] Her diagnosis is echoed soon thereafter by the Physician, who confirms that 'We cannot die wholly against our wills'; Hygd has grown 'impatient of enduring'.[90] This willed death is never romanticized. Rather than empathizing with the plight of her mistress, rather than mourning her imminent demise, Merryn contemplates her own fear of death: she is horrified at the thought of the humiliation that comes with sudden death, of 'the hard will of fumbling corpse-watchers'.[91] The play concludes by dramatizing – and emphasizing – the inevitability of that humiliation in an extended scene of Dickensian black humour. The exchanges between Bottomley's elderly corpse-washers resemble those in *Martin Chuzzlewit* between Sarah Gamp, alcoholic layer-out of the dead, and her companions.[92] Bottomley's corpse-washers are indifferent both to the rank of the Queen and to the poignancy of death: they try to rob her but find they have been beaten to it; they urge each other to hurry, as the body 'is setting'; they pray for help from the 'friend of the worms'; they remind each other of the difficulty of putting 'damp linen on a corpse'.[93] The play ends with the elder of the two singing of an unhappy wet louse:

He's looking for us, the little pet;
So haste, for her chin's to tie up yet,
And let us be gone with what we can get –
Her ring for thee, her gown for Bet,
Her pocket turned out for me.[94]

In their 'black hoods and shapeless black gowns with large sleeves that flap like the wings of ungainly birds', in their action around 'a heavy cauldron of hot water',[95] the two women also resemble the witches in *Macbeth*. Rather than prophesying the rise or fall of kings, however, they reinforce the crude reality of the queen's corpse and the heartless indifference of those to whom her body is now entrusted.

The corpse-washing scene garnered considerable attention from critics upon publication; as Ross notes, the primary objection seemed to be that 'the brutality was too deliberate, too conscious'.[96] Similar objections greeted the staged play: in a letter to Marsh, Drinkwater noted of the Birmingham production, 'The Censor added to our gaiety by sending horrified protests on Saturday about the louse and the lady's shift, in a letter which I have given as an heirloom for ever to the clan Bottomley'.[97] The censor was not alone: the production at His Majesty's Theatre was stymied considerably by the refusal of the actress Viola Tree (who played Goneril) to accept the ending of the play. In a letter to Nash, Bottomley notes, 'she wanted me to have the curtain at Lear's exit two lines after her own, and to cut out the finale of the corpse-washers; and when I wouldn't she cut out half of it all by herself'.[98] In response to Nash's supposition that Tree was too 'neat-minded' to appreciate the ending,[99] however, Bottomley concludes, 'I doubt if Viola Tree is neat-minded: she simply wanted the curtain for herself'.[100] Such responses point to the relative novelty of the play not only in its naturalist bleakness, but also in its structural refusal to prioritize the conventional focus of the commercial theatre: Bottomley dispatches his star performers and instead concludes with a final, grotesquely humorous tableau of death and grim reality.

King Lear's Wife is thus much more than a simple prequel to Shakespeare or a deliberately brutal rejection of the lyrical sentimentalism of Victorian poetic drama. In its very invocation of Romantic conventions, in its simultaneous exploitation of aesthetic beauty and naturalist theme, the play points to its critical engagement with preceding traditions. These traditions are literary, visual and dramatic; the play evokes the art of the Pre-Raphaelites, the romanticism of Yeats, the black humour of Dickens and the Arthurian and Shakespearean sentimentalism of the Victorian stage and its poets. It also, however, invokes an ideal of Shakespearean expression and theme – direct, animalistic, brutal, bleak, blackly humorous *and* poetic – that contests many of those traditions and that places Shakespeare himself within a more emphatically modern frame. As Bottomley himself was to explain:

The Jacobeans had established that drama of patterned, unrealistic speech on the basis of a realistic plot which might serve a prose drama equally well. I fell in with this, and was only conscious of innovation in adopting Maeterlinck's early experiments with a one-act form for poetic writing of grave and even tragic import.[101]

As he was to recognize soon thereafter, however, that Jacobean method (or 'pattern'), particularly as developed through allusions to Shakespearean plots and characters, was not enough to sustain the development of a distinctly contemporary dramatic art in verse.

Like Monro, Bottomley eventually concluded that such an art could only come into being through a reform of theatre conventions and the theatre space itself. Central to that reform would be an essential re-examination of the relationship between dramatic verse and the other theatrical arts: the first translations of early Maeterlinck and the 'revolutionary first productions' of Craig had confirmed for him that 'poetry might live in the theatre, in a way that it had never done, by a synthesis of arts'. For Bottomley, one of those arts was the music of verse speaking – not the histrionic Victorian 'organ-playing' derided by Trewin, but rather a more nuanced articulation of verbal sound as art in itself. In attending a first performance of *Gruach* 'at Glasgow, by the new and promising Scottish National Theatre Society', Bottomley became aware of the extent to which 'their fine vowels and trained diction made listening a delight': 'If poetic drama had an affinity it was with the opera-house, theatre of vocalised sound, rather than with the theatre of uncontrolled speech.'[102] Rather than marking a radical departure, the realization of that recognition on the English stage would itself induce a much-needed restoration of the Shakespearean legacy: 'At last I knew that the beauty of spoken sound was that factor of Shakespeare's theatre which had dropped out of our consciousness. Its presence had been the element which had made crowded auditoriums willing to listen to still poetry.'[103]

Bottomley's perception of an inherent musicality to Shakespeare's plays echoes that of Archer, who, in applauding the modern divorce of 'imitation' from 'lyrical passion', had conceded 'that the highest drama known to us, the drama of Aeschylus, Sophocles, Euripides and Shakespeare, is, as a matter of fact, in measure operatic':

In such masterpieces as *Macbeth* and *Antony and Cleopatra* we are moved quite as much by miracles of verbal melody, as by the dramatic action, magnificent as that often is. ... we confess freely and unreservedly that the greatest tragedies as yet known to us were produced at a time when the drama still came trailing clouds of musical glory from the rites of nature-worship and ancestor-worship in which it took its rise.[104]

For Archer, 'the experience of three centuries has shown us that the spirit of modern man can no longer produce masterpieces in the impure form in which Shakespeare worked'.[105] For Bottomley, however, this very 'impurity' was essential to the realization of a more authentic and contemporary definition of theatrical art. Equally essential was a recognition of the extent to which musicality in verse would necessitate formal change: 'The execution of *aria* or *scena* in opera by a supreme singer in complete stillness is still as acceptable as the execution of a blank verse soliloquy was of old, when audiences were in regular training for listening to verse.'[106] Now, however, the realist drama does not allow for that staging of stillness: 'producers of the realistic theatre use the possibilities of stage-movement to the point of restlessness', and in so doing, 'prejudice speaking'.[107]

Like many others, Bottomley was relatively pessimistic as to the verse-speaking abilities of English actors (only those 'of the older generation, who had had their youthful training in Shakespeare' knew how to speak verse at all).[108] This state of affairs was the natural consequence of a critical and creative climate that no longer recognized the dramatic and musical role of poetry and that consequently blamed the poet for its theatrical failure: 'the picture-frame theatre had so steadily diseducated [actors and critics] ... that they had never understood or conceived that poetry could have a relationship to drama at all.'[109] Bottomley began to suspect 'that the fault' might be elsewhere than his verse and that '[he] had been, as it were, offering an ancient, natural vintage to a *clientèle* that honestly believed the wine-trade's best blended port to be a natural wine too'.[110] He found considerable solace in Scotland, where he wrote dramas almost consistently on themes of Celtic and Northern legend, and eventually became president of the Scottish Community Drama Association. He also found a sympathetic environment at Masefield's theatre. For Bottomley, that theatre was unique in England for recognizing the musical imperative of verse-speaking and the relationship between dramatic verse-speaking and staging. It was also unique in its construction, whose two prosceniums, one smaller and slightly raised, with a gallery in the back, ensured a stage that 'would have fulfilled Stakespeare's [sic] requirements'.[111]

Notwithstanding his own movement away from national traditions of verse drama, particularly through his exploration of Noh drama, Greek chorus and dance, Bottomley consistently articulated his evolving aesthetic in relation to a more authentic reading of Shakespearean poetic drama. Where the Victorians had read Shakespeare as literature, Bottomley (like many of his Georgian peers) read Shakespeare as inherently dramatic and inherently musical.[112] For Bottomley, that legacy offered an essential model for the restoration of verse drama within a modern context. Rather than promoting imitative verse or perpetual allusions to Shakespearean plays, Bottomley insisted on the revitalization of poetic drama through the incorporation and *unification* of poetic verse with music, movement and the visual arts. Deeming painting to be 'too formidable a competitor with poetry to be allowed such a dangerous start' on the stage, Bottomley concluded that as in Shakespeare's plays, 'performed poetry [must] begin again, and trust the scenery to the poetry'.[113] Rather than delegating theatrical effect and drama to poetry alone, however, he demanded a more integrated, collaborative interaction between the arts. In so doing, he embraced a much more abstract ideal of representation. As in Shakespeare, poetic drama must avoid the strictly representational (or 'pictorial'); instead, its music, art and subject must unite to present a coherent 'world for poetry':

> Almost everything can be done by the miracles of modern lighting, playing upon properties and well-imagined symbols; rear-curtains . . . can contain all poetry. Curtains may even carry a little painting . . . add to these a few four-leaved tall screens . . . light will transform them into a world for poetry. Finally, as the painted picture has been left out, let us do away with the picture-frame; and begin.[114]

This definition of 'beginning', with its celebration of abstract setting, suggestive lighting, musical speaking and intimate proximity to the audience, is very distinct from that which inspired nineteenth-century perpetuations of a Shakespearean ideal. It is also very different from the New Drama advocated by Shaw and Archer. That Bottomley would continually legitimate his evolving aesthetic in relation to a Shakespearean legacy, however, points both to its informing presence and to its very malleability within changing and experimental conceptions of dramatic verse, dramatic heritage and the theatre-space itself.

CHAPTER 4
RELIGIOUS DRAMA: THEATRICAL EXPERIMENTATION AND SPIRITUAL RENEWAL BETWEEN THE WARS

In 1922, Laurence Housman (1865–1959) published his first series of *Little Plays of St Francis*, eighteen short dramas built upon imaginative re-workings of the life of the saint. In the preface to that publication, he noted:

> Not all of these plays are intended primarily for the stage – not at least for the stage as it exists to-day; they have nevertheless all been written with an underlying sense of stage requirements and stage effect; and some of them depend so much on these that it is with some regret that I place them before readers instead of before an audience.[1]

The long career of Housman – illustrator, novelist, prominent pacifist, founder of the Men's League for Women's Suffrage and co-founder of the Suffrage Atelier – extended considerably beyond the writing of drama. To some extent, that eclectic career was undertaken of necessity: at one time, thirty-two of his plays had been refused a licence. This refusal was most notoriously centred around Housman's (lightly irreverent, prose) play *Victoria Regina* (1934), which, due to a ruling of the Lord Chamberlain, received its first British production three years after its mainstream success in the United States.[2] Housman was also the author of *Bethlehem*, privately produced by Craig through the rapidly formed Bethlehem Society in 1902, but refused a public licence due to a ban on representations of biblical characters. As James Woodfield speculates, 'officially, the subject matter and the play's content determined the censor's verdict, but there is little doubt that the author's name and reputation swayed his decisions'.[3]

In his own preface to the published *Little Plays*, Housman's friend and occasional collaborator Barker recognizes in both the subject and form of the plays an essentially political act against a dominant 'theatrical industry'.[4] While Housman's plays (like those of Shaw) were of necessity reaching the public first through publication, this did not mean that 'they are more fitted for the study than the stage'; they have merely 'not been fitted to the

Procrustean bed of the commercial theatre'.[5] Barker identifies a 'so-called renascence of the English drama' in the last twenty-five to fifty years ('you may date its beginning according to your particular sympathies').[6] This renascence is both aesthetic and ideological: it has seen the rejection of the values of the commercial theatre and the 'upspringing all over England of bodies of people so hungry for a little simple, wholesome, unhocussed dramatic art, that, denied it by the professional providers, they are ready to see to the supply themselves'.[7] The modern amateur associations now 'stand clean upon their own theatrical feet', free of commercial concerns and considerations: 'here is a theatre for which any dramatist of to-day, with his eye upon the immediate tomorrow, may well sit down to write'.[8]

For Barker, this freedom is particularly enabled by religious drama: 'It is surely a very salient sign both of our new drama's vitality and of the fact we have alleged that its life is now truly a part of the people's life, when it turns – and quite simply and normally turns – to religion for a topic'.[9] To some extent, Barker mirrors Gray's similar association of religion with a shared popular mythology: where the 'Celtic nations' had retained their oral traditions and myths, England had seen its 'vague legends' and 'early history' die out 'with the Arthurian cycle in the Middle Ages'.[10] Nonetheless, 'on the religious side', 'the Bible stories and the heroes of biblical tradition are still part of the family education'.[11] Barker also, however, extends that reading to align the perpetuation of modern drama itself with an essential spiritual renewal. Nowhere is that association more evident than in the humble performance of religious drama by the 'people':

> But let half a dozen actors, thinking more of their art than of themselves, and for the time being more of St. Francis than of either – let them give such life as is in them to any one of these plays, and . . . they will find without fail that the life of the play's art and the intenser life of its purpose will give increase tenfold.[12]

Writing before the renewal of cathedral drama only six years later, Barker notes that the Church had thrown away 'a weapon' in distancing itself from drama. Drama, however, 'may still offer her service': 'One sees, very shortly, a Guild of the Players of St. Francis being formed, with these plays for its text-book. Will they tramp, bare-footed and brown-frocked, round the English country as their prototypes tramped Italy?'[13]

Barker's preface hints at the extent to which the reform of modern drama could be aligned with the reform of society itself, and not necessarily in religious terms. Built upon an innately spiritual sense of community, legitimated by its origins in the 'family mythology', that drama might awaken a natural, cohesive and communal instinct for self-expression. In so doing, it might also encourage the questioning and (gentle) overthrow of the tyranny of established institutions. For many self-conscious reformers of modern drama (many of them also Fabians), the commercial theatre itself represented these larger institutions, both in its determining, profit-orientated operations and in the nature and focus of its apparently superficial, staid and empty productions. For Barker, therefore, the amateur theatre and the 'small' religious play, ostracized from that larger stage, could be aligned with a growing movement that was as much political as it was aesthetic. Unlike the dramas of Galsworthy, Shaw and even Barker himself, the very origins and subject of that theatre ensured its *manifestation* of political argument. In this context, it is unsurprising that poet-dramatists such as Masefield, Bottomley and Housman should have participated so actively within the promotion of amateur and community theatre.

It is also unsurprising that those poets should have turned so readily to religious drama as a means of promoting verse drama itself. In 1925, Masefield's introduction to his verse plays refuted the common assumption that 'nobody wants plays in verse: nobody goes to them':

> That is not true. All over England, little companies of people are playing plays in verse because they enjoy them and prefer them. Great movements begin among little companies. Eighteen hundred years ago little companies of Christians looked at the majesty of the pagan world as a thing almost impossible even to attempt to overcome. In direct conflict, it would perhaps have been impossible to overcome, but by the patient endeavour of little companies for a thousand years the thing was done, and those companies raised themselves theatres where their rites could be fittingly performed.[14]

In Masefield's assessment, verse drama constitutes the innately dramatic, intuitive expression of the common man. This expression, overlooked by governing authorities, continues to grow in confident opposition to that larger prosaic reality, sure of ultimate triumph. As such, it can apparently be aligned with the early growth of Christianity itself within a pagan world.

Such constructions are blatantly rhetorical, and Masefield's own activities suggest a slightly more moderate conviction of the instrumental role of verse drama as a whole. His assertion does intimate, however, the fundamental inaccuracy of contemporary associations of both verse drama and religious drama with an established, conservative dogmatism. It also implicitly refutes a contemporary tendency to assume in that drama an equally conservative aesthetic. As manifest in the intensive involvement of actors, directors, designers, musicians and poets, the development of religious verse drama in the first decades of the twentieth century constituted a distinct movement of aesthetic, dramatic reform. As manifest in the overwhelming success of *Murder in the Cathedral*, as reinforced by the relatively mainstream status of religious verse drama soon thereafter, that movement would eventually achieve a cultural status for verse drama not entirely unlike that predicted by Masefield. In so doing, however, it would also ensure its status as one of the dominant targets for the next movement of dramatic reform.

The following pages offer an overview of some key developments in the 'rise' of religious verse drama to its informing position within the new drama of the 1940s. Those developments were many and rarely linear, but they can be said to have been emboldened in many ways by the commissioning of Masefield's *The Coming of Christ* for performance in Canterbury Cathedral. The critical, cultural and commercial status of *Murder in the Cathedral*, performed in the same space five years later, is well-known, and the play itself is a rare example of a verse drama that has not suffered from scholarly neglect. It is not, however, the first or only manifestation of modern religious verse drama and its cultural position is perhaps better considered in relation to other developments within that form. The primary focus of this chapter is the perpetuation of religious verse drama in the church-space over the 1920s and 1930s, and its evolving formulation by a diversity of literary and dramatic voices.

In his postscript to his *A Stage for Poetry*, Bottomley records his keen interest, as developed in discussions with George Bell, Abercrombie and Binyon, in the recent movement to formulate 'a new religious drama'.[15] After having witnessed the dramatic result of that movement at Canterbury Cathedral, he is now convinced that in 'no other type of building now existing is a quarter so sympathetic to dramatic poetry as a great Gothic church, or offers it so perfect a home: formal drama can be performed there with an ease and acceptance never attained in a modern theatre-building'.[16] For Bottomley, this conviction resonates with the established interest of many poet-dramatists in Greek ritual drama, and with his own increasing appreciation of the relationship between verse drama and opera. He consequently describes his vision for an ideal Theatre of Poetry, as yet unborn:

my ideal building might best adopt the auditorium of the Greeks and Wagner, though on a smaller scale for the fostering of subtle and delicate effects ... I would build ... a new stage afresh for every play, dictated by production needs and potentialities; as intimately connected with the play by its shape as the High Altar is with the High Mass.[17]

Bottomley recognizes in Wagnerian opera a translation of Greek ritual within the contemporary (and modernized) theatre space. He also, however, points to the influence of recent religious drama – its ritualistic element, its theatrical intimacy and its invocation of a larger, controlling authorship through artistic presentation itself:

I would give life to this stage by light from above, from every side, from afar off and over the auditorium at will ... creating an all-controlling 'gulf of mystery' *behind* the stage, as Wagner sought to do in front of his stage, between that and his audience. His gulf could only be bridged by a torrent of sound, which it was to control; my gulf should be that darkness in which an act of creation can emerge, can arise and take shape as a human action does in an unseen eternity.[18]

As Bottomley's response suggests, the experience of religious drama in the cathedral space could do much to support evolving conceptions of a more secular ideal of poetic theatre.

It also, of course, did much to support the theatrical growth of religious verse drama itself. In what is as yet the only concerted discussion of the rise of the modern cathedral play, Pickering provides an invaluable overview of the formative and influential revival of religious drama at Canterbury Cathedral.[19] To some extent, the aesthetic foundation of this movement was rooted in the rediscovery of medieval drama at the turn of the century, which appealed to poets already bent upon the reform of poetic drama. Medieval verse was not blank verse: 'its most obvious quality was its apparent simplicity and yet it combined both biblical paraphrase with a simulation of colloquial speech'.[20] While the influence of this recognition is apparent in many Georgian plays, it would become most strikingly articulated in the cathedral plays of both Eliot and Masefield, despite some otherwise striking differences in idiom between the two. Furthermore, as we have seen, productions such as Poel's *Everyman* provided an affirmation of alternative, native forms of dramatic writing beyond the Elizabethans, aligning those forms with a modern movement of dramatic reform. In suggesting 'that the roots of medieval drama, and of any new religious drama, lay in the Liturgy',[21] *Everyman* also provided an implicit model for contemporary explorations of dramatic structure, choral speech and ritualistic action independently of the conventional stage. Pickering attributes both Bottomley's subsequent experiments in ritual drama and Eliot's *A Dialogue on Dramatic Poetry* (1928), in which Eliot identifies a relationship between drama and the Mass, at least in part to the pervading influence of that medieval revival.[22]

Much of the development of religious verse drama as a distinctly modern genre, however, can be traced to the energies of Bell, who as Dean of Canterbury between 1925 and 1929 initiated the annual Canterbury Festival of the Arts. From his subsequent position as Bishop of Chichester, Bell appointed Browne as Director of Religious Drama for the diocese and became the first president of the Religious Drama Society. As Pickering notes, between them, the two men 'were to determine largely the development of verse drama in England for the next decade'.[23] Where Bell continued to develop the direction of the Festival from Chichester, Browne would help to form the touring Pilgrim Players in 1939. Under the auspices of the government-funded CEMA (Council for the Encouragement of Music and the Arts), the professional Players performed primarily religious drama and verse drama around the country, in local air-raid shelters, barns, schools and local churches, before disbanding in 1948.

Browne directed all of Eliot's verse dramas, and as his invaluable accounts of those productions reveal, he proved to be a seminal collaborative presence. In 1945, he took on an influential three-year residency at the Mercury Theatre from Dukes. Dukes had used the small, intimate theatre (150 seats, with no proscenium arch) primarily for the Ballet Rambert (run by his wife, Marie Rambert). As evident in his own dramas, his attempt to establish a Poets' Theatre, his sponsorship of *Murder in the Cathedral* at the Mercury and his published essays, he was also strongly invested in the support of contemporary poetic drama. At the Mercury, Browne commissioned and staged readings and productions of modern verse dramas (many of them religious) from poet-dramatists such as Anne Ridler, Christopher Fry, Norman Nicholson and Ronald Duncan. In 1946, he established the Poets' Theatre Guild, where he organized Saturday meetings between dramatists, directors, actors and members of the audience to discuss contemporary productions. Browne was director of the British Drama League from 1948 to 1957, and later oversaw the revival of the mystery plays at York and Coventry Cathedral.

John Masefield's *The Coming of Christ*

Many of these later developments can be attributed to the commissioning, by Bell, of Masefield's *The Coming of Christ*. Produced in 1928 under the direction of the author, with costumes by Ricketts and original music by Holst, the production was an unprecedented event in the history of the Church and the larger theatre. As Pickering notes, 'six thousand people saw the play and, like the cast, were fully aware that they were involved in something quite revolutionary'.[24] The revolutionary nature of this phenomenon can be attributed in large part to the very fact of the play's commission and performance. Furthermore, the event did not just constitute the first production of a drama in an English cathedral since the Middle Ages; it was also the first modern, overtly religious *spectacle* in many years.

Dramatizations of biblical characters and events had, as we have seen, been largely banned from the commercial stage. *The Coming of Christ* was produced after some years of relative liberalization of that particular form of censorship (not least to allow for the production of medieval religious drama). The play did, however, constitute the first 'mainstage' acknowledgement by the Church of the affiliation between religion and theatre. It was also a testament to the vital position of the Church itself in the promotion not only of contemporary dramatic writing, but also of contemporary music and design: theatrical art as a whole. With its songs, incidental music, varied verse idioms and spectacular exploitation of the church-space, *The Coming of Christ* went some way to signal the effective liberation of religious drama from its relatively exclusive association with the theatrically static (if musically powerful) form of the oratorio. In so doing, it encouraged the celebration of a more vibrant, interdisciplinary definition of modern religious theatre – and of the contemporary spiritual and dramatic resonance of verse drama more generally.

In keeping with the activities of a playwright who had overseen the design of his own (much smaller) private theatre, Masefield's play made significant use of the theatre space, thus ensuring an alignment of that drama with the experimental initiatives of contemporary dramatists, designers and producers. Freed of the traditional proscenium stage, the production enabled an exploitation of space and setting that reinforced the intimate relation between audience, subject and theatre itself. The play was staged primarily on the steps of the Cathedral that lead from the nave to the quire screen. Separated by three large landings, the steps essentially led to three separate stages. The middle of these stages, framed by an arch, could also be reached by steps from the north-east and south-west transepts; the other two could only be approached from the middle stage, the nave, or the quire.[25] As exploited by Masefield, those stages enabled the dramatic presentation of simultaneously diverse and complementary themes and expressive idioms. This setting also allowed for experimentations in natural light (as filtered through the building's stained glass) and floodlighting that resonated with the increasing interest, amongst anti-realist directors and dramatists, in the dramatic exploitation of colour as a symbolic, signifying presence. As manifest in the cathedral space, as articulated through the themes of a Nativity play, that theatre was rendered ritual to an extent often invoked and only rarely achieved by the diverse experimental attempts, in writing and production, of such relative contemporaries as Craig, Yeats, Poel and Gray.

In its close prescription of sound and movement, in its staging of symbolic, archetypal figures, Masefield's play immediately underscores his interest in ritual drama:

At the closing of the preluding music the two trumpeters of the Host of Heaven enter from the Quire Door, walk each three paces to his side, blow a short blast, descend to the Middle Stage, halt, blow a long salute, turn, each to his side, and go off into the transepts. As they disappear, the Angel called The Power enters from the Quire Door, comes down five steps and says:

> I bring the Power of God as God directs,
> My hand is on the stars and on the tides
> What Man least hopes or proud Man least expects,
> That Power I bring, which being brought abides.[26]

Where many of Masefield's dramas employed conventions from Greek drama, any appreciation of their immediate, contemporary relevance could suffer from the alignment of those earlier conventions with historical subjects. For many then (and particularly now), the effect of plays such as *Philip the King* and *A King's Daughter* was to suggest a mildly experimental, if not eclectic, interest in archaic tradition. In *The Coming of Christ*, however, Masefield was enabled by the Christian context to reinforce the significance of that ritualistic drama itself to the dramatization of shared, spiritual 'truth'. In so doing, he was also able to align some of his own rather distinctly political interpretations of that truth with the communal experience of ritualistic worship.

The play is unconventional for a Nativity play: in an opening that resembles more the structure of *Everyman* than that of Housman's *Bethlehem* or traditional amateur dramatizations,[27] Masefield eschews the three kings, the shepherds, or heralding angels in favour of four angel spirits: The Power, The Sword, The Mercy and The Light. Each spirit declares his identity and role in verse that is characteristic of Masefield. As apparent in the declaration by The Power quoted above, that verse is direct, economical, sufficiently structured as to suggest its ritualistic origins – but never overtly stylized as literary poetry. The four then speak in choral unison: in keeping with the acoustic demands of the cathedral space (and in somewhat notable contrast to the later use of the chorus in *Murder in the Cathedral*), the language remains simple and spare. It also, however, establishes a distinctive pace and auditory impression. Four voices in choral unison have a very different effect on listeners than one. Furthermore, where the preceding statements had been relatively staid and controlled within a rhyme scheme of ABAB, that scheme shifts to AABA, suggesting a restlessness and incentive towards resolution. This rhythmic, rhyming effect complements a new thematic focus on the violence and restlessness of the contemporary, human world:

> We see the world of men seizing and slaying,
> Lusting for wealth, destroying and betraying,
> With neither hope nor peace,
> Save greed, between their darkness and decaying.[28]

This statement precedes the entry of the Anima Christi, who is readying himself for his arrival on Earth, and finds himself '[quaking]' as he enters 'Life with its griefs and sin ... Man with his love and hate.'[29]

Rather than confirming the power of God on Earth, rather than hailing the imminent salvation of humankind, the spirits assert the danger of entering a human world of violence and despair. The subsequent exchange between the spirits and the Anima Christi comes to resemble the structure of a Tudor interlude, with the Anima asserting that humans will 'be one with [him] in exaltation'[30] while the spirits consistently, individually, argue his impending, violent fate. In thus calling prominent attention to the inevitability of the Crucifixion as a manifestation of human violence (rather than imminent human salvation), Masefield tempers any simplistic celebration of Nativity. He also calls attention to what later becomes a more extensive condemnation of human brutality and injustice. The primary emphasis, in this debate, is on the sacrifice of Christ. Asked if, 'being a Man,' he will be able to 'endure the end', the Anima asserts, 'God's mercy will not fail me, being a Man.'[31] Nonetheless, almost overcome by repeated assertions of the impossibility of helping mankind – 'Men are but animals, and you will fail' – the Anima begs for 'comfort in [his] going': he is told that 'We have no comfort: for your task will bring none.'[32] The Anima eventually finds some hope in the appearance of the 'shapes' of Peter and Paul, who bear witness both to their own flaws and their spiritual faith. As reinforced in the consistent warnings and pleadings of the spirits, however, the overall effect is to emphasize the sacrifice of Christ in choosing to enter this cruel, thankless world.

Towards the end of the scene, the Anima is sent forth in song by the Host of Heaven, who – in another dramatic exploitation of the theatre-space – sing from the quire door and the gallery above. The song hails the coming of Christ to save humankind. It also, however, consistently tempers that celebration with a reminder of, if not emphasis on, the violence of humanity:

> So will an April snow assail the spring;
> So pain attends each Changer of the Course
> In which Man feels the shadow of God's wing.[33]

This emphasis is again reinforced by the final plea of the Anima Christi: 'O all you host of heaven, be beautiful / About my going, that I do not fail.'[34] This plea for beauty is realized in the subsequent song of the spirits, who individually and then collectively herald the coming of Christ in language that invokes the tone and imagery of more conventional Nativity pageants:

> To the oxen lowing
> In a night of snowing
> This friend is going
> To lift Man's curse.
>
> . . .
>
> A star shall shine[35]

The song is characterized by established Nativity images and by the harmonious comfort of its musical setting. Ultimately, as juxtaposed against the thematic and dramatic context of the preceding exchanges, the effect is less to reinforce the transcendent power of this aesthetic beauty than to underline its limitations.

In this first scene, therefore, Masefield implicitly deconstructs conventional celebrations of the Nativity in an attempt to re-animate the significance of that myth. In his focus on the (legitimate) fear and sacrifice of the Anima Christi, he invites a renewed appreciation of the gift of and need for salvation: as the Anima passes through and into the quire, he states, 'O brother Man, I come; hate me not / always.'[36] The Host of Heaven then sing of the coming of Christ in verse that invokes the heralding joy of nature:

The cock of glory lifts his crest of fire:
Far among slumbering men his trumpet rings:
Awake, the night is quick with coming things[37]

The verse is much more expressive, emphatic in its celebration of the impending Nativity, 'The Beauty, within touch, of God the king.'[38] It is equally emphatic, however, in its attempt to awaken humanity itself – nature is awake, Christ is come, but the imperative remains: 'O mortals, praise Him; O awake and sing.'[39] In the context of the play's presentation within the Cathedral, that imperative is implicitly addressed as much to the contemporary audience as it is to the unseen subjects of the play itself.

Rather than dramatizing this awakening, the play proceeds to a lengthy chorus that describes the limited progress of man from darkness into 'light': he has built cities, conquered nature and mastered science. He yearns, however, for peace on earth, for the voice of a 'friend' 'from a city more lasting than his', 'and he dies, crying out in his need, and his son cries anew'.[40] The play constantly associates the resolution of such despair with the Incarnation, but forestalls its dramatization to focus on the human need for salvation.[41] The next section of the play presents the three kings as morality figures; their individual declarations expand upon this restless, unhappy state of mankind. Baltazar has killed and conquered and now fears death; Gaspar is wealthy and now despairs of the value of material accumulation in the face of imminent death; Melchior is more existential in his desire to find 'Some link that will forever bind / Our minds to an eternal mind.'[42] As they eventually follow the star, they sing of being 'waters without plan' and of seeking 'that simple thing / Under the eyes of every day' that they might find 'where the glittering waters go.'[43]

When the star appears, the three kings become more conventional, familiar characters – and the play itself moves from ritualistic drama to 'realist' narrative (but always in verse). As the kings process off the stage, the shepherds Rocky, Earthy and Sandy enter in a scene that bears overt resemblance to the Towneley Second Shepherds's play. Rather than rooting these rustics in a medieval setting, however, Masefield translates that play's emphasis on the human, demotic experience of the Nativity into a setting that is simultaneously contemporary and timeless. This elision is effected by the verse, whose language is vaguely rural, but otherwise suggests both a contemporary reality and a ritualistic transcendence of time and place. The shepherds echo their dramatic forebears in their colloquial language, irreverence and immediate complaints about the cold: 'the ground is all rimed with the white, / And the frost is all crisp on my fur.'[44] They also, however, voice complaints and convictions that would have resonated in an inter-war environment marked by political and social unrest. As he complains of working for another man without respite from the cold, Sandy declares: 'what we want is a good revolution.'[45] Earthy then responds:

> It's time they did, the rich and great,
> To pay for what they did to me:
> They said that I must serve the State
> And fight poor heathen over-sea.
> And there I stayed among the mud
> In beds of lice and deeds of blood,
> Until they chose to let it be.
> Four years they kept me, 'serving,' so they said;
> Ordered like dogs, and Death to all who disobeyed.[46]

Unlike the earlier angels and kings, these shepherds are characters rather than exemplary figures, and as such, they talk to each other. The effect is not only to render these implicitly archetypal workers more immediately contemporary in their discourse and idiom, but it is also to dramatize the collective potential of their convictions and social condition. In response to Earthy's barely concealed reference to the recent war, Sandy takes on the cause of the workers: it is time that they 'should command / and have the wealth they make. We are the ones who till the land, and / what we grow they take'; Earthy replies that 'one thing' he can let future kings know is that 'in the next war the workers will not go'.[47] Sandy reflects that 'war isn't any glory: it's a crime', and Earthy remembers the cruelty of the generals towards their soldiers in the last war – '"Serving the State", they called it.'[48]

Rocky differs from Sandy and Earthy in his willed subservience to governing structures; he rebukes his companions that 'the government of men [is not] easy' and that all men govern with the help of God.[49] The intervention enables a return to the theme of the Incarnation as salvation; Sandy and Earthy are convinced that 'this talk of God is used by Kings and priests / To frighten people' and send them to war,[50] while Rocky is convinced that he has felt the power of God protecting him. Rather than resolving these doubts and apparent contradictions, the play interrupts the exchanges between the shepherds by staging the announcement of the Nativity by the Power, while the Angels of the Host appear at the quire door, on the upper stage, and in the gallery and clerestory. As presented in the themes and shifting idioms of the play, the drama inspires the realization of the Incarnation within the theatre space itself, both within and outside the framework of narrative presentation. The play transforms into a spectacle of worship grounded equally in narrative and contemporary liturgical celebration: the kings process in song, celebrating the potential realization of their hopes in the Christ-child ('We have lived by knowledge and wealth and spear, / And are weary of all, if change might be').[51] The shepherds pay similar devotion. Throughout, Masefield has suggested the contemporary resonance of the social themes and moral crises articulated within the play. At the conclusion of the play, he dramatizes the transformation of those doubts and realities through the miracle of the Incarnation.

The play concludes in an act of performative, liturgical celebration with which the audience is invited to identify – and in which, with the musical procession of the litter through the nave, the quire and the transept – it is assumed to be a participant. The Sword re-invokes the 'angry blood' of man that 'was once the guide', but suggests a fundamental transformation of mankind through the ritualistic celebration of the Nativity. Where once the spring connoted an assailing 'April snow', 'perish boughs are thrust aside / In the green fever of the Spring'.[52] The play concludes with a final address to the characters and to the audience of the play, again enforcing the inseparability of art and ritual, audience and performer:

> Friends, Christ is come within this hall;
> Bow down and worship, one and all,
> Our Father for this thing.[53]

As Pickering notes, this final 'shift from dramatic entertainment to liturgical enactment' made a strong impression on those who attended the play, testifying to the success of Masefield's apparent aim to reawaken 'an in-built desire to confirm our faith in symbolic acts'.[54]

Read in the context of Masefield's other dramatic projects, *The Coming of Christ* can be assessed as a successful realization of the affective possibilities of verse drama, ritual and art. The play works to instigate spiritual reflection through the definition and development of theatrical experience itself. It also suggests a movement away from verse alone as the dominant language of poetic drama, towards a more interdisciplinary dramatic realization of heightened truth – Abercrombie's 'emotional reality' and Drinkwater's 'passionate life'. Equally central is the enabling of this drama through reference to different dramatic traditions: medieval mystery play, medieval morality, Christian liturgy, Greek drama and, to a more subtle extent, the contemporary social problem play. The work can also be read in relation to Barker's invocation of the transformative potential of religious drama in more political, social terms. Masefield foregrounds the ultimate fate of Jesus at the hands of a violent and cruel humanity. In so doing, he tempers any overall tone of simplistic jubilation. *The Coming of Christ* celebrates the eternal, saving presence of Christ and the transformative power of liturgical ritual as developed and ultimately manifest through the contemporary art of a musical, spectacular and poetic drama. It also, however, dramatizes the perpetual need for that presence in a society that continues to perpetuate war, that continues to exploit its workers, and whose kings refuse to recognize the spiritual emptiness of their actions.

Not everyone was content with this manifestation of the cathedral play, either as an aesthetic manifestation of a modern drama in verse, or as a spiritual affirmation of religious doctrine. For some, the play could be seen as excessively reliant on earlier traditions in order to signify its own contemporary – and spiritual – relevance. It could also be seen as moving the art of modern poetry itself too far from a central, defining role in drama. Others objected to the play on theological grounds. One of the most trenchant criticisms of *The Coming of Christ* came from Eliot, who had not seen the play in performance, but questioned

> whether such an entertainment serves any cause of religion or art. The poetry is pedestrian, machine made Shakespearean iambics; the imagery is full of Birmingham spirits and Sheffield shepherds. The theological orthodoxy is more than doubtful? The literary incompetence is more than certain.[55]

Aside from critiquing Masefield's verse, Eliot aligns himself with those religious voices that objected both to the very dramatization of the Anima

Christi and to Masefield's imagining of the Anima's need for support from the angel powers. According to the critic of the *Patriot*, it might be that 'poets have great licence, but it misrepresents Christian theology, and is, therefore, not conducive to Christian worship'.[56] As manifest in subsequent developments, this potential tension between theology, the development of modern poetic art, and theatre itself was to become increasingly more apparent.

The years after *The Coming of Christ* saw the performance of other successful plays for the Festival at Canterbury, including a 1932 production of Tennyson's *Becket* in the Chapter House and another in 1933, with designs by Irving. Bell, however, had become increasingly convinced of the need to commission plays that 'explored the Christian faith in twentieth century terms', rather than merely dramatizing Christian history.[57] The result was his commission of *Murder in the Cathedral*, which went some way to establish contemporary religious drama as a distinct (and distinctly modern) genre. The very subject of the play, the martyrdom of Thomas Beckett, was not just appropriate to the Canterbury setting: it offered an implicit response both to the recent revival of Tennyson's work at Canterbury and to the cultural position of its author. Many in the Canterbury audience would have seen the Tennyson revivals, and, as Pickering argues, the scenes in Eliot's play in which the knights enter the Cathedral 'are a conscious reworking of the final two scenes in Eileen Thorndike's acting edition of *Becket*'.[58] For those bent upon the assertion of verse drama as a contemporary art, the play seemed to signal a deliberate break from earlier, implicitly more tired manifestations of the form.

The initial performance context was overtly religious, and in its focus on the spiritual nature of martyrdom (and the witnessing of martyrdom), the play did much to reinforce Eliot's declared interest in theological orthodoxy and literary competence. As Speaight suggests, however, the larger success of *Murder in the Cathedral* can also be attributed to the fact that it had taken as its subject 'a well-known story whose melodramatic outline is familiar to every British schoolboy'.[59] With its eventful narrative, powerful choral voices and striking juxtaposition of contemporary prose and verse, the play ensured a dynamic re-imagining of that story in terms that translated easily onto a mainstream stage. The play experienced an almost seamless transition into the contemporary repertoire. While the importance of Masefield's *Coming of Christ* continues to be overlooked in most historical assessments, it was undoubtedly *Murder in the Cathedral* that established a larger recognition of verse drama as a powerful and potentially contemporary dramatic art.

Notwithstanding the cultural position of Eliot's play, that art – and particularly as manifest in the religious verse drama of the 1930s and 1940s – was exceptionally diverse. Many of the verse dramatists of the 1930s and 1940s were concerned with the active reinvigoration of dramatic expression in verse itself, in the re-alignment of the 'poetry' of theatre with its articulation through a distinct, recognizably modern verse idiom. Others – most notably Auden – insisted equally on rendering that drama more authentically contemporary by building from current theatrical forms, none of which were wholly independent of music and dance. Not all writers of religious verse drama identified primarily as poets or poet-dramatists, however, and not all chose to engage with (or seemed to be aware of) the larger movements that had theorized verse drama in relation to prevailing theatrical practice and/or dramatic and poetic writing.

The result could be works that seemed to rely upon the signifying, heightening role of verse primarily in order to validate the presentation of theological argument. It could also be dramas that differed considerably from the anti-realist, anti-argumentative aesthetic that had dominated the exertions of many poetic dramatists thus far. As religious verse drama evolved into a relatively mainstream genre in the late 1930s and early 1940s, it would at times establish a very close relationship with other movements in dramatic and theatrical art. It would at other times come very close to manifesting a new, contemporary version of the much-derided drama of ideas.

Zeal in the House: Charles Williams and Dorothy L. Sayers

To some extent, the critical and popular recognition of *Murder in the Cathedral* only gave strength to what had already become a minor tradition amongst literary figures to develop an intellectualized, theological culture in literary writing. Nowhere, perhaps, had that instinct been more manifest than in the activities of the Inklings, an informal group at Oxford University whose primary, most well-known denizens (C.S. Lewis, Charles Williams, J.R.R. Tolkien) were committed to various explorations, in literature and thought, of religious consciousness and doctrinal truth. Amongst these writers and intellectuals, Williams was undoubtedly the most prolific, and alongside works of literary criticism, poetry, biography, history and lay theology, he produced a number of what Eliot himself was to term 'supernatural thrillers', popular novels dedicated to the exploration of contemporary experience with the sacred.

From the late 1920s until his death in 1945, Williams was also the writer of a number of religious plays. Most of those dramas were written for publication alone. In 1936, however, he was commissioned to write the first drama for Canterbury to follow *Murder in the Cathedral* (*Thomas Cranmer of Canterbury*). The play is considerably more ambitious than that of Masefield in both its theology and its dramaturgy, and while subsequent critical voices may have hailed the work's anticipation of Brechtian techniques, the overall impression at the time was of a drama that, in the words of Philip Hollingworth (who played Henry VIII), was 'obscure and pretentious'.[60] According to the *Kent Messenger*, the play was fundamentally 'unsatisfactory': 'Its form is hard to follow; its language ... is obstruse, its action is slow in the extreme, and it develops, really, into an exhibition ... of elocution by two men.'[61] Speaight, who portrayed Cranmer, characterizes it as 'torturous in thought and expression, but dramatically powerful in an expressionist convention'.[62] In 1937, Williams was nonetheless commissioned to write *Seed of Adam*, for the Chelmsford Diocesan Religious Drama Guild. His later works were written for the Rock Theatre Company at Oxford, an offshoot of Browne's Pilgrim Players.

In 1946, Ridler conceded that 'it is difficult to judge Charles Williams by contemporary standards other than those of his own work, and this is one result of his originality'.[63] Noting his relative lack of experience in the theatre before *Thomas Cranmer*, she also observed that Williams never 'consciously acquired dramatic technique': nonetheless, 'drama was natural to him because ideas existed in a state of tension in his mind'.[64] This state of tension had been developed in many of Williams's other writings, and he found in religious drama a means to expound upon his ideas primarily through the imaginative staging of embodied abstractions. Williams's dramas are thus very much in keeping with a creative genre whose thematic focus on religion had ensured that it did not just appeal to poets, poet-dramatists and churchmen eager to re-align the Church with contemporary art. At times, that drama could seem to develop almost entirely independently of contemporary stage traditions and dominant movements in poetic expression. As subsequent assessments of the 'Brechtian' and 'expressionist' theatre of *Thomas Cranmer* suggest, that very independence could also encourage the development of less traditional ways of envisioning the contemporary stage.

In his notes on *Seed of Adam*, Williams rather grudgingly acknowledges that he has turned his Shepherds into a Chorus. This decision went against his own instinct; it was a concession to the commissioners of the piece, who had hoped for a choral effect similar to that in *Murder in the Cathedral*. For

Williams, the result could be inhibiting: Eliot 'has made choruses a little difficult. I know all about the Greeks, but they do not prevent one being told one is copying Mr. Eliot.'[65] Williams's comments underline the extent to which *Murder in the Cathedral* was assumed to have established certain formal expectations of religious drama in verse. Notwithstanding this one concession, however, Williams's drama, like *Thomas Cranmer*, constitutes an intriguing manifestation of a drama written almost wholly independently of prevailing trends.

Seed of Adam is overtly mystical in its themes and theology: where Masefield assumed a need to coerce his audience into Christian experience (and affirmation), Williams assumes a certain familiarity with his own particular theology, his tendency as he describes it, 'in my usual way [to abolish] Time and Space.'[66] The play is a Nativity play. While Masefield disrupts conventional expectations of the Nativity play in his opening dramatization of the Anima Christi and the four Powers, he uses that initial framework to inform the ultimate pageant of Christ child, shepherds, kings and Mary at the end of his drama. For Williams, however, a more spiritually and dramatically authentic representation of the Nativity demands a more significant rewriting. He concedes that there may be 'profound and awful possibilities' in the conventional Nativity image of 'the old man leading a devout girl on a donkey', but not for him: the thought resounds too much with 'the later plays of Shakespeare, and as a rule it is safer not to go trying to reap what He left. I will put S[hakespeare] into a novel when I want him but I will not chase after him.'[67]

Seed of Adam certainly does nothing to invoke Shakespeare and very little to invite comparison with more traditional Nativity pageants. As Glen Cavaliero observes, Williams was bent on overcoming the 'mummified complacency' of the conventional Nativity play by '[obliterating] the simper of lethargic piety.'[68] According to Williams himself, he intended not so much to present 'historic facts' as to dramatize their spiritual value.[69] Like Masefield, Williams identifies the spiritual value of the Nativity primarily in the Incarnation, in the presence of Christ amongst humankind. Unlike Masefield, however, he is considerably less invested in rooting that drama within a contemporary social or moral context; the focus of the play is on reinforcing the doctrine of the seed of Adam, the presence of God in Man. The play begins with the entrance of the Tsar of Caucasia ('King of Gold') who, like many opening characters in religious dramas of the time (and mummers plays of old), proclaims his identity to the audience: he is 'Gaspar', who '[sprang] from our father Adam's loins / in a bright emission of coins' and is

now devoted to commercial trade and expansionism.[70] He is followed by
'Melchior, Sultan of Bagdad', whose father Adam and mother Eve 'construed
[him] aloof from sister and brother / through a post-paradisal afternoon',
and who is preoccupied with art and philosophy.[71] In a characteristically
Williams-esque conflation of time and space, he is then followed by Adam
himself, who reprimands the two kings – his children – for their failure to
adhere to his own attempt to seek a way back into heaven.

Discouraged by his children, Adam – who represents Man – hopes to save
his daughter Mary from the inevitable persecution of his sons. Mary is
betrothed to Joseph, and is soon thereafter visited by the angelic Chorus who
announce the Incarnation in Hebrew.[72] Rather than prophesying the coming
of God, however, the Chorus (Williams's original Shepherds) cry out in fear
of impending disaster: 'Father Adam, save us or we perish.'[73] Adam's authority
is nonetheless limited, and derives primarily from his tenacity in seeking the
Way of Return rather than giving in to fear or despair. This limited power is
emphasized in his own return in the shape of Augustus Caesar: he will
conduct a census to ascertain if he can find the Way of Return through
human means. Adam's attempts are interrupted by the Third King (and thus
his third son), who is in despair and is accompanied by a cannibalistic
'negress' (who, in Williams's notes, represents Hell). The play concludes,
however, 'with the overthrow of the destructive cannibal nature of man at
the moment of the Nativity, and with the adoration of the Omnipotence'.[74] In
an affirmation of Adam's identity as 'seed of Christ', both Man and God
unified in Salvation, Joseph calls out: 'Father Adam, come in / here is your
child, / here is the Son of Man, here is Paradise.'[75] The characters variously
reinforce this fundamental unification ('return') of man to God: 'blessed be
he who is the earth's core', 'he consumes and is consumed', 'he is the womb's
prophecy and the tomb's' and, in the words of Eve, 'Blessed be he who is sown
in our flesh, grown / among us for our salvation: blessed be he.'[76]

As this brief summary can only begin to suggest, Williams's play builds
upon morality traditions, Renaissance allegory and the conventional figures
of the Nativity to present the distinctly symbolic reading of the Incarnation
that he perpetuated in many of his other works. It also suggests a relatively
different understanding of audience, where the play is as much theological
argument as it is communal affirmation. With its scimitar-baring Joseph,
singing chorus of Angels and cannibalistic Mother Myrrh, the play is not
without a sense of stageable drama; indeed, Grevel Lindop identifies a work
that is 'profoundly imaginative and visually spectacular'.[77] The primary roots
of that profound imagination, however, seem to lie less in recent explorations

of poetic drama (or modern drama more generally) than they do in poetic tradition – most particularly, perhaps, in the allegory of Spenser and the imagery of Milton. When Adam first enters to berate his two sons, his language is dominated by interior rhymes that call immediate attention to its expression as poetry:

> Dullards of darkness, light's lazy-bones,
> poor primitives of our natural bareness,
> where's your awareness? Will moans and groans
> for gold of brawn or brain regain
> the way to the entry of Paradise?[78]

When the Third King arrives, he uses language whose imagery echoes that of *Paradise Lost*, and whose use of enjambment to dramatize movement enforces a primarily literary appreciation of drama *within* poetry:

> You saw me
> when you breathlessly slid down the smooth threshold
> of Paradise gate?
> . . .
> Did you remember, ungrateful that you are,
> how you threw me away, with such a swing
> I flew over Eden wall, dropped,
> and stuck between two stones?[79]

While these excerpts point to a primarily literary sensibility, they are not impossible to imagine as staged performance. Joseph's realization of his 'appointment' as husband to Mary, however, suggests a rather more daunting challenge, both to actor and audience:

> Do not with descent, O altitude, even of mercy,
> sweeten the enhanced glance of those still eyes
> which to my lord's house, and to me the least,
> illumine earth with heaven, our only mortal
> imagination of eternity,
> and the glory of the protonotary Gabriel.[80]

As Cavaliero suggests, *Seed of Adam* 'labours under Williams's tendency to cram his text with words, to make his idea bring forth the verse rather than to let the verse carry the idea'.[81] The verse of Masefield tended towards a deliberate simplicity, an economy of expression that might evoke (if not effect) ritualistic declamation. As we shall see, Eliot was similarly focused on developing a form of poetic expression that would speak directly to an innately contemporary sensibility, albeit within a very different verse idiom. Williams, however, embraces an overtly poetic diction that calls attention to itself as poetry and acts to affirm the significance of its drama in primarily literary and theological terms. He was relatively alone amongst his peers in this regard, and the majority of religious drama in verse – while at times equally invested in theological exploration – tended much more consistently towards an ideal of drama focused on a larger, less specialized imagining of dramatic audience.[82]

In 1937, the Canterbury Festival staged *The Zeal of Thy House* in the Chapter House of the Cathedral, based upon the story of one of the Cathedral's original architects. The play, by Dorothy L. Sayers, proved immensely successful, transferred to London and the provinces, was revived on several occasions, and achieved significant popularity in print. It also undoubtedly led to the wartime commissioning of Sayers's twelve-part radio drama, *The Man Born to Be King*, in 1941. *Murder in the Cathedral* had taken as its subject the historical Thomas for a religious examination of martyrdom and faith. The next year, Williams's *Thomas Cranmer* had effected a similar dramatization of an Anglican martyr, admittedly within a very different poetic and dramatic idiom. In the year following, Sayers built both upon the aesthetic expectations established by *Murder in the Cathedral* and her own close theological affiliation with Williams to engage with the subject of religious art and the religious artist.[83] In so doing, she also composed a play that seemed implicitly to assert a parallel between the building of Canterbury Cathedral and the recent emergence of religious drama as a contemporary art-form. While the play never asserts that parallel directly, that reading is encouraged both by the drama's production within a critical context that would see *Murder in the Cathedral* hailed as 'a kind of *Hamlet* of our times'[84] and by the very poetic diversity and dramatic allusiveness of the play itself.

The Zeal of Thy House centres around the character of William of Sens, his selection by committee to work on the Cathedral and his growing hubristic assumption that his art – the working of God through Man – is in fact a manifestation of his own equality with God. Building upon historical material, the play represents the crippling fall of William from the archway of the Cathedral as the Fall of Man: it is, as Michael tells William, 'The sin that is so much a part of thee / That thou know'st it not for sin.'[85] Ultimately, after much discussion with the angels, William recognizes:

> O, I have sinned. The eldest sin of all,
> Pride, that struck down the morning star from Heaven
> Hath struck down me from where I sat and shone
> Smiling on my new-world [86]

He also recognizes that where he may have sinned, the art itself did not: 'The work is sound, Lord God, no rottenness there.'[87] That art can never be completed by one individual alone: William repents, begging only that he might one day be given 'one glimpse, one only, of the Church of Christ / The perfect work, finished, though not by me.'[88] The play concludes with a reminder from Michael of the relationship between holy creation and artistic creativity: the Creative Idea 'is the image of the Father', the Creative Energy 'is the image of the Word' and the Creative Power 'is the image of the indwelling Spirit'.[89] Notwithstanding the dynamic effect of much of the verse and its imagery, the play is rooted in doctrine to an extent that Masefield's play is not, and its essentially parable-like focus ensures an emphasis on message that renders it considerably more didactic than the plays of Eliot or Williams.

This message, however, is not the sole focus of the play. *The Zeal of Thy House* employs a diversity of expressive idioms, ranging from exchanges in prose to direct quotations from the bible, to declamatory pronouncements, to a blank verse characterized by an emphasis on action and development of argument. While these diverse stylistic modes serve the dramatic focus and action of the play, they also underline the status of the play itself as art. Furthermore, in the context of a drama essentially about a man 'whose waxen wings did mount above his reach', the play seems to invoke comparison with Marlowe's over-reaching Faustus. In Sayers's play, William goes so far as to claim that God himself 'over-reached Himself and gave away / His Godhead': 'Man stands equal with Him now, / Partner and rival.'[90] In its dramatization of a craftsman motivated by a self-willed belief in his own powers, drawn to great heights upon a holy edifice, the play also recalls Ibsen's *The Master Builder* (1892); at one point, William declares: 'We are the master-craftsmen, God and I— / We understand one another.'[91] In constructing this allusive resonance, Sayers both emphasizes her central themes and locates the play's own expression of those themes within a larger tradition of dramatic expression. In so doing, she ensures that her play calls attention to its own status within a tradition of dramatic art.

In the context of the play's commission, that art is, like the Cathedral, an essential monument to human faith. Given the recent rebirth of cathedral drama within that very space, the play can be seen as similarly aligning that new dramatic tradition with a collective act of worship and creation. Unlike many other works within that tradition, however – and unlike the Cathedral itself – *The Zeal of Thy House* is a work of art created by a woman. Sayers's play contains a number of seminal exchanges on the theme of gender and creative ambition between William and Ursula, a wealthy widow and patron. In their first conversation, William questions the ability of women to even understand 'the passion of making' and 'the love of knowledge': where women create passively from the womb, 'borne on a wind of lust', only men create 'with the will, with the blood, with the brain / All the desire of the soul, the intent of the mind.'[92] Ursula replies by returning to the theme of the Fall: Eve, 'careless of peril, careless of death' seized knowledge both for herself and man – 'knowledge, like God; Power to create, like God.'[93] Where her reward was sorrow, that of Adam

Was work—of which he now contrives to boast
As his peculiar glory, and in one breath
Denies it to the woman and blames her for it,
Winning the toss both ways.[94]

For Ursula, the role of Eve can be likened to that of Prometheus: in 'snatch[ing] the torch / Of knowledge from the jealous hand of God' she ensured 'that the fire runs in man's blood for ever.'[95] She also implicitly ensured that woman is left to suffer, in chains, for having given that creative freedom and ambition to man.

The play goes some way to redress the passive construction of woman voiced by William. Ursula herself articulates a forceful understanding of the traditional binary between men and women, and claims a much more active and self-conscious role for woman in the enabling of the creative impulse. The play's very resonance both with *Doctor Faustus* and *The Master Builder* further underlines this thematic emphasis. In the Marlowe play, Helen is a passive, sensual ideal summoned up by the sinful and hubristic Faustus. In *The Master Builder*, the over-weaning ambitions of Solness are largely inspired and encouraged by the youthful presence of Hilde Wangel, whose influence ultimately ensures his death. In *The Zeal of Thy House*, however, Ursula observes, understands and comments upon the sinful ambitions of William. She also offers to marry him, in an act of love. As Crystal Downing notes, when William rejects Ursula by associating her presence with sensual distraction, Sayers has the Archangel Michael convince him both of his hubris and 'of his lack of connection both to God and to woman'.[96] Furthermore, as written by a woman, the play itself shatters the conception – perpetuated in much Christian art, literature and drama generally – of man alone as capable of acting upon the 'Power to create, like God'. It also implicitly aligns that artistic creation with the selfless, communal affirmation of God's guiding presence as reiterated didactically throughout the play.

These diverse projects point to the variety of artistic expression enabled by the 'form' of religious drama in the 1920s and 1930s, by its theatre space, and by its presumed audience. Rather than representing the entrenched social conservatism with which it now tends to be associated, much of that drama was actively critical and socially engaged. As manifest in the dramas of Williams, it could also develop independently of the prevailing 'movement' of verse drama with which others were so closely associated. Rather than representing a niche area of theological endeavour, therefore, this religious drama emerged to complement, expand upon and help to realize many of the artistic and social formulations of a vital contemporary theatre that characterized these decades.

CHAPTER 5
MUSIC, POLITICS AND THE MODERN POET: T.S. ELIOT AND W.H. AUDEN IN THE 1930s

By the early 1920s, Yeats's dramas were well on their way towards an exclusive ideal of total art theatre centred around ritual and the Noh (or, in Bentley's words, 'Parlor games *à la japonaise*').[1] Bottomley similarly came to envision a closer 'synthesis of arts' that would break from both the structure and content of existing theatres and, with its use of cyclorama, suggestive lighting, movement, 'liberal costume' and musical poetry, effect an ideal not entirely distinct from Cocteau's more-recognized 'poetry of the theatre'.[2] These instincts complemented the directorial emphases of Craig and Gray,[3] not to mention the experimentations in dance-drama and ballet taking place in England, in Ireland and on the Continent. The 1930s also saw the first seminal collaborations between Britten and Auden on the poetic song-cycle *Our Hunting Fathers* (1936) and on the film *Night Mail* (1936), with verse and music working together with documentary image. From 1932 to 1939, such collaborative enterprises were further encouraged and developed by the (London) Group Theatre, whose many creative voices included Auden, Isherwood, Robert Medley, Guthrie, Britten, Henry Moore, Stephen Spender, Louis MacNeice and Eliot himself; from 1936, the Unity Theatre promoted an openly political theatre, whose use of agitprop techniques frequently aligned and juxtaposed dance, song and verse.

Group Theatre: Politics and collaborative art in the 1930s

Such developments point to a recognizable pre-war movement, amongst many poets, artists and directors, towards an ideal of verse in dramatic performance that could embrace a greater theatrical collaboration or interaction between the arts. That interest, as we have seen, was not exclusive to experimental artists of the 1930s: it was apparent in the ambitions of the turn-of-the-century Literary Theatre Club, and it is clearly evident in the religious drama developed at Canterbury and in various church spaces.

Verse Drama in England, 1900–2015

Despite its exploitation of theatre space and diverse theatrical and verse idioms, despite its seminal use of music and movement and its overt breaking of the fourth wall, a drama such as *The Coming of Christ* is unlikely to be associated with the secular verse dramas of the 1930s. In that decade, the most vocal advocates of a self-consciously experimental, contemporary drama tended to position their art in relation to a clear political agenda. While that agenda could often be equally doctrinaire, the secular (and leftist) emphasis of that art has tended to ensure its greater valuation as a representation of more contemporary trends – as in many ways the spiritual antecedent of the Joan Littlewood Workshop and the political dramas of John Arden and Margaretta D'Arcy.

Read in this context, the plays of Eliot can come across as distinct and isolated from that movement. In 1934, Eliot had identified the need to formulate both a new poetic drama and a new audience that would be free of complacent assumptions about the role of the poet and poetry in drama:

> The young dramatist to-day . . . does not want to write a play merely to please a small audience of poetry-lovers many of whom he will know, and the faces of those of whom he remembers having seen before and is tired of seeing. The best opportunity that presents itself seems to be the opportunity to appeal to those who are interested in a common cause which the poet and dramatist can also serve.[4]

For Eliot, 'There are only two causes now of sufficient seriousness, and they are mutually exclusive: the Church and Communism.'[5]

This assumption of mutual exclusivity is embodied in Eliot's verses for the Christian pageant *The Rock* (performed that year at Sadler's Wells Theatre), which position the builders of the church against an environment marked by the group appeal of contemporary political movements. Nonetheless, while 'the Church and Communism' might constitute two very different common causes, they are also united by the very fact of their 'sufficient seriousness', by their informing presence within contemporary efforts to formulate a tradition of modern drama in verse. That potential affinity is suggested in *The Rock* itself, whose use of song, as Sidnell has argued, simultaneously invokes and subverts the emphasis on choral singing that characterized much of the socialist movement at the time.[6] The result is a work whose aesthetic language acknowledges, works within and develops the expressive modes of the dominant political theatre against which it is otherwise ideologically opposed.

Ultimately, *The Rock* points less to Eliot's rejection of the Workers' Theatre Movement than to his close, reciprocal relationship with the experimental productions of the Group Theatre. The Group had been formalized in 1932 by Doone, whose experience in ballet and whose previous collaborations with Cocteau and Diaghilev complemented his extensive enthusiasm for poetry, and particularly for poetry in performance.[7] To some extent, the Group was a logical extension of Yeats's earlier attempts to found a Theatre of Beauty, and like that earlier project, it attracted a number of contemporary artists – including, briefly, Yeats himself.[8] According to an early appeal for members:

the GROUP THEATRE is a co-operative. It is a community, not a building.

the GROUP THEATRE is a troupe, not of actors only but of
Actors
Producers
Writers
Musicians
Painters
Technicians
etc, etc, and
AUDIENCE[9]

In words that echo the earlier emphasis of directors and playwrights such as Yeats, Masefield and Gray on theatre as communal ritual, the declaration concluded: 'Because you are not moving or speaking, you are not therefore [merely] a passenger. If you are seeing and hearing you are co-operating.'[10]

The political implications of this emphasis on community and art were gradually developed and promoted by Doone. They were not always at the forefront of the Group, however, whose initial focus was much more centred on creative collaboration and experimentation. The individual enthusiasms of those within the Group were rarely cohesive; Guthrie, for example, resisted any attempt at political theatre. Many of the poet-dramatists in the collective remained aloof from the Theatre's more everyday promotion of aesthetic community: in *The Dance of Death* (1933), Auden satirizes the Group's summer retreats. He also 'made it clear from the start that he detested ballet'[11] despite the centrality of Doone and Medley to the Group as a whole. Most of the plays produced by the Group did make extensive use of its collaborative ethos and exploited the dynamic between audience and performer. Spender's political *Trial of a Judge* (1933), however, was marked by what the poet had identified as his conviction that 'the whole apparatus of the Expressionist stage' could be replaced with 'a calmer, more permanent form'. For Spender, 'the form that should take the place of Expressionist experiments is poetic drama',[12] and his play essentially ignores the larger Group in favour of its own poetry. These distinct appreciations of art and authorship within the nominal collective doubtless contributed to the eventual collapse of the Group – but not before that Theatre had influenced the initial development of a number of leading artists.

Eliot was a member of the Group from 1934. Long after his aesthetic had apparently mirrored his politics by moving away from the most publicized values of that Theatre, he continued to support its dramas and dramatists: the majority of plays produced by the Group were published by Eliot, and he was a frequent attendee at performances.[13] He had also provided strong initial encouragement to Auden, whose first drama (*Paid on Both Sides*, 1928) had been published in *The Criterion* – and whose *The Dance of Death* was published by Faber and Faber at the time that Eliot was working on *The Rock*.[14] In 1934, Eliot's *Sweeney Agonistes* was performed by the Group at their London Rooms. The next year, the Group produced *Sweeney* at the Westminster Theatre in a double-bill with *The Dance of Death*, which (in yet another acknowledgement of continuity between 'experimental' traditions) had been performed originally with the Chester mystery play *The Deluge*. In apparent contradiction of Eliot's own identification of mutually exclusive causes, the enthusiasms of Group members could extend to religious drama: while *Murder in the Cathedral* had been commissioned for Canterbury Cathedral, its first performance had been planned initially for the Group, directed by Browne.

Eliot's dramas have often been appraised as conservative, both in their aesthetic and in their themes.[15] As these pre-war projects suggest, however, any such assumption risks overlooking the extent to which Eliot's dramatic aesthetic in fact evolved from his experience within a more intermedial and collaborative creative environment. It also risks overlooking his reciprocal influence on that environment. As Sidnell has argued:

> It is fascinating to observe, through the thirties, Auden converging on Eliot, Eliot borrowing from Auden, Auden and Isherwood attempting to finesse Eliot's new Christian dramaturgy, and Yeats, at one point, offering to join the dance.[16]

The mutual influence of Eliot and Auden has been traced forcefully in Sidnell's history of the Group Theatre. Equally revelatory, perhaps, is the eventual trajectory of each dramatist's career. Auden's last verse drama was completed in 1938; Eliot continued to theorize about and compose successful dramas into his last years. Despite their clear differences, the aesthetic of both poets was to evolve as a reaction against a pre-war theatrical environment marked by intermedial exploration and an increasingly politicized, social ideal of verse in drama. Ultimately, both would recognize in that experience a fundamental challenge to the role of the poet himself in the creation of a vital contemporary art.

Eliot: rhythm, chorus, aria

Like many who had come before him, Eliot identified verse drama as uniquely capable of both expressing and manifesting an essential communal identity. He also recognized that the social (and thus spiritual) role once occupied by poetic drama had become eclipsed by more popular forms. Rather than retreating into the exclusive salon, Eliot aimed to revivify poetic drama by effecting a renewal of both the modern stage and the modern audience. With verse drama, he wanted to appeal to 'as large and miscellaneous an audience as possible', to experience 'at least the satisfaction of having a part to play in society as worthy as that of the music-hall comedian'.[17] In so doing, he would coerce – and educate – that collective into a poetic sensibility:

> The audience should find, at the moment of awareness that it is hearing poetry, that it is saying to itself: '*I* could talk in poetry too!' Then we should not be transported into an artificial world; on the contrary, our own sordid, dreary daily world would be suddenly illuminated and transfigured.[18]

Thus aiming to speak directly to contemporary sensibilities, Eliot attempted a consistent rapprochement between verse drama and the subject and aesthetic of more popular dramatic forms.

As early as 1920, Eliot had contemplated an Elizabethan public that had 'wanted entertainment of a crude sort, but would stand a good deal of poetry'; the contemporary goal was 'to take a form of entertainment, and subject it to the process which would leave it a form of art'.[19] Eliot's first plays identify that form of entertainment in the tradition of the music hall and revue; his later dramas gravitate towards the middle-class drawing room. According to Speaight, Eliot was 'anxious to write the kind of play that could be accepted in the West End'; after the war, 'the plays he liked to go and see in London were plays by Terance [sic] Rattigan'.[20] This movement entailed a gradual distancing from the interactions between music and verse that had characterized both the popular 'forms of entertainment' and the overtly experimental dramas of the 1930s. Eliot saw this developing aesthetic as a consistently evolving attempt to reach a large and miscellaneous audience. In increasingly identifying that audience with a text-based ideal of theatrical expression, however, he also retrenched the poet-dramatist within a considerably less experimental theatrical idiom. That evolution may well have been inspired by an increasingly greater valuation of the drawing room over the music hall. It also, however, points to Eliot's growing and negative recognition of the independent musicality of verse itself when performed on stage.

From page to stage

As strikingly evident in works such as *The Love Song of J. Alfred Prufrock* (1920), 'Portrait of a Lady' (1915) and *The Waste Land* (1922), Eliot's own poetry was often characterized by its experimentation with dramatic voice and situation. By 1924, Eliot was working on *Sweeney Agonistes*. Never completed and arguably never envisioned for actual production, this formative drama in verse nonetheless points to the beginning of Eliot's movement away from the solely metaphorical stage of the page.[21] Of the original scheme for *Sweeney*, Arnold Bennett records that Eliot 'wanted to write a drama of modern life ... in a rhythmic prose "perhaps with certain things in it accentuated by drum beats".'[22] The latter aspiration resonates with Eliot's idea of poetry as beginning with a 'savage beating a drum' and with his frequent metaphorical invocations of rhythm.[23] It also resonates with his critical and creative preoccupation with intermedial readings of poetry itself, particularly in relation to poetic musicality.

Eliot's poetry, essays and correspondence reveal a consistent engagement with ideas and images of music and music-drama, and have gone some way to support the critical commonplace that he was a 'musical' poet, if not dramatist. Notwithstanding his interest in and frequent allusion to musical structure, rhythm, instrumentation and composers, that interest was always characterized by a reading of musical creativity as a distinct art from that of the poet and verse dramatist. Like many poets before and since, Eliot recognized a potential affinity between verse and music. Yeats had both invited and attempted to control that affinity in his musical experimentations with bardic chanting, in his collaborations with Florence Farr and Arnold Dolmetsch.[24] Eliot, however, was much more focused on poetry as a literary, rather than oral, tradition. In *The Use of Poetry and the Use of Criticism* (1933), 'The Music of Poetry' (1942) and 'Poetry and Drama' (1951; reprinted with an additional note, 1957), he consistently resists any confusion of musical analogy with the idea that poetry itself might be rendered (or render itself) musical. When he writes of 'the music of a word' in 'The Music of Poetry', Eliot is emphatic that the term does not refer to sound, which is 'as much an abstraction from the poem as is the sense'.[25] In 'Poetry and Drama', he explicitly challenges Pater's famous assertion that all art 'constantly aspires towards the condition of music': 'We can never emulate music, because to arrive at the condition of music would be the annihilation of poetry'.[26] This reading was to become increasingly more entrenched in Eliot's dramas – an implicit response both to the musical setting of his own verses in *Sweeney* and *The Rock*, and to the distinctly musical effect of verse on stage.

The first section of *Sweeney* was published as 'Fragment of a Prologue' in 1926; the second appeared in 1927 as 'Fragment of an Agon. From Wanna Go Home, Baby?', thus reinforcing the play's Jazz Age affiliations. Collected together, the fragments were published with the subtitle 'Fragments of an Aristophanic Melodrama'. This subtitle implies an attempt to (re-)unite 'melos' and drama within the form of a self-consciously new, contemporary form of verse drama. In its dramatic scenario, use of the vernacular, sexual innuendo and swift rhythmic exchanges, *Sweeney* invokes comparison with the music hall. It also contains scripted songs, all of which reinforce in their lyrics and rhythm their origins in popular forms. The play also contains scripted moments of sound effect without specifying who (or what) utters the words that create that sound. In one moment, for example, 'Telephone' is represented with 'Ting a ling ling / Ting a ling ling'. The second fragment of the play concludes with a full chorus in which the lyrics of the characters slowly evolve into rhythmic utterances, their auditory effect implicit in the use of alliteration, line divisions and capitalization: 'And you wait for a knock and the turning of a lock for you / know the hangman's waiting for you . . . Hoo ha ha . . . Hoo . . . KNOCK KNOCK KNOCK.'[27] In identifying the play's engagement with the linguistic, rhythmic and theatrical idiom of the Jazz Age, many have consequently read the fragments as music-drama itself:

> The drumbeat, the stamping and shuffling of feet, the stylized gesture and speech of the English music hall and probably also of American vaudeville and minstrel show, together with the patterned rhythms of [Kipling's] *Barrack Room Ballads* – these are what we hear, with strains of Gilbert and Sullivan occasionally breaking in . . .[28]

Ultimately, however, such readings point to what Eliot always emphasized as a problematic tendency to associate poetic metre and rhythm – not to mention musical allusion and musical imagery – with a literal musical effect in poetry itself.

As published, *Sweeney* is an autonomous work marked by its poetic *suggestion* of musical effect and idiom. *Sweeney* does not just invite comparison to the rhythm and idiom of popular musical forms, however; it is a drama that contains scripted songs. When those songs are set for the stage, music becomes a distinct dramatic presence. In 1934, the Group Theatre staged the fragments of *Sweeney* as a play. The production was not the first; *Sweeney* had been produced by Hallie Flanagan the year before at the Vassar College Experimental Theatre – Eliot had attended and contributed a concluding passage. (Flanagan had also produced Auden's *Paid on Both Sides* only two years previously.) As staged, the fragments of *Sweeney* hint at the extent to which Eliot's movement towards realized, staged theatre might problematize his invocations of music (and ordered, rhythmic sound) as an analogous but distinct art to that of the poet. Indeed, for their more well-known and influential production, the Group commissioned music from William Alwyn for the songs and billed the performance as a 'revue'.

The production in many ways enacted Eliot's earlier ambition 'to take a form of [popular, crude] entertainment, and subject it to the process which would leave it a form of art'. In its fragmentary structure, colloquial use of jazz and popular song, and seedy suggestiveness, the production ensured a definition of that art that resonated with much European experimental theatre at the time – and perhaps most particularly with that of Brecht. Auden had attended an early performance of *The Threepenny Opera* in Berlin in 1928, and in 1934, he took Priscilla Thouless to task for having omitted Brecht from her study of *Modern Poetic Drama*: 'though their influence in this country has so far been slight, some account of the continental writers like Cocteau, Obey, and Bert Brecht would have been welcome'.[29] A few years later, Isherwood asserted that 'if the poetic drama has a rebirth in England . . . the movement will be largely German in inspiration and origin'.[30] He also contended that his first collaboration with Auden, *The Dog Beneath the Skin*, had been 'much influenced' by *The Threepenny Opera*.[31] That influence, no doubt, would have received significant encouragement from the 'Brechtian' realization of Eliot's play by the Group Theatre. Indeed, Brecht himself attended the third performance of *Sweeney* and was reportedly so impressed that he promised to send the Group 'a play of his, with music by Hindemith'.[32]

Notwithstanding his support of the production, Eliot consistently emphasized a distance between the Group's realization of *Sweeney* as a 'preconceived Expressionist montage'[33] and his original conception and meaning. Indeed, the fact that he persisted in publishing the fragments as poems rather than fragments of a play suggests an attempt to contain the primary achievement of the play to the literary page. The production and critical reception of *Sweeney* nonetheless gave strong encouragement to the Group Theatre's development of an experimental, expressionist drama built around verse, song and non-linear (if not absent) narratives. Ironically, Sidnell attributes the post-war curtailment of this expressionist (and political) influence to Eliot himself: 'Under Eliot's influence, "poetic drama", as it was so infelicitously called, acquired utterly un-Brechtian connotations and an odour of sanctity.'[34] This 'odour of sanctity' implies a conservatism that it is both aesthetic and social. As Eliot developed his own practical involvement within the theatre, his plays became invested primarily in religious themes. They also became increasingly resistant to the very fragmentary, non-linear and intermedial stagings that had positioned his first dramatic work at the forefront of contemporary theatrical experimentation in verse.

Murder in the Cathedral: the anxiety of intermediality

In a 1949 interview, Eliot identified two essential levels in poetic drama – 'the dramatic and the poetic':

> The first and perhaps the only law of the drama is to get the attention of the audience and to keep it. . . . But there was a more poetic side to it, treating it according to the way in which we treated poetry as distinct from the drama. . . . No explanation in the ordinary sense of a poem is adequate. If you can completely explain a poem . . . then it just is not poetry.[35]

For Eliot, theatre was the 'ideal medium for poetry', the form through which the performative realization of unity – between audience-members and poet, between the 'dramatic' and the 'poetic'– could be effected.[36] By 1951, he was reflecting upon his own apparent failure to realize that ultimately 'unattainable' ideal. The goal must nonetheless remain as 'an incentive towards further experiment and exploration':

> For it is ultimately the function of art, in imposing a credible order upon ordinary reality, and thereby eliciting some perception of an order *in* reality, to bring us to a condition of serenity, stillness, and reconciliation . . .[37]

Eliot articulates this ideal of unity and reconciliation in musico-dramatic terms: at its most intense moments, dramatic poetry can 'touch the border of those feelings that only music can express'.[38] This poetry cannot 'emulate music', as in so doing it would annihilate its own language.[39] It must, however, work towards 'a kind of mirage of the perfection of verse drama, which would be a design of human action and of words, such as to present at once the two aspects of dramatic and musical order'.[40]

The articulation of this goal is significant not only for its theorization of an ideal of expressive perfection, but also for its use of musical *analogy*. In an added note to the essay, Eliot expands upon this analogy when he writes of a 'musical pattern' in the balcony scene of *Romeo and Juliet,* of an 'arrangement of voices' in which Juliet 'has the leading part'.[41] The musicality of this passage is signified by a pattern ('as surprising in its kind as that in the early work of Beethoven') that underlies a verse that is simultaneously natural and 'raised to great poetry'.[42] This 'musical pattern' underpins and enables genuine poetic expression and affect. Eliot describes this ideal in similar terms in *The Use of Poetry* when he identifies 'several levels of significance' in a play of Shakespeare:

> For the simplest auditors there is the plot, for the more thoughtful the character and conflict of character, for the more literary the words and phrasing, for the musically sensitive the rhythm, and for auditors of greater sensitiveness and understanding a meaning which reveals itself gradually.[43]

Again, Eliot invokes an ideal of aesthetic unity in drama. Again, 'music' constitutes an essential element (or signifying 'level') within that drama. Again, however, that music is essentially figurative, contained and controlled within the authorship of the literary poet, and thus implicitly heard and experienced within.

This exclusively figurative construction was challenged, however, by Eliot's practical experience in the theatre. That experience began with his collaboration on *The Rock* with Browne, the Reverend Webb-Odell and the composer Martin Shaw. Envisioned (primarily by Browne and Webb-Odell) as a church pageant-as-revue, the work was again a fragmentary drama with music – and one whose very conception was focused on the practicalities of its staging. As Browne observed: 'At that time, producers like Charles Cochran and Andre Charlot were making a success with a type of revue which . . . had a thread of plot. Might it not be possible to weave a thread out of the building of a contemporary church . . .?'[44] Browne's account of the composition and production of the drama is replete with references to Eliot's awakening into an awareness of the complications of the collaborative nature of theatre. In his prefatory note to the publication, Eliot distances himself from creative authorship: the scenario was devised by Browne based on scenes suggested by Webb-Odell, and Eliot wrote 'and rewrote' his contributions 'submissive to the direction' of Browne.[45] Browne similarly notes Eliot's resigned subjugation of his poetic instincts to the 'craft' of writing for the theatre:

> he wanted to write for the stage; well then, he would do what the stage asked of him . . . And he would find out by experience how far the writer has to give in to the dictates of the others who are in the job with him, and will give his work the only true life it can have, by putting it on the stage.[46]

Throughout his account, Browne observes how this acquiescence with the 'demands' of theatrical production inhibited Eliot's instinctive attempts to write verse drama to his own ideal.

Equally inhibiting, it would seem, was both the fragmentary nature of the revue structure and the fact that many of the verses were to be completed by musical setting. Eliot wrote to Shaw, complimenting him on his 'versatility and adaptability' during the process: 'I have myself been irked by having to write bits and snippets, seeing how I should have liked to develop them dramatically if I had had the scope.'[47] As Eliot was to experience in the staging of both *The Rock* and *Murder in the Cathedral*, the music of the composer was not the only musical dramatic presence in the play. As Browne observes, in a speech chorus, 'the poet does not, as the composer does, determine the sound . . . to be heard at each moment. This falls to the director.'[48] In the spoken chorus of *The Rock*, those directors were Elsie

Fogerty and Gwynneth Thurburn who, as Browne details, would make extensive musical use of the colour and tone of the mixed-voice chorus.[49]

In *Murder in the Cathedral*, Eliot experienced an even more fundamental conflict between his attempt to effect a figurative, 'poetic' musical understanding through drama and the very musical effect of his own verse on stage. For Eliot, modern verse drama should (re)awaken the 'most intense and subtle kinds of feeling'[50] that had validated the artistry of earlier poetic traditions, 'a kind of doubleness in the action, as if it took place on two planes at once.'[51] This contemporary awakening into a greater sensibility could only be effected by a reinvention of the modern drama, a movement away from the dominant realist mode into an 'abstraction from actual life' with the materials of that 'actual life'. This aesthetic demands stylistic consistency: 'In a play of Aeschylus, we do not find that certain passages are literature and other passages drama'; 'It is essential that a work of art should be self-consistent, that an artist should consciously or unconsciously draw a circle beyond which he does not trespass.'[52] In *Murder in the Cathedral*, Eliot broke emphatically from the realist drama – but in so doing, he also problematized his own ideal of aesthetic unity. He would later critique the drama's use of a historical setting, its moments of emphatic contrast between verse and prose, and its very use of a chorus. The result, he concluded, was a work that had enforced a distance between idiom, audience and religious argument. It had also imposed a contrast of dramatic aesthetics that, rather than enforcing the focus of the play, only distracted into a contemplation of the drama's diverse modes of expression.

The play is written consistently in verse, with two notable exceptions: a lengthy prose interlude in which the Archbishop preaches his sermon – and a vital moment towards the conclusion of the play, when the Knights turn and address the audience directly. The Knights reason out their motivations in an informal language that aims to enforce a relationship between their actions and the instincts of the contemporary audience:

> You are hard-headed sensible people, as I can see, and not be to be taken in by emotional clap-trap. . . . We have served your interests; we merit your applause; and if there is any guilt whatever in the matter, you must share it with us.[53]

Following these lengthy, direct addresses, the play returns to its earlier 'mode' as the three priests pray individually to God: 'Who shall now guide us, protest us, direct us?'[54] The play concludes with a final prayer by the Chorus, whose verse slowly effects a transition from praise, to thanks, to final litany (a *Te Deum* is sung in Latin in the distance). As Speaight observes, the prose addresses by the Knights 'are calculated to shatter any stained-glass window in which the audience may have been tempted to confine the Canterbury epic', and they can always come 'as something of a shock to a public which might be … expecting nothing further from the play than a rhetorical apotheosis of its hero'.[55] At the same time, however, the play essentially returns to that 'stained-glass window' in its conclusion: the prayer for mercy and intercession is re-absorbed within what the play itself has now suggested to be a more distant, aestheticized mode of religious expression and experience.

At the conclusion of *Murder in the Cathedral*, Eliot aligns the aesthetics of liturgy with the aesthetics of a choral verse that, in its contrast with the preceding prose intervention, had been exposed as a distanced, historicizing and potentially consolatory 'beauty' not entirely unlike that sought by Masefield's Anima Christi. For many, those moments of expressive beauty constituted the primary accomplishment of the play. For others (including Eliot), they inhibited dramatic development and coherence. Reynolds, for example, identifies the choruses as perhaps 'Eliot's finest achievement in dramatic poetry. They have the restraint of Sophoclean tragedy, and the simplicity and depth of their imagery makes them poems of permanent interest'.[56] In thus identifying the choruses independently of their larger dramatic context, however, Reynolds gives some force to Donoghue's assessment that *Murder in the Cathedral* 'evades, rather than solves, the problems of dramatic verse': the play's 'structural flaws' resemble those 'of certain late nineteenth-century verse plays', with their similarly static moments of poetic effusion.[57] Eliot himself later confessed that in *Murder in the Cathedral* he had 'hoped to make up by choral effects what was lacking to the strictly dramatic action'.[58]

Equally problematic, it would seem, was the independent musicality of the chorus in performance. In *The Coming of Christ*, Masefield's choruses invite musical setting through the very simplicity of their language and the regularity of their rhythm. Eliot's choruses already manifest that musicality in the demands they place upon the choral performers, in their scripted variations in tone, rhythm, sound effect and metre:

A rain of blood has blinded my eyes. Where is England? Where is
 Kent? Where is Canterbury?
O far far far far in the past; and I wander in a land of barren boughs[59]

Browne provides an extensive account of the difficulties faced by Fogerty and Thurburn, who trained the choral performers for the production. Identifying an 'orchestral' complexity and ambition in the play's verse, they recognized a literal musical challenge that was simultaneously melodic and rhythmic. As Browne observed of the production:

> . . . each speaker has her distinctive tone of voice. This means also that when they are blended, each, by preserving her own pitch and timbre, can contribute a distinctive sound to a whole which is not an anonymous unison but the harmony of persons thinking together, expressed in a series of chords.[60]

Fogerty essentially took on the role of a music director for these seminal choral passages, recounting that 'each speaker had to be like an instrument, in harmony with the other voices during the ensemble passages, but repeating a recurring phrase in an individual tone – just as flute or horn would do in an orchestra'.[61] For one line alone, 'we tried four voices'.[62]

Fogerty recounts her insistence that 'the musical note must never be the dominant effect, and the group must work until they can *speak* with harmonious inflection – not chant'.[63] These sensibilities accord with Eliot's instinct towards 'unity' in both drama and poetry, where sound never allows for the annihilation of poetry. Fogerty's comments also indicate, however, that those sensibilities had become *translated* into the practical realities and distinct language of the theatrical stage over which Fogerty presided as a self-confessed tyrant. This translation underlines the theatrical viability of Eliot's aesthetic. It also, however, offers an implicit challenge to the autonomous authority of the poet and his verse. In 1945, J.C. Crum remarked to the choral performers: 'Your music haunts us. We float on your supporting sentences, from mood to mood, always imagining – which is perhaps not what we do most easily in this time and country'.[64] Ultimately, this literal musical invitation to 'imagining' exists independently of the 'dramatic' and 'poetic' authorship of the poet himself. In so doing, it offers an implicit challenge to the self-consistency of his art, a musical distraction that risks transporting his audience 'into an artificial world'.

Murder in the Cathedral is the last of Eliot's plays to have required the musical direction of a choral trainer. His next drama, *The Family Reunion* (1939), employed a considerably reduced Chorus: aunts and uncles occasionally break out of their drawing-room setting to comment on a drama of spiritual crisis and guilt within the form of a modern detective story. According to Browne, the lines of the chorus were occasionally spoken individually in productions, and his aim (with Eliot) was to suggest their natural incorporation within their idiomatic setting, rather than to advertise their origins in Greek traditions.[65] The Chorus, prose interventions and temptation scene in *Murder in the Cathedral* in many respects signalled the play's attempts to unite diverse levels of experience (historical, social, spiritual) through its stylistic variety. *The Family Reunion*, however – notwithstanding its drawing-room chorus and the staged appearance of the Eumenides – points to Eliot's increasing instinct towards a more consistent verse form, a 'rhythm close to contemporary speech', and towards a more 'unifying' dramatic structure and form. It also points to his deliberate reduction of the intermedial dynamic between verse and staged musical effect in the dramas. As Browne notes, music in the production, 'concrete or otherwise, is, I am sure, misleading'.[66]

The Family Reunion was not a success with critics or audiences, who generally objected to the play's philosophizing, apparent lack of narrative and Greek interventions. In *Poetry and Drama*, Eliot condemns the play for continuing to rely on techniques that he identifies with opera: the 'device of a lyrical duet' between two characters is excessively unnatural, ensuring passages that 'are too much like operatic arias. The member of the audience, if he enjoys this sort of thing, is putting up with a suspension of the action in order to enjoy a poetic fantasia ...'.[67] Eliot's reflections offer a fascinating contrast to the contentions of Bottomley, whose very appreciation of verse drama was rooted in the 'operatic' moments that allowed for such 'enjoyment'. Contemplating the subsequent weaknesses of his next play, *The Cocktail Party* (1949), Eliot can only conclude that he must continue to 'discipline[e] his poetry' and put it 'on a very thin diet in order to adapt it to the needs of the stage'.[68] This conviction in many ways supports Sidnell's assessment of Eliot's 'curtailment of the sensuousness of the theatre'. It also reveals an aesthetic that insists on an essentially anti-musical dramatic poetry in order to unify 'the two aspects of dramatic and musical order' central to any 'condition of serenity, stillness, and reconciliation'.

Auden: from Brecht to Britten

In a 1938 Paris lecture on 'The Future of English Poetic Drama', Auden, like Eliot, identified poetry as 'a medium which expresses the collective and universal feeling'.[69] Despite that similarity, the two poets approached the dramatic realization of that collective feeling in very different terms. In his Thouless review, Auden complains that 'those who would write poetic drama, refuse to start from the place where they can start, from the dramatic forms actually in use':

> These are the variety-show, the pantomime, the musical comedy and revue . . . the thriller, the drama of ideas, the comedy of manners, and, standing somewhat eccentrically to these, the ballet. . . . Poetic drama should start with the stock musical comedy characters . . . and make them, as only poetry can, memorable.[70]

Rather than coercing the audience into a recognition of poetic drama by adopting popular forms, the poet should embrace those forms as a manifestation of shared feeling and expression. Auden concludes with what seems to be a deliberate critique of both Yeats and, as Mendelson observes, Eliot's earlier appraisal of what the public might 'stand':

> If the would-be poetic dramatist demands extremely high-brow music and unfamiliar traditions of dancing, he will, of course, fail; but if he is willing to be humble and sympathetic, to accept what he finds to his hand and develop its latent possibilities, he may be agreeably surprised to find that after all the public will stand, nay even enjoy, a good deal of poetry.[71]

For Auden, the material for poetic drama already exists in the public taste; it is up to the dramatist to exploit that potential and to remove any semblance of cultural authoritarianism from the relationship between audience and poet. It is also up to the dramatist not to draw attention either to himself or to his individual characters through poetry: 'All characters who speak verse are as flat as playing-cards. So are they also in the popular dramatic forms today.'[72] In this assessment, only poetry in service to dramatic form and popular genre can approximate 'collective feeling'.

In keeping with Eliot's recognition of exclusive causes, Auden's appeal to that collective feeling tended to be political rather than spiritual or emotional. As Mendelson observes, he had essentially chosen poetic drama 'as his didactic vehicle'.[73] By 1938, however, Auden was sufficiently uncomfortable with that didactic role as to identify an inherent danger to the use of poetry (if not verse) in drama: 'poetry unalloyed tends, if one is not very careful, to introduce a rather holy note . . . faith is never unalloyed with doubts, and requires prose to act as an ironic antidote.'[74] Auden's later verse plays, written in collaboration with Isherwood, had indeed employed prose (usually written by Isherwood), and often as 'an ironic antidote'. As Mendelson observes, however, the achievement of a balance – stylistic, thematic, and argumentative – between the two often proved difficult: the dramatists 'always concluded by emphasizing one side or the other, either ascending on hymns of poetic vision, or collapsing in the flat necessity of prose. Then, recognizing the imbalance, they would rewrite the endings to reverse the emphasis, and leave the plays just as imbalanced as before.'[75]

That Auden moved away from verse drama entirely soon after his 1938 lecture suggests a dissatisfaction both with that imbalance and with the expectation of a didactic 'common cause' in drama itself. Like many of his contemporaries (including Eliot), Auden identified verse drama as precluding the writing of poetry 'with a capital P': the poet must pretend not to '[make] a scene'.[76] The verse in many of Auden's dramas tends towards the recognizably theatrical or overtly colloquial rather than the conventional 'spoken language' poetically invoked by the later dramas of Eliot and Duncan. It also, however, tends towards a deliberate juxtaposition of styles that, in keeping with Auden's emphasis on popular forms and flat characters, calls attention to the manipulation of dramatic genre rather than the unique voice of the dramatist. By the end of the 1930s, Auden had clearly tired of thus subjugating individual poetic expressivity to the apparent aesthetic expectations of the 'common cause'.

Dance of Death: collaboration and collectivity

Auden's first published play had been *Paid on Both Sides: A Charade*.[77] In its dramatization of a feud between North Country families, in its emphasis on rural tradition and the cyclic nature of life, the drama suggests a tenuous link to the rural tragedies of Masefield and Abercrombie and – with its invocation of Norse sagas – the more elemental, mythic emphasis developed by Bottomley. That emphasis is similarly suggested in Auden's expanded version for publication, which incorporates characters from the traditional mummers play. As Sidnell observes, however, rather than reinforcing these traditions, mythical subjects and rural settings as the ritualistic foundation for a contemporary communal drama, Auden subjected them to 'a modernizing process of irony, harsh juxtaposition, thematic overlaying and verbal discordance'.[78] Central to this ironizing process, it would seem, was a much more emphatic alignment of both poetry and narrative with the more totalizing, collaborative theatre promoted (variously) on the Continent by Cocteau, Obey and Brecht. As Auden concluded in a 1929 journal entry: 'A play ... is poetry of action. The dialogue should be correspondingly a simplification.'[79] Throughout the 1930s, that conclusion would be taken up enthusiastically by the Group Theatre, aided and abetted by its leading – and increasingly disillusioned – poet-dramatist.

Auden's first piece for the Group was *The Dance of Death*. The work originated from a request from Doone for a ballet on the theme of Orpheus – and (perhaps in keeping with Auden's distaste for ballet) evolved into a much more intermedial drama in verse, with the figure of the dancer at its centre. Rather than dramatizing the death of Orpheus, the play presents, through a series of choral scenes in dance, song and verse, a fundamental critique of the hypocrisy behind middle-class appropriations of socialist ideology. As proclaimed unambiguously at the beginning of the play:

Announcer   We present to you this evening a picture of the decline of a class.
Chorus (*behind curtain*)   Middle class.
Announcer   Of how its members dream of a new life.
...
But secretly desire the old, for there is death inside them. We show you that death as a dancer.[80]

The result is a work that does not so much embrace a common cause as deconstruct its assertion amongst many of Auden's own peers. It does so, moreover, by adopting many of the signifiers of agitprop drama and workers' theatre. As Sidnell observes, 'with its political message couched in blatantly didactic terms, its use of chorus in a collective role, strict choreography on a bare stage, doggerel verse and simple words, caricature and revue structure, *The Dance of Death* was the first attempt to forge a link between "bourgeois" and workers' theatre in England'.[81] In keeping with Auden's declared instinct to qualify and temper any 'holy note' in theatre, however, the play forges that link by satirizing its middle-class subjects, performers and audience alike. In so doing, it inevitably redefines the social, political and artistic role of the very theatrical conventions it invokes. Rather than advocating vital social change, rather than dramatizing popular solidarity, the play ultimately focuses its satire on contemporary attempts at political theatre itself. That theme is forcefully emphasized at the end of the play, when Death offers congratulations to the performers: 'as soon as [the performance] is done / May engagements be offered them by everyone'.[82]

Despite this cynicism towards its own medium, the play also articulates that theme within a self-consciously theatrical idiom. The play defies the reader to an extent that differs considerably from the contemporaneous verse drama by Yeats or Eliot. Written specifically for the Group's small and intimate theatre space, the play stages characters amongst the audience, behind curtains and on a bare stage 'with a simple backcloth, in front of which are the steps on which the ANNOUNCER sits, like the umpire at a tennis tournament'.[83] In keeping with Group productions, it also makes considerable use of its dancers, its singers and its musicians, all of whom constitute signifying presences within the drama itself: 'Downstage is a small jazz orchestra. In front of the conductor a microphone. When BOX and COX are to speak the conductor sits down and they take his place'.[84] This relatively experimental theatricality is complemented by a fragmented, barely perceptible narrative within a work that constantly disrupts any sense of a consistent aesthetic mode, both in its action and within the verse itself.

In the initial scene, the members of the Chorus enter, shedding their dressing gowns to reveal two-piece bathing suits. In what Auden's synopsis describes as a presentation of the 'present day cult of athleticism', they invite (in song) 'Gents from Norway / Ladies from Sweden' to 'join in our dance', to 'sing in harmony / Come out into the sun':

> Here on the beach
> You're out of reach
> Of sad news, bad news
> You can refuse
> The invitation
> To self-examination
> Come out into the sun.[85]

This ironized invitation from the middle class to refuse self-critique through group performance constitutes an essential theme of the play. The Chorus sing of building the future 'With no more sorrow': they will do this by continuing to stay in the sun, out of reach of bad news.[86] This theme is also reinforced in the aesthetic of the play, which in its allusions to contemporary dance, the nineteenth-century comedy of Box and Cox, jazz, 'old-time Waltz', folk dance, Mendelssohn's 'Wedding March', and sundry other forms of popular performance and theatrical tradition, aligns the performance language of the play itself with the self-delusional dance, song and aesthetic beauty of the opening chorus.

Soon thereafter, the Chorus find themselves without clothes. They are offered uniforms from a 1916 musical revue. A group in the 'Audience' sings of 'red front ... red united fighting front', and another of united workers: 'Down with the bosses' class, / Up with the workers' class.'[87] The Chorus, dressed in costume uniforms, then adopt the sentiment, singing of overthrowing the capitalist state. Ultimately, however, the play suggests that they have been transformed less by ideology than by the theatrical trappings of costume and choral song. When both groups are reminded by the Announcer that such ideological challenges to capitalism are fundamentally un-English, they consequently espouse violence and intolerance, recognizing a duty 'to keep the race pure, and not let these dirty foreigners come in and take our jobs.'[88] The middle class has thus willed itself into a collective, unthinking performance of nationalism that is blindly adherent to dominant disseminated narratives:

We are all of one blood, we are thoroughbred,
We'll not lose our courage, we'd sooner be dead.

. . .

The ship of England crosses the ocean
Her sails are spread, she is beautiful in motion.
We love her and obey her captain's orders
We know our mind, no enemy shall board us.[89]

Auden thus implicitly aligns the fascist rhetoric of Hitler's Germany with an equally engrained and unthinking intolerance within England itself. Soon thereafter, the staged Theatre manager (a German Jew) is assaulted and beaten by the English Chorus: 'Take your place, take your place, / To save the Anglo-Saxon race.'[90]

In the final scene, after having become disillusioned with the enactment of various modern causes (athletic beauty, communism, patriotism, fascism, escape from machine civilization, feminism), the Chorus asks for a pilot to the very heart of reality. As Auden himself explains in his synopsis: 'Death presents himself. But he collapses through the inanition of a class.'[91] To the popular tune of 'Casey Jones', the Announcer proclaims the last will and testament of Death, who (performed by Doone) has enacted his final death-throes. Death has bequeathed 'all England's estates, raw materials, industry and money. ... To work their will among the working class.'[92] That bequest only reinforces a status quo, however: the middle class Chorus sings repeatedly of 'Alma Mater on the door / Like a secret sign inviting / All the rich to meet the poor'.[93] The play ends by interrupting this 'Betjemanic paean to the status quo'[94] with the sound of offstage noises. Karl Marx enters with two young communists to proclaim (in prose) before the final 'Exeunt to a Dead March': 'The instruments of production have been too much for him. He is liquidated'.[95] As Mendelson contends, 'Any Marxist who found this satisfying was deaf to irony'.[96] Rather than presenting Marx as the imminent saviour of either the proletariat or the stagnant middle class, the play ironizes the 'common cause' of communism as a deus ex machina, its power already critiqued within a drama bent upon exposing the illusory appeal of group theatre as a whole – on stage and in society. Auden's play does not just offer a Brechtian critique of social and moral complacency; it enacts an implicit critique of the very transformative, political power of the collaborative drama of the Group Theatre itself.

Wistful Poetics: *The Ascent of F6*

Unsurprisingly, this definition of a 'new' poetic drama proved difficult to sustain, and Auden's dramas moved increasingly towards more linear and vaguely realist plot-lines. Where *The Dance of Death* was very much a Group Theatre production, its authorship – the scripted, thematic relationship between dance, song and theatre-space – was essentially in the hands of Auden. By the time of *The Ascent of F6* (1936), however, Auden was working much less closely with Doone's Group and much more closely with Isherwood alone in determining the essential structure and themes of his work. Much can be said – and has been said – of the politics of the Auden-Isherwood plays, not least in relation to the experience of both playwrights outside of England in the years immediately preceding the outbreak of war. Plays such as *The Dog Beneath the Skin* (1935), *F6* and *On the Frontier* can also be examined in the context of Auden's gradual withdrawal from the ethos of the Group itself into an ideal of art that was to become much more focused on verse as poetry. Where *The Dance of Death* demanded a staged interaction between various theatrical arts, *F6*, with its clearly delineated moments of poetry, prose and song, ultimately points to a movement, on Auden's part, from the 'poetry of the theatre' to 'poetry in the theatre'.

The Ascent of F6 takes as its subject the ascent of a mountain in Sudoland, a British colony 'about as big as Ireland' whose natives believe that whoever reaches the summit will rule the land for a thousand years.[97] Michael Ransom is an adventurer and climber. He has been removed from the concerns of petty politics, patriotism and state-craft by the careful nurturing of his mother; his brother James, in contrast, is Colonial Secretary to Sudoland and hopes to coerce Michael into climbing the mountain to secure the allegiance of the natives: 'the future of England, of the Empire, may be at stake.'[98] Michael rejects the approach: although he knows the mountain to be his 'fate', he will not ascend for the wrong reasons.[99] He is finally persuaded by his mother, however, who has been summoned by James and invokes her withheld love as a symbolic aim for the ascent. In a lengthy verse speech, Mrs Ransom explains that her intention had always been to make Michael 'unlike [his] father and [his] brother', and thus to give him 'the power to stand alone'.[100] Ironically, of course, she invokes this freedom in order to manipulate Michael into fulfilling his brother's political ambitions.

The play's politics are at their most obvious in their critique of British colonial power. In its dramatization of the influence of Michael's mother over her son, it also emphasizes (without fully developing) its Freudian themes; a similar fragmentary presentation characterizes the homoerotic love triangle between Michael and his fellow adventurers, companions from public school. Equally central is the persistent choral voice of Mr and Mrs A, representatives of a mundane suburban everyman that attempts to live vicariously through the heroes constructed by national poets, media and state. Unsurprisingly, the play ends with the death of Ransom, whose final ascent is rash and ultimately pointless, a capitulation to the lure of fame (another form of power) and mother fixation. In one of many endings, Michael is eulogized by a final Chorus and by Mrs Ransom who, Agave-like, mourns and idealizes her son in hopelessly romanticized terms that serve to reinforce the cynicism of the play's authors:

And in the castle tower above,
The princess' cheek burns red for your love,
You shall be king and queen of the land,
Happy for ever, hand in hand. [101]

As E.M. Forster remarked in a review in *The Listener*, 'Mother-love, usually sacrosanct, becomes a very nasty customer.'[102]

The play went through many endings that variously but always incompletely reinforced its many themes. Its cynicism always remained a constant, however, directed variously at familial love, imperial adventure and the social role of the artist-as-hero. As Mendelson observes, Auden tended to be uncharacteristically silent in offering explanations of the play: 'he left the explanations to Isherwood, who thought the play was all about T. E. Lawrence and contemporary dictators'.[103] Later, Isherwood acknowledged 'definite obscurantist elements' in the play 'which seemed designed simply to confuse critics, professors, members of the audience'.[104] Ultimately, the play is best read as a manifestation of Auden's increasing frustration with the very didactic expectations of the drama he had helped to promote – and particularly with its curtailing of the individual poetic voice of the dramatist himself.

Auden dramatizes this theme within a work that also critiques the contemporary danger of indulging the individual poetic voice as social and moral authority. The play begins with Michael Ransom, seated on 'the Summit of the Pillar Rock', reading aloud from Dante: 'Consider your origin: ye were not formed to live like brutes, but to follow virtue and knowledge.'[105] Ransom then wonders at the right of Dante – 'to whom the Universe was peopled only by his aristocratic Italian acquaintances and a few classical literary characters' – to invoke Virtue and Knowledge.[106] For both Ransom and Auden, that assumption of moral authority from a position of elitist withdrawal wields a dangerous power:

with a stroke of the pen to make a neighbour's vineyard a lake of fire and to create in his private desert the austere music of the angels or the happy extravagance of a fair. Friends whom the world honours shall lament their eternal losses in the profoundest of crevasses, while he on the green mountains converses gently with his unapproachable love.[107]

Mendelson identifies in the speech (and the play) Auden's discomfort with his own increasingly Lawrence-like celebrity as a political poet and dramatist. Even more significant, however, is the play's clear engagement with Eliot. As Sidnell observes, in his 1929 'Dante' essay, Eliot had quoted the passage from the *Inferno* with which Ransom's speech begins.[108] He had also, of course, begun to occupy a similarly exalted cultural position. That that position could assume a certain moralizing power was no more evident than in the recent success of *Murder in the Cathedral*, with its presentation of contemporary, collective spiritual crisis through the mediating poetic and spiritual 'authority' of one capable of creating 'in his private desert the austere music of the angels'.

At the same time as the play condemns conventional constructions of the artist as hero or as spiritual, didactic authority, it attempts 'to face up to the [contemporary, social] vision of *The Waste Land*, from which Eliot, in *Murder in the Cathedral*, had averted his eyes'.[109] Where Eliot's 'Everyman' consists of a Chorus of historicized women in Canterbury, Auden's choral voices are rooted within a present defined by contemporary British imperialism, class hierarchy and empty suburban dreams.[110] The play addresses this political, social and cultural reality, however, within an aesthetic that in many respects comes closer to that of Eliot by re-appropriating the art and authorship of the poet-dramatist from that of the theatrical collective. The earlier dramas are often characterized by doggerel verse or by a deliberate pastiche of popular song, ballad or music hall. In their overtly poetic evocation of mundane urban reality, however, the lines of Mr and Mrs A are not entirely dissimilar from the language of *The Waste Land*. In their dramatic escalation of emotional tension and movement, they can also resemble the choruses of *Murder in the Cathedral*, while the emphasis on the poetry beneath quotidian urban reality resonates clearly with the imagery and themes of *Prufrock*:

> Evening. A slick and unctuous Time
> Has sold us yet another shop-soiled day,
> Patently rusty, not even in a gaudy box.
> . . .
> I have spoken with acquaintances in the Stores;
> Under our treble gossip heard the menacing throb of our hearts
> . . .
> Throbbing raggedly, fitfully, scatteredly, madly.
> We are lost. We are lost.[111]

Later in the play, the themes, rhythm and imagery of the Chorus again resonate with the choral focus in *Murder in the Cathedral* on nature, time and the traumatizing disruption of order by heroic acts:

> Let the eye of the traveller consider this country and weep,
> For toads croak in the cisterns; the aqueducts choke with leaves
> . . .
> The weasel inhabits the courts and the sacred places;
> Despair in our faces[112]

While these passages might suggest pastiche or parody, they also reveal Auden's increasingly more literary openness towards what might constitute primary material for poetic development – what the poet-dramatist 'finds to his hand and [might] develop [from] its latent possibilities'.

The play reveals – and indulges – a creative, poetic restlessness on the part of the poet-dramatist. The dialogue of Ransom and Mrs Ransom is characterized by irregular blank verse, and Ransom is given to soliloquies that, as Sidnell observes, come remarkably close to resembling those of Stephen Phillips.[113] In one passage, for example, Ransom expostulates against the 'senseless hurricanes' that waste themselves against nature instead of 'find[ing] some employment proper' by pressing 'murdering thumbs' 'on the neck of Man'.[114] The idiom is consistent to character type and theme. The verses of Mr and Mrs A are the most Eliotesque in their poetic images of suburban drudgery and in their occasional, emotive attempts to relieve natural, cyclic despair. In keeping with his position as a flawed romantic, Ransom's speeches evoke an earlier age; his blank-verse exchanges are more mundane, alleviated primarily by the content of the dialogue. *The Dance of Death* elided contemporary theatrical performance with contemporary social performance. The poetic variety of *The Ascent of F6*, however, acts primarily to theatricalize the poet's own wistful indulgence of a poetic instinct towards creative experimentation hitherto rendered 'drab' in the service of a 'common cause'. In so doing, it implicitly redefines that cause to focus much more overtly on art itself, independent of its didactic or political role.

The final Auden-Isherwood play, *On the Frontier* (1938), is by all accounts a relatively minor work, its ideas clearly stated and its verse stylistically simple, written almost exclusively for setting as a variety of popular forms of song. With the exception of the songs, most of the play is written in prose, suggesting a certain exhaustion with the very idea of drama in verse. Given the rapidity with which Auden and Isherwood produced their dramas, that exhaustion had no doubt been precipitated by the more concerted exploration of the role of verse itself within *F6*. *On the Frontier* would not so much end Auden's dramatic career, however, as encourage its revitalization within a different theatrical idiom.

Subtitled *A Melodrama in Two Acts*, the play contains numerous songs and interludes scored by Britten, and verses deliberately written for musical enhancement. In the assessment of Keynes, who oversaw production of the play at the Cambridge Arts Theatre, the play text was admirably less clever than the previous Auden-Isherwood dramas, successfully 'crude and obvious throughout'.[115] In the final realization, however, that obviousness was subjected 'to the process which would leave it a form of art' through the expressivity, dramatic variety, and distinct modernity of the composer.

Towards the end of his life, Auden gave a grudging interview to William B. Wahl. Asked about 'the future of poetic drama in the world of today, especially in England', Auden replied that 'he had some time ago perceived little future for it, which was why had changed to writing libretti'.[116] For Auden, it would seem, the 'rather holy note' of dramatic poetry could best be 'alloyed' not through its juxtaposition with prose, not through musical setting, but through its liberation into operatic form and tradition. As Mendelson observes, where Yeats withdrew 'to the symbolic intensities of the drawing-room, Eliot took the opposite road to Broadway and the West End, bringing drama with him but leaving behind much of the poetry'.[117] Although Auden did not write any more verse dramas after On the Frontier,[118] he did not abandon drama; he left the country and he moved into a different collaborative medium.

A new poetry: Auden and opera

In 1941, Auden and Britten collaborated on the operetta Paul Bunyan: in its episodic structure, in its satirical political focus, the work suggests the legacy of the Group Theatre experience. Britten himself had been closely involved with the Group, and as intriguingly reinforced by his later dramatizations of Noh drama and mystery plays, his own operatic aesthetic clearly evolved out of and in relation to that larger, diffuse movement of verse drama in England.[119] Auden's career as an opera librettist, however, reveals an enthusiastic transformation of his initial involvement within an intermedial, collaborative and political verse theatre into what he identified as a very different dramatic tradition. Auden's projects embraced opera as an art-form whose origins could be traced to the Florentine Camerata, Purcell, Verdi and Wagner rather than the indigenous poetic or political voices of contemporary Britain. For Auden, that very independence seems to have enabled the liberation of poetry (and the poet) from the debates about the political, spiritual and aesthetic role of poetry in drama to which he had so actively, creatively contributed in earlier years.

It is perhaps significant that Auden's most frequent operatic collaborators thereafter were Stravinsky and Hans Werner Henze, composers for whom the debates about the role of verse in drama and contemporary political theatre in England meant very little. The legacy of those debates lingers in some of Auden's most well-known libretti, all written with Chester Kallman. The episodic, social satire of *The Rake's Progress* (1947–8), undoubtedly the most successful of the operas, in many ways resonates with the Brechtian enthusiasms of the Group Theatre. As translated into the distinct musical idiom of Stravinsky, as staged through the conventions of the opera-house, however, those enthusiasms become appropriated into a tradition for whom episodic narrative, song and stylistic variety carry very different artistic and political connotations. In *The Bassarids* (1963), a loose rewriting of *The Bacchae* with Henze, Auden and Kallman return to much of the psycho-sexual material invoked in *F6*, particularly in their dramatization of the relationship between Pentheus and his mother. They also align that dramatization with the play's larger theme of unhealthy repression. In the opera, that theme is enforced in the libretto's emphasis on sexual identity and throughout the work's larger exploration of musical and poetic expression itself.

Auden did not merely compose verse dramas for musical setting; his numerous writings about opera, his translations of Mozart and his programme notes to specific libretti reveal a clear engagement with (and firm, often controlling opinions about) a diversity of musical idioms, operatic conventions and debates about drama as opera.[120] Consistent throughout, in fact, is a confidence in his own ability to demand particular musical forms and styles. Equally consistent – and contradicting his proclaimed subservience to the musical authority of the composer – is his persistence in writing a verse whose conceits, arguments and ideas could often render text-setting a distinct challenge. In one characteristic passage from *The Bassarids*, Agave recounts:

> Savoury odors in the noon silence
> Rose from the goat-herd's galloping pot;
> A white cloud drifted; a cliff echoed
> To the axe-chant of a charcoal burner:
> Lost-happy were earth and I.[121]

This persistence with complex poetic conceit might suggest Auden's ignorance of musical setting. It is more likely, however, to point to his enthusiastic embrace of the occasional inaudibility of the poet's words within a medium dominated by music.

In *Elegy for Young Lovers* (1959–60), Auden and Kallman present a thinly veiled critique of Yeats as an artist-genius poet-celebrity, thus echoing the earlier preoccupations of *F6*. They do so, however, within a work whose medium and whose librettists are much more distanced from the conventional medium of the poet himself. In *Elegy*, Auden and Kallman come close to dramatizing the liberation of the poet's voice within what is identified as a larger, more expressive, and more selfless collaborative form. In their notes on the genesis of the libretto, Auden and Kallman underline the representation of 'great poetry' in the opera through its *suggestion* and *evocation* in musical setting:

> Our hero, Gregor Mittenhofer, is a great poet. . . . Unless, at the end, the audience are convinced that the poem is a very good one, the whole dramatic and moral point of the opera is lost. We believe that this conviction can be secured by having the poem represented in another artistic medium – as a man, Mittenhofer sings words; as a poet he is dumb, and his poem is represented by orchestral sound and pure vocalisation.[122]

For Auden, it would seem, the primary appeal of operatic collaboration was its release of the dramatic poet into a medium where truly 'great poetry' is defined by 'orchestral sound and pure vocalisation'. Within that medium, the literary poet becomes free to indulge his affection for opera as the 'last refuge of the High style' – the 'only art to which a poet with a nostalgia for those times past when poets could write in the grand manner all by themselves can still contribute'.[123] Ultimately, that indulgence is enabled by the poet's concession of the primary, authoring voice in the staged drama to that of the composer.

In his 1968 memoir, Duncan recounts an incident in which Britten showed him a prospective oratorio libretto that had been sent to him by Auden. Familiar with the success of Auden's libretti, Duncan was surprised at Britten's perpetual unwillingness to collaborate with the poet. Looking at the libretto, however, he could only conclude that 'Auden must have been suffering from some temporary aberration. It was as long as the *Ring* and almost as incomprehensible. Auden must have known that it was unsuitable.'[124] Such indulgences, however, were relatively characteristic of the Auden-Kallman libretti, and were generally excised by their musical collaborators with the willing agreement of the librettists.[125] When they were not, they were nonetheless often effaced by the music setting itself. As Kallman notes of the setting of *Elegy*, 'Henze's musical setting and distribution of crucial stresses in several of our scenes *were* a surprise for us.'[126]

Such practices point to the willed subservience of the poet to the subsuming presence of music. As manifest in the publication of the libretti, however, they also point to a certain exploitation of that theatrical process as a means to justify the writing of a literary-dramatic poetry more in keeping with the poet's 'nostalgic' yearning. The published editions of the Auden-Kallman libretti often restored the cuts made by composers and often with detailed, explanatory program-notes. When Henze insisted on cuts to the *Bassarids*, for example, Auden wrote, 'C[hester] and I are vain enough to believe that our text is worth reading an-und-für-sich'; he asked that the original text be printed with an indication of 'which bits have not been set.'[127] Ironically, the effect of such practices is to suggest in the libretti of one of the most collaborative, intermedial and experimentally theatrical verse dramatists of the 1930s a new manifestation of the closet drama in verse.

CHAPTER 6
RENAISSANCE AND FALSE DAWN: MAINSTREAM SUCCESS ON THE POSTWAR STAGE

By the end of the war, critics, commentators and politicians alike were adamant in identifying both a nation and a contemporary culture in need of revivification and renewal. To some extent, the cultural focus of that rhetoric had been apparent in the wartime formation of CEMA. In its democratizing emphasis on communal creativity and a regional participation in the arts, the Council's focus resonated strongly with the efforts of many proponents of amateur and community theatre. In 1945, however, the transformation of CEMA into the Arts Council saw a pronounced centralization of that focus and an emphasis on cultural excellence as national renewal. The arts consequently became aligned much more emphatically with the formulation and eventual manifestation of a modern national identity – an association pronouncedly on display at the simultaneously performative, optimistic and celebratory Festival of Britain, in 1951. In the years leading up to the coronation of Queen Elizabeth II, that rhetoric became translated into one that anticipated a 'new Elizabethan age' to be manifest in the cultural expressions of new Shakespeares, Marlowes and Sidneys. At the time, some of the most well-known contemporary dramatists assumed to inherit that role were verse dramatists: Eliot and Fry figured prominently in cartoon renderings of 'new' Elizabethan courtiers and in more serious discussions of modern theatre by commentators such as A.L. Rowse and Philip Gibbs. While this cultural position was to prove fleeting, it nonetheless attests to the relative centrality of verse drama within mainstream discussions of a contemporary dramatic tradition at the time.

Much of that reception can be attributed at least in part to the success of a programme of verse dramas at London's intimate Mercury Theatre. These plays built upon a pre-war culture marked by its active and varied exploration of theatrical aesthetic, theological argument, political propaganda and dramatic verse-form. The success of *Murder in the Cathedral* had also ensured that Christian subjects and themes could go some way to associate that drama less with doctrinal rigidity than with an active engagement with modern sensibilities and post-war realities. As manifest in the plays of Norman Nicholson and Anne Ridler, for example, they allowed for the dramatic exploration of more broadly defined contemporary preoccupations. Many of Duncan's explorations continued to advocate for a more intermedial contemporary stage. As particularly evident in the popularity of Eliot and Fry, these immediate postwar years also witnessed a brief, if ultimately very fleeting, moment of mainstream and international success for verse drama as a whole.

Mercury rising: *The Old Man of the Mountains* and *The Shadow Factory*

In contrast with the Canterbury plays, the post-war dramas written for Browne's residency at the Mercury Theatre were not religious commissions. Nonetheless, the first year of that season (1945–6) saw a number of plays that embraced Christian subjects and themes from a variety of perspectives. Amongst those plays were Duncan's *This Way to the Tomb*, Fry's *A Phoenix Too Frequent* (a light exploration of life, death and the afterlife, framed as a loose adaptation of Petronius' story of the matron of Ephesus), Nicholson's *The Old Man of the Mountains* and Ridler's *The Shadow Factory*. The relative success of these plays attests to the resilience, if not popularity, of religious themes in the immediate post-war era.[1] It also points to the effective translation of those themes into a secular setting whose dramatists were equally bent upon establishing verse drama itself as a mainstage, contemporary tradition.

Nicholson's *The Old Man of the Mountains* takes as its narrative framework the biblical account of Elijah. It sets that story in contemporary Cumbria and evokes its setting in a verse that replicates regional cadence and colloquialisms. In Nicholson's play, Elijah is not an aloof prophet, but a statesman farmer whose language and actions are rooted within a contemporary local reality. Asking for a drink of water, for example, he knocks at a neighbour's door, professing to feel 'as dry as a haddock' and 'fair hungered'.[2] The play begins with The Raven and The Beck, who introduce themselves as if they were characters in a morality drama. Rather than embodying distinct human qualities, however, they embody nature itself – and specifically the nature of the Lake District:

I gaze down on the larks, I gaze on the tops of the larches,
I gaze into the long cleft of the dale, and see
The dalefolk crawl like ticks in an old sheep's wool.[3]

They also embody the voice of a primal entity, God-in-nature:

It is not often that you hear my voice, for I am the voice
Of the One who is older than I even as I am older
Than the voices you hear.[4]

The language of the characters is consistently informed by this natural setting, which is both mystical and commonplace. As the Raven notes towards the end of the play, 'In the preoccupation of day by day / They shall find grace and a glint of glory.'[5] That assertion is then reinforced by Ruth's exclamation that the rivers are now running, after a long period of drought: 'Hark at the beck again – like the bairns running out of school.'[6] Rather than reflecting upon this grace and glory, Rebecca replies, 'It's a real treat to have some pure water for your tea.'[7]

In keeping with this dramatization of the divine amongst the commonplace and everyday, the verse of the play avoids ritualistic presentation and is flexible and idiomatic, overtly dramatic in its pace and variety.[8] The action of the beck is represented in the rhythm and alliteration of its verse, 'Bouncing over cobbles, hobbling over ferns; / Bubbling, babbling, chittering and chattering.'[9] This verse and this nature are never quaint or picturesque: recognizing the too-frequent containment of nature within poetic convention itself, the Raven observes to the audience, 'When you hear the rain on the window you say it sounds / Like "Pitter patter or what does it matter".'[10] Both the Raven and the play contest such representations and receptions, reasserting the primal and divine power within nature. In his address to the audience from his 'tabernacle towers of rock',[11] the Raven also gives voice to the poetic aesthetic of the dramatist intent on countering more conventional, superficial (and Southern) representations of the natural sublime:

But when you hear my voice there is no need to read it in words;
You know what it means without interpretation.
Down in that hidden gully of your soul,
Where words never trickle and eyes never probe[12]

As this initial declaration suggests, the play is emphatic in aligning nature with God, and nature with the natural instinct of humanity itself. That emphasis is reinforced both in the thematic emphasis of the play and in the imagery, sound and developed metaphors of its verse.

Speaight likens the effect of this rural setting and idiom to that of Synge: in its 'power to adapt a popular speech to a poetic usage', the play approximates 'a genuine folk-drama'.[13] Unlike the dramas of Synge or the more historical folk-dramas of Masefield and Abercrombie, however, Nicholson's play is set emphatically within the middle of the twentieth century. The play's dramatization of the tension between rural characters builds upon traditional conflicts in folk-drama. The play also, however, roots those tensions within a more modern rural context – not least in relation to the environmental concerns brought about by industrialisation and irresponsible farming. This treatment is tantamount to blasphemy: the Raven rebukes the audience for having torn the crops 'like hair from the living skin' – 'The hills which were your altars have become your middens; / The becks which were your temples have become your sewers.'[14] In its dramatization of Elijah as a regional prophet bent upon the restoration of man to the responsible treatment of nature (and thus God), Nicholson's play is considerably less dated than its biblical framework might initially suggest. In its translation of a contemporary rural idiom and reality onto the mainstream stage, it also provides a prescient anticipation of the 'revolution' more often than not associated with the staging of working-class voices and regional identities in the more realist (and prose) drama of the 1950s and 1960s.

Ridler's *The Shadow Factory*, while very different in idiom, setting and theme from *The Old Man of the Mountain*, reveals a similar focus on post-war realities. The subtitle of the work is 'A Nativity Play', and in its final dramatization of the performance of a Christmas play in a factory, it conforms to that description. Ultimately, however, the notion of nativity invoked in the play can be applied equally to the drama's focus on the creation of modern art and the 'birth' of a modern, post-war society. (The scene is 'A Factory, a year or two after the War'.)[15] The play is in many ways a satire of the paternalist approach to the arts, of a bureaucratic assumption of improvement and education, if not social appeasement, through culture. With its commissioned Artist, Education Officer and overriding Director, the play's factory represents a microcosm of the contemporary (and potentially totalitarian) state. Listening to the drills of his workers, the Director reflects, 'This is the music / I like to hear. Rising, falling – / Isn't it the beat of England's heart?'[16] In an ironic expansion of this metaphor, the

Director commissions an Artist ('Garnish') to help him perpetuate this music by creating a mural for a new canteen that, in '[striking] a note of optimism', will also help to build 'a factory still in the making'.[17]

The play is also in many ways a critique of the dehumanizing nature of 'the factory' itself, whose nameless female workers adhere blindly to an order imposed upon them by the equally nameless, aloof Director. The industry of the factory is never specified. By representing this implicit archetype in gendered terms, the play also provides a significant dramatization of male power and control. The factory is staged somewhat abstractly to reinforce its larger representative significance. The Director's office is in the foreground, behind which are three indistinct figures behind screens, 'sitting at drills', with 'a large wheel across the top right-hand corner'.[18] As one worker observes, 'You'd hardly tell where the drills end / And the hands begin.'[19] Contemplating her fellow workers, the '2nd Girl' notes that 'they look like ghosts'.[20] As enforced by Ridler's set directions, the 'art' of the theatrical presentation itself encourages the audience to look for the individuals and humanity behind these screens and dehumanizing structures.

In language that forcefully juxtaposes the spiritual significance of Nativity with the perpetuation of an essentially inhuman structure, Garnish accepts the commission to paint 'The essence of the Works'.[21] He also, in a direct address to the audience, acknowledges the complexity of creating an art that is fundamentally representative, neither realist nor individualist in its artistic manifestation of that 'essence'. In this emphasis on a larger artistic truth beyond the individual artist and experience, Ridler's play resonates with the themes of *The Zeal of Thy House*. It also, however, translates that emphasis into an emphatically contemporary context that is simultaneously spiritual, social and aesthetic. Garnish begins by acknowledging the solipsism of his own artistic instincts, the artist's construction of his own autonomy through a refusal to engage and to thus reduce:

> If I put a picture on a wall
> I like it to make a man feel small.
> That's quite out of date, to be sure –
> A man needs nothing beside himself any more.[22]

He identifies in the commission, however, a temptation to depict a larger, human truth whose very recognition demands a participation from the artist himself:

And yet – I'm tempted. Surely here
Is a symbol not yet alive in paint.
Human hand, machine's skeleton –
What is the true articulation?
Live in this place and learn its secret,
Without liking and without hatred
Paint its secret?[23]

At the end of that first scene, the Artist is torn between his need to engage with the reality that he must represent and his desire to remain similarly aloof, like the Director himself: 'Can I put my hand in the cogwheel / And still claim freedom?'[24] That thematic emphasis in many ways echoes that of the Romantic artist, necessarily distant from reality in order to understand and translate its spiritual essence. For Ridler, however, any such willed, individualistic distance is in many ways akin to that so wrongly espoused by William in Sayers's play.

In the seminal scene in which the new mural is unveiled, Ridler juxtaposes the Christian theme of Nativity with the artificial manifestations of promise and birth both in the contemporary factory and in contemporary art itself. The unveiling immediately follows the laying-out of the props for the Nativity play in the factory; in verse whose imagery and urgent questioning emphasize the significance of that moment, the Parson (and the play) underline the contemporary imperative of that re-enactment:

No need to search
In such a world at such a time
For cold, when cold is in every heart.
Yet ice can burn, the icy stars
Can flame, and so our hearts at coldest
May be found on fire with love.
Who will stand at the farthest pole
Of frost, and stand enflamed with love?
. . .
Who will encompass the birth of Christ?[25]

This verse immediately contrasts with the effect and emphasis of the Director's announcement (in prose): 'I use no high-sounding metaphors; I do not demand supernatural powers; I only ask of you that you that you should become modern citizens, with all that those words connote: I only ask that you should assist at this new birth.'[26] The mural, as the audience (but not the factory) has been led to expect, is ruthlessly critical of the factory's structure; as the Artist admits (again in prose): 'It's a propagandist picture . . . but it's good. I hate your humanitarian your superman-among-the-guinea-pigs State, and I had to say so.'[27] Ultimately, however, in dramatizing the Artist's own emphasis on contemporary structures, in contrasting that emphasis with the Parson's invocation of a more 'legitimate' Nativity, the play invites a more positive, spiritual realization both of a contemporary Christian art and of a contemporary Christian experience. That art, the play suggests, exists independently of 'propagandist' art – critical or otherwise – and its roots are to be found in a verse, drama and social experience focused on the miracle of the Incarnation.

The Director is eventually convinced by the Parson to allow the mural to stand, as a sign of the factory's strength in allowing (and thus containing) satire. This intervention is not motivated by a belief in the factory itself, but by a realization on the part of the Church that it 'cannot undo the past' and so 'Making the best of a bad job / She works on what she finds.'[28] Faced with the (abstractly represented) reality of his own 'monstrous' control in the mural as a 'figure, groping his fingers downward',[29] the Director acknowledges in the mural an art that has begun to 'pierce' with the 'smallest knowledge'.[30] His choice, the play suggests, is whether or not to acknowledge that intervention. Thus awakened by the critical art of the mural, the Director wills himself into a more passive acceptance of a potentially larger Fate:

I'll turn with the tide, which way it swings –
Let the sea flow over,
Wait for the Crib, see what the moment brings.[31]

The consequences of the Director's decision are dramatized symbolically in the next scene, when he instinctively takes part in the Nativity pageant: 'Child, take [my power] and teach me to give.'[32] By the end of the play, the Director has not been fully converted into a hatred of industry structures, but he has been made to recognize his own relative lack of controlling power: 'I've lost all that I had before', 'I simply wander about in the dark.'[33]

The play thus offers a qualified dramatization of the transformative effect of the Nativity, ensuring its perpetual re-enactment in factory Christmas pageants to come. It also, however, uses that larger framework to expose and condemn the spiritual implications of encroaching bureaucratic attempts to manage both art and the individual in the contemporary factory and the contemporary state. In its valuation of religious drama as a spiritually transformative force, in its juxtaposition of that art against the social propaganda of the modern artist, it also presents an implicit critique of a contemporary art that has as yet to recognize the importance of engaging with its origins in 'the mind of the maker'. In so doing, *The Shadow Factory* reinforces the social, spiritual and dramatic significance of the very idiom of religious verse drama itself.

Ronald Duncan: intermedial instincts after the war

Of the many overlooked literary and theatrical careers of modern poet-dramatists, that of Duncan was undoubtedly one of the most prolific and broad-ranging. By the time of *This Way to the Tomb* (1945), one of the most popular verse dramas of the 1940s, Duncan was emerging as a relatively well-known poet, pacifist and writer. In 1937, under the encouragement of Pound, he had set up the modernist magazine *Townsman* (later to become *The Scythe*). At Faber and Faber, Eliot published Duncan's *Journal of a Husbandsman* (1944; a characteristically anecdotal collection of essays about his first-hand experiences in farming), and he published much of Duncan's poetry and drama thereafter. Throughout his career, Duncan produced short stories, reviews, poetry and numerous plays. In the 1940s, his drama received extensive critical and public attention, and by 1946 he had achieved what he identified as a 'hat trick': *The Eagle has Two Heads* transferred to the Theatre Royal, *This Way to the Tomb* transferred from the Mercury to the Garrick and *The Rape of Lucretia* was staged at Covent Garden. As Duncan observes: 'I was on what is known as the "crest of a wave": I didn't perceive the trough beneath it. I was in fashion: but because that fashion was me, I mistook it for good taste.'[34] By the time of his indicatively entitled second autobiography, *How to Make Enemies* (1968), he was bemoaning a 'sense of "failure" now that fashion has farted in my face . . .'[35]

Like Auden and Isherwood, Duncan extended his theatrical enthusiasms considerably beyond the English stage, most particularly in relation to the non-realist drama of Cocteau, Obey and Brecht. In 1947, he published two translations of Cocteau plays as *The Eagle has Two Heads* and *The Typewriter*.[36] His interests also embraced music and music-in-theatre: before the war, he had persuaded Dukes to lend him the Mercury Theatre so that he and Pound could stage 'one of his Noh plays for our own private pleasure': 'Britten produced a musician who could play gongs, and Henry Boys, who had composed some music for Michel St Denis ... suggested a dancer.'[37] Duncan was also in frequent correspondence with Stravinsky. Excited at the prospect of Stravinsky's *The Rake's Progress*, he was, 'of course, envious of Auden for having written the libretto'.[38] Furious at the indifference of London organizers to the prospect of the first English performance of Stravinsky's *Jeu de Cartes* and *Symphony of Psalms*, he reflects: 'I didn't understand then that it takes precisely twenty-five years, one full generation, for any new idea, either in music, literature or paint, to perforate the island fog'.[39] These convictions would become more entrenched over the years, Duncan's most common target being the cultural parochialism of England and its apparent refusal to acknowledge Continental thinkers, artists and musicians.

Equally vexing was the apparent resistance of the English stage to a more intermedial definition of drama that he hoped to promote both through verse drama and through collaborative projects with contemporary composers. Duncan became one of Britten's most frequent collaborators: in the 1930s, he recounts, 'we used to sit for hours discussing operas that we were going to write, or ballets in which I would write verse-commentaries and he would be delegated to making a few noises off'.[40] According to Duncan, in keeping with his early, formative experience with Auden and the Group Theatre, Britten himself wanted 'to find as many opportunities for music on the stage as possible'.[41] Duncan assisted on the completion of the Montagu Slater libretto to *Peter Grimes* (1945), composed the libretto to Britten's *The Rape of Lucretia* (1946; based on the play by Obey), and was sufficiently inspired both by Britten's establishment of the English Opera Group and his own increasing disdain for the mainstream stage as to establish the English Stage Company, in 1956. That this latter role tends to be forgotten (if not excised) from most histories of the theatre continues to suggest a significant omission in favour of a critical narrative that prioritizes the realist social drama so emphatically, vocally despised by Duncan himself.

Shortly after the first success of *This Way to the Tomb*, Duncan refused an offer to review theatre for the *Daily Express* on the pretence that he never attended: 'the plays make me too angry'.[42] Equally infuriating 'was the ridiculous way the theatre had been truncated into religious plays, social plays, thrillers and so on'.[43] By the time that Duncan came to compose *Stratton* (1950), he had identified a theatrical climate innately hostile to his ambition to write a verse play that could be set in modern times, contain elements both of the thriller and of the miracle play, and be 'permanent to the human dilemma and not dependent on frivolous topicality'.[44] For

Duncan, the primary obstacle was the artificial organization of the West End theatre, which 'divid[ed] sensibility in such a way that we had a separate theatre for every aspect of it: the Old Vic for the serious; the Windmill for the bawdy; the Mercury for the poetic; and the Haymarket for the plush. Life is entirely empty if it doesn't contain the whole, I shouted.'[45] In the 1950s and 1960s, Duncan would become even more disillusioned, bemoaning a theatre scene now dominated by an exclusionary expectation of social realism and argument: 'the values of Shaftesbury Avenue merely shifted to Sloane Square ... the New Establishment was now established.'[46]

As Duncan was only too aware, this New Establishment had been enabled by his own early efforts. In 1953, he had combined energies with Britten and George, Earl of Harewood and director of the Royal Opera House, to run the Taw and Torridge Festival in Devon, with the aim of promoting a dramatic art that could not otherwise establish itself on the West End stage. He then became convinced of the need for a London management that 'would stage non-commercial plays'.[47] In Duncan's account, the English Stage Company (ESC) took its name from the English Opera Group with which he had worked so closely: hoping that 'it would achieve for the theatre what the Group had done for chamber opera', he also aimed 'to encourage serious composers and artists to write and design for the stage again'.[48] Duncan contacted Cocteau, Bébé Bérard and Fry. With Oscar Lewenstein, then manager of the Royal Court, he drew up 'lists of plays which had never been seen in England though they'd been produced on the Continent a generation previously. Brecht, Montherland, Betti, Sartre, Cocteau and many more'.[49] Duncan's aims in many ways complemented the energies of George Devine and Tony Richardson, who had similarly hoped to establish a new home for modern drama, but whose enthusiasms were primarily focused on English drama. These directors also increasingly resisted the theatrical tradition apparently represented by Duncan and the dramatists he had hoped to support. In Duncan's account, at his first meeting with Lewenstein he 'acquired a theatre'; in meeting Devine, imminent Artistic Director of the ESC, he 'lost it at another'.[50]

According to Duncan, his primary differences with Devine centred around 'what drama should be about'.[51] Where Devine and his supporters on the Artistic Committee of the Royal Court demanded a drama of social consciousness, Duncan advocated a drama focused on 'the dilemma of being, the limitations of humanity, the frailty of our nature, yet the strength of our vision'.[52] Like many of his predecessors, Duncan identified 'meaningful' drama as that which refuses to engage with 'transitory social equations: the human problem, not the social background, interested me'. Frustrated at the expectation that a known left-wing, pacifist writer should write plays with 'a strong political flavour', he objected that for drama, the only 'vital' problems are 'those to which there [are] no solutions'.[53] As Duncan repeatedly (and often justifiably) complained, his own work consequently tended to be 'derided and dubbed the stuff of religious drama':

> Occasionally I would ask these Fabian-conceived intellectuals, who stood with one hand on the bible of Brecht and the other on the *Observer*, to consider the derivation of the word 'religion'. It derives, I reminded them, from the Latin 'to connect'.[54]

Duncan professed himself 'nauseated' to be labelled a religious poet: 'If religious meant "to connect" how could any poet not be religious?'[55] Both the subject of *This Way to the Tomb*, Duncan's first and most successful produced drama, and the joint commission of *Our Lady's Tumbler* for Salisbury Cathedral and the Festival of Britain (1951) had nonetheless earned him the apparently permanent epithet of 'highbrow religious poet'.[56] As Duncan ruefully observes, this label 'was not a description but a restriction: in the commercial theatre, it amounted to the sentence of death'.[57] It little mattered that *This Way to the Tomb* had been 'written more from unbelief than belief'.[58]

Such objections have done little to counteract Duncan's persistent reputation as one of the many religious verse dramatists of the post-war years. They have also done little more generally to encourage a reconsideration of the very idea of religious drama itself, particularly in relation to the evolution of verse drama as a self-consciously contemporary art, emphatically distinct from the realism, political argumentation or escapism variously promoted in the 'secular' theatre of the time. Although Duncan would soon dismiss *This Way to the Tomb* as a misguided work, excessively rooted in its historical subject and poetry, the play was not just his most commercially successful work, but also one of the most popular verse dramas of the 1940s.[59]

In its dramatization of the life of a saint, in its formalistic presentation of the temptations of that saint through distinct character types, the play, as Duncan openly acknowledged, reflects the clear influence of *Murder in the Cathedral*. In its adoption of the form of the masque, it also reflects and expands upon the tendency of many modern verse dramatists to exploit pre-existing theatrical traditions for the elucidation of a contemporary aesthetic and theme. In its recognition and exploitation of the musico-dramatic expectations of that form, it also suggests a sympathy with the aesthetic enthusiasms of Auden. Where Auden would move into opera in an apparent attempt to escape the political expectations of the verse dramatist, Duncan's dramas emerged within a post-war climate whose three most dominant poet-dramatists (Eliot, Fry and Duncan himself) acknowledged no greater imperative than to dramatize 'the dilemma of being'.

This Way to the Tomb

This Way to the Tomb was written in some respects as a corrective to *Murder in the Cathedral*, which Duncan admired but also criticized for presenting its saint in intellectual, rather than human terms. According to Duncan, his aim was to 'to try to give Saint Antony an ordinary man's emotions and regrets', and he built upon his personal experience in meeting Gandhi to dramatize the natural human temptations of hunger and sensuality.[60] Just as Auden had been inspired by Hogarth's images in the composition of *The Rake's Progress*, Duncan had taken original inspiration from a book of reproductions of Hieronymus Bosch paintings.[61] He had 'no synopsis, only the vaguest idea of what the play was about'.[62] He also, however, 'had Ben Jonson's Masques in the back of [his] mind as a form which [he] wished to use'.[63] The work consists of a masque and anti-masque. The first section loosely dramatizes the temptations of Saint Antony, its verses interpolated with a cappella song, Gregorian chant and offstage solos in Latin, scored by Britten. The second, set in the present-day and scored within a jazz idiom, dramatizes the search for the tomb of Saint Antony by modern pilgrims; it is doubtless no coincidence that Duncan was at the same time 'hatching up another opera' with Britten, based on *The Canterbury Tales*.[64]

In its stylized action, with characters taking up distinct, 'statuesque' positions on stage 'in stylised movement',[65] in its personification of temptation-figures and in its incorporation of Latin verse, the first section of the play demonstrates the influence not only of the masque form, but also of the mystery play and classical drama. It also suggests the influence of such predecessors in contemporary poetic drama as Yeats and Bottomley – not to mention the stagings of Gray and Craig. The masque section of *This Way to the Tomb* does not so much trace the dramatic evolution of its character as explore his spiritual condition through various artistic presentations of movement, voice, music and verse. Like Auden (and Isherwood), Duncan presents a variety of verse idioms within that first section. Unlike Auden, however, he renders that verse audibly and emphatically poetic; indeed, he consulted F.R. Leavis about some of the lines that came to him.[66]

In his verse dramas, Auden tends to evoke a diversity of contemporary, popular idioms to ensure that the 'poetic' element of the play is rooted less in the individual quality or expression of those verses than in the totalizing effect of their presentation and performance within the larger drama. Duncan, however, is much closer to the Eliot of *Murder in the Cathedral* in his conceptualisation of those verses as poetry. 'Nauseated with the flood of so-called "free verse",' he consciously decided 'to use various verse forms with strict limitations'.[67] Antony's meditations are modelled on Pound's translation of Guido Cavalcanti's *Canzone, Donna me Pregha*, chosen deliberately 'because of its complicated structure, its division into five strophes, each subdivided into three stanzas with sixteen internal rhymes'.[68] Duncan thus aimed to explore (and dramatize) the art that evolves from the acceptance of limitations. In so doing, he ensured an aesthetic that sought essentially to mirror the ascetic path of his dramatic subject.

The second section is very different; as befitting the conventions of the anti-masque, it eschews the ritualistic action of the earlier section and parodies the theme presented in the masque. It does so, moreover, by choosing a contemporary setting that enforces its author's contemporary social satire. The anti-masque does not do away with 'poetry'; its various, perpetually satirized characters invoke Christian litany, unite in choral pronouncements and versify their misguided faith (now rooted within a commercial and implicitly Americanized culture). As the character of the Announcer declares:

Our Masque's no more a Miracle. It is no Play,
For Television's here, and here to stay
Making all Art, impromptu shall we say
. . .
. . .
Instead of Art and the unnatural
We've now the hideously actual.
The play's no more.[69]

In its cynical presentation of contemporary pilgrims incapable of differentiating between fashionable trends and individual spiritual quest, the play implicitly endorses this sentiment, aligning real Art with the perpetuation of 'Miracle', with the resistance of the 'hideously actual'.

That resistance is ultimately manifest in the art of the play itself, which presents its satire within a carefully constructed form 'with strict limitations'.

That form, as the Announcer reminds the audience in both parts of the play, is that of the masque and anti-masque; together, the sections imply the presence of a larger design. The play resolves its satire of contemporary materialism and culture by concluding with a return that is both thematic and aesthetic. Antony reappears on stage as the carekeeper of his own shrine, reciting a canzone that reinforces – in both theme and aesthetic – the central preoccupation of the play:

> To live is to remember,
>   to die is to forget;
> Present existence
>   is all reminiscence,
>
> . . .
> Behind the forgotten poem lies the remembered vision.[70]

In the narrative context of the drama, this final song of Antony is addressed to God; its invocation of renewal, the revolving wheel and the return of life through death reinforces and implicitly validates that character's assertion of faith. In the context of a play whose primary preoccupation is the articulation of a 'remembered vision' through the recuperation of 'forgotten poems', that song also manifests a final *aesthetic* return as 'rebirth'. The play itself dramatizes and effects the renewal of the canzone, of the masque, of 'Art and the unnatural' against a contemporary, implicitly artless world hitherto in thrall to television and 'the hideously actual'.

Leeming identifies in *This Way to the Tomb* an 'undramatic paralysis of the action while the poetry is going on'.[71] Ultimately, however, the action of that drama *is* its poetry, its triumphant re-emergence through received, conventional forms in the face of an essentially hostile, ignorant reality. Nowhere, perhaps, is that argument rendered more clear than in the figure of the contemporary Man of Culture, who declares a taste for 'muddy' painting, 'obscure' verse and 'music without melody': 'you see I'm most mature'.[72] While these tastes may mark him as a follower of contemporary and fashionable trends, they also reveal a fundamental spiritual emptiness: declaring that he has 'lost [his] destination', the Man of Culture reflects: 'But I'm on the telephone / Searching for Faith and Love.'[73]

This faith and love for what the Chorus (and Duncan) identify as the 'new illiterate' is not forthcoming from the play. The Chorus excoriates the Man of Culture for writing free verse, eating in foyers at the ballet and writing mediocre novels while drunk: 'verbose reaching and diarrhoea'.[74] For

Duncan, poetry was not 'a flabby decoration to life but an axe, the only tool to hand with which [he] could try to swipe at some of the inarticulate undergrowth'.[75] It was 'a crowbar, not a parasol', and 'no tool could be tough or sharp unless it had form ... You cannot carve wood with wood'.[76] The salvation for the contemporary everyman pilgrims in *This Way to the Tomb*, the play implies, is to be found less in God or the example of St Antony than in the example of the poetic, ascetic idiom of the saint – now triumphantly revived in the structured verses of the contemporary, self-consciously resistant aesthetic of Duncan himself.

While Duncan remained emphatic in his conviction of the importance of formal discipline in verse drama, he was soon to see *This Way to the Tomb* as a failure. He consistently aligns himself with Eliot in this regard: 'we both saw that by writing plays about saints in a remote period we had evaded the essential challenge, which was to find a flexible verse form to express the age we lived in, on the stage'.[77] Both consequently attempted to find an idiom through which to dramatize contemporary sensibilities, and both, in Duncan's assessment, had initially failed: Eliot's *The Family Reunion* and his own *Stratton* were 'overloaded ... with either Greek or Viennese overtones'.[78] Duncan professed himself pleased with the accomplishment of *The Catalyst* (1957), a critically unsuccessful drama about a contemporary ménage à trois whose morality ran afoul of both the censor and Eliot, who refused to publish the play. For Duncan, however, the ultimate achievement was the fact that 'none of the critics had spotted that the play was in verse'.[79] Notwithstanding the divergent thematic interests of both poet-dramatists, their careers shared this increasing conviction of the transformative potential of an 'unobtrusive', controlled and disciplined verse within a contemporary idiom. Where Duncan applied himself to *Stratton* and *The Catalyst*, Eliot was to assert this aesthetic in *The Cocktail Party*, one of the most successful verse dramas of the post-war years. In a telling reassertion of verse drama as a vital, violent form of righteous resistance, Duncan observes in Eliot's play a sympathetic movement towards 'language which had the discipline of prose but could carry the charge of a hand grenade when required'.[80]

The Cocktail Party

In a caustic (but not unusual) 1954 assessment of Eliot's dramatic career, the prominent arts editor and commentator J.W. Lambert suggested that by the time of *The Confidential Clerk* (1953), with its 'undecorative' verse and conventional setting, Eliot had 'embraced deliberate banality with almost scornful deliberation'.[81] As early as 1946, Bentley was asking, 'Why is [Eliot] not an important playwright?'[82] Over fifty years later, few voices have emerged to contest what Spencer (who seems to have a particular hatred of verse drama) assumes to be a critical commonplace: Eliot's 'preachy verse dramas may once have been seen as the way forward for British drama, but they now look like the deadliest of dead ends'.[83] Reinforcing the presiding assumption of the way forward that British drama was to take, Gill Plain observes of *The Cocktail Party*: 'brittle people, stylised dialogue, middle-class mores, and no sign as yet of the angry young man'.[84]

Nowhere, perhaps, is the general association of verse drama with 'theological orthodoxy' more prominent than in critical assessments of Eliot's dramas. To a considerable extent, that association (not always anticipated by Eliot's contemporary, often mainstream audience) seems to have been ensured both by Eliot's public religious conversion and by the fact that his first two dramas for performance were written for a religious setting. As the above assessments suggest, however, the idea of orthodoxy has also been applied in relation to the evolution of Eliot's dramas to embrace contemporary settings, popular West End idioms (social comedy, detective drama, farce) and a more flexible verse form that could often be mistaken for prose. As we have seen, that evolution asserts a break from the more experimental, intermedial instincts that had characterized much verse drama before the war, and that Auden and Duncan continued to explore in their operatic collaborations. It also aligns Eliot much more closely with the very mainstream theatre that so many verse dramatists had set out to challenge – and that the subsequent social 'revolutionaries' of the 1950s would identify as the primary target of their much-mythologized anger.

The Cocktail Party was Eliot's most successful, oft-revived post-war drama; the New York production received the 1950 Tony Award for Best Play, and when broadcast on British television in 1952, the play was 'watched by an estimated three-and-a-half million people'.[85] Much of that popular success has been attributed to the play's contemporary setting, to what many saw as its barely detectable verse and to its clear affiliation with the popular West End drawing-room comedy. In keeping with his ambition to express 'a kind of doubleness in the action, as if it took place on two planes at once',[86] Eliot himself identified the play as manifesting a relatively successful development. After *The Family Reunion*, he had 'made a good deal of progress in finding a form of versification and an idiom which would serve all [his] purposes, without recourse to prose, and be capable of unbroken transition between the most intense speech and the most relaxed dialogue'.[87] He had therefore determined on 'no chorus, and no ghosts,' and on a play in which 'something should happen'.[88] By thus seamlessly positioning the 'poetic' element of his drama within the narrative conventions of the middle-class drawing-room play, he had also come closer to realizing his conviction that 'if the poetic drama is to reconquer its place, it must ... enter into overt competition with prose drama'.[89]

For Eliot, it would seem, that competition was most manifest in the drawing-room comedies and dramas of Terence Rattigan and Noël Coward. While maintaining his earlier emphasis on taking 'a form of entertainment, and subject[ing] it to the process which would leave it a form of art', Eliot no longer looked to the music hall, with its problematic fragmentary structure, its combination of music and verse, and its inherently social emphasis. He also abandoned the historical drama and a more detectably poetic verse, which (like Duncan) he criticised for imposing an artificial distance between audience and play:

> What we have to do is to bring poetry into the world in which the audience lives and to which it returns when it leaves the theatre; not to transport the audience into some imaginary world totally unlike its own, an unreal world in which poetry is tolerated.[90]

In moving his subsequent dramas into a modern setting, 'with characters of our own time living in our own world', in finding 'a rhythm close to contemporary speech, in which the stresses could be made to come wherever we should naturally put them', Eliot aimed to meet his audience on what he identified as its own terms.[91] To a certain extent, however, by turning to the more narrative-based, contemporary settings of detective drama and drawing-room comedy, he also risked eliding that form of entertainment with his emphasis on modern experience itself. As the Royal Court 'revolution' of the 1950s was to assert most emphatically, the contemporary social realities represented by the conventional drawing-room drama were no more relevant to the 'world in which the audience lives' than those of 'some imaginary world'.

In an interview with the *Glasgow Herald* following the Edinburgh premiere, Eliot reiterated his distinction between the 'dramatic' and the 'poetic' element of the play. The dramatic element is 'the immediate situation and the troubles and conflict which agitate people', and as such 'the characters should not be on the surface unusual or different from ordinary human nature'.[92] The poetic element of the play 'is that which each individual takes from his experience', that which is intuitively awoken by the balance between verse, drama and theme: 'I would not want to say to anyone that this or that is the meaning, because the whole interest of the process is in getting your own meaning out of it.'[93] As Smith argues, the play nonetheless provides a fairly strong indication of its author's 'desire to destroy and clear away conventional modes of thought and interpretations of events in order to reveal the hidden meaning and the divine plan behind appearances'.[94] Browne concurs: 'however much the author insisted that each interpreter must be free to find his own meaning, those who penetrated furthest into the play's thought were the critics who were willing to recognise its Christian basis.'[95]

The Cocktail Party in many respects conforms to the formal expectations (such as they are) of the drawing-room comedy: it is populated by middle-class characters whose love-triangles and marital tensions evolve over witticisms and drinks; it constantly hints at a (humorous) repression of emotional and sexual experience within those exchanges; and it is inevitably resolved – as befitting the 'comedy' pronounced in the play's subtitle – in a superficial restoration of social and marital order. As Speaight observes, 'the rectification of four disordered lives by a quizzical psychiatrist was calculated to put even Broadway at its ease.'[96] From the very beginning of the play, however, Eliot constantly pushes at these conventions, inviting the audience to acknowledge their disruption and in so doing to contemplate the realities that exist beneath the surface of lived, social routine. The play opens with a typical cocktail party: Peter is being asked to 'tell us that story' about how the butler of Lady Klootz 'found her in the pantry, rinsing her mouth out with champagne'.[97] Ten years later, such a line would have provided the focus for social critique or satire; in Eliot's play, however, it serves primarily to establish an idiom and a setting for characters who are not 'on the surface unusual or different from ordinary human nature'.

As the act proceeds, it becomes apparent that Edward, the host of the party, has been left by his wife Lavinia, and that he has been obliged to continue with the party nonetheless. When the guests have departed, Edward is left to converse with the 'Unidentified Guest', whose air of authority immediately tempers the conventionalism of the setting. That authority is first manifest in his adoption of the role of psychiatrist, when he urges Edward to 'Breathe deeply, and adopt a relaxed position': 'Now for a few questions.'[98] Soon thereafter, he adopts the tone of a lawyer: 'But I put it to you.'[99] That Eliot is drawing attention to conventional modes of discourse and social roles is emphasized by Edward's retort: 'I have often used these terms in examining witnesses, / So I don't like them.'[100] It is also emphasized by Edward's confession, 'I don't think I want to know who you are', and the stranger's cryptic – and decidedly unconventional – introduction of mystery:

> I know you as well as I know your wife
>
> . . .
>
> But let me tell you, that to approach the stranger
> Is to invite the unexpected, release a new force,
> Or let the genie out of the bottle.[101]

The visitor speaks directly to Edward's essential self, urging him to recognize that this approach will help him to discover 'What you really are' and 'What you really are among other people': at the moment he is 'nothing but a set / Of obsolete responses.'[102]

Rather than invoking the drawing-room comedy to 'trick' his audience into an appreciation of his larger themes, Eliot exploits the thematic importance of this idea of conventional and thus potentially obsolete responses. The Guest urges Edward to recognize that the absence of his wife has made him see that he is nothing more than an object, or a 'type': he no longer feels 'quite human', he is 'A living object, but no longer a person.'[103] In a potential allusion to *Prufrock*'s patient 'etherised upon the table',[104] he likens the condition of Edward to that of a patient in an operating room, 'stretched on the table': 'For those who surround you, the masked actors; / All there is of you is your body / And the "you" is withdrawn.'[105] In many respects, therefore, Eliot aligns the rote conventions of the drawing-room comedy with those that characterize the 'ordinary' social world inhabited both by Edward and (implicitly) by the play's audience. In exposing the limitations of those objectifying conventions, he also implicitly critiques the contemporary West End play itself, which relies exclusively on those conventions instead of revealing the necessarily 'poetic' reality of life – and the poetic potential of drama itself.

Unlike *The Rock* or *Murder in the Cathedral*, *The Cocktail Party* is not *explicitly* Christian. Speaight observes that the Christian members of the audience 'knew what they were in for and complied; the pagans complained and few, one guesses, were converted. Both combined to assure a theatrical success.'[106] As Smith convincingly details, those familiar with the Anglo-Catholic theology of Charles Williams and John Heath-Stubbs would have recognized in the respective fates of Celia, Edward and Lavinia a dramatization of the Affirmative Way and the Negative Way to salvation.[107] The Negative Way is ultimately epitomized by Edward and Lavinia in their decision to – like the Church in *The Shadow Factory* – 'make the best of a bad job',[108] in this case to know themselves and each other, to acknowledge their own limitations, and to recognize in that knowledge a manifestation of God's grace as design. In contrast, Celia seeks unity with a larger, selfless love, where 'desire is fulfilled / In the delight of loving'.[109] Disillusioned by her earlier affair with Edward, she is overcome both with an indescribable urge to atone more broadly and to identify an object of love that is not simply 'created by our own imagination'.[110] As Smith observes, she chooses 'to conduct her love affair with God rather than be content with the reflection of God's love in the love of creature for creature'.[111]

In the play, all of these characters ultimately seek a path to salvation through love. Edward and Lavinia end the play reconciled, relatively content to resume the perpetual conventions of the cocktail party in a state of greater knowledge. Julia recognizes that Edward and Lavinia have been 'stripped naked to their souls / And can choose, whether to put on proper costumes / Or huddle quickly into new disguises'.[112] The play ends with another party, two years later; despite their familiar costumes, the protagonists are now aware, as Edward states, 'that every moment is a fresh beginning'.[113] Celia, in contrast, eschews the social world to join an austere religious order in Kinkaja. Her fate is very different: she is taken by pagan villagers and crucified close to an ant-hill – only remnants over her body are found. As Reilly emphasizes, that fate is ultimately a triumph, the manifestation of Celia's decision to accept 'the way of preparation' and thus to refuse to allow 'the body to become a *thing*'.[114] The account of that fate also effects the more conventional characters at the end of the play: in their mutual recognition of the importance of finding a 'way', they come closer to recognizing the inherent presence of this larger design.

At the same time as the play is invested in these larger Christian themes, it also clearly engaging with dramatic aesthetic itself. Central to that engagement is Eliot's apparent identification of a mainstream, 'competitive' prose drama that refuses to allow for the articulation or aesthetic representation of more metaphysical themes. In a retrospective lecture, Eliot noted with some pride that no-one seems to have recognized the source of his story in the *Alcestis* of Euripides.[115] In his mysterious retrieval of Lavinia, in his later role as Reilly, the Guest, like Heracles, wrestles his charges from the finality of Death. Where the Euripides reference is relatively oblique, Eliot consistently presents his character as one who disrupts convention – social *and* dramatic – and in so doing calls attention to a poetic mystery otherwise unacknowledged within that drama and within that society. Soon after noting that 'nobody likes to be left with a mystery',[116] Reilly erupts into a song whose subject and 'lower-class' idiom reinforce this sense of disruption, if not mystery, in aesthetic terms.[117] This association is acknowledged by Julia, who observes, 'were you singing songs all the time? / There's altogether too much mystery / About this place today.'[118] Tellingly, when Edward apologizes, Julia – who has hitherto embodied the type of the busybody aunt – declares that she loves mystery before returning to the subject of her missing spectacles.[119]

These mysterious moments continue to present themselves within the play. At the end of Act Two, Reilly is joined by his fellow guardian-figures, Julia and Alex. The three together drink a libation to their charges, 'The words for the building of the hearth.'[120] Peter Quilpe, the next charge for these guardians, returns at the end of the play: he is now employed by Hollywood, and has been sent to scout for 'some typical English faces', but 'only for minor parts'.[121] As Julia observes and as the play consistently enforces, with the exception of Celia, 'We're all very typical.'[122] While the role of that 'type' might be defined as 'minor' in American films, however, Eliot presents these characters as representative of a fundamental human condition. In the thematic and aesthetic context of the play, that condition demands acknowledgement within a form that might allow for the overt presence of poetry as unrealist, metaphysical expression. Towards the end of the scene, Reilly quotes a passage from Shelley's *Prometheus Unbound*, which resonates with the 'two worlds of life and death' respectively chosen by Celia and by Edward and Lavinia.[123] In *The Cocktail Party*, these two equally essential worlds are invoked by the dramatization of the perpetual, if only occasionally visible, presence of mystery as 'poetry'. This poetic presence is suggested in Reilly's guardianship and in the characters' own realization of a larger design. It is also manifest aesthetically in the incursion of Euripides, Shelley and music-hall song within the larger, totalizing creation of the poet-dramatist himself.

Notwithstanding its success at the time, *The Cocktail Party* did very little to establish a dominant idiom for future manifestations of drama in verse, religious or otherwise. Eliot clearly manipulates the conventions of the drawing-room entertainment to invoke other, more poetic forms of drama. He also, however, has his characters *explain* their spiritual and moral preoccupations within a language whose idiom comes very close to that of prose. In so doing, he comes very close to aligning his self-consciously distinct, poetic drama with the aesthetic conventions of the drama of ideas. As suggested by Spencer's dismissal of Eliot's preachiness, those ideas may have resonated in the immediate post-war years, but they were soon to be superseded by a drama focused on very different contemporary realities and a more politicized social argument. Equally problematic, in that context, are the contemporary setting and dramatic conventions through which the play works. Eliot's ideas are rooted in what he identifies as a universal spiritual reality, the stuff of Duncan's 'dilemma of being'. In *The Cocktail Party*, however, he positions that reality exclusively in relation to the experience and rituals of the very social class whose legitimacy would be so overtly challenged by the Angry Young Men of the English Stage Company.

Ultimately, the most resilient legacy of *The Cocktail Party* can be identified in its incorporation of absurdist elements within a conventional form; to that extent, it acts as a potential precursor to Pinter's *The Birthday Party*, *The Caretaker* and *The Homecoming*. According to Browne, *The Cocktail Party* is a deliberate riposte to Sartre's existential *Huis Clos*: Edward's line 'Hell is oneself' echoes and refutes Sartre's 'Hell is other people'.[124] Ironically, however, Eliot's play also concludes with lines that, in their terse, rhythmic invocation of repetition, anticipation and unknown beginning, seem to have provided an implicit template for such explorations of the existential condition as Beckett's *Waiting for Godot*, *Happy Days*, and *Endgame*:

Edward	And now for the party.
Lavinia	Now for the party.
Edward	It will soon be over.
Lavinia	I wish it would begin.
Edward	There's the doorbell.
Lavinia	Oh, I'm glad. It's begun.
	CURTAIN[125]

Christopher Fry

In 1950, addressing the question of 'Why Verse', Christopher Fry echoed Eliot's 'doubleness of action' when he identified two roles to poetry in the theatre: 'it must have a direct surface meaning, an immediate impact of sense, but half its work should be going on below that meaning'.[126] Like Eliot (and like Abercrombie, Masefield and Bottomley), Fry suggests that '[t]he truth of poetry deepens under your eye. It is never absolute.'[127] Also like Eliot, he often guided his audience into an appreciation of such 'truth' in plays whose thematic explorations of birth, death, love and renewal resonated – at times explicitly, more often only implicitly – with the preoccupations of Christian drama. Like Duncan, Fry rejected the easy categorization of these thematic concerns: 'this has been an age of signposts, of ideologies, of patent cures . . . [we must] draw clear lines between this or that . . . But we have been looking at the possibility that poetry has another, deeper law.'[128]

Fry's first acclaimed drama was *The Boy with a Cart* (1938), a commission for a local church festival to celebrate the life of St Cuthman. In keeping with a cultural and theatrical environment that had yet to assert a definitive break between the professional theatre and either the amateur theatre or religious drama, the success of that play garnered him a 1939 commission from the Tewkesbury Festival (*The Tower*) and influenced his appointment as artistic director of the Oxford Playhouse. In 1950, *The Boy with a Cart* was revived on the West End, starring Richard Burton. In 1951, *A Sleep of Prisoners* was commissioned by the Religious Drama Society for the Festival of Britain.[129] By that time, Fry had already established himself as a prominent presence in contemporary theatre: his religious-historical drama *The Firstborn* (1948) had been staged at the Oxford Playhouse, with songs specially written by Leonard Bernstein, and that year had also seen the performance of his Canterbury play, *Thor, with Angels*. It had also seen the premiere of *The Lady's Not for Burning*, commissioned in 1947 on the strength of the Mercury's 1946 production of *A Phoenix Too Frequent*, starring Paul Scofield.

Unquestionably Fry's most popular and successful play, *The Lady's Not for Burning* was taken on tour by John Gielgud before it transferred to the West End for a nine-month run. The production opened on Broadway in 1950, where it was awarded the New York Drama Critics' Circle Award as Best Foreign Play of 1950–1. That year had also seen the premiere of *Venus Observed* as part of a Fry season at the St James Theatre; starring and directed by Laurence Olivier, the play transferred soon thereafter to New York, where it too won a New York Drama Critics' Circle Award. In 1950, Fry's image graced the cover of America's *Time* magazine. That year, the London productions of three of his plays (*Venus Observed*, *The Lady's Not for Burning*, and his highly successful translation of Anouilh, *Ring Around the Moon*, directed by Peter Brook) ensured a 'hat-trick' even more prominent than that enjoyed by Duncan a few years previous.

By 1954, however, Fry was beginning to meet with a more tempered reaction. Moving away from his characteristically pastoral or whimsical

English settings, *The Dark is Light Enough* was set in the distant context of the Hungarian Revolution of 1848. A self-styled 'Winter Comedy' written for Edith Evans, the play saw an inevitable Broadway transfer that starred Katharine Cornell and Tyrone Power. While the play achieved some success, many critics noted a shift in tone and idiom, with a verse now 'bent more closely to the rise and fall of the story',[130] 'less like an illuminated missal, less astounding'.[131] By 1960, an even more significant shift in tone had come to define the critical climate of the London theatre: Fry's *Curtmantle* was offered to the ESC through Olivier; much to the lasting ire of Duncan, it was refused. Philip Roberts now identifies this decision approvingly as 'a defining moment in the Court's history', a seminal recognition that the drama represented by Fry and promoted by Duncan 'no longer existed'.[132]

Notwithstanding his personal friendship with Fry and his anger at the direction of the ESC, Duncan laid much of the blame for this reception fairly evenly at the feet of the taste-makers of the 1950s and Fry himself. Where Fry shared with Eliot and Duncan a conviction of the suggestive importance of poetry in drama, he differed significantly in his belief that that suggestion could be achieved with a verse that was overtly poetic in its linguistic exuberance, poetic conceits and wit. Both Eliot and Duncan 'deprecated [the] verbal fireworks' of Fry, his apparent 'concern with imagery for the sake of coining it'.[133] Rather than 'over-decorat[ing]' as Christopher Fry does', verse in drama should '[carry] the idiom and run of spoken language',[134] all the while contesting a reductive realism. In a prescient anticipation of this increasingly entrenched expectation, Auden had retreated to opera to 'return' to the writing of 'poetry with a capital P'. Fry, however, resembled earlier dramatists such as Bottomley in his conviction that an audibly poetic idiom could – and should – flourish on the contemporary spoken stage: 'poetry in the theatre is the action of listening. ... sound itself, pure sound, has logic, as we know in music, and what does that logic accord to if not the universal discipline felt along the heart?'[135] While Duncan acknowledged the dramatic effect of modern(ist) music in his collaborations with Britten, where Auden moved exclusively into a musico-dramatic form, Fry tended to indulge the musical, sonorous potential of staged poetry itself. Rather than distancing the verse from the drama, that musical effect would essentially mirror the drama's thematic emphasis on harmony, resolution and a larger design.

Equally central to Fry's reading, therefore, was his recognition of a musically analogous effect to his drama as a whole. In that reading, the suggestive imagery, poetic conceit and overtly non-realist idiom of his verse would reinforce both the play's consistent movement towards comic resolution of plot and theme and its service to a 'deeper law'. This law depended upon an essentially absolute, traditionalist ideal of music (and art more generally) rooted not in discordant modernity or jazz improvization, but rather in an ideal of order, structure and harmony. This traditionalism was enforced in the tendency of Fry's language towards a hitherto unfashionable indulgence of poetic conceit, its metaphors and imagery consistently tempered by a tone of humour and wit. It was also suggested by his settings, which tended either towards the vaguely historical or classical, or towards a contemporary setting constantly informed by earlier aesthetic traditions. As Peter Brook observed, 'Fry finds his poetry in the England that still has echoes of the middle ages in its villages. . . . The melancholy of *Venus Observed* is that of the Elgar cello concerto and *Brideshead Revisited*.'[136] In a post-war Britain marked by austerity, increasing debates about modern(ist) culture, urban renewal and mass technology, the effect would undoubtedly have been to suggest a reassuring continuity. As Fry himself contended, 'The period, (except in a strictly historical play) is merely the colour on the brush: the extra illumination of the idea.'[137]

Post-war Elizabethan comedy: *The Lady's Not for Burning*

Nowhere, perhaps, are these various tendencies more immediately manifest than in *The Lady's Not for Burning*. The play in many respects builds upon the themes and structure of *A Phoenix Too Frequent*, a one-act, three-character play in which Dyname is convinced (through love) by Tegeus-Chromis of the joy to be had in living. The cast of *The Lady's Not for Burning* is more populous, but the drama, set in '1400 either more or less or exactly',[138] follows a similar trajectory: Thomas Mendip, a former soldier in his early twenties (and thus not unlike many of the audience-members in the 1940s), demands to be hanged. He claims to have killed two men, but the play makes clear that he has invented these crimes in an attempt to end his life; the world disgusts him:

> I have left
> Rings of beer on every alehouse table
> From the salt sea-coast across half a dozen counties,
> But each time I thought I was on the way

To a faintly festive hiccup
The sight of the damned world sobered me up again.[139]

In one of many self-conscious acknowledgements of his own poetic style, Fry has Thomas reflect that life 'is the way / We fatten for the Michaelmas of our own particular / Gallows. What a wonderful thing is metaphor.'[140] The effect is to embrace an exuberantly non-realist mode of representation. It is also to contain the play's very serious, potentially resonant themes of despair and disillusionment within a larger comic structure and tone whose very generic conventions promise a drama of resolution.

The antithesis to Thomas in the play is Jennet Jourdemayne, chased to the same location by a mob of witch-hunters: unlike Thomas, she is desperate to live. The essential drama of the play revolves around the transformation of Thomas, through love of Jennet and an experience of life, into an equal acceptance of love. It is populated by many other characters, who enact various subplots of comic misunderstanding, thwarted love, misplaced desire and half-hearted blackmail in such a way as to position the central situations of Thomas and Jennet within a larger, totalizing context. The very liveliness of this context serves as a persistent foil to the disillusionment of Thomas. So too does the play's constant, developed invocation of nature imagery, and its gently persistent association of that imagery with a larger Christian design. Alizon enters the play half-blind from having been in 'the light' of nature:

Such white doves were paddling in the sunshine
And the trees were as bright as a shower of broken glass.
Out there, in the sparkling air, the sun and the rain
Clash together like the cymbals clashing
When David did his dance. I've an April blindness.[141]

Her suitor, Humphrey, is 'prone in the flower-bed' after having been hurtled 'like Lucifer into the daffodils' by the jealous Nicholas.[142] The setting, tone, and light-hearted treatment of this rivalry also invokes Chaucer, not least the rather more bawdy adventures of Alisoun and Nicolas in *The Miller's Tale*. While none of the characters are paragons, their very ebullient, varied participation in life, love and music – their very aestheticized presence within a pastoral context marked by 'spring sunlight, hatching egg after egg'– reinforces their presence within a comedy defined by the promise of a regeneration that is simultaneously spiritual, natural and poetic.[143] Fry would later retrospectively label the work one of his 'spring' comedies.

The play is ultimately resolved in the deus ex machina appearance of the alleged victims of both Thomas and Jennet; both protagonists are vindicated, and they are resolved into love of each other. Thomas remains disillusioned with the larger world and society: 'I love you, but the world's not changed.'[144] He had been 'nicely tucked up for the night / of eternity,' but 'with a rainbow' where her face should be, Jennet has ensured that 'presto! The bedclothes are on the floor.'[145] Hearing the 'pickaxe voice of a cock, beginning / To break up the night,' Jennet asks Thomas if she is an 'inconvenience' to him; he replies that she is – 'as inevitably as original sin' – but she is also the implicit means to his salvation: 'I shall be loath to forgo one day of you, / Even for the sake of my ultimate friendly death.'[146] Jennet reminds him that she 'is friendly too.'[147] She is also apprehensive of the future: the world looks frozen beneath the moon, but she is resolved, with Nicholas, to 'begin again', 'who knows where.'[148] To a considerable extent, therefore, Fry reiterates the thematic emphasis of both Eliot and Ridler on making the 'best' of a bad job – and the fate of Edward and Lavinia, with its simultaneously new and familiar beginning, is not unlike that of Jennet and Thomas. In Fry's play, however, that 'bad job' is presented within a drama that *continually* contests any disillusionment with a world that is so clearly, manifestly characterized by beauty, comedy and regenerate nature.

Equally regenerate, of course, is the very ideal of an overtly poetic expression clearly informed by preceding traditions. For Fry, those expressions, like his own, are rooted in an ideal of the public, the popular and the community. Fry's medieval setting and allusions invoke a Chaucerian world. He also supports his aims for verse drama with a quotation from *The Merchant of Venice*: 'The man that hath no music in himself . . . is fit for treasons. . . . Mark the music.'[149] Dwelling upon that later statement, Fry aligns his embrace of a buoyant, non-realist idiom with that of Shakespeare, a poetic dramatist to whom overt allusions in verse drama had been conspicuously absent since the initial re-workings of Bottomley.[150] The popularity of Fry's plays coincided with a moment that had seen Olivier and Gielgud gain an increasing cultural dominance, that had seen Shakespeare himself revitalized in the productions of the Old Vic and the films of Olivier, and that was soon to crown its new queen as the 'second' Elizabeth. In that context and in the context of a post-war environment marked by austerity and the recent trauma of war, both the themes and the audibly poetic, comic and optimistic aesthetic of Fry's dramas found a particular resonance. In 1953, a book-length study by the journalist Philip Gibbs looked for the re-emergence of a contemporary poetic tradition to define a new Elizabethan age: 'English poetry is not dead. It is very much alive, and one day, soon, perhaps – tomorrow! – a new Elizabethan poet will be revealed and acclaimed, giving us a new vision, some touch of ecstasy, a call to the spirit of the people.'[151] For Gibbs and many others at the time, that call and 'vision' was manifest in the dramas of Fry, a poet who is nearest to the Elizabethans 'in robust spirit and in playfulness with words and joy in them, as though they were glittering jewels'.[152]

For Duncan (and apparently Eliot), however, the success of Fry's *The Lady's Not for Burning* had dealt a decisive and ultimately fatal blow to the establishment of a modern tradition of drama in verse. The very popularity of the work had 'put the clock back' on verse drama as a whole: 'The damage was done. Fry's brief success associated poetry on the stage with rhetoric and verbal puff again.'[153] Duncan's assessment is refuted by Fry's clearly-developed alignment of 'verbal puff' with theme and dramatic structure, and many of his themes resonate with those of his more 'contemporary-minded' peers. Like Eliot and Duncan, however, Fry found himself unable to establish an aesthetic for verse drama beyond that brief moment of a post-war 'false dawn'. Indeed, he confessed himself to having undergone, in the late 1950s, 'a crisis of confidence in [his] own ability to express the world as [he] saw it in terms of the modern theatre'.[154] The subsequent development of Fry's aesthetic was characterized by a relative restriction of the poetic conceit and image in his verse. That evolution, however, did very little (if anything) to align his drama with the perceived direction of the modern theatre in subsequent decades.

Unlike Eliot, Fry cannot be said to have inspired other dramatists – no matter how tangentially – to develop certain elements of his aesthetic or sensibility. Furthermore, as Leeming observes, Fry was not an established poet or writer before he wrote plays, and unlike the plays of Yeats, Auden and Eliot, his works have not had 'their life prolonged by reflected interest in other works, after verse drama grew out of fashion'.[155] Duncan himself is rarely acknowledged in studies of modern poetry or poetic drama. Fry's fall from critical and popular grace, however, is all the more striking for his brief, spectacular popularity on both sides of the ocean – with critics, actors, directors and mainstream play-goers alike. As Duncan reports with a certain amount of schadenfreude, 'Within five years [of *The Lady's Not for Burning*] both Eliot and I found it difficult to get a production – Fry himself found it impossible.'[156]

CHAPTER 7
ANGER AND AFTERMATH: ROYAL COURT, NATIONAL THEATRE AND VERSE DRAMA AFTER 1956

Before the war, the culture of serious dramatic writing had been relatively fluid, marked primarily by a self-conscious movement – in London, in amateur and touring theatre, in literary circles, in festival programs, in repertory theatres – against the commercialism and apparent complacency of the West End. The post-war years, however, saw the emergence of an increasingly powerful nationalist instinct in relation to the definition and subsequent historiography of modern 'British' theatre. Nowhere, perhaps, is the influence of that moment more strikingly evident than in the effective eradication of verse drama (and dramatists) from the contemporary stage and from any discourse of a modern national tradition.

The modern English stage

Central to that phenomenon was the emergence of a particularly strong national(ist) sensibility in the theatre and reviewing culture of the 1950s and 1960s, itself a reflection of a renewed investment of the state in an ideal of national culture. As Dan Rebellato observes, one consequence of this shift was that the amateur and community work of the forties and early fifties was relatively ignored in attempts to formulate a national tradition in contemporary writing and theatre practice.[1] The first decades of the twentieth century had been marked by diverse attempts – in stage societies, repertory theatre and amateur drama – to counteract the centrality of a mainstream commercial theatre in London. They had seen Barker staging Shaw's socially argumentative plays, collaborating with Housman on the writing of *Prunella*, promoting Maeterlinck, and advocating for the revitalization of Shakespearean performance. They had seen de Valois working with contemporary composers, poet-dramatists and experimental directors at the same time as she was forming a modern national ballet. Playwrights such as Auden were just as likely to capitalize upon the living traditions of the mummers play as they were to invoke the influence of the mystery play, Brecht or Eliot.

By the middle of the century, however, as 'London became a focus for displaying the nation',[2] the valuation of modern drama became increasingly more centralized and the diversity of its explorations and collaborations relatively discouraged in favour of a larger, nationalizing instinct. As Trewin observed in 1965:

> Hardly any of the test-tube club theatres, so numerous in the late Forties, remain today upon the outer circle. We have lost the converted church halls, the basements, the attics . . . Outside London, with the old touring system in wreck, the provinces rely increasingly upon the subsidized theatre: a growing battalion of regional Repertories (never an attractive title) aided by the Arts Council or the municipalities or both.[3]

Throughout those decades, repertory theatres encouraged considerable diversity, new theatre-spaces promoted innovations in staging, and the founding of such alternative London venues as the short-lived but influential Arts Lab in 1967 attested to a lively and explorative artistic culture. Those years also, however, saw the critical and historiographical (re)definition of national drama become increasingly confined to its apparent manifestation within national, primarily London-based institutions. Ironically, much of that transformation can be attributed to the slow but steady development of the National Theatre, whose official opening in 1963 marked both the acknowledgement and inevitable containment of the amateur, community-based ideals initially promoted by Geoffrey Whitworth and the British Drama League.[4]

Complementing that institutionalization was the received emergence of the Royal Court Theatre as the prominent, decisive home of vital modern drama. The end of the 1950s consequently saw the emergence of a dominant critical consensus not only as to the very national position of drama as representative modern art, but also as to its informing social and aesthetic values. As Styan notes, the ESC 'made English drama a subject for debate as it had not been since the advent of Ibsen. After six years nearly a hundred plays had been tried out . . . [and John Osborne, Arnold Wesker and John Arden] had come to the surface, their plays often of working-class life and resolutely "kitchen-sink".[5] While this emphasis on kitchen-sink realities would itself become a cliché of the moment, the presiding English ideal of contemporary British theatre as primarily realist (if occasionally, nominally, Brechtian), socially engaged and nationally focused would not. Its resilience is apparent in Aleks Sierz's recent identification of 'a very British aesthetic' in the tradition that marks today's (English) drama, an aesthetic marked by its 'strongly naturalistic style and a social realist agenda'.[6] This drama is 'New Writing Pure': 'often difficult, sometimes intractable ... it usually has something to say about Britain today'.[7]

Such assumptions signal a certain regression to the drama of ideas and the problem plays that had been so strenuously challenged by the verse dramatists, Continental playwrights and experimental directors of the first half of the twentieth century. In Duncan's reading, the drama promoted by the Royal Court and its critical supporters had essentially assimilated mainstream, West End conventions and aligned them with an argument-driven ideal of modern, left-wing theatre: 'The only change was that the convention of Shaftesbury Avenue duchesses fiddling with flower vases was replaced by Jimmy Porters picking their noses in public':

> Filling the sails in the wings was Mr Tynan with his facility for reaching the wrong conclusions. He eventually propagated the idea of the Committted Theatre. This was not precisely novel: Brecht had discussed the notion thirty years before. But it provided a talking point. It now became fashionable.... The language in a play was not noticed so long as it had the tone of protest within it ...[8]

Most alarming, however, was the extent to which this emphasis on contemporary settings, naturalist language and political argumentation had limited any variety of theatrical and dramatic creativity. In his letter of resignation to the ESC (1966), submitted after years of conflict with his administrative peers, Duncan notably claimed that 'it is not the plays that we have produced that makes me wish to withdraw from the Company, but the plays we have not produced'.[9]

Informing this exclusionary critical consensus – clearly endorsed by the very terminology of a 'New Writing Pure' – was (and is) the almost instantaneous mythologization of John Osborne's *Look Back in Anger* (1956). While the play may not have effected the revolution with which it is often credited, it did ensure a reading of a fundamental cultural and aesthetic divide, what Trewin identified less than ten years later as a 'gulf that seems as deep as that between the Swaying Stone and the Trembling Spur'.[10] As Rebellato has argued, the force of such critical perceptions ensured that in most assessments of modern British drama, 1956 is 'year zero', and time seems to flow both forward and backwards from it'.[11] The reception of Osborne's play was such as to associate the received social anger, colloquial vehemence and contemporary focus of that play and its immediate successors with the emergence of a definitive dramatic modernity. It was also to align those dramatists on the other side of that 'gulf' with both a 'pre-modern' aesthetic and an out-dated, blinkered resistance to inevitable social change. David Pattie identifies an essential fault-line, with the popular, successful dramas of Eliot and Fry, Rattigan and the West End on one side, and 'on the other, the Royal Court generation – the radical, impatient, questioning, and clear-eyed anatomists of post-war Britain'.[12] The consequence of such readings was – and continues to be – the relegation of both verse drama and its oft-assumed adversaries, the middle-class drawing-room play and the popular musical, to a position of inauthenticity.

This presumed inauthenticity was both social and aesthetic. The much-mythologized radicalism and questioning of the 'Royal Court generation' was marked by its association with a youthful frustration and impatience, with the angry awareness of a post-war generation traduced by its elders into an artificial 'myth of British coherence'.[13] Nowhere, perhaps, was this anger more articulate than in its reaction (at times implicit, at times explicit) against an establishment that was as much cultural as it was social or political. Osborne's Jimmy Porter rants against the Sunday papers, with their 'different books – same reviews'.[14] The stagnancy of that critical discourse, Osborne and his protagonist suggest, is the marker of a generation and class still in thrall to hierarchies and still bent on making readers 'feel ignorant' in order to bolster their own position.[15] Osborne's play is by no means unique in this regard, and the work of those 'angry young men' who despised that very title is characterized by a persistent challenging of established elites, those whom Kenneth Allsop identified in 1958 as the Cyril Connolly generation, 'sad synthetics', 'culture disc-jockeys of the Thirties and Forties … collective-farm fetishists with their etiolated sensitivities and their penthouse patter' who represented in their 'exhaustion and inbreeding' the 'fag-end of a cultural period'.[16]

In this context, some of the most recognized recent representatives of verse drama were easy targets: many had attended Oxford or Cambridge; many had published and broadcast about poetry, drama and aesthetics in literary journals, on the BBC Third Programme and in invited university lectures.[17] Eliot was an established public intellectual and poet; in 1956, Auden became Oxford Professor of Poetry; two years before, Spender had become Elliston

Chair of Poetry. No matter the declared (and differing) politics of these artists, this established cultural status served to align them and their chosen dramatic idiom with the intellectual elite against which the angrily realist, self-consciously young 'revolution' was so swiftly entrenched. Furthermore, in those years, poetry itself – particularly the structured, often highly allusive poetry of Eliot and Auden – had come to occupy an increasingly rarefied position within contemporary valuations of national culture.[18] In this context, prose – particularly as manifest in the emphatically colloquial expressions of the Royal Court 'generation' – was not only more realist, but it was also more populist, direct, honest and contemporary. As Sean O'Brien notes, by mid-century at the latest, the assumption came to be that 'if the common man and the working classes were to be heard, it would happen in prose'.[19] Years later, histories of the modern British theatre continue to reinforce a critical commonplace that the verse drama of the mid-century, despite its manifest popular success, spoke only to 'academically elite audiences'.[20]

Equally elite, it would seem, was the very prioritization of theatre as art – particularly as a 'poetic', non-realist art. In 1955, Devine (also an Oxford graduate) wrote to the Earl of Harewood. Asking Harewood not to share the correspondence with Duncan, Devine asserted that it 'will be important to show the kind of thing [the ESC is] after': 'The so-called highbrow public now seeks a new form of nostalgia in the "new intellectual theatre theatrical" (Betti, Beckett, Eliot, Fry, Whiting). We have to drive beyond this point to keep going.'[21] Devine identifies the drama promoted by Eliot, Duncan and Fry as marked by its social exclusivity, by its necessarily nostalgic, outmoded appeal to a cadre inherently at odds with the more authentic definition of national audience being formulated at the Court. Characterized by intellectual ideas rather than social convictions, by a resistance to naturalism, by a taste for verse and by an emphasis on poetry as a totalizing theatrical ideal, that drama could only ensure 'phoney "poetry"; phoney "theatrical situations"; turgid wallowings in the mud of the "poetic soul"'.[22] As Roberts observes, 'Duncan's notion of theatre was thus comprehensively destroyed before the ESC gave its first performance.'[23]

It is telling that Devine does not just include Eliot and Fry (and Duncan) within his critique: he aligns their sensibilities with an implicitly foreign aesthetic embodied by Beckett (whose *Waiting for Godot* had been translated into English that year) and Ugo Betti. With the potential exception of Beckett, none of these playwrights occupied a highbrow position in London at the time; most were popular.[24] By the early 1950s, Jean Anouilh had been established as 'probably the most successful playwright in Britain': close behind were Jean Giraudoux, Jean Genet, Eugène Ionesco, Obey and Betti.[25] This success had been aided and abetted by some of the most prominent verse dramatists of the time. In 1950, Fry translated Jean Anouilh's *L'Invitation au Château* as *Ring Around the Moon* for production by Peter Brook – who would himself eventually decamp to France. He had also translated Anouilh's *l'Alouette* as *The Lark* (1944) and adapted Jean Giraudoux's *La guerre de Troie n'aura pas lieu* (as *Tiger at the Gates*, 1955), *Pour Lucrèce* (as *Duel of Angels*, 1955) and *Judith*, in 1962. Duncan had translated two Cocteau plays; ten years later, he translated Giraudoux's *L'Apollon de Bellac*. *The Rape of Lucretia* was a translation of Obey's *Le Viol de Lucrèce*, and in 1972, he also translated Sartre's adaptation of Euripides' *The Trojan Women* (1972).

Rather than representing a distinct sensibility, the work of these French dramatists was diverse, unified primarily by the anti-realism of its subject or style. It also complemented a developing English interest in the experimental theatre and staging traditions of leading European companies. Where the recognition of expressionist theatre, Brecht and surrealism had hitherto been restricted to stage societies, club theatres and repertory theatres, the post-war decades saw these manifestations of European theatrical modernism emerge belatedly onto a more mainstream platform, primarily through touring productions.[26] Many of these techniques – some of them pointing to the reciprocal influence of Craig – would prove a seminal influence on the theatre of the Joan Littlewood Workshop and the productions of Brook.[27] They would also, however, help to enforce a distinct, implicitly foreign emphasis on drama as *theatre* that could prove disconcerting to the promoters of an indigenous contemporary tradition.

Notwithstanding the overt theatricality of such Royal Court dramatists as Ann Jellicoe and John Arden, the first years of the Royal Court saw a retrenchment of what Claire Armistead has identified as a 'traditional textual patriotism' in English theatre, an instinct immediately enforced by the ESC's self-advertised remit to promote contemporary *writers*.[28] Again, the legacy of that moment (in many respects merely a retrenchment) is suggested by the contemporary assumption of Sierz that 'What characterizes British theatre during its golden age of creativity . . . is not its actors, nor its directors, nor its theorists, but its writers': 'the writer defines the Britishness of British theatre.'[29] As Harvie notes, such assertions can invoke literary pedigree to 'defend [the] sovereignty [of British theatre] from other national theatre practices and traditions.'[30] Rebellato identifies a similar instinct in the rhetorical repatriation of Brecht that occurred within the theatre culture of the 1950s.[31] He also notes the swift revisionism that has characterized the writing of the history of the Royal Court – a revisionism aided in no small measure by some of its founding members. While the early press releases for the Court 'give equal weight to its interest in presenting new British and European work', the ESC would 'soon be written about as if it had only ever been interested in domestic writing'.[32]

In *Look Back in Anger*, Jimmy Porter excoriates the cultural establishment both for its confined social insularity and for the foreignness of its cultural tastes: 'I've just read three whole columns on the English Novel. Half of it's in French. Do the Sunday papers make *you* feel ignorant?'[33] For Porter (and implicitly Osborne), this reliance on 'foreign' models disguises a fundamental national absence. It also fails to recognize an urgent imperative to formulate a contemporary cultural identity in the face of a waning Empire, American cultural imperialism, and larger social and political change:

> The old Edwardian brigade do make their brief little world look pretty tempting.... Phoney too, of course.... Still, even I regret it somehow, phoney or not. If you've no world of your own, it's rather pleasant to regret the passing of someone else's. I must be getting sentimental. But I must say it's pretty dreary living in the American Age—unless you're an American of course. Perhaps all our children will be Americans. That's a thought isn't it?[34]

As further reinforced in Osborne's *The Entertainer* (1957), the phoniness of 'the old Edwardian brigade' is more to be eulogized than rejected, its ability to enforce a confident, if not triumphalist, ideal of national identity ideally to be revived and translated into a contemporary cultural and political idiom. These sentiments reflect a general, oft-cited anxiety about the encroachment of American mass culture on a post-war Britain. They also associate Continental influence with an equally invasive presence and inherent inauthenticity. As reinforced by the Artistic Committee of the ESC and the declarations of Devine, that foreignness was marked by a theatre that had embraced symbolism, allusion, poetry – and theatricality itself.

By 1956, therefore, the majority of English verse dramatists had proven themselves emphatically on the wrong side of any theatrical defence of the realm, often in very different ways. Despite the emergence of a revolutionary theatre focused on the centrality of the writer as dramatist, verse drama could not define 'the Britishness of the British theatre'. The metaphysical themes and drawing-room settings of Eliot's popular post-war plays immediately discounted their participation within the new drama. So too did the overt poetry, historical settings and ebullient optimism of Fry – not to mention the religious and thus implicitly preachy focus of Ridler or Nicholson. While Eliot and Duncan focused increasingly on adapting their verse to contemporary spoken idioms and dramatic form, they did so to effect a drama that eschewed the very political, social specificity that came to be associated with the most celebrated plays of the Royal Court. Equally problematic was the enthusiasm of many of these verse dramatists for Continental theatre, and particularly for its manifestation of a more intermedial, interdisciplinary ideal. In 1946, Bentley's *The Playwright as Thinker* had noted Yeats's inability to unite poetic drama with dance and music, attributing that failure less to the plays than to the cultural environment in which he had attempted to work:

> Had he lived in Paris or Vienna he might have come up against composers and choreographers who would have been colleagues in a great enterprise. The fact that he lived in Great Britain was a limitation. It was probably the ultimate limitation.[35]

As manifest in the collaborations between Auden and Britten and in the projects of Britten and Duncan thereafter, England had afforded some climate for intermedial, interdisciplinary explorations. With the brief exception of *This Way to the Tomb*, however, it had tended to do so at a certain remove from the mainstream spoken stage.

Duncan's angry retrospective does not just condemn the prevailing naturalism of this 'New Establishment in Sloane Square', what Coward similarly identified as a new 'intelligentsia'[36]: it contrasts that exclusionary aesthetic with a more vital artistic culture. The ESC had aimed initially to 'encourage the theatre of imagination and poetry as against the theatre which predominates today'.[37] This culture exists in Europe – and it is signified not exclusively by the use of verse, but by its open and interdisciplinary embrace of theatricality: 'It is too much to hope that we can find the equivalent of a Diaghilev', someone who could 'put a Cocteau in touch with a Stravinsky. But it is not too much [to] hope that we could find somebody who is aware of contemporary trends in art.'[38] In the emergent definition of new drama that defined and now enshrines the achievements of the Court and its established representatives, such complaints would fall on relatively deaf ears. They would also mark the effective end of the concerted, if diffuse, movement towards a modern tradition of drama in verse that had characterized the first half of the twentieth century.

Aftermath and legacies

Since the 1960s, the primary dramatic manifestation of verse has been as one element within a larger socially critical or political drama, deployed variously as a mode through which to achieve stylistic contrast, to emphasize particular themes or characterizations, or to assert a more Brechtian effect of alienation. Many playwrights (Bond, John McGrath) have aligned verse with popular song: at times, that technique resonates with earlier dramatic forms (medieval, Elizabethan), while at others it invites comparison with the instincts of Auden and Isherwood (themselves influenced by Brecht, cabaret, music-hall, jazz, agit-prop and collaboration with Britten).[39] It also suggests the influence of the collaborative productions of the Joan Littlewood Workshop, rooted as much in an ideal of popular tradition and communal creativity as the Brechtian aesthetic with which they become more prominently (and at times erroneously) associated. Notwithstanding the use of verse in these productions and plays, the informing creative impetus for that verse – unlike that which characterized the poetic drama of the Group Theatre – does not tend to originate from a conventional poetic tradition, let alone a recognized heritage of verse drama.

Like the most acclaimed theatre of the ESC, much of this drama has been openly political. It has also, however, been anti-naturalist and anti-realist – a fact that has at times been enough to ensure its association with an even more radical – and thus 'fringe' – theatre. In 1969, Jane Arden's *Vagina Rex and the Gas Oven* made prominent use of this assumption (and the abolition of censorship) at the Arts Lab in a work that aligned itself with the growing Women's Liberation Movement. In its embrace of theatricality (vaudevillian song, strobe lights, Furies cast as people of the streets), multimedia (film, radio, slideshow) and sung and spoken verse, the play also provided an implicit riposte to the primarily male-centred, naturalist presentation of social anger that could often characterize the most acclaimed political theatre at the Royal Court.

Arden's play positions the psyche of 'Woman' as contemporary archetype against the equally archetypal 'Man' and the controlling, patriarchal modes of social representation that dominate contemporary life and society. Central to the play is the Woman's assertion that 'We have no language. The words of women have yet to be written': 'We must destroy the language.'[40] Micheline Wandor sees Arden as appealing 'to Greek mythology as if she has to turn away from contemporary society to find metaphors for issues she cannot yet name clearly'.[41] Ultimately, however, the play appeals less to Greek mythology than to alternative theatrical modes – verse, song and dance – as a means to destroy the language that continues to oppress, control and dominate. In so doing, it aligns itself (doubtless inadvertently) with the aims of those verse dramatists who saw in the social realism and argumentation of the 'progressive' contemporary theatre a fundamental indifference to a more essential and urgent reality. Unlike those verse dramatists, however, Arden's play insists on aligning that theatrical and verse aesthetic with a focus that is also unequivocally political and argumentative.

Not all of the plays at the Royal Court in the 1950s were exclusively naturalist, and not all were as propagandist as Duncan's objections might suggest. Prominent amongst these exceptions were the plays of John Arden, whose conspicuously non-realist, historical and ideologically ambiguous *Serjeant Musgrave's Dance* (1959) is now central to many contemporary mythologizations of the revolution effected by the Court.[42] At the time, however – and despite his swift promotion to manuscript reader at the ESC – Arden's relationship with the new 'intelligentsia' promoted by the Court was ambivalent at best. *The Waters of Babylon* (1957) was given one unfortunate Sunday-night production at the Court; the seventeen-scene, episodic *Live Like Pigs* (1958), his most naturalistic drama, ran for twenty-three performances and to mixed reviews. With the exception of *The Workhouse Donkey* (1963; commissioned by the Court but ultimately performed at Chichester) and the relatively notorious *The Island of the Mighty* (1972), which saw its authors picketing the Royal Shakespeare Company production,[43] the majority of Arden and Arden/Margaretta D'Arcy plays were composed for and performed away from the mainstage London theatre. The later plays were almost all written for community theatre. Indeed, while Arden is often invoked in passing identifications of the 'New Wave' of drama at the time, he can be more accurately positioned as one of the most prominent representatives of a self-consciously resistant and self-consciously poetic radicalism in the theatre of the late 1950s and subsequent decades.

Poetic radicalism and the people: John Arden and Margaretta D'Arcy

In 1960, Arden declared in *New Theatre Magazine*: 'People must want to come to the theatre because of the artificiality, not despite it. . . . I am pleading for the revival of the Poetic Drama.'[44] This theatre is not a Theatre of Beauty, but rather of the 'Dionysian' life of society itself: in his introductory note to

The Workhouse Donkey, Arden imagines an ideal production lasting 'six or seven or thirteen hours', allowing audience-members to come and go within a 'casual or promconcert conception'.[45] Informing these ideals – like the instincts that motivated Masefield and Bottomley decades before – is Arden's appreciation of theatre as the organic manifestation, representation and expression of communal identity. For Arden, that community cannot be idealized, nor can it be fixed within uniform modes of representation or a consistent, authorial imposition of political perspective. Any such instincts traduce the essential function of a 'Vital Theatre' that 'consists of plays which must be organic events – to get hold of their audiences by laughter, by pain, by music, dancing, poetry, visual excitement, rhythm'.[46] The language of this theatre is innate, rooted in history and legend, in a past and present disseminated through English poetry and popular traditions: 'What I am deeply concerned with is the problem of translating the concrete life of today into terms of poetry that shall at the one time both illustrate that life and set it within the historical and legendary tradition of our culture'.[47]

Where Yeats invoked oral traditions and legends, Arden argues that 'the bedrock of English poetry is the ballad'; like Masefield, he identifies storytelling and the communal experience of that storytelling as essential to poetry and to theatre.[48] He cites Chaucer, Shakespeare, Jonson and Brecht as poets who 'have known, almost as an unnoticed background to their lives, the enormous stock of traditional poetry, some of it oral, some of it printed and hawked at street-corners, some of it sung from the stages of the music-halls'.[49] This reading is both aesthetic and political: 'seen through the eyes of the sort of writers I have mentioned, the English prove to be an extraordinarily passionate people, as violent as they are amorous, and quite astonishingly hostile to good government and order'.[50] Arden's dramas – both single-authored and with D'Arcy – are similarly diverse in their theme, style and subject, their most prominent unifying characteristic being an emphasis on the relationship between historical representation and contemporary experience, popular expression and communal identity, and the role of the authoring collective in society and in theatre. This latter conviction – and its relationship to the subject, cultural position and structure of the ballad – was represented most prominently in plays that often entailed large casts, that tended to be structured episodically and that used song, verse and prose as a means to present the variety of experience and expression that confounds a single, authorial representation. Rather than manifesting a nationalist celebration of essential Englishness, Arden identifies in this re-invocation, revivification and dramatic return of the ballad form a fundamental, unifying link with other cultures: 'Other countries have similar traditions, so without deliberately straining for it, the effect of the poetry *becomes* universal.'[51]

Nowhere, perhaps, are these convictions more thoroughly assembled than in the Arthurian play that Arden had been working on since the 1950s and that was developed with D'Arcy into the epic – and epic controversy – *The Island of the Mighty*, eventually staged by the Royal Shakespeare Company (RSC). In 1955, Arden had submitted a version to Devine that already incorporated some of his key political and cultural themes, and whose language was a characteristic mixture of prose and verse. Variously responding to and developing the Arthurian scholarship of R.G. Collingwood and Robert Graves, Arden focused on the implications of invasion and 'civilization' to more established traditions of expression and belief. (He and D'Arcy would later expand this theme in relation to Britain's imperialist position in India by incorporating strong elements of Indian folk theatre into the play.) He also developed a critique of military endeavour through the representation of squabbling rival British generals. Notwithstanding the clear resonance between the play's themes and the imperial and domestic politics of the time, the play's perceived idiom was such as to ensure its rejection by the Royal Court. Arden later discovered the assessment of the reader: 'boring historical play written in phoney verse'.[52]

To the extent that Arden openly aligned his theatrical ideal with a pre-existing poetic form and tradition, to the extent that his verse was intended to elicit more than a disruption of dramatic mode – and to the extent that his 'verse' drama was rejected by the Royal Court – his plays suggest a certain affinity with modern verse drama. Although many of Arden's plays manifest a clear engagement with Brecht (he once declared that *Mother Courage* was the twentieth-century play he would most like to have written),[53] they differ in their dramatic valuation of both verse and song. For Arden, rather than serving an alienation effect, verse heightens expression:

> In a play, the dialogue can be naturalistic and 'plotty' as long as the basic poetic issue has been crystallized. But when this point is reached, then the language becomes formal (if you like in verse or sung), the visual pattern coalesces into a vital image that is one of the nerve-centres of the play.[54]

Arden and D'Arcy distinguish between their use of song, which attempts to 'draw on collective experience', and verse, which presents 'the character talking as a rule'.[55] For Arden, such effects ensure that the theatre does not just employ poetry, but that it *is* poetry: playwriting can be thought of 'as an offshoot of poetry. I think it is all part of the same craft'.[56] As early as 1963, Irving Wardle acclaimed Arden as 'the first writer of the post-Fry generation to succeed in restoring verse to the stage, and the first to have assimilated Brechtian method into a style that is entirely his own'.[57]

The verse in much agitprop theatre and in the productions at Stratford East tended towards the simplistic, the didactic or doggerel. Many of Arden's plays, however, contain passages in what Trussler identifies as a 'whimsical, house-arrested free verse',[58] and the very variety of his verse points to Arden's extensive engagement with poetic tradition and convention.[59] (One of his earliest schoolboy attempts at drama had been a verse play based on the death of Hitler, written 'in the style' of *Sweeney Agonistes*.) Throughout his career, however, Arden's definition of poetic drama never acknowledged its potential to exist *as* verse drama. Doubtless the closest that Arden and D'Arcy came to writing a complete verse play was *Friday's Hiding* (1965). Commissioned by the Glasgow Citizens' Theatre as a play without words, the work contains minimal dialogue and consists primarily of stage directions in a lively, idiom-inflected blank verse, the effect of which is to establish rhythm of action, mood and setting:

> They grab him up, he slumps under,
> they hoick his feet, his arms hang heavy,
> they stoop and lift his head, they shake it and it lolls.
>> Good God have they murdered him?
>> It looks damn well like it.[60]

The effect is also, of course, to suggest the populist tone, rhythmic regularity and narrative incident that characterizes the ballad form:

> Of course the man's not dead at all,
> (this is a comedy)
> and after a while he lifts back the cloth
> peeps out, sits up. They're all at their tea.[61]

Subtitled 'An Experiment in the Laconic', *Friday's Hiding* is less a verse drama than it is a dramatization of its own attempt to direct the *translation* of the verse ballad into the voices, physical movement and collaborative energies that define the theatrical stage.

Unlike the poet-dramatists who preceded him, Arden identified verse as but one of many modes through which to achieve the re-invigoration, through theatre, of the informing vitality of the English ballad. Indeed, as early as 1961, he doubted that it was now possible for anyone 'to write satisfactory plays in verse from beginning to end'.[62] Central to that doubt was his consistent resistance to the individual, authoring presence of the theatrical poet. Where Eliot, Duncan and Fry could aim towards a uniformity of rhythm and idiom, for Arden any such stylistic regularity risked traducing the political and social imperative of theatre, which was to reintegrate the expression of the poet with that of the people. Eliot aimed to appeal to a heterogenous audience to some extent by hiding beneath mainstream dramatic forms in order to coerce them into a recognition of poetry. Auden's manipulation of popular and traditional forms comes much closer to the politics and aesthetics of Arden and D'Arcy. The very showmanship of that manipulation in the Auden-Isherwood plays, however, tends to call attention to the presiding authorial role and perspective of the dramatists. In Arden's dramas, the individual (and the individual poet-dramatist) is at his or her most authentic as a manifestation of the community, and both the language and the thematic focus of that drama must derive not from the poet, but from a collaborative theatrical ethos and from the organic expressions and traditions of an informing communal reality.

In *The Island of the Mighty*, the character of Arthur himself is set against the vital theatrical background and expressivity of the peasants such that he is neither a tragic nor a focal hero. Much more central to the play is the contrast established between three poet figures. Taliesen is Arthur's official poet and Aneurin a 'vagrant ballad-singer possessed of a certain secret poetic lore'.[63] In his notes to the play, Arden aligns Merlin with 'the liberal intellectual who no longer knows what is liberality and what is tyranny, who is unable to draw a distinction between poetic ambiguity and political dishonesty'– and who in many respects mirrors some of Arden's central concerns (shared with Auden) about the potential tension between individual creativity, social identity and political statement.[64] Towards the end of the play, Merlin fails to act when called upon and goes mad, retreating into the woods. The play ends with his death: in a confirmation of Aneurin's pronouncement to the audience that 'The poet without the people is nothing. The people without the poet will still be the people,' Merlin is drawn out of the woods into innocent, human interaction with a Cowman's Wife: 'I am welcome at last for the man that I am / And neither for craft nor art!'[65] This state of happiness cannot last, however, and he is killed soon afterwards by her jealous husband.

The play concludes not with a final eulogy to a great poet (or to Arthur), but rather with a dramatic validation of the role of the poet as that of the anonymous, integrated, voice of the people. Aneurin's closing song tells the tale of Lazarus who, risen from the dead, condemns those who are alive for having put 'Two thousand or three / Of stinking corpses / Just like me' into the earth before allowing them first truly to live.[66] Rather than celebrating the miracle of one man's rebirth (let alone the presence of God), the play ends with an expression of collective anger and strength, and with a reinforcement of the essential role of the people's poet, the 'vagrant ballad-singer' with a 'certain poetic lore'. In the context of the play and in keeping with the politics of 'radical' theatre at the time, that role is to articulate an anger that is not entirely dissimilar to that voiced within a much more naturalist idiom by Arden's more 'conventional' peers:

> We are going to come back
> And we are going to take hold
> So hideous and bloody greedy
> We take hold of the whole world![67]

In keeping with much radical political theatre at the time, Arden rejected both the authorial supremacy of the writer and the very idea of a coherent, consistent drama entirely in verse *or* prose. Within this collaborative ideal of theatre as communal tradition, the 'craft' and 'art' of the dramatist must derive from and reflect the collaborative energies and traditions of the community. As Auden had acknowledged decades before, that social conviction necessarily entailed a certain suppression of the individual and literary expressivity of the poet. Where Auden eventually turned away from verse drama to embrace the opera-house and the published page, Arden and D'Arcy would retreat from the professional theatre in an attempt to root their 'poetic' drama ever more organically within the community from which it derived.

Any association of Arden with a preceding generation of verse dramatists is thus tenuous at best. The plays of Arden and D'Arcy stand relatively alone in their persistence with an ideal of *poetry* in drama, a poetry to be manifest in the theatricality of drama and in the variety and expression of their verse. This ideal is nonetheless at a considerable remove from that promoted by the representative generation of verse dramatists that had preceded them. Rather than disappearing entirely, however, the legacy of that earlier modern tradition of verse drama can be traced, if somewhat tangentially, to a rather unlikely quarter.

A new stage: Michael Tippett and English verse drama

In 1959, the composer Michael Tippett identified verse drama, 'the theatre of Auden, Eliot and Fry', as a vital tradition for the formulation of a contemporary opera in England.[68] He writes of opera and drama within a shared continuum, 'from the Camerata in Florence to the time when verse-drama returned in English theatre, through figures like Christopher Fry, W.H. Auden and T.S. Eliot'.[69] As suggested by the collaborations between such prominent writers as Auden, Duncan, Forster and Christopher Hassall and such leading composers as Britten and Walton, by the middle of the twentieth century, opera in England had become a key site for intermedial exploration. Rather than replicating the traditional role of the librettist as craftsman and of the composer as author, many of these works – from the Britten-Forster-Eric Crozier *Billy Budd* (1951) to the Christopher Hassall-William Walton *Troilus and Cressida* (1954) – redefined and developed the traditional hierarchies within music-drama itself.[70]

Within this cultural environment, Eliot was considered a strong candidate for similar ventures. Collaborations with Britten, Tippett and Stravinsky were suggested; more unique was the approach of theatre impresario C.B. Cochran with the idea that Eliot, Duncan and Britten together compose a musical revue.[71] The invitation alone reveals the extent to which traditional divisions between the revue, the opera and verse drama had been challenged by the various projects of these three artists. It also suggests the perception of a distinct creative role for the literary artist within musico-dramatic forms traditionally deemed the sole domain of the composer or subservient lyricist. Eliot consistently resisted these approaches, generally by pleading insufficient expertise or time. An experienced perception of tensions between distinct artistic languages and creative instincts may well have informed Eliot's decision (as recounted by the impresario Lincoln Kirstein) to contemplate a ballet version of *Sweeney Agonistes* with Stravinsky – but 'without any spoken words'.[72]

That Eliot was a vital influence on this culture of intermedial exploration can nonetheless be argued by citing contemporary readings of the musical and dramatic qualities of his poetry, his support of modern music and modern opera at Faber and Faber, his reiterated enthusiasm for modern ballet, and his promotion in criticism of an analogous relationship between musical expression and a dramatic ideal. An even more immediately evident and yet more curious influence is to be found in Eliot's interactions with Tippett. Although the collaborative relationship between the two artists was always restricted to one of consultation, on numerous occasions Tippett was to identify Eliot as his 'spiritual and artistic mentor'.[73] Already well-read in Eliot's poetry and drama, Tippett initially approached Eliot to write the libretto for his oratorio *A Child of Our Time* (1939–41). Eliot eventually recommended that the composer write the words himself, 'as any words [Eliot] might write would be of such greater *poetic* quality, they would "stick out a mile" and impede the music'.[74] Tippett wrote his own libretti thereafter, consulting frequently with Eliot about their setting and dramatic viability.[75]

As recounted by Tippett, this mentorship was characterized by Eliot's insistence on the conventional subjugation of poetry in opera, on the inevitable conflict between a poet's art and the role of music in opera and oratorio: 'Guided by Eliot . . . I took the view that whatever words I had, the music I wrote would swallow up their intrinsic poetry: if I took the words of a fully-fledged poet or dramatist, there would be conflict'.[76] Eliot 'suggested a *schema*' to Tippett through which to understand the 'relationships that are possible between the various ingredients in opera and drama':

> Suppose (he said) we imagine that there are three genres of action upon a stage: the stage-play as such, the ballet and opera. There are three expressive ingredients that belong in each of these three genres: the drama proper – the story, that is, or dramatic action – gesture, and music. In each genre, these three means of expression are in a certain hierarchy. . . . In opera, music is on top, the story is second and gesture third.[77]

These appraisals of the dynamics within stage-drama, ballet and opera reinforce Eliot's reading of the autonomous language and expressive role of different arts. They also reinforce his own suspicion, as a poet and poet-dramatist, of any movement towards music-drama, which he identifies as a distinct dramatic art. According to Tippett, however, Eliot was 'above all others' in having helped him to 'clarify [his] notions of the aesthetics of theatre and opera': 'Sometimes he even guided my reading'.[78] This reading included the work of Suzanne K. Langer, whose philosophy Tippett cites as essential to his (and Eliot's) understanding of the role of the literary artist in opera:

> 'Every work of art has its being in only one order of art . . .' So that, while drama eats up all incidental music and painted stage sets, 'music' in Miss Langer's words, 'ordinarily swallows words and action creating (thereby) opera, oratorio, or song.'[79]

Eliot's influence may well have encouraged Tippett into this relatively conventional assumption of the secondary role of the poet in opera. It also, however, encouraged him to assume the mantle of libretto-writing himself – and in so doing to assume a totalizing creative role.

Auden seems to have embraced opera for its implicit encouragement of an unbridled poetic expressivity that would be safely subsumed on stage within the larger authorship of the composer. Tippett's response was not to write the serviceable libretti conventionally expected of opera. Instead, he seems self-consciously to have attempted a literary project within those libretti in order to emulate the philosophical and poetic accomplishment of contemporary drama in verse. Indeed, at times, his reiteration of that project goes so far as to suggest 'an apparent indifference about music as an innovative, vital, and dramatic participant in opera.'[80] Where the collaborations between Britten, Duncan, Auden, Forster and Stravinsky often moved to redefine the dramatic aesthetic of contemporary music-drama through intermedial collaboration, Tippett's originality can be more easily identified 'in his rhetorical reinvention of the role of the opera composer as that of the literary intellectual.'[81] For Tippett, this role was not analogous to but in fact the very *same* as that represented in contemporary verse drama. Tippett identifies his indebtedness to Eliot in the poet's assertions about the dominance of musical effect in opera. As his statements about drama and opera suggest, however, that indebtedness is more evident in his acceptance of Eliot's rhetorical idealization of verse drama in *figurative* terms, where drama achieves a 'musicality' less through sound than through the literary and intellectual strength of its poetry.

Central to Tippett's dramaturgy is a literary libretto whose words will naturally generate a musical setting. In a letter to Ernest Newman in 1946, Tippett notes that in writing *A Child of Our Time* he had 'found with pleasure that the rhythms of the words [he] had invented were specially suitable to the music.'[82] In terms not entirely dissimilar from those of Bottomley in describing the composition of *King Lear's Wife*, he writes, 'I had the music unconsciously there subliminally when "discharging", as it happened, the word pattern.'[83] Now embarking upon what was to become *The Midsummer Marriage* (1955), he fears 'the greater degree of purely literary imaginative resource required for the newer venture.'[84] By thus looking to the poetry of his own libretto as the source of both the drama and musical direction of his opera, Tippett explicitly contradicts the teachings of his mentor Eliot. He also ignores that mentorship by positioning his attempt in relation to the 'verse-drama tradition' of Eliot himself: 'echoes of [the] prosody [of Eliot and Yeats] sound in everything I have written for myself to set to music.'[85] According to Tippett, 'the opera, however much it seems to us a mainly musical experience, is always ultimately dependent on the contemporary theatre'.[86]

Rather than differentiating between that spoken theatre and opera, Tippett explicitly likens *The Midsummer Marriage* to the dramas of Auden, Eliot and Fry.[87] Eliot's verse drama – not just his correspondence – 'had the apple' in influencing his work.[88] This influence, this acknowledged dependence, is such that Tippett's own libretti are replete with references to that theatre: as Robinson notes, 'judged merely from the number of quotations from Eliot in the draft of *A Child*, Tippett had evidently studied *The Rock* and *Murder in the Cathedral*'.[89] In his operas, Tippett expands upon his sources for allusion; in *King Priam*, he cites Yeats directly, borrows Eliot's concept of the 'loop in time' from *The Family Reunion*, and specifies that his chorus sing of Dylan Thomas's 'force that through the green fuse drives the flower'. Tippett's libretti thus suggest the perpetuation of contemporary verse drama through the *literary* enthusiasms of the contemporary composer. The ultimate effect is less an aesthetic transformation than a certain subjugation of music itself to the dramatic and intellectual authority of written verse.

Tippett is relatively unique amongst English composers in his tendency to write his own libretti. As the diversity of Britten's projects and collaborations reveal, however, he is not unique in having identified a potentially vital relationship between modern opera and the creative projects of contemporary poets. More recently, this instinct has continued to be explored in mainstream contemporary English opera, which has seen collaborations between such well-known poets as Simon Armitage, Harrison and David Harsent and such prominent composers as Harrison Birtwistle, Stuart MacRae and Henze. Unlike earlier poet-librettists, very few of these poets have engaged in theorizing a lasting and formative relationship between poetry and music in relation to the contemporary stage. In the very fact of their operatic collaboration, however, they can nonetheless be seen as perpetuating – however unconsciously – a similar lineage to that initially explored by Britten, Auden, Duncan and Tippett, between 'the Camerata in Florence to the time when verse-drama returned in English theatre.'

CHAPTER 8
TRADITION AND TRAJECTORY: VERSE AND DRAMATIC HERITAGE IN CARYL CHURCHILL, STEVEN BERKOFF AND TONY HARRISON

The roots of the first modern movement in verse drama can be traced variously (and sometimes simultaneously) through late nineteenth-century extensions of poetic Romanticism to a self-consciously reforming culture of poetic and dramatic creativity. That movement also encouraged a strong social emphasis on popular community and expression, often relating that communal aesthetic to the 'rediscovery' of Greek, medieval and Renaissance drama in contemporary staging practices and writing. Equally significant, as we have seen, was the emergence of a modern religious drama whose invocation of contemporary spiritual experience could resonate with less specific ambitions to 'connect' beyond the surfaces of lived social experience. Far from representing a school of dramatic composition or a coherent genre, the primary exponents of a modern verse drama in these first decades typically embraced a variety of themes, subjects and appreciations of theatre – not to mention a diversity of approaches towards versification itself.

This diversity has continued to characterize more recent verse drama, from the work of Caryl Churchill through to that of Ted Hughes, Steven Berkoff, Tony Harrison and Mike Bartlett. Nonetheless, as recent receptions only begin to suggest, the presiding critical instinct has been to approach any drama written entirely in verse as inherently distinct from a more dominant, established tradition whose otherwise diverse expressions comprise a contemporary national stage. This instinct has arguably increased since 1956 to identify in verse drama a self-conscious otherness, a willed distance not merely from drama written in prose, but from what that received tradition, Gardner's 'broad church', is assumed to signify. Rather than attempting to redress that assumption, some of the most prominent verse dramas in recent decades have actively engaged with that reputation, to very different ends.

Serious Money: Caryl Churchill's city comedy in verse

Unlike the majority of verse dramas written in the last decades, Caryl Churchill's *Serious Money* (1987) was an unambiguous success. As critics have been swift to point out, the play was in fact so successful (first at the Royal Court, then in its transfer to the West End, then in its Broadway transfer the following year) that while its subject may have appealed as much to capitalist conservatives as to the Court's traditional left-wing audience, that 'pleasuring of right-wing City audiences helped to make "serious money" for left-wing theatre'.[1] Central to this 'pleasuring' of both ideological perspectives, it would seem, was the play's relative accuracy in depicting the intricacies of the contemporary financial culture that followed the Big Bang. Where the self-styled left-wing responded enthusiastically to the play's unambiguous and topical critique, the City audiences – not unlike those who responded in a similar fashion to the recent film *The Wolf of Wall Street* (2013) – seemed to respond to the very fact of their being represented in drama.

Rather than focusing her drama on character, Churchill creates an explicitly argumentative play – developed through collaborative workshop – with multiple plots, settings and characters (actors doubled roles). The structural focus of the work is the mystery of the death of Jake, a commercial paper dealer who had traded in information, and whose dealings had been the subject of a DTI (Department of Trade and Industry) investigation. That investigation, we learn, has been enabled by a tip from Frosby (played by the same actor who portrayed Jake), a 'reactionary' jobber. Frosby's disillusionment is not moral, but class-based, a traditionalist response to the new forms of money-making in the City that emerged after the deregulation of the Stock Exchange: 'I thought the sun would never set. / I thought I'd be extremely rich'.[2] Later, Frosby observes:

My lovely city's sadly changed.
Sic transit Gloria! Glory passes!
Any wonder I'm deranged,
Surrounded by the criminal classes.[3]

Rather than leaving the audience to appreciate the irony of this observation, Churchill has the gilts dealer Grimes reply:

You've all been coining it for years.
All you fuckwits in the City.

It just don't look quite so pretty,
All the cunning little jobs,
When you see them done by yobs.[4]

Although the play condemns Grimes and what he represents as much as it does Frosby, it also reinforces the truth of his observation throughout.

Heading the investigation of Jake's death is his sister Scilla, a member of the privileged classes who has turned her back on her family by choosing to work in the 'new' City as defined by 'yobs'. Rather than embracing her self-emancipation from that class, Scilla merely conforms to a new mode of repression; in working as a LIFFE (London International Financial Futures Exchange) dealer, she accepts a gendered definition of strength and power that is just as corrupt, limiting and inhumane as the background that she has abandoned. At the end of Act One, Churchill emphasizes this theme in a scene in which women traders attempt to integrate themselves within the profession by adopting the language of the men who have defined it. Reinforcing Scilla's acknowledgement that they're a 'very chauvinist bunch',[5] Brian tells Dave that he's trading 'like a cunt' – and Jill reveals that she does not call Dave 'Dick because he's got spots'; she calls him 'Spot because he's a dick'.[6] The act concludes with the characters singing the 'Futures Song', scored by punk/rock musician Ian Dury, in *unison*. In a direct celebration of corruption that would not have been out of place in *The Threepenny Opera*, they proclaim: 'I'm a Romford scholar in Eurodollars'; 'I fucked that runner she's a right little stunner so I pulled her off / the floor'.[7]

One explanation of the popularity of the play across the ideological divide is the fact that it does not stage a foil who reacts against the values of this sexist, corrupt and corrupting system. Instead, *Serious Money* relies on the convictions of the audience to provide that foil. The characters (all representative types) consistently conform to and enact the totalizing world critiqued by the play. Nowhere, perhaps, is that conformity rendered more forceful than in the presentation of Scilla's investigation of her brother's death. While the mysterious death of Jake attests to the literal dangers of a corrupt profession, so too does the eventual fate of Scilla, whose investigation becomes increasingly determined by greed rather than familial love or personal conviction. Scilla proclaims to the American arbitrageur Marylou Baines: 'I had been wondering if you killed Jake, but now I hardly care ... The main thing's to get my share': 'I'm greedy and completely amoral'.[8] Not only does Scilla have 'the cunning and connections of the middle class', but she is able to combine that empowered and corrupting lineage with a proud embrace of the fact that she is also 'tough as a yob'.[9] By the end of the play, Scilla has been named Wall Street's rising star by *Business Week*, Marylou Baines has run for president and the entire cast of characters has reunited in a rousing song that proclaims 'five more glorious years' to be defined by the gleeful indulgence enabled by unfettered money, consumption and greed.

For Churchill, the financial environment of the City acts as both the power-base and the microcosm of a ruthless capitalist and imperialist structure, of the continuing presence of a class-based social hierarchy, and of a fundamentally gendered environment built upon chauvinism and misogyny. While the play thus presents various characters, financial cultures and social structures as being in apparent opposition to each other (America/ Britain, new traders/old traders, men/women), it does so to emphasize their essential conformity to this larger, determining environment. The play excoriates the cliquish, class-orientated practices of the old guard for their social snobbery and xenophobia, while the equally cliquish, more openly ruthless practices of the new are condemned for their crassness, blatant misogyny and Americanization. The influence of these practices extends beyond the 'old' colonial power of Britain and the 'new' dominance of America. Through the figure of Jacinta, Churchill presents the colonizing influence of a capitalist system in which a Peruvian businesswoman abandons the concerns of her own country to make money in London: 'I do not want to help, I want to be rich, I close my mines and sell my copper on the London Metal Exchange.'[10] In a characteristically explanatory passage, Churchill has Jacinta detail her motivation:

> It is all because of the debt that will never be paid because we have to borrow more and more to pay the interest on the money that came from oil when OPEC had too much money and your western banks wanted to lend it to us because who else would pay such high interest, needing it so badly?[11]

Serious Money is thus unambiguously didactic, its polemical tendencies tempered primarily by the energy of its execution – and its use of verse. The play begins with a brief prologue that re-enacts a scene from Thomas Shadwell's posthumous *The Volunteers, or The Stockjobbers* (1692). For Aston, this 'imaging of late-seventeenth-century trading among the mercantile classes ... provides a historical example which underscores Churchill's critique of capitalism'.[12] It also suggests the influence of Brecht, whose 1928 adaptation of *The Beggar's Opera* as *The Threepenny Opera* invited a similar critique of contemporary ruthlessness and social amorality. Churchill's drama, however, is superficially more realist in its presentation, relatively linear in its narrative, and (notwithstanding its punctuating use of song at the end of its acts) generally uniform in its aesthetic. The allusion to Shadwell's play at the beginning of *Serious Money* does much more than provide a 'historical example' of the rampant corruption of the country's financial system or suggest material ripe for contemporary re-dramatization. The effect of that initial presentation is to establish a satirical tone both within and *towards* the drama to come. Both plays are city comedies and both focus their satire on contemporary society. Only *Serious Money*, however, ironizes its own aesthetic idiom in order to establish that satirical emphasis.

According to Churchill herself, the play originated with its subject: for weeks, she had immersed herself in research about the City to provide material for a workshop with the Royal Court and director Max Stafford-Clark. She continued to research material thereafter, 'and only finally got a purchase on the material when [she] decided to write the play in verse'.[13] Unlike those earlier poets who identified drama in verse as an essential mode for the representation of 'truth' and larger realities, Churchill identifies verse primarily as a means through which to order and present her factual material as dramatic. In *Serious Money*, that transformation is established through the presentation of a tone and argument about that factual material, which it otherwise fictionalizes through representative types enacting representatively corrupt scenarios. Ultimately, Churchill's play actively presents verse as an essentially outdated mode of dramatic expression in order to effect this comic, satirical emphasis.

That reading is particularly exploited in the play's frequent use of rhyming couplets, a form of dramatic verse whose associations with serious dramatic expression had been virtually extinguished by the end of the eighteenth century. It is also reinforced in the play's exploitation of the anachronistic qualities of that verse for humorous effect, primarily through the use of contemporary colloquialisms and deliberately awkward rhymes. In one instance, for example, Jake observes:

Bob Geldof was a silly cunt.
He did his charity back to front.
They should have had the concerts in Zaire
And shipped the money to banks over here.[14]

The management of the verse within the play tends to vary; in some exchanges, characters finish each other's rhymes, while in others they are given to more lengthy cogitations. Not all of the verse is rhyming, and not all of it is in couplet form. The primary effect of that variety is to establish and vary pace and to reinforce the satirical potential of verse by calling perpetual attention to its presence. It is not, however, to differentiate its speakers as characters – let alone to suggest the development of a contemporary mode of dramatic expression. *Serious Money* does not confine its satirical focus to the financial world; its opening reference to Shadwell and its comical presentation of rhyming verse establish a similarly satirical tone towards earlier modes of dramatic expression. The play actively establishes a distance between that verse aesthetic and its own contemporary subjects and themes, and in so doing implies the anachronistic, outdated nature of verse drama as a whole.

Nowhere, perhaps, is that conviction more thematically enforced than in the play's hunting scene, which satirizes the familiar, empty conventions of the established 'ruling class' by dramatizing those conventions within regular, rhythmic exchanges and repeated lines:

Greville
> Good morning
Major
> > Good morning
Greville
> > > Good morning
Mrs Carruthers
> > > > Hello
Greville
> Good morning
Lady Vere
> Good morning
Greville
> > > I don't think you know Mr Zackerman
> here, my colleague and guest
Mrs Carruthers
The hound that I walked goes up front with the best.[15]

Throughout that scene, Mrs Carruthers repeats (of her horse), 'He's terribly clever, won't put a foot wrong', while Lady Vere perpetually comments, 'We've lost our head gardener, bit of a chore.'[16] By thus aligning what it presents as a hopelessly outdated, predictable social tradition and class with a similarly cohesive, regular form of expression in verse, the play again dramatizes its distance from the very mode through which it presents its satire.

Although *Serious Money* does not advocate for the development of a more contemporary form of drama in verse, it was to become one of the most popular verse plays of the last few decades. The very nature of its success, however, points less to the revitalization of verse drama than to the general acceptance of that idiom as a contemporary subject for satire itself.

Steven Berkoff, Greek drama and the modern Elizabethan aria

In its use of rhyming couplets to critique the greed and corruption of the ruling classes of Thatcherite Britain, *Serious Money* bears some resemblance to the social satire promoted by Steven Berkoff in his verse play *Decadence* (1981). In the famous restaurant scene of that play, the upper-class Steve monologizes:

> We escape to the restaurant / at last some repose / throw off your coat darling / powder your nose / put on some lip gloss / I'll splash my toes ... our table is ready / how simply hooray .... (*Aside*) (hallo Charles, hallo Di) just the sauce that lends a perfect flavour to all / a small royal sprinkling seems to draw from the rest a flavour that's absolutely the best ...[17]

As Berkoff explains in his author's note, *Decadence* can be read as a 'study of the ruling classes or upper classes, so called by virtue of strangulated vowel tones rather than any real achievement.'[18] In what amounts to an effective summation of the theatrical language of the play itself, built around an anti-naturalist aesthetic of mime and exaggerated gesture, Berkoff further describes his decadent, ruling class:

> They move in awkward rapid gestures or quick jerks and sometimes speak at rapid speeds to avoid appearing to have any feeling for what they say. They achieve pleasure very often in direct relation to the pain they cause in achieving it. Particularly in causing intolerable suffering to achieve exquisite pâtés; boiling lobsters alive with other crustaceans,

and hunting down defenceless animals to give them (the hunters) a sense of purpose on Sundays.[19]

The play presents two couples differentiated by class, their roles played by the same actors. Where *Serious Money* presents similar social caricatures in relation to a larger action, *Decadence* is much more contained in focus. The action, such as it is, centres on the exploits of the adulterous Helen and Steve, and those of Sybil (Steve's wife) and Les (a private detective hired by Sybil). Like Churchill, Berkoff does not present rounded characters in *Decadence* so much as he does types; although all of the characters are presented for scrutiny, the primary subject of that critique is the perpetual existence of the class system. Equally central, however, is Berkoff's *personal* response to that class system – a response that demands a very different aesthetic from the more developed argumentation presented in *Serious Money*.

Much of the effect of Berkoff's plays depends upon their performance, and productions have often featured Berkoff himself as actor and director. Those productions – influenced variously and openly by mime, music hall, Greek drama and relatively unfashionable ideals of the actor as histrionic personality – are marked by what Berkoff consistently emphasizes as a theatrical and social background that is inherently oppositional. Central to that opposition – like that of many experimental writers and directors who emerged in the 1960s – is an emphatic anti-naturalism. Relatively unique, however, is Berkoff's engagement with the development of that anti-naturalism through a consistently emotional and subjective theatrical language. Berkoff cites Elia Kazan's maxim that 'what is most personal is most universal' as a means to criticize those contemporary plays that 'are dissertations proclaiming their values . . . with little heat but much rant. . . . I have seen too many plays which left me frozen and unmoved, the characters merely mouthpieces for certain correctly held attitudes.'[20] These plays, 'socially conscious' and with 'worthy scenarios', do not just omit the personal voice, but they prohibit the necessary theatricality of theatre itself: they assume that drama is 'a kind of forum reflecting political and social events'.[21] Not only do these plays contain 'no daring or experiment with form', but they forget the imperative of theatre 'to be the last resort of an overburdened imagination'.[22] For Berkoff, that imagination is frequently 'overburdened' with a sense of poetry in language itself.

Like *Serious Money*, *Decadence* is written primarily in rhyming couplets. Like Churchill, Berkoff focuses his satire on the immorality of the ruling classes. Rather than satirizing that class by aligning its empty traditions with an outdated, conventional and consequently comic verse, however, Berkoff implicitly re-appropriates rhyme – and particularly the rhyming couplet – as a means through which to heighten dramatic effect. Much of that effect is achieved by the very length of what Berkoff likens to arias,[23] by his indulgence of both language and actor in such a way as to demand a visceral, inevitably emotional response to their expressivity. In *Serious Money*, characters are given to pithy articulations of horrific attitudes: 'One thing I've learned from working for Marylou: / Do others before they can do you.'[24] In *Decadence*, however, they expand upon such attitudes, revelling in imagery and an expressive idiom that simultaneously invokes, ironizes and rewrites 'poetic' language in such a way as to demand its contemporary acceptance as theatrical effect.

Decadence concludes with a final dialogue between Steve and Helen whose short, rhythmic exchanges resemble those in Churchill's hunting scene:

Steve   I like to dance.
Helen   I like tea in the Ritz.
Steve   I like to fly / sipping champagne in the sky.
Helen   I like to wriggle my hips to the beat in my heart / turn and twist.[25]

Churchill's scene depends upon a regularity of rhythm and a certain repetition of imagery and form to dramatize the stagnancy of the upper class she satirizes. Berkoff's passage, in contrast, indulges in poetic conceit to dramatize the nature of the upper-class imagination he condemns:

Helen   We leave the murder and crime in crunched newspapers never to begrime the spotless lives that are yours and mine.
Steve   They belong in the other place where people walk in arsenic and hate.
Helen   Where envy follows greed and becomes the seed that seeks to flower in our pot.[26]

While the characters in this passage remain representative types, their indulgently poetic, anti-naturalist and rhythmic language calls attention to the 'overburdened' poetic sensibilities of their author – and invites the audience to share a similar, visceral response to his subjects.

Berkoff develops this poetic instinct in relation to a very different theme in his plays *East* (1975) and *West* (1983). *Decadence* and the later *Sink the*

Belgrano! (1986) are satirical, focused on the corruption of the ruling classes. In *Sink the Belgrano!*, Berkoff centres his critique on Margaret Thatcher and her aggression in the Falklands; the play articulates this satire on one level by aligning the jingoism of that moment with the received patriotism of *Henry V*: 'Oh for a brace of Exocet missiles / That would ascend the brightest heaven of intention / The sky would be their stage / Super Etendard jets to fly.'[27] The subjects of *East* and *West* are much more personal and considerably less satirical, taking as their inspiration the working-class London of Berkoff's youth. *East* was Berkoff's first play in verse: by his own account, it was written to exorcize personal demons 'and is less a biographical text than an outburst of revolt against the sloth of my youth and a desire to turn a welter of undirected passion and frustration into a positive form.'[28] This 'revolt' became manifest in verse:

> one day, for no reason that I can explain, I started to write the whole thing in verse and even to obey the pentameter in many places … my pen literally flew across the paper as if the structure of this style completely liberated me.… I know not why I did it, just doodling perhaps and with a fondness for Shakespeare since I had never given up the hope of thespian glory and would incessantly practise the big soliloquies.[29]

Likening his embrace of verse to the street presence of rap in San Francisco, Berkoff sees in this natural development of idiom a subconscious manifestation of his 'desire to be different, to be dangerous and entertaining.'[30]

Like many of the modern poet-dramatists that preceded him, Berkoff identifies verse with the expression of a greater reality, with a liberation from superficial representation. He differs notably, however, in his relative fearlessness in invoking Shakespeare as a direct influence. Eliot insisted on developing a verse that might translate the effect of Shakespearean drama into contemporary terms: his essays analyse the modulations in form and verse-structure of the plays. For Berkoff, however, that influence derives from the experience of Shakespearean language (and thus Shakespearean acting) in the theatre. That experience in itself – particularly as disseminated in the performances of Laurence Olivier – renders Shakespeare a *contemporary* presence. Where Drinkwater (via Galsworthy) invoked 'the shadow of the man Shakespeare', and others attempted to distance themselves as far as possible from any comparison, Berkoff openly appropriates Shakespearean lines and his reading of Shakespearean form, 'the big soliloquies'.[31] He aligns the effect of his 'arias' to that of the 'long speech' in Elizabethan drama, an opportunity 'to get a run, if you like, to give the actor a chance to get up some speed and sum up the situation so far, a chance to unburden himself and confess his essential being to the audience': 'It is the time when the heat lifts the lid off your socially acceptable being and you ultimately reveal *you!*'[32] The emotional nature of this revelation is inextricable from its revelation of the art (and thus 'overburdened imagination') of the dramatist: the soliloquy/aria 'gives the writer a chance to flow and weave, to elaborate, to run with the ball all the way to the goal'.[33]

Rather than demanding reverence or overt imitation, Berkoff plays with his allusions to Shakespeare and his suggested pastiche of Elizabethan language, often to violent and profane effect.[34] In *West*, for example, Mike is told that the face of a fellow gangster 'doth resemble the asshole of an elephant'; he acknowledges that 'A face like that won't launch a thousand ships or pull the scrubbers to their beds in Edmonton / Gants Hill / or Waltham Cross'.[35] This suggestion of a contemporary Elizabethan argot constitutes only one of many non-realist theatrical devices through which Berkoff looks to express his self-conscious revolt. *East* and *West* are rooted within Berkoff's own experience and his artistic response to that experience. They are also blatantly theatrical and non-realist: as Berkoff notes, he stylized *East* 'by some cross-fertilization with Shakespeare and threw in a few classical allusions – this seemed to help to take it out further into a ritual and yet defined it with a distinct edge'.[36]

This interest in ritualistic theatre, and in Greek theatre especially, is particularly evident in *Greek* (1980), a loose rewriting of *Oedipus Rex* set in the 1970s, in 'the unimaginable wastelands of Tufnell Park' that Berkoff likens to the plague-ridden city in the Sophocles drama.[37] As the working-class father in the play observes of his contemporary society (and theatre):

The rats march across Piccadilly avoiding Soho where the food is dangerous even for rats, heading down to the Strand / collect the Savoy contingent, overfat rats not sleek for battle but just good germ carriers with rotten teeth head across Waterloo Bridge and the National Theatre ... try to wake the theatre rats who have been long in coma from a deadly attack of nightly brainwash.[38]

Berkoff's version of *Oedipus* contains a number of such attacks on a contemporary London characterized by greed, class warfare and empty commercialism. It also perpetuates its critique of the contemporary mainstream theatre through an adaptation that simultaneously establishes parallels with the original and exploits those parallels in order to articulate a very different thematic emphasis.

Berkoff notes that the first production of *Greek* (which he directed) emphasized both the play's inspiration in classical theatre and its relevance to the contemporary, stylized, non-realist theatre that he looked to promote and develop. The play was staged in a white-walled box, the faces of the actors were whitened in such a way as to '[give] the feeling of the Greek mask', the 'strong use of gesture' was 'close to dance but nearer to drama', 'a table surrounded by four chairs became the centre-piece and it sometimes had a feeling of oratorio': 'the whole production was an invention'.[39] Equally central to this invention was the language. Where *Decadence* satirizes the upper classes and *East* and *West* give voice to the 'natural' poetry inherent in working-class life, *Greek* aligns that natural, working-class poetry explicitly with a tradition whose dissemination in English (pace Gilbert Murray) has been conventionally considered to be the province of the cultural elite. As early as 1971, Berkoff had identified classical translations as being 'stuffed full of that stilted, over-respectful heroic verse with no resonance of human life'.[40] Making an exception for Ted Hughes, he dismisses those translations as 'staid, posy and archaic'.[41] *Greek* implicitly redresses that situation by aligning such 'archaic' practices with class. Thus, the play is written 'in the language of the people, a demotic tongue, with a working-class poet in the character of Eddy, showing that the middle classes are not the only ones who are allowed poetic flights of imagination'.[42]

In his writings about the play, Berkoff emphasizes the personal nature of this class appropriation of classical tradition by associating himself with Eddy: the play became his 'credo for the young, the frustrated, the idealists, the romantics, the renegades'.[43] This renegade role is most evident in Eddy's rejection of the authority of the Sphinx – and in his ultimate refusal to accept that he cannot love the woman he has married now that she has been revealed as his biological mother: 'Yeh I wanna climb back inside my mum. What's wrong with that. It's better than shoving a stick of dynamite up someone's ass and getting a medal for it':

> It's love I feel for your breast, for your nipple twice sucked . . . for your thighs, for your cunt twice known, once head first once cock first, loving cunt holy mother wife / loving source of your being / exit from paradise / entrance to heaven.[44]

In Berkoff's rendition, Eddy does not just react against a conventional narrative; he reacts against the received authority of that narrative as disseminated through the mainstream culture he now rejects. That rejection is articulated in his question, 'Why should I tear my eyes out Greek style, why should you hang yourself.' Eddy then repeats the conventional 'story' of Oedipus to himself only to conclude, 'Bollocks to all that.'[45]

This rejection is equally enforced by the idiom of the play, which simultaneously aligns itself with the conventions of classical drama and subverts those conventions in its narrative and language. The play's use of verse and lengthy monologues invites comparison with the ritualistic speeches and action of classical theatre. From the very opening of the play, however, the language of that verse is not only contemporary, but imbued with Berkoff's characteristically fanciful and profane poetic conceits: 'So I was spawned in Tufnell Park that's no more than a stone's throw from the Angel / a monkey's fart from Tottenham or a bolt of phlegm from Stamford Hill / it's a cesspit, right.'[46] Rather than meeting with the uniform outrage of a staid and over-respectful critical class, *Greek* proved to be one of Berkoff's most popular and critically successful plays. When that play was later transformed into an opera libretto by Auden's old collaborator, Hans Werner Henze, Berkoff could only note with glee:

> Eventually, my scatological piece of vituperative spleen, enriched of course with passages of lyricism, inspired [an opera]. I was to see at last my reviled child set to music and delighting the well-heeled aficionados of the opera at the ENO [English National Opera].[47]

As Berkoff himself has been more than willing to acknowledge, his plays (unlike those of Churchill) have yet to garner him a position within mainstream assessments: 'I read Irving Wardle's yearly round-up of the year's best writers, leaving me out, of course, they all do and I am not only used to this but really don't mind.'[48] He concludes that his plays are ostracized by those who are only impressed 'by cleverness or literary brilliance', by 'writers of polemics and people telling them what to feel or what to think,' who 'like to be taught.'[49] Although Berkoff slightly exaggerates that critical rejection, his plays have yet to achieve a central position in mainstream histories.

Ultimately, that omission overlooks a seminal creative voice in the development of a contemporary theatre in verse. Like many contemporary verse dramatists, Berkoff has essentially discarded the aesthetic legacy of twentieth-century drama in verse. For Berkoff, today's drama must take inspiration from a more ritualistic, theatrical ideal inspired equally by the Elizabethan theatre, classical drama and contemporary working-class idioms. It must also be informed by the poet's expressive independence from prevailing expectations and from a cultural establishment that continues to promote an inauthentic, fundamentally literary ideal of theatrical tradition and contemporary relevance. On the surface, the very individualism of this self-consciously experimental, resistant aesthetic distances Berkoff from other theatrical traditions. Nonetheless, many of his aesthetic and social values resonate with the instincts of the earlier self-consciously community-oriented, anti-realist verse dramatists who had been equally bent on a theatre of beauty, ritual and innate popular expression. Furthermore, Berkoff's particular interest in reworking the conventions of classical drama to contest cultural elitism and to articulate a more socially inclusive sensibility has found strong, implicit support in some of the most mainstream manifestations of verse drama in recent years.

Contemporary trends in modern English verse drama

With a few notable exceptions, the most vocal objections to the very idea of a contemporary drama in verse have tended to greet those (relatively rare) plays that attempt an entirely original scenario on the mainstream national stage. As manifest in the negative criticism of Harrison's *Square Rounds* (1992) and the general derision that greeted his *Fram*, Frayn's *Afterlife* and Laurent's *Five Gold Rings* in the national papers, such attempts – no matter the nature of their verse or themes – seem to invite immediate comparison with the decidedly unfashionable work of Eliot or Fry. Perhaps as a result, a much more prevailing trend has seen such recognized poets as Harrison, Hughes, Roger McGough and Peter Oswald translating and occasionally expanding upon classical Greek, medieval English, seventeenth-century French and German Romantic drama. Projects such as McGough's translations of Molière, Oswald's translation of Schiller, and Maxwell's satyr-play *Lily Jones's Birthday* (2009) argue implicitly for the contemporary resonance of earlier theatrical traditions – and occasionally specific dramas – in which poetic expression was a more dominant, natural idiom.

They also implicitly liberate the modern poet-dramatist from any direct engagement with the social, political and aesthetic expectations of the contemporary naturalist stage. Where Eliot and Duncan eventually attempted to subsume their dramatization of the 'religious' within contemporary realist settings, the late 1950s and 1960s saw an emphatic recognition of the social connotations of those settings. In adapting or invoking earlier dramatic traditions, today's more mainstream verse dramatists are more likely to eschew such settings entirely – along with their social connotations – in favour of dramatic forms and traditions whose 'natural' nonrealism mirrors that of poetry itself. In so doing, they align themselves with the instincts of the more experimental theatre represented by Berkoff, and with those many twentieth-century poet-dramatists who positioned drama in verse against an apparently reductive social realism, that 'preference for ordinary appearance over spiritual reality'.[50] Where some translations foreground a primarily revivalist instinct, others have exploited this received distance between verse drama and social naturalism in order to articulate contemporary themes within an implicitly more universalizing aesthetic.

As Berkoff acknowledges, nowhere is the prevailing assumption of the universal, emotional power of drama in verse more frequently (if obliquely) acknowledged than in contemporary stagings of Shakespeare. Nowhere does it find more creative and critical support as a contemporary form, however, than in modern translations and adaptations of classical drama. The last decades have seen numerous adaptations and translations by Harrison, the acclaimed publication and production of Hughes's interpretative translations of the *Alcestis* (1999) and *The Oresteia* (1999), and Maxwell's contemporary retelling and conflation of *Women of Troy* and *Hecabe* as *After Troy* (2011). Many dramatists have also, like Yeats, Gray, Masefield and Bottomley before them, continued to embrace such conventions of classical drama as the use of mask, the messenger speech and the chorus.

More often than not, today's verse dramatists tend to confine such techniques either to the adaptation of classical drama or to works that draw attention to the earlier traditions or specific dramas from which they take inspiration. Masefield reassigns the role of the Greek messenger to that of a Spanish nobleman in *Philip the King*, Bottomley dramatizes British origin myths through stylized movement modelled after Greek choral dances, and Eliot stages the Furies at the windows of a contemporary country house. Subsequent verse dramas by contemporary poets, however, have characteristically positioned their appropriation of earlier conventions in relation to earlier traditions. This tendency may suggest a relative conservatism and resistance to experimentation. It may also, however, reflect the very legacy of the anti-realist, experimental political theatre of the preceding decades, where – as in Jane Arden's play – the contemporary presence of Furies, masks and choruses could be associated as much with social argumentation and political statement as could the more naturalist tirades of the Angry Young Men.

This instinct towards a more universalizing theatre clearly informed the 1971 collaborative theatre-piece *Orghast*. Developed through the International Centre for Theatre Research (ICTR; founded in France by Brook and Micheline Rozan), the work was created by Hughes and Brook for the Shiraz/Persepolis Festival in Iran. The piece is a dramatization of the myth of Prometheus written partly in an invented language ('Orghast'), partly in ancient Greek, and partly in the ancient ceremonial language of Avesta. In its engagement with language, myth and a variety of dramatic (and national) modes, in its formulation and staging outside of England (and Europe), the drama reinforced the multinational, internationalist explorations of the ICTR. It also suggested a unique opportunity for the contemporary English poet bent upon returning myth, poetry and drama to a more universalizing significance. For Hughes, the project enabled him to take dramatic verse beyond the literary confines he identified as hindering any poetic drama now written in English. In a telling echo of the spiritual aims of many verse dramatists that came before – and in an even more telling reinforcement of Auden's operatic invocation of the master poet's 'pure vocalisation' – Hughes aligns this ideal effect with that of music:

> The purpose of *Orghast*, play and language, is an inner transformation, an opening to a lost world. . . . Music is already such a language, precise and mysterious. Like music, Orghast is at no point meant to engage the cerebration which cuts us off from this deeper world.[51]

Orghast was an openly experimental work, and while Brook was to continue to push his directorial explorations of a theatrical poetic drama outside of England, Hughes would relocate his subsequent dramatic projects within a more familiar literary approach to verse drama and its inspiration in classical traditions.

Nonetheless, this instinct to align Greek classical drama with an experimental, internationalist and contemporary definition of theatre continues to characterize the work of some of today's most prominent poet-dramatists. Nowhere has that instinct been more apparent than in the work of Harrison. In 1988, Harrison premiered a single performance of *The Trackers of Oxyrhynchus* at the stadium of Delphi in Greece. Two years later, the play was a critical and commercial success at the National Theatre.

Rather than adapting a known classical work, Harrison based his play partially on fragments of *Ichneutae*, a satyr play by Sophocles, positioning that adaptation within a larger narrative about the turn-of-the-century discovery of those fragments by Bernard Pyne Grenfell and Arthur Surridge Hunt. As Rosemary Burton notes, 'if Greek tragedy had been ruined by reverence, Greek satyr plays were, until the premiere of [*Trackers*], virtually extinct.'[52] Harrison's play builds upon the fact that satyr plays had been considered 'the unacceptable face of classicism.'[53] Rather than positioning one 'face' of classicism against another, Harrison advocates a rethinking and expansion of that tradition to enable its more authentic representation and appreciation. As Harrison himself explained in an address to the Festival of Greek Drama at Delphi: 'tragedy and satyr play have to be conceived as unity if we are to understand how the ancient Greeks could confront dark realities without wallowing in that darkness. . . . We have to remember that the same imagination created both.'[54]

In *Trackers*, Harrison does not just revive an ancient satyr play or make a plea for a reconsideration of the classical tradition. He positions the satyr play and its contemporary cultural connotations within a drama whose plot and theatre exploit the tensions between the Apollonian and the Dionysian, between 'high' culture and 'low' culture, in relation to mainstream English culture and class. Harrison focuses these tensions around the conventional cultural position of classical theatre (as high culture) more generally in contemporary England. For Harrison, this position is exclusionary; it omits the Dionysian and populist element of the satyr play, and it appropriates that incomplete – essentially fragmentary – classical tradition for the establishment class. The satyrs of today are left to languish on the margins, listening to ghetto-blasters whose music they do not understand. In the play, this condition reflects the rejection of the satyrs from high art (and thus 'culture'). It also reflects their refusal to claim their own position within that culture. When the satyrs rebel at this ostracization, they destroy the papyrus that has (incompletely) enshrined their cultural existence thus far, ensuring their perpetual ostracization. Harrison's play thus works more broadly to expose and contest contemporary cultural hierarchies and their perpetual acceptance on both sides of an artificial and destructive social divide. Nowhere, of course, is that divide rendered more artificial than in the theatre of the play itself, whose own elision of satyr and classical drama, time and place, advocates for a more cohesive, inclusive definition of society and culture built upon a perpetual openness to art.

In 1995, Harrison returned to Delphi to premiere *The Labours of Herakles*, a play based on fragments of tragedies by the dramatist Phrynichos. As in *Trackers*, Harrison exploits the contemporary thematic potential of this material – its subject, its cultural connotations (in England and in Greece), and the very fact of its theatrical revival. In *Labours*, Harrison invokes these associations to dramatize larger themes about contemporary attitudes towards war and the role of art and the poet. In the first production of that highly meta-theatrical play, Harrison himself took on the role of the spirit of Phrynichos. In that role, he delivered a speech whose contemporary resonance with the war in Bosnia was much-noted at the time. Rather than suggesting a simply didactic or propagandist interpolation, however, that speech was contained within a drama that, when the poet leaves the stage, has one of the Labourers exclaim, 'Who the fuck was that?'[55] Despite this staged qualification, Harrison also reinforces the imperative of the modern poet to exploit the tragic forcefulness of classical drama, to enforce its universal resonance as contemporary, potentially transformative myth. As in *Trackers*, that resonance is not just cultural, but social and political; in *Herakles*, it is also much more internationalist. Towards the end of the play, one of the Labourers gets caught in cement and asks for a shirt to keep him warm: that shirt becomes the Shirt of Nessus that killed Herakles. It is also described by the two other Labourers as having been made by the victims of the Bosnian war: 'The mother of the mortared mosque's dismembered muezzin, assisted by the convoys of the cleansed of Knin.'[56] The description is unambiguously political. It is also, however, presented in relation to the containing but incomplete narrative of Herakles – and within the expressive idiom of what the play itself presents as the self-questioning voice of the contemporary poet.

As such projects only begin to suggest, these contemporary engagements with classical drama bear no resemblance to the 'stilted, over-respectful heroic verse' that Berkoff condemns in contemporary attitudes towards Greek drama. Instead, they exploit the presumed distance between source text and contemporary audience to effect a rapprochement between that audience and the conventional cultural position of earlier traditions. They also engage consistently with the social and necessarily *artistic* role of the poet within the community. Arden and Auden translate that awareness into an idiom that insists upon collaboration and the negation of the individual voice of the poet within a larger culture defined by established popular forms. Harrison, in contrast, works much more explicitly to reassert the relevance of more established traditions of poetry and poetic drama – and to promote their artistic continuation and development within a theatre actively engaged with its contemporary society. For Harrison, the drama of Eliot and Fry fails as theatre: where he has always 'had a passion for Greek drama', he could never 'understand the language' of the modern poet-dramatists: 'if people can't understand you lose them very quickly'.[57] This emphasis on accessibility and understanding can only be developed through a theatre that acknowledges and develops a much more natural poetic affinity between earlier traditions and the modern poet.

Tony Harrison and the return of the poet

Of contemporary poet-dramatists, Harrison is undoubtedly the most prolific and ambitious. Aside from *Square Rounds*, *Fram* and *Trackers*, Harrison's work for the National Theatre has included a 1973 adaptation and re-setting of Molière's *Le Misanthrope* (in the 1960s) that was so successful as to be re-translated into French; an adaptation of Racine's *Phèdre* (*Phaedra Britannica*, 1975), set in British India under the Raj; a translation of the *Oresteia* (1981) with music by Birtwistle that Harrison has described as an opera 'where the words are primary'; a reworking of medieval mystery plays as *The Mysteries* (1985); and *The Prince's Play* (1996), an adaptation of Victor Hugo's *Le roi s'amuse* set in Victorian London. Other adaptations have included a 1964 reworking and resetting of the *Lysistrata* (Aikin Mata) set and staged in Africa: for Harrison, 'by restoring music and dance to an integral place in a production of a Greek Comedy, the play itself could be performed in a manner nearer to the Greek than the kind of productions one has in European theatre and on radio with effete angelic choral speaking and emasculated dancing'.[58] This enthusiasm for the restoration of music to Greek drama is also apparent in Harrison's work on the unperformed but published *Medea: a Sex-War Opera* (1985).[59] In 1986, he composed the libretto for *Yan Tan Tethera*, Birtwistle's chamber opera based on an English folk tale.

Harrison often prefaces the published editions of his plays with lengthy discussions of the rationale behind his adaptation, of his critical negotiation with and assessment of pre-existing translations, and of the desired effect of the verse form that he has chosen. In *The Misanthrope*, for example, he can only achieve the 'almost Chekhovian tension between farce and anguish' through rhymed verse: 'I have made use of the occasional Drydenian triplet, and, once in Act Three, of something I call a "switchback" rhyme, a device I derive from the works of George Formby.'[60] In *Phaedra Britannica*, Harrison 'wanted a more organic model' for his iambics after 'the metronome, the comic-pace-maker of the *Misanthrope* couplet'.[61] The project is much more than a literary exercise, however, and Harrison's preface analyses the numerous difficulties posed by the translation of French classical drama. Identifying a seminal line in the original, Harrison recognizes that a literal translation or approximation is insufficient to convey its dramatic force in English. Instead, he has 'had to redistribute the energies of that renowned line over [his] whole version', and this instinct to some extent informs his re-contextualization of the play in India.[62] Where Berkoff takes *Oedipus* as his inspiration to present a contemporary drama of self-expression and class identity, Harrison roots his translations within an (often scholarly) appreciation of the poetics, metre and cultural origins of what is clearly treated as a source text. He is also, however, unafraid to recognize that the most accurate translation is that which 'radically' reconfigures its source in such a way as to assert a contemporary relationship with a contemporary audience.

Harrison is relatively alone amongst contemporary verse dramatists in his critical and creative engagement with a diversity of poetic forms and traditions. In that respect, his plays suggest a clear affinity with the earlier creative explorations and theorizations of such poets as Auden, Eliot and Duncan. Like Eliot and Duncan, he also insists upon a mastery of verse forms, convinced that the rhythmical element of poetry 'is like a life-support system': 'The metre itself is like the pulse. . . . I don't have the heart to confront some experience unless I know I have this rhythm to carry me to the other side.'[63] Unlike those poets, however, Harrison has not struggled to identify a single, coherent mode of dramatic expression in verse. In his primary focus on dramatic adaptation and translation, Harrison appeals to a contemporary audience through the very tradition of poetic drama that these dramatists had sought to surpass in modern forms and contemporary settings. Furthermore, unlike those earlier poets – and like Berkoff – Harrison aligns his engagement with verse, form and audience much more emphatically with his own social background.

Born in 1937 Leeds to a working-class family, Harrison won a scholarship to Leeds Grammar School, completed a Classics degree at Leeds University, took a diploma in linguistics, and began preliminary research (on translations of Virgil's *Aeneid*) for a PhD thesis (never completed). As reinforced in his poetry, interviews and essays, this keen appreciation of education, poetry and literary creativity was constantly informed by a familial upbringing that had been 'very loving' and 'rooted', but that had been to some extent 'disrupt[ed]' by education and poetry: 'I've been trying to create new wholes out of that disruption ever since.'[64] As Ken Worpole has noted, 'if [Richard] Hoggart was the benign chronicler of the "scholarship boy", Brian Jackson and Dennis Marsden the sociologists, Raymond Williams the novelist, then Tony Harrison is pre-eminently the poet of that major cultural (and disintegrative) experience.'[65] In an oft-quoted interview, Harrison observes, 'because of my background poetry is not something I can take for granted.'[66] In terms that resonate with the thematic focus of *Herakles*, he declares that because of that background, he demands that his work 'be exposed to all the gale-force winds of what negates poetry: social indifference, self-destructiveness, time, nothingness – the whole fatuity of the belief that writing poetry will *do* anything.'[67]

All of Harrison's work is informed by a strong social politics motivated by his self-confessed need to validate the role of the poet and to (re)connect. His poetry and drama are rooted in his early experience as an 'outsider' both from a family that did not own books and from the literary and poetic tradition with which he sought to engage and participate. At school, that outsider position was defined by his class and by his Northern accent. As Harrison recounts in his poem 'Them & [uz]': 'Poetry's the speech of kings. You're one of those / Shakespeare gives the comic bits to: prose!'[68] In an interview with Hoggart (to whom he dedicated 'Them & [uz]'), Harrison identifies 'a kind of aggro' in his writing not unlike that of Berkoff: in translating classical literature as a student, he had always wanted to 'do it, make things that were classically formed, but in [his] own voice'.[69] For Harrison, that interest in translation – like his interest in poetry and drama – was always articulated in relation to a contemporary social voice and implicit audience; he 'always thought about the way people spoke'.[70] When he translated Plautus, he would use colloquial idioms – and he would always be 'corrected' by his teachers. In 'Them & [uz]', Harrison presents an implicit manifesto that rejects that teaching and that embraces contemporary colloquialisms and Northern idiom: 'So right, yer buggers then! We'll occupy / your lousy leasehold Poetry.'[71]

To some extent, therefore, the very diversity of Harrison's theatrical projects attests to his constant exploration of the forms and traditions through which best to both 'occupy' the leasehold of Poetry and address the 'gale-force winds of what negates poetry'. In both *The Oresteia* and *The Mysteries*, he comes closest to dramatizing this poetic manifesto through the use of a Northern, colloquial idiom. In *The Mysteries*, he also comes closest to aligning that idiom with the very innate, ritualistic community drama so consistently sought and invoked by English dramatists at the beginning of the century – and so enviously identified in the Irish theatre of Synge. Harrison recounts having been angered at a production of mystery plays at York, where 'God and Jesus were played by very posh-speaking actors from the South, and the local people again played the comic parts.'[72] In language that echoes his invocation of a more expansive and unifying tradition in *Trackers*, he insists that one of the most important elements of the mystery plays is the homogeneity of their language: 'God, Christ, and everybody else speak in the language of the time, which is also colloquial.'[73]

Declaring a project to 'restore Yorkshire's great classic to itself',[74] Harrison produced a translation that capitalizes upon the natural resonance of Yorkshire colloquialisms and rhythms with their earlier manifestation in Middle English. Harrison's alliterative verse positions the origins of those colloquialisms and rhythms within a drama whose language is simultaneously familiar and ritualistic. In so doing, he implies a 'doubleness of action' in the verse itself:

Since I am maker unmade, and most high in might,
And aye shall be endless, and nought is but I,
Unto my dignity dear shall duly be dight
A bliss all-abundant about me.[75]

Equally central to that doubleness was the play's exploitation of the theatre-space in performance. The production cast Yorkshire actors (itself still a distancing effect in the London theatre) in the contemporary working-class garb of modern carpenters, painters, fishmongers and construction workers. Rather than merely enacting the mystery plays, these characters – integrated amongst the audience both in an initial staging on the terrace of the National Theatre and in an indoor promenade concept – were presented as the enablers of that drama. In the first play, God was elevated by this company-within-a-company on a fork-lift truck; Lucifer was carried in a chair. The production was constantly accentuated by music, to which members of the company clapped along – and in which they invited the audience to participate. In the context of its staging at the National Theatre, the play did much more than 'restore Yorkshire's great classic to itself': it positioned that classic in the heart of the London cultural establishment. In its performative, theatrical alignment of North and South, actor and performer, past and present, it also suggested a contemporary ritualistic affirmation of national community, a 'new whole' created poetically through 'the language of the time, which is also colloquial'.

Little has changed in the intervening years to contest Leeming's 1989 assessment that 'the struggle of poetic drama for acceptance is over – defeated, if seen as a struggle for dominance'.[76] As evident in the essays, collaborations, and plays of poets as otherwise diverse as Yeats, Bottomley, Masefield, Abercrombie, Eliot and Duncan, the majority of the most vocal, prolific and theoretically engaged verse dramatists did indeed see 'the struggle of poetic drama' as 'a struggle for dominance'. Subsequent poet-dramatists have rarely, if ever, acknowledged the potential for such an ambition to exist in relation to today's mainstream stage. As nonetheless manifest in the experimental personal theatre of Berkoff, as reinforced by the classical translations and creative re-workings of Maxwell and Oswald, as perpetuated in Harrison's explorations of community, theatre and poetic tradition on the national stage, the apparent fight for precedence may have ended – but today's theatrical environment continues to be characterized by a flourishing culture of drama in verse that is far removed from any 'pastel shades of twee'.

CONCLUSION
THE RETURN OF THE KING: *KING CHARLES III* AND SHAKESPEAREAN POWER AND PASTICHE

In 2014, the popular and critical success of Mike Bartlett's blank-verse *King Charles III* provided a significant riposte to any who would associate drama in verse with the drama of the past. Although the play was never hailed as marking the rebirth of contemporary verse drama, its very success – and particularly its reception as vital *national* drama – certainly qualifies any assumption that modern drama in verse cannot succeed with critics or audiences. Intriguingly, while some noted its use of blank verse, *King Charles III* was rarely acknowledged as a verse drama – and certainly not as a work in the same modern tradition now apparently represented by Eliot, Fry and Harrison. Ironically, both the play's apparent escape from this unfashionable association and its overwhelming success seem to have been ensured by its enthusiastic invocation of the very Shakespearean legacy from which most other modern verse dramatists had been at pains to distance themselves.

In the first half of the twentieth century, that legacy was seen as having inhibited the creativity of nineteenth-century poet-dramatists: artists from Keats to Tennyson had apparently confined themselves to the sonorous imitation of the perceived achievement and idiom of that 'national poet'. In so doing, they had traduced the contemporary imperative of both the modern stage and the modern poet. As we have seen, such perceptions encouraged the exploration of alternative theatrical traditions in verse, not to mention the development of a stage verse that might develop, if not derive from, a more innate and contemporary idiom. For poet-dramatists from Yeats through to Masefield, Auden, Eliot and Arden, this emphasis demanded a much closer engagement with what Gray identified as the materials of the 'family education', the common narratives, myths and modes of expression that informed the identity of the essential community. As Bartlett's play implicitly contends, however, the most prominent manifestation of such a shared cultural and national language, its stories and idiom perpetually re-invoked and re-reworked in contemporary culture, is the 'Shakespearean tradition' itself.

King Charles III

In its Shakespearean allusions, in its pastiche and parody, *King Charles III* both exploits and critiques the pervading familiarity of Shakespearean drama as a signifier of contemporary identity. For the majority of the play's critics, however, it was that very familiarity rather than Bartlett's critique that seemed to confer a 'Shakespearean' status upon the play itself. The work was universally acclaimed: it experienced a sold-out run at the Almeida Theatre before transferring to the West End, moving to Broadway, and being subsequently revived as a touring production from September 2015. In 2016, a BBC television adaptation was announced. In 2015, the play won an Olivier award for Best New Play and the Critics' Circle Award for Best New Play of 2014. The reviews were laudatory without exception: according to *The Times*, 'theatre doesn't get much better than this'[1]; *The Independent* acclaimed a 'bracingly provocative and outrageously entertaining new play'[2]; Michael Billington included the play in his book *The 101 Greatest Plays: From Antiquity to the Present*; and Spencer himself hailed 'the most spectacular, gripping and wickedly entertaining piece of lèse-majesté that British theatre has ever seen.'[3]

In the vast majority of these reviews, the success of the play was marked not only by its ability to entertain, but also by its apparently topical exploration of the role of the monarchy. According to Sarah Crompton in the *Daily Telegraph*, 'Suddenly, the monarchy and its rule is an urgent matter for debate and understanding – and history not a dusty tome or a dim candle but a blazing torch, a beacon to guide us into the future.'[4] *King Charles III* is not in fact a history play: it imagines a contemporary Britain faced with a constitutional crisis after the death of the Queen. It can apparently be likened to a history play, however, due to its use of blank verse and its numerous Shakespearean allusions. As Crompton explains: 'Technically, this isn't a history play at all ... But it is written in blank verse, quotes Richard II – the "hollow crown" – and is consciously Shakespearean both in tone and purpose.'[5] In this relatively characteristic assessment, the 'blazing torch' to 'guide us into the future' is not that of history itself, but that of Shakespearean drama.

Most reviews identified a vital and profound significance to the play's allusion to (and thus implicit association with) Shakespeare. Almost all – like Crompton – were somewhat ambiguous as to what the play was articulating in its use of that allusion beyond signalling an 'urgent matter for debate and understanding'. For Billington, the play dramatizes the 'inviolable solitude of monarchy and uses a dense tissue of Shakespearean references to acquire a tragic dimension'.[6] Dominic Cavendish identifies 'knowing, deft references to many of Shakespeare's political works' and a blank verse 'that combines jolting colloquialism with pastiche Bardic brilliance': the effect of such allusions is to ensure a drama that 'moves by weirdly plausible degrees to a place of spiralling civil strife'.[7] According to Spencer, the play is 'heavily and often wittily in debt to Shakespeare's history plays'.[8] Where Billington identifies the play as a tragedy, these other receptions identify in the use of Shakespearean allusion and blank verse a more nebulous *signifier* of contemporary expressive and political vitality.

The play contains many overt and often parodic references to Shakespeare's plays, the majority of which in fact derive from *Macbeth* rather than the history plays. In a humorous reference to the witches in that play, the ghost of Diana appears both to her ex-husband and to her son – manipulating them both with the same prophecy. The effect of that prophecy is to awaken what the play implies to be the innate Lady Macbeth in Kate, who urges her husband to usurp his father and thus fulfill her own ruthless ambition. The wrangling of the young Harry in local night clubs and with a working-class girlfriend suggest the tavern scenes in *Henry IV*, with no recognition of an imperative that that prince, second-in-line, do anything other than enjoy himself. The most political – and tragic – allusions are focused on the figure of the King. Charles is given to John of Gaunt-like eulogies of a beautiful nation now traduced by its political class. In his questioning of his own role and identity within that nation, in his ultimate capitulation to those politicians and his abdication of the Crown, he also echoes the concerns and language of Shakespeare's Richard II.

Ultimately, Bartlett's treatment of the King hints at a certain ambivalence about the general tone of pastiche and parody towards Shakespeare that otherwise characterizes the drama. Charles has ascended the throne, determined to influence matters of state, to 'ascend' and 'rise to how things have to be'.[9] He intervenes in the passing of a bill that attempts to restrict the freedom of the press. In a topical reference to the recent phone-hacking scandal, the Labour Prime Minister insists on the value of a bill that will prevent 'phones belonging to the dead [from being] hacked'.[10] As Charles observes, the bill is opposed by the Conservative Leader of the Opposition not on the basis of principle, but on the basis of his friendship with newspaper editors. When Charles attempts to stop the bill, the two leaders unite in what they articulate as a defence of democracy – but in what the play cynically, consistently exposes to be a fundamental defence of an unchanging status quo. This critique of the status quo is also enforced in relation to the monarchy, which is shown to be nothing more than decorative, a visual and *theatrical* signifier of a national identity that languishes in its own stagnant, uncritical acceptance of custom. Through the character of Charles, Bartlett underlines the extent to which the monarchy is not the cause of this condition, but rather a hitherto willing participant, the passive subject of an equally passive nation.

Towards the beginning of the play, Charles speaks of ascent, insists on social hierarchy and recognizes in any acquiescence to the politicians a potential loss of power and identity. In a simultaneous echo of Shakespeare's Claudius, Richard II and melancholy Jaques, he observes:

The pen dries up, my hand it cannot write.
For if my name is given through routine
And not because it represents my view
Then soon I'll have no name, and nameless I
Have not myself, and having not myself,
Possess not mouth nor tongue nor brain . . .[11]

Charles identifies with both the agency and the tragedy of Shakespearean kings (and their courtiers), not all of them historical. The awkward and eclectic conflation of these various Shakespearean references also suggests that the play is satirizing that identification, presenting Charles as an outmoded manifestation of monarchy, inaccurately rooted in the fragments of an aesthetic and historical past.

Nonetheless, immediately after this speech, Charles turns to the Prime Minister to explain his actions. His explanation is focused not on his personal sense of identity and kingship, but rather on his sense of duty towards a nation that has been traduced by its elected leaders:

I'm not sure if ever in the past,
That there was such a bill, that changed the way
That speech is granted freedom.[12]

Such assertions of principle are relatively exclusive to Charles, who condemns those 'fragile politicians' who insist on censorship for their own agenda:

it will
Be easier to govern as corrupt
Than bother being held unto account.[13]

Both Charles and the play itself see him as standing 'outside the rough / And tumble of expedience'.[14] In contrast, the politicians object to the challenge of the King on constitutional grounds, but they do so in perpetual defence of their own vested, established interests. When Charles concludes Act II with a principled reassertion of his necessary duty, his lines again echo those of Shakespearean kings: 'Without my voice, and spirit, I am dust, / This is not what I want, but what I must.'[15] In the thematic context of the play, this 'Shakespearean' idiom calls attention to the anachronism of such convictions within a superficial, contemporary society. The effect is to ensure that the tension between the King's mode of expression and that of his modern courtiers implicitly validates rather than satirizes the strength of his 'outdated' convictions *and* of his kingly Shakespearean idiom.

Bartlett thus presents the Shakespearean king as a flawed voice for contemporary national performance and reform. He also dramatizes the impossibility of his ideals within a society characterized not by progressive, democratic reform, but rather by an acceptance of unchanging governing structures. In the play, William and Kate ultimately help to stage a peaceful coup against the King: William cedes to the prophecy of his dead mother and the will of his ambitious wife, while Kate acts as the primary – and 'populist' – foil to the definition of monarchy espoused by Charles. Charles initially recognizes her essential 'gift' to the royals: 'A sense of fashion, better hair as well'.[16] This humorous remark also reveals a significant truth, and one that Kate herself fully appreciates. Noting the presiding misogyny that dominates the 'rooms of power' and their 'white, and southern, likely Oxbridge men', Kate identifies the limited agency of women within society as a whole:

But I know nothing, just a plastic doll
Designed I'm told to stand embodying
A male-created bland and standard wife.[17]

Rather than accepting that role as passive, Kate is determined to manipulate its conventions for herself, to reinforce the superficiality of contemporary society in order to define her own power. In yet another ironic allusion to the 'Ages of Man' speech from *As You Like It*, she observes:

We're told the world's a play of surfaces
Where meaning's made through only what is shown
You must then focus 'pon the public eye
Your dress your best. And so, of course, shall I.[18]

The play concludes with the triumph of this definition of the contemporary age of humankind. Kate rebukes Charles with the truth that the way she dresses 'should not be thought as vanity / but is part of the substance only we provide'.[19] That substance might be 'airy', but in a contemporary culture ruled by superficial performance and theatre, 'Our column inches are / The greatest influence we possess',[20] and Charles cedes power to what he identifies as 'a pretty plastic picture with no meaning'.[21]

King Charles III presents Charles as both a slightly absurd figure and as an unlikely hero, as the champion of the 'country's unique force and way of life' against the restrictive authoritarianism of its politicians and the superficial gloss of its media.[22] It also, however, satirizes his assumption of the vital role of the contemporary ruler (elected or not): the power of kings, queen-consorts and governments in the modern age is now defined by their self-conscious, decorative and familiar performance of passivity. Nowhere, perhaps, is that complacency – that assumption of the world as 'a play of surfaces' – more dramatically represented than in the play's very use of Shakespearean allusion and blank verse. The society of the play is willingly contained within an empty, ritualistic enactment of its contemporary identity, divorced from its own history and indifferent to what were once its defining values. As Kate observes at the beginning of the play:

So coronation day itself is just
The ancient costumes worn, and lines to learn,
A slice of theatre, that's played for fun?[23]

In its use of Shakespearean pastiche, the play suggests that this idea of empty, conventional state theatre – misunderstood, blindly re-enacted, perpetually fragmenting and socially manipulative – is forcefully reinforced within the chosen idiom of the play itself.

As Bartlett recognizes, the plays of Shakespeare continue to occupy a powerful position in national culture, associated as much with the mythical, common language of the national collective as with theatrical excellence alone. In *King Charles III*, he deliberately plays with that expectation: the parallels between Kate and Lady Macbeth are primarily comic, coercing the audience into a comfortable recognition of a continuous, familiar language. In the play's many incomplete, jumbled allusions to Shakespeare, however, Bartlett disrupts that familial recognition. He further disrupts that recognition by inviting a complexity of reactions to his Shakespearean allusion, where anachronistic reference to Lady Macbeth might amuse, but allusions to Richard II apparently enforce the tragic position of a contemporary king. These various invocations of Shakespeare and the Shakespearean legacy thus invite a constant critical engagement with the play's allusions, their sources and their re-working throughout the play. To a much greater extent, they also reinforce the drama's larger thematic preoccupation with the 'play of surface' that defines today's passive expectations (and acceptance) of its national institutions: its politicians, its monarchy *and* its national theatre.

As manifest in the ecstatic critical recognition of Bartlett's apparently Shakespearean 'tone and purpose', however, this resonance between the social themes of the play and its chosen idiom seems to have gone virtually unnoticed. Ultimately, that reception reinforces the established strength of Shakespearean drama as an immediate, ritualistic signifier of an innate identity – and of the unchanging mode of collective performance that Bartlett sets out to question. Considered in the context of historical attempts to formulate a modern tradition of drama in verse, it also hints at the perpetual challenge faced by those who might yet hope to establish 'more than one poet in the national drama' on the contemporary English stage.

Nonetheless, rather than fading into ignominy, many of the instincts of the self-consciously modernizing verse dramatists have persisted well into the twenty-first century. The first decades of the twentieth century saw an identifiable movement marked by a diversity of creative voices, many of which espoused different readings of poetry, tradition, audience and the stage itself. While that diffuse movement was effectively eradicated after the received theatrical revolution of the 1950s, its legacy nonetheless continues to resonate in contemporary theatre.

The most prominent legacy of that moment can be traced through the collaborative energies of those poets and artists who recognized and exploited the creative dynamic between verse, movement, art and music in performance. In the first half of the twentieth century, such energies often pushed at the very boundaries between ballet, opera and the spoken stage, encouraging a larger redefinition of drama and dramatic creativity. Subsequent decades have seen a certain retrenchment of these apparently disciplinary divides, both in practice and particularly in the historiography of contemporary drama. As manifest in much contemporary opera, ballet and experimental performance theatre, however, those divisions continue to be challenged within fundamentally interdisciplinary, intermedial forms.

An equally significant legacy of the modern verse drama movement is the persistence of what can be identified as the two defining ideals of modern drama in verse. Then as now, 'poetry' in drama signified a means to challenge a dominant national aesthetic – 'New Writing Pure' – focused on social argumentation and naturalist staging. In the first half of the twentieth century, that challenge was often aligned with spiritual reform; as promoted by Yeats and Bottomley, drama must appeal to the 'poignant significance at the heart of the matter' through experimental formulations of a contemporary theatre of beauty. As envisioned by dramatists as otherwise diverse as Masefield, Housman, Barker and Abercrombie, that appeal to the spirit held the potential to effect social change; for others, it was much more aligned with the invocation and experience of religious truth. In more recent years, the challenge, through verse, of a potentially reductive realist aesthetic has been perpetuated individually by many poet-dramatists: it is overtly signalled in the self-consciously subjective theatre of Berkoff; the contemporary reworkings of classical structures and themes by Maxwell, Hughes and Harrison; and the established tension between Shakespearean idiom and contemporary theme in *King Charles III*.

The first half of the century also saw verse dramatists attempting to revivify an ideal of community and communal ritual through theatre. This ambition was variously perpetuated by Yeats, Gray and the Georgians; by numerous amateur societies; by the religious verse dramatists at Canterbury and the Mercury; and by the political dramatists of the 1930s Group Theatre. In later decades, it was manifest in the ballad theatre of Joan Littlewood, the epic and populist verse plays of John Arden and Margaretta D'Arcy, and the socially informed and self-consciously poetic 'translations' of Greek, medieval and French classical theatre by McGough, Harrison and Oswald. Where Arden and D'Arcy felt forced to picket the RSC, where the political plays of the Group Theatre and Stratford East have yet to be recognized within dominant histories of the 'development' of the modern English stage, the relative prominence of Harrison's work at the National Theatre hints at the possibility for a larger revival of such aesthetic and social definitions of theatre on a mainstream English stage.

Since the very beginning of that twentieth century, however, many verse dramatists have also been acutely aware of the extent to which the dramatic traditions of other eras, languages and nations can implicitly challenge entrenched definitions of the English 'national' stage. This awareness was manifest in the exploration of Noh drama by Yeats, Binyon, Bottomley and Masefield, not to mention the Georgian fascination with 'Celtic' myth and idiom. It was reinforced in the middle of the century by the creative translation of much contemporary European poetic drama by such verse dramatists as Duncan and Fry. It has been more recently epitomized by the fascination of Harrison and Hughes with African theatre and with a contemporary Greek performance-space. It has also received striking support in the very cynicism of *King Charles III* about the contemporary vitality of England's 'one poet in the national drama', particularly in relation to the dramatization of 'national' themes.

Ultimately, these various, prevailing enthusiasms suggest that the most hopeful possibility yet for English contemporary drama in verse might be found in a more emphatic rejection of the very idea of a national, rather than world, stage. In their very variety and breadth, they also advocate implicitly for a much more thorough appreciation – in theatre practice, criticism and scholarship – of the many, surprisingly overlooked, voices and aesthetic formulations that have contributed to the recent history of drama in England.

NOTES

Introduction

1. Andrew Haydon, 'Poetry in Motion: Why Poetic Drama Has Something New to Say', *The Guardian*, 2 March 2011, http://www.theguardian.com/stage/theatreblog/2011/mar/02/poetic-drama-theatre-andrew-motion (accessed 14 January 2016).

2. Charles Spencer, review of Joanna Laurens, *Five Gold Rings, The Daily Telegraph*, 24 December 2003. According to Laurens, the critical response killed her career. She speculates, 'if I had written a play using naturalistic language that had not been a success, I can't imagine that the response would have been so extreme'. Hannah Silva, interview with Joanna Laurens, 10 September 2012, http://hannahsilva.co.uk/interview-with-joanna-laurens (accessed 14 January 2016).

3. Spencer, review of Michael Frayn, *Afterlife, The Daily Telegraph*, 11 June 2008.

4. Lyn Gardner, 'Rhyme and Punishment', *The Guardian*, 11 July 2005, http://www.theguardian.com/stage/2005/jul/11/theatre1 (accessed 14 January 2016).

5. Wilfrid Wilson Gibson, 'Some Thoughts on the Future of Poetic-Drama', *Poetry Review* 3 (1912): 119.

6. Halcott Glover, *Drama and Mankind: A Vindication and a Challenge* (Boston: Small, Maynard & Co., 1924), 39.

7. Desmond MacCarthy, *Criticism* (London: Putnam, 1932), 99.

8. Christopher Fry, 'Why Verse?' *Vogue*, March 1955.

9. David Pattie, *Modern British Playwriting: The 1950s: Voices, Documents, New Interpretations* (London: Methuen, 2012), 47.

10. Ibid., 48.

11. Arnold P. Hinchcliffe, *Modern Verse Drama* (London: Methuen, 1977), 37.

12. Simon Trussler, *The Cambridge Illustrated History of British Theatre* (Cambridge: Cambridge University Press, 1994), 307.

13. A.T. Tolley, *The Poetry of the Forties in Britain* (Ottawa: Carleton University Press, 1985), 203.

14. Christopher Innes, *Modern British Drama: The Twentieth Century* (Cambridge: Cambridge University Press, 2002), 436.

15. Ibid., 437.

16. Glover, *Drama and Mankind*, 44.

Notes

17. Harley Granville Barker, *On Poetry in Drama* (London: Sidgwick & Jackson, 1937), 13.

18. Ibid., 3.

19. Ibid., 15.

20. Glover, *Drama and Mankind*, 40.

21. Barker, *On Poetry in Drama*, 36.

22. Denis Donoghue, *The Third Voice: Modern British and American Verse Drama* (Princeton: Princeton University Press, 1959), 10.

23. Glenda Leeming, *Poetic Drama* (London: Macmillan, 1989), 205.

24. Peter Hall interviewed by Catherine Itzin and Simon Trussler, 'Directing Pinter', *Theatre Quarterly* 16 (1975): 4.

25. Hinchcliffe, *Modern Verse Drama*, 52.

26. Tolley, *The Poetry of the Forties in Britain*, 204.

27. Edward Bond, *Selections from the Notebooks of Edward Bond*, vol. 2, 1980–95 (London: Bloomsbury, 2013), 291.

28. Ibid.

29. E. Martin Browne, 'The Poet and the Stage', in *The Penguin New Writing* 31 (1947), 82.

30. Kenneth Tynan, cited in Hinchcliffe, *Modern Verse Drama*, 14.

31. Donoghue, *The Third Voice*, 18.

32. John Masefield, *So Long to Learn: Chapters of an Autobiography* (London: William Heinemann, 1952), 105.

33. Robert H. Ross, *The Georgian Revolt 1910–1922: Rise and Fall of a Poetic Ideal* (Carbondale: Southern Illinois University Press, 1965), 80.

34. Ibid., 119.

35. John Drinkwater, *Discovery: Being the Second Book of an Autobiography* (London: Ernest Benn, 1932), 230.

36. Ross, *The Georgian Revolt 1910–1922*, 121–2.

37. Ibid., 121.

38. Christopher Hassall, *Edward Marsh, Patron of the Arts: A Biography* (London: Longmans, 1959), 277.

39. The plays of the Georgians became known primarily through publication. Some of their plays did, however, receive a modest staging at either the Liverpool Repertory Theatre (where Abercrombie became a reader, in 1913), the Birmingham Repertory Theatre (where Drinkwater was the first manager) and at Masefield's Boars Hill Theatre (for which Abercrombie, Binyon, Masefield and Bottomley wrote specifically). Of these playwrights, only Bottomley and Masefield achieved some early critical recognition for their plays in production – Masefield

for his first two dramas in prose, and Bottomley for *King Lear's Wife*, *Gruach*, and *The Riding to Lithend*.

40. A useful exploration and contextualization of the play is offered in Kevin J. Wetmore, '"Avenge me!" Ghosts in English Renaissance and *Kabuki* Revenge Dramas', in *Revenge Drama in European Renaissance and Japanese Theatre: From Hamlet to Madame Butterfly*, ed. Kevin J. Wetmore (New York: Palgrave Macmillan, 2008), 75–90. See also Helen Phillips, 'Gordon Bottomley and the Scottish Noh Play', *English Studies 3: Proceedings of the Third Conference on the Literature of Region and Nation*, Part 1, eds. J. J. Simon and Alain Sinner (Luxembourg: Publications du Centre Universitaire de Luxembourg, 1991), 214–33.

41. The productions at Rutland Boughton's Glastonbury Festivals provide a strong manifestation of this instinct, most particularly Boughton's own *The Immortal Hour* (1914). Rather than existing within an exclusive disciplinary context, these projects were of considerable interest to many modern dramatists, composers and poets, and reflected a larger environment of interdisciplinary and occasionally intermedial interaction. See Michael Hurd, *Rutland Boughton and the Glastonbury Festivals* (Oxford: Clarendon, 1993) for a useful introduction.

42. Paul Cornwell, *Only by Failure: The Many Faces of the Impossible Life of Terence Gray* (Cambridge: Salt, 2004), 100.

43. The term itself is more often than not attributed to theatre critic J.C. Trewin, and was a commonplace throughout the first, formative years of the BBC. See, for example, John Drakakis, *British Radio Drama* (Cambridge: Cambridge University Press, 1981).

44. MacCarthy, *Criticism*, 99. Not everyone agrees about Shelley; *The Cenci* is often cited as a potential exception to the general rule that nineteenth-century poets could not write literary or stageable drama. See, for example, Trewin, *Verse Drama Since 1800* (Cambridge: Cambridge University Press for The National Book League, 1956): 'The Cenci stands alone', 8.

45. J.W. Lambert, 'The Verse Drama', in *Theatre Programme*, ed. Trewin (London: Frederick Muller, 1954), 61. Robert Speaight provides a useful summary of the play's 'phenomenal' success: 'It was first produced in the Chapter House of Canterbury, and then ... the same company played over 800 performances in London, the main provincial cities of Britain and in the United States. During the war Mr. Martin Browne ... has toured the play throughout Britain, presenting it not only in theatres but also in churches and cathedrals. It was again successfully revived in 1947. No other modern English play in verse has had a comparable success ...' Robert Speaight, *Drama Since 1939* (London: Longmans Green, 1947), 35.

46. Henzie Browne, *The Pilgrim Story: The Pilgrim Players, 1939–1943* (London: Frederick Muller, 1945), 20.

47. William Poel, quoted in Speaight, *William Poel and the Elizabethan Revival* (London: William Heinemann, 1954), 196.

48. Harold Hobson, *Theatre in Britain: A Personal View* (Oxford: Phaidon, 1984), 84.

Notes

49. Hinchcliffe, *Modern Verse Drama*, 32.

50. E. Martin Browne, 'The Poet and the Stage', 81.

51. William B. Wahl, *Poetic Drama Interviews: Robert Speaight, E. Martin Browne and W.H. Auden* (Salzburg: Institut für Englische Sprache und Literatur, 1976), 14.

52. Ibid., 68.

53. In a recent overview of post-war British theatre, Michael Billington openly declared his bias: he 'focuses more on England than Scotland, Wales and Northern Ireland' because that is the 'territory' with which he is most familiar. He seems to have had no compunction, however, in entitling his book: *State of the Nation: British Theatre Since 1945* (London: Faber, 2007). Billington's account only exploits an established critical tradition that tends to assume the essential centrality of England (and the London stage) to the trajectory of British theatre. Despite advertising a comprehensive history of the modern British stage (and 'state of the nation'), such narratives characteristically marginalize the independent dramatic history and traditions of Scotland and Wales.

54. Gordon Bottomley, quoted in Claude Colleer Abbott, 'Introduction', *Gordon Bottomley Poems and Plays* (London: Morrison and Gibb, 1953), 17.

55. Ibid. Bottomley became associated with several movements and societies whose aim was to foster the performance of drama beyond the limits of the established theatre: the Community Theatre, the Village Drama Society, the Arts League of Service, the Scottish National Theatre, the Scottish Association for the Speaking of Verse.

56. For more on Gullan's career, see Ronald E. Shields, 'Noble Poetry, Nobly Spoken: Marjorie Gullan and the Glasgow Nightingales', *Literature in Performance* 7.2 (1987): 34–45.

57. The premiere of Eliot's *The Cocktail Party* inaugurated the Edinburgh Festival in 1949.

58. David Atkinson, 'A Great Welsh Literary Tradition', *The Daily Telegraph* (online), 19 June 2014, http://www.telegraph.co.uk/sponsored/travel/wales-dylan-thomas/10909071/welsh-literary-tradition.html (accessed 14 January 2016).

Chapter 1

1. Barker, *On Poetry in Drama*, 4.

2. Ibid., 9.

3. In Hardy's nineteen-act *The Dynasts* (1903), 'the noblest of all closet-plays', Trewin argues, 'we are moved by the prose directions as much as by the verse' (Trewin, *Verse Drama Since 1800*, 13).

4. Robert Bridges, *The First Part of Nero*, in *The Poetical Works of Robert Bridges*, vol. 3 (London: John Murray, 1901), 86.

5. Hallam Tennyson, *Alfred, Lord Tennyson: A Memoir* (Cambridge: Cambridge University Press, 2012), 174–5.

6. Henry Irving, quoted in Laurence Irving, *Henry Irving: The Actor and his World* (London: Faber & Faber, 1951), 265.

7. Hallam Tennyson, *Alfred, Lord Tennyson*, 175.

8. Barker, *On Poetry in Drama*, 3.

9. Ibid.

10. Clifford Bax, 'Stephen Phillips. Poetic Dramatist', in Bax, *Some I Knew Well* (London: Phoenix House Ltd., 1951), 27.

11. Barker, *On Poetry in Drama*, 39.

12. As many apologists have been keen to point out, Lamb was responding to the theatrical conventions of his day, many of which saw a striking misrepresentation (if not alteration) of the original plays.

13. George Rowell, *The Victorian Theatre, 1792–1914: A Survey* (Oxford: Oxford University Press, 1956), 32.

14. Trewin, *Verse Drama Since 1800*, 7.

15. Edward Bulwer-Lytton, *Richelieu. Or, The Conspiracy, A Play in Five Acts* (London: Saunders & Otley, 1839), 55.

16. Alfred Lord Tennyson, *Becket* (London: Macmillan, [1884] 1885), 60–1.

17. Donoghue, *The Third Voice*, 25.

18. Priscilla Thouless, *Modern Poetic Drama* (Freeport: Books for Libraries Press, [1934] 1968), 1.

19. Ernest Reynolds, *Modern English Drama: A Survey of the Theatre from 1900* (Greenwood: Greenwood Press, 1950), 53–4.

20. Trewin, *Verse Drama Since 1800*, 11.

21. Ibid., 5.

22. Terry Otten, *The Deserted Stage: The Search for Dramatic Form in Nineteenth-century England* (Athens: Ohio University Press, 1972), 3.

23. Augusta Webster, *Disguises: A Drama* (London: C. Kegan Paul & Co., 1879), 202.

24. Stephen Phillips, in William Archer, *Real Conversations. Recorded by William Archer. With Twelve Portraits* (London: William Heinemann, 1904), 83.

25. William Archer, 'Drama', in *The Reign of Queen Victoria: A Survey of Fifty Years of Progress*, vol. 2, ed. Thomas H. Ward (London: Smith & Elder, 1887), 561.

26. Reynolds, *Modern English Drama*, 63.

27. Glover, *Drama and Mankind*, 39.

28. Trewin, *Verse Drama Since 1800*, 11.

29. Barker, *On Poetry in Drama*, 10.

30. Ibid., 28.

Notes

31. Thouless, *Modern Poetic Drama*, 10.

32. Trewin, *Verse Drama Since 1800*, 12.

33. Reynolds, *Modern English Drama*, 62.

34. Bax, 'Stephen Phillips. Poetic Dramatist', 26.

35. Reynolds, *Modern English Drama*, 63, 66–7.

36. Richard Le Gallienne, review of *Paolo and Francesca*. Reprinted at back of Stephen Phillips, *Paolo and Francesca. A Tragedy in Four Acts*, 10th ed. (London: John Lane, [1900] 1902), n.p.

37. Reprinted at back of Phillips, *Paolo and Francesca*, n.p.

38. Ibid.

39. Ibid.

40. Ibid.

41. Thouless, *Modern Poetic Drama*, 15.

42. Ibid., 19.

43. Phillips, *Paolo and Francesca*, 24.

44. Alfred Lord Tennyson, *Queen Mary* (New York: Robert M. De Witt, 1875), 34.

45. Phillips, *Paolo and Francesca*, 25.

46. Ibid.

47. Ibid., 120.

48. Letter from Stephen Phillips to Laurence Binyon, 1886, quoted in Richard Whittington-Egan, *Stephen Phillips: A Biography* (High Wycombe: Rivendale Press, 2006), 42.

49. Ibid.

50. Archer, *Real Conversations*, 77–8.

51. Ibid.

52. Thouless, *Modern Poetic Drama*, 25.

53. Hesketh Pearson, *The Last Actor-Managers* (London: Methuen, 1950), 31.

54. N.a., review of *Paolo and Francesca*, *The Times*, reprinted at back of Phillips, *Paolo and Francesca*, n.p.

55. Manchester Literary Club, *Papers Manchester Quarterly, 1902: A Journal of Literature and Art*, vol. 28 (London: Forgotten Books, [1902] 2013), 410–1. For Pratt, such differences are resolved by noting the similarity between the drug scene in *Paolo and Francesca* and the apothecary scene in *Romeo and Juliet*.

56. According to Sidney Colvin, 'Mr Phillips has added that which was hitherto lacking . . . namely, a poetical play of the highest quality, strictly designed for, and expressly suited to, the stage' (reprinted at back of Phillips, *Paolo and Francesca*, n.p.). Indeed, a recent biography continues this trend when it identifies in his plays a 'sort of highly simplified Elizabethan rhetoric that could

be absorbed by his audience without strain or irritation' (Whittington-Egan, *Stephen Phillips*, 126).

57. N.a., review of *Paolo and Francesca, Stage*, reprinted at back of Phillips, *Paolo and Francesca*, n.p.

58. Harold Monro, *Some Contemporary Poets* (London: Simkin, Marshall, 1920), 3.

59. Bax, 'Stephen Phillips. Poetic Dramatist', 26.

60. Phillips, *Herod: A Tragedy* (London: John Lane, 1901), 126.

61. N.a., review of *Paolo and Francesca, Morning Leader*, reprinted at back of Phillips, *Paolo and Francesca*, n.p.

62. Ibid.

63. Pearson, *The Last Actor-Managers*, 10–11.

64. Arthur Symons, *Plays, Acting, and Music* (London: Duckworth, 1903), 95.

65. Ibid., 96.

66. Ibid.

67. Ibid., 97.

68. Ibid.

69. Ibid., 98

70. 'I felt that the Jacobean form was the British form ... and that Browning and Tennyson and Stephen Phillips had practised it just as much as Marlowe and Shakespeare and Webster and Jonson.' Gordon Bottomley, *A Stage for Poetry: My Purposes with my Plays*, Kendal: Titus Wilson & Son Ltd (1948), 2.

71. Reynolds, *Modern English Drama*, 68.

72. Trewin identifies in *Don Juan* 'the Theatre of Ideas pressing upon the theatre of Stephen Phillips (but Flecker was a far better poet)' (*The Edwardian Theatre*, Oxford: Basil Blackwell, 1976, 124).

73. Alec Macdonald, 'James Elroy Flecker', *Fortnightly Review* 115 (February 1924): 274–84.

74. Tree died in 1917, and never saw the revised manuscript.

75. Basil Dean, 'Introduction' to James Elroy Flecker, *Hassan, An Acting Edition prepared and Introduced by Basil Dean with Commentary and Notes by E.R. Wood* (London: Heinemann, 1951), xii.

76. Flecker, letter to Dean, 18 June 1914, quoted Ibid., xiv.

77. Ibid.

78. Dean, 'Introduction', *Hassan*, xviii.

79. Martin Lee-Browne and Mark Elder, *Delius and His Music* (London: Boydell & Brewer, 2014), 401.

80. Reynolds, *Modern English Drama*, 67.

81. Trewin, *Verse Drama Since 1800*, 13.

82. E.R. Wood, Commentary and Notes, in Flecker, *Hassan* (London: Heinemann, 1951), 97.

83. Reynolds, *Modern English Drama*, 13–14.

84. Ibid., 99.

85. Ashley Dukes, *The World to Play With* (London: Oxford University Press, 1928), 123.

86. Trewin, *Verse Drama Since 1800*, 13.

87. Wood, Commentary and Notes, in Flecker, *Hassan*, 89.

88. Flecker, *Hassan*, 23–4.

89. Ibid., 69.

90. Ibid.

91. Ibid., 70.

92. Ibid.

93. Ibid., 73.

94. Ibid.

95. Ibid., 79.

96. Ibid.

97. Ibid., 80–1.

98. Ibid., 81.

99. Ibid.

100. Ibid., 86.

101. Ibid., 83.

102. Ibid.

103. Ibid., 85.

104. Ibid., 1.

105. Ibid., 11.

106. Ibid., 33.

107. Ibid., 12.

108. Ibid., 13.

109. Ibid., 6.

110. Ibid., 39.

111. Ibid., 40.

112. Ibid., 15.

113. Wood, Commentary and Notes, in Flecker, *Hassan*, 98.

114. Ibid.

115. Lee-Browne and Elder, *Delius*, 405.

Chapter 2

1. Leeming, *Poetic Drama*, 188.

2. Norman Marshall, *The Other Theatre* (London: John Lehmann, 1947), 14.

3. Trewin, *The Birmingham Repertory, 1913–1963* (London: Barrie & Rockliff, 1963), 10.

4. Trewin, *The Edwardian Theatre* (Oxford: Basil Blackwell, 1976), 133.

5. William Bridges-Adams, letter to Arthur Colby Sprague, quoted in Bridges-Adams, *A Bridges-Adams Letter Book*, ed. with a memoir by Robert Speaight (London: Society for Theatre Research, 1971), 35.

6. Barker, *Prefaces to Shakespeare*, vol. 6, ed. Edward M. Moore (London: B.T. Batsford, 1974), 36.

7. Kenneth Pickering, *Drama in the Cathedral: A Twentieth-Century Encounter of Church and Stage*, 2nd edition (Colwall, Worcestershire: J. Garnet Miller, 2001), 35.

8. Speaight, *William Poel and the Elizabethan Revival*, 165.

9. Ibid.

10. Drinkwater, *Discovery*, 210.

11. Gilbert Murray, quoted in Ashley Dukes, *The World to Play With* (London: Oxford University Press, 1928), 116.

12. Terence Gray, *Dance-Drama: Experiments in the Art of the Theatre* (Cambridge: W. Heffers & Sons Ltd., 1926), 13.

13. Dukes, *The World to Play With* (London: Oxford University Press, 1928), 27.

14. William Archer, *The Old Drama and the New: An Essay in Re-Valuation* (London: William Heinemann, 1923), 369.

15. E. Martin Browne, 'British Drama League', *Educational Theatre Journal* 5.3 (1953): 203.

16. Ibid.

17. Claire Cochrane, *Twentieth-Century British Theatre: Industry, Art and Empire* (Cambridge: Cambridge University Press, 2011), 113.

18. See Cochrane, *Twentieth-Century British Theatre*. Ironically, that divide – and the generally derogatory implications of the term 'amateur' – now attests to the realization of many of the theatrical, if not social, instincts of that amateur movement on a professional stage that is no longer exclusively in thrall to a commercialized West End.

19. Pickering, *Drama in the Cathedral*, 24.

20. E. Martin Browne, quoted in Pickering, *Drama in the Cathedral*, 88.

21. Leeming, *Poetic Drama*, 5.

Notes

22. W.B. Yeats, 'Samhain: 1906 – Literature and the Living Voice', in Yeats, *The Irish Dramatic Movement*, ed. Mary FitzGerald and Richard J. Finneran (New York: Scribner, 2003): 96.

24. Yeats, 'A People's Theatre: A Letter to Lady Gregory', ibid., 131.

25. Ibid., 131.

26. Ibid., 132–3. Indeed, for Yeats, it was the very democratizing success of Irish nationalism that had ensured its consequent myopia in matters of art: 'Ireland has suffered more than England from democracy, for since the Wild Geese fled, who might have grown to be leaders in manners and in taste, she has had but political leaders' (133).

27. Ross, *The Georgian Revolt 1910–1922*, 131.

28. Lascelles Abercrombie, 'Preface', *The Poems of Lascelles Abercrombie* (London: Oxford University Press, 1930), vi.

29. Gordon Bottomley, letter to Edward Marsh, 1 October 1915, quoted in Ross, *The Georgian Revolt 1910–1922*, 131.

30. Bottomley, *A Stage for Poetry: My Purposes with my Plays* (Kendal: Titus Wilson & Son Ltd., 1948), 18.

31. Bottomley, 'To W.B. Yeats', in Bottomley, *Lyric Plays* (London: Constable & Co., 1932), v.

32. Allardyce Nicoll, *English Drama, 1900–1930: The Beginnings of the Modern Period, Part 2* (Cambridge: Cambridge University Press, 1973), 303.

33. Chaman Lall, 'Shaw, The Show, and the Shawm, or, What's Wrong With the Theatre?' *Coterie* 3 (1919): 77.

34. Ibid., 77.

35. Glover, *Drama and Mankind*, 40.

36. Ibid.

37. Ibid.

38. Symons, *Plays, Acting, and Music*, 97.

39. Abercrombie, 'The Function of Poetry in the Drama', *Poetry Review* (March 1912): 109.

40. Ibid., 114.

41. Drinkwater, *Prose Papers* (London: Elkin Mathews, 1918), 213.

42. Dukes, *The World to Play With*, 29.

43. Eric Bentley, *The Playwright as Thinker: A Study of Drama in Modern Times* (New York: Reynal & Hitchcock, 1946), 225.

44. James Agate, *A Short View of the English Stage, 1900–1926* (Freeport, NY: Books for Libraries, [1926] 1969), 58, 55.

45. Donoghue, *The Third Voice*, 31.

46. Katharine J. Worth, *Revolutions in Modern Drama* (London: G. Bell & Sons, 1972), 105.

47. Monro, 'Dramatic Poetry and Poetic Drama', *Poetry Review* 3 (March 1912): 132.

48. Abercrombie, 'The Function of Poetry in the Drama', 113.

49. Abercrombie, *An Essay Towards a Theory of Art* (London: Martin Secker, 1922), 110–11.

50. Yeats, '*Beltaine*: February 1900 – Plans and Methods', in *The Irish Dramatic Movement*, ed. FitzGerald and Finneran, 154.

51. Drinkwater, *Prose Papers*, 221.

52. Laurence Binyon, 'The Return to Poetry', *Rhythm* 1.4 (1912): 1.

53. Bottomley, *A Stage for Poetry*, 70.

54. 'For the purpose of this discussion, however, let me use a name which allows it to be more easily handled. ... I do not entirely mean the plane of such named and recognizable emotions as love, anger, hate, but rather the general substratum to all existence, emotion nameless and unappointed.' Abercrombie, 'The Function of Poetry in the Drama', 112.

55. Ibid.

56. Gibson, quoted in Drinkwater, *Discovery*, 214.

57. Ibid., 214.

58. George Bernard Shaw, 'Preface' to *Mrs Warren's Profession*, in *Plays Pleasant* (London: Penguin, 2000), 196.

59. Archer, *The Old Drama and the New*, 387.

60. Ronald Schuchard, *The Last Minstrels: Yeats and the Revival of the Bardic Arts* (Oxford: Oxford University Press, 2008), 189.

61. Drinkwater, *Discovery*, 217.

62. Ibid., 154.

63. Masefield, *So Long to Learn*, 157.

64. Ibid.

65. Gray, *Dance-Drama*, 13.

66. Ibid.

67. Drinkwater, *Discovery*, 172.

68. Masefield, *So Long to Learn*, 141-2.

69. Martin Ellehauge, *Striking Figures Among Modern English Dramatists* (Copenhagen: Levin & Munksgaard, 1931), 27.

70. Ibid., 28.

Notes

71. T.S. Eliot, 'Poetry and Drama' [1951 with additional notes, 1957], in Eliot, *On Poetry and Poets* [1957] (London: Faber & Faber, 1969), 77.

72. Schuchard, *The Last Minstrels*, 147.

73. For an account of the Poets' Theatre project and its collapse, primarily under the tension between Ashley Dukes and Rupert Doone, see Michael J. Sidnell, *Dances of Death: The Group Theatre of London in the Thirties* (London: Faber & Faber, 1984), 266–9.

74. Eliot, 'Poetry and Drama', 78.

75. Schuchard, *The Last Minstrels*, 17.

76. Ibid., 41.

77. Masefield, *So Long to Learn*, 154–55. Intriguingly, the dramas by Masefield that are most clearly influenced by the subject and themes of that Irish movement are in prose: *The Campden Wonder* and *The Tragedy of Nan* are indebted to Synge in particular. Masefield's *Tristan and Isolt* shows a strong affiliation with the Pre-Raphaelites, although its earthy 'Chaucerian' realism also points to the influence of a more realist poetic aesthetic.

78. Schuchard, *The Last Minstrels*, provides an extensive and valuable account.

79. Masefield, *So Long to Learn*, 193.

80. Ibid., 194.

81. Masefield, 'Words Spoken at the Music Room Boars Hill in the Afternoon of November 5th, 1930 at a Festival Designed in the Honour of William Butler Yeats, Poet'; reprinted as 'On Mr. W.B. Yeats' in Masefield, *Recent Prose* (New York: Macmillan [1932] 1933), 194.

82. Masefield, *So Long to Learn*, 207.

83. Bottomley, *A Stage for Poetry*, 20. Yeats had been mistaken in his emphasis on stillness in dance, had 'failed to evolve that sufficiency of movement which is necessary to keep an audience interested' (ibid.).

84. Gray, quoted in Cornwell, *Only by Failure*, 51.

85. Gray, quoted ibid., 132.

86. Gray, quoted ibid., 152. Gray's theories and stagings suggest the influence of Adolphe Appia, Jacques Copeau and Charles Dullin, amongst others.

87. Marshall, *Other*, 54.

88. Ibid., 57.

89. Cornwell, *Only by Failure*, 151.

90. See Ninette de Valois, *Step by Step: The Formation of an Establishment* (London: W.H. Allen, 1977), 181.

91. Reynolds, *Modern English Drama*, 89.

92. de Valois, 'Introduction' to *The Ballet in Britain. Eight Oxford Lectures*, ed. Peter Brinson (London: Oxford University Press, 1962), 1. For further discussion of

de Valois's involvement with Gray, Yeats and the formation of the National Ballet, see Melanie Bigold, 'English Ballet: A National Art for the New Elizabethan Moment', in *The New Elizabethan Age: Culture, Society and National Identity after World War II*, ed. Irene Morra and Rob Gossedge (London: I.B. Tauris, 2016), 243–64.

Chapter 3

1. Binyon, 'The Return to Poetry', 1.
2. Binyon, *Attila: A Tragedy in Four Acts* (London: John Murray, 1907), 15.
3. N.a., review of *Attila*, His Majesty's Theatre, *Spectator*, 7 September 1907, 11.
4. Ibid.
5. Ibid.
6. 'Georgian revolt' is a term coined by Robert H. Ross in his study of the same name.
7. See Ronald E. Shields, 'Voices inside a Poet's Garden: John Masefield's Theatricals at Boar's Hill', *Text and Performance Quarterly* 16.4 (1996): 301–20.
8. E. Martin Browne, *The Making of T.S. Eliot's Plays* (Cambridge: Cambridge University Press, 1969), 1.
9. Kenneth Muir, quoted in Shields, 'Voices inside a Poet's Garden', 317.
10. Richard Badenhausen, 'Drama', in *T.S. Eliot in Context*, ed. Jason Harding (Cambridge University Press, 2011), 129. For a more detailed consideration of Masefield's influence on drama-in-education, see Shields, 'Voices inside a Poet's Garden'.
11. Shields, 'Voices inside a Poet's Garden', 302.
12. Dennis Kennedy, *Granville Barker and the Dream of Theatre* (New York: Cambridge University Press, 1989), 51.
13. Ibid.
14. Bentley, *The Playwright as Thinker*, 67. Donoghue, on the other hand, terms it 'one of the most embarrassing plays in the modern theatre' (*The Third Voice*, 29).
15. Masefield, *So Long to Learn*, 182.
16. As Trewin notes of Pompey, the play 'is classical, not domestic, tragedy. Pompey is an idealist with more of Masefield in him than the historical original, just as Shaw's Caesar is ineradicably Shavius. A chronicle without bombast. . . . Most of the action is, classically, offstage; *Pompey* is a play of the mind' (*The Edwardian Theatre*, 121–2).
17. Joan Tasker Grimbert, 'Introduction' to *Tristan and Isolde: A Casebook*, ed. Joan Tasker Grimbert (London: Routledge, 2013), lxxxv.

18. Masefield provides a description of the Victorian recitation against which he (and Yeats) reacted: 'The old-fashioned reciters ... were to be heard on many stages and at entertainments, reciting tales in verse, that lasted about ten minutes, with a slow delivery and much interspersed fervour of theatrical action: "pump-handle", as it was called' (*So Long to Learn*, 131).

19. Ibid., 169.

20. Elsie Fogerty, quoted in Marion Cole, *Fogie: The Life of Elsie Fogerty* (London: Peter Davies, 1967), 29–30.

21. Masefield, *So Long to Learn*, 169–70.

22. Gray, *Dance-Drama*, 26.

23. Masefield, *So Long to Learn*, 235.

24. Ibid., 224.

25. Masefield, *Philip the King*, in *Verse Plays* (New York: Macmillan, 1925), 60.

26. Ibid., 60–1.

27. Ibid., 61.

28. Drinkwater, *The Storm*, in *Collected Plays*, vol. 1 (London: Sidgwick & Jackson, 1925), 97.

29. Ibid., 112.

30. Ellehauge, *Striking Figures Among Modern English Dramatists*, 88.

31. Abercrombie, *The Adder*, in *The Poems of Lascelles Abercrombie* (London: Oxford University Press, 1930), 363.

32. Ibid., 365.

33. It is worth noting, however, that the division between Georgian and modernist can often be artificially absolutist, not least in relation to Binyon's influence on Pound.

34. George Bernard Shaw, 'Preface' to *The Admirable Bashville; or, Constancy Unrewarded, Being the Novel of Cashel Byron's Profession Done into a Stage Play in Three acts and in Blank Verse with a Note on Modern Prizefighting* (New York: Brentano's, [1901] 1909), 7.

35. Masefield, 'Play-Writing', in *Recent Prose* (New York: Macmillan, [1932] 1933), 123.

36. Shaw, 'Preface' to *The Admirable Bashville*, 9.

37. Ibid.

38. Ibid., 126.

39. Thouless, *Modern Poetic Drama*, 8.

40. Reynolds, *Modern English Drama*, 62.

41. Ibid., 55.

42. Thouless, *Modern Poetic Drama*, 8.

43. For Yeats, that irrevocable past was an essentially oral tradition, one in which 'poetry was a part of the general life' of the people. By 1916, Yeats – unlike many of his English followers – had declared the impossibility of restoring this larger social and cultural environment. 'The First Performance of *At the Hawk's Well*', in Yeats, *The Plays. The Collected Works of W.B. Yeats*, vol. 2, eds. David R. Clark and Rosalind E. Clark (New York: Scribner, 200), 691–2.

44. Ronald Peacock, *The Poet in the Theatre* (New York: Harcourt, Brace & Co., 1946), 119.

45. Drinkwater, 'Preface' to *The Collected Plays of John Drinkwater* vol. 1 (London: Sidgwick & Jackson, 1925), vi.

46. Dukes, *The World to Play With*, 119.

47. Ibid., xi, xiii.

48. Ibid., 79.

49. T.S. Eliot, *The Aims of Poetic Drama*, The Presidential Address to the Poets' Theatre Guild (London: The Poets' Theatre Guild, 1949): 4.

50. Monro, 'Dramatic Poetry and Poetic Drama', 132.

51. Ibid.

52. Ibid.

53. Bottomley, *A Stage for Poetry*, 3.

54. Bottomley, quoted in Abbott, 'Introduction', 15.

55. Bottomley, *King's Lear's Wife*, in *Poems and Plays* (London: Morrison & Gibb, 1953), 133.

56. Ibid., 139.

57. Ibid., 141, 142.

58. Ibid., 137.

59. Ibid., 139.

60. Ibid., 139–40.

61. Ibid., 140.

62. Ibid., 133.

63. Ibid., 133.

64. Ibid., 137.

65. Ibid., 144.

66. Ibid., 149.

67. Ibid., 102.

68. Ibid., 194.

69. Ibid., 147.

70. Ibid.

71. Ibid., 146.

72. Ibid., 143.

73. Ibid., 142.

74. Ibid., 149.

75. Ibid., 155.

76. Ibid., 155, 156.

77. Ibid., 153.

78. Ruby Cohn, *Modern Shakespeare Offshoots* (Princeton: Princeton University Press, 2015), 252.

79. Bottomley, *King Lear's Wife*, 157.

80. Ibid., 161.

81. Ibid., 140.

82. Ibid., 161.

83. Ibid.

84. Ibid.

85. Ibid.

86. Ibid., 162.

87. Ibid., 163.

88. Ibid., 163.

89. Ibid., 133.

90. Ibid., 135.

91. Ibid., 133.

92. Cohn also identifies a similarity between the scene and that between the Blind Man and the Fool in Yeats's *On Baile's Strand* (*Modern*, 251).

93. Bottomley, *King Lear's Wife*, 163.

94. Ibid.

95. Ibid., 158.

96. Ross, *The Georgian Revolt 1910–1922*, 129.

97. Drinkwater, letter to Edward Marsh, 27 September 1915, quoted in Ross, *The Georgian Revolt 1910–1922*, 131.

98. Bottomley, in *Poet and Painter: Being the Correspondence between Gordon Bottomley and Paul Nash, 1910–1946*, eds. Claude Colleer Abbott and Anthony Bertram (London: Oxford University Press, 1955), 133.

99. Ibid.

100. Ibid., 139.

101. Bottomley, *A Stage for Poetry*, 2–3.

102. Ibid., 19.

103. Ibid.

104. Archer, *The Old Drama and the New*, 386–7.

105. Ibid., 387.

106. Bottomley, *A Stage for Poetry*, xiv.

107. Ibid.

108. Ibid., 18.

109. Ibid., 4.

110. Ibid., 19.

111. Ibid., 21.

112. In so doing, of course, he again echoes the assertions of Yeats: 'Shakespeare's art was public, now resounding and declamatory, now lyrical and subtle, but always public' (Note to *At the Hawk's Well*, 692).

113. Bottomley, *A Stage for Poetry*, xvi.

114. Ibid.

Chapter 4

1. Laurence Housman, 'Preface' to *Little Plays of Saint Francis*, First Series, (London: Sidgwick & Jackson, 1931), xix.

2. As Duncan Marks observes, the play 'is the first example of a new, intentionally unhistoric and fictitious depiction of WANA [We Are Not Amused].' 'We ARE Amused! The Comical Uses and Historical Abuses of Queen Victoria's Infamous Approach "We are Amused"', in *History and Humour: British and American Perspectives*, eds. Barbara Korte and Doris Lechner (Bielefeld: transcript Verlag, 2014), 141.

3. James Woodfield, *English Theatre in Transition, 1881–1914* (London: Routledge, 2015), 120.

4. Barker, 'Preface' to *Little Plays of Saint Francis*, vii. One of Housman's most successful and oft-revived plays to have escaped any problem with the censor is his co-authored verse play with Barker, *Prunella: Or, Love in a Dutch Garden* (1906), a lightly satirical pierrot romance with music. Housman reported to Margery Morgan that he had collaborated with Barker on six or seven plays; only *Prunella*, however, was produced and published as a co-authored work. See Margery M. Morgan, *A Drama of Political Man: A Study in the Plays of Harley Granville Barker* (London: Sidgwick & Jackson, 1961), 82.

5. Barker, 'Preface', viii.

6. Ibid., ix.

Notes

7. Ibid., xi.

8. Ibid., xii–xiii.

9. Ibid., xiv.

10. Gray, *Dance-Drama*, 14.

11. Ibid.

12. Barker, 'Preface', xv.

13. Ibid.

14. Masefield, 'Introduction' to *Verse Plays*, v–vi.

15. Bottomley, *A Stage for Poetry*, 69.

16. Ibid.

17. Ibid.

18. Ibid.

19. The studies of William V. Spanos and Gerald Clifford Weales remain the most thorough works thus far to engage with the theology of a number of religious dramas from the period under discussion.

20. Pickering, *Drama in the Cathedral*, 40.

21. Ibid., 39.

22. Ibid.

23. Ibid., 97.

24. Ibid.

25. See Ibid., 121–2 for a more detailed description of the staging and stage-space.

26. Masefield, *The Coming of Christ* (New York: Macmillan, 1928), 1.

27. Housman's play begins with a choral figure that offers a relatively conventional narrative promise. The audience will see:

    The manger where in great humility
    Lieth that Babe, the Maker of us all,
    By Mary's side, amid the beasts in stall.
    And ye shall see the coming of the Kings,
    Led by a star; and Gabriel that brings
    Unto St. Joseph in a dream by night
    Word of King Herod's fear, and counsels flight.

    (*Bethlehem, a Nativity Play* [New York: Macmillan, 1902], 4).

28. Masefield, *The Coming of Christ*, 3.

29. Ibid., 5.

30. Ibid., 8.

31. Ibid., 10.

32. Ibid., 13.

33. Ibid., 19.
34. Ibid., 20.
35. Ibid., 21.
36. Ibid., 22.
37. Ibid., 23.
38. Ibid., 24.
39. Ibid.
40. Ibid., 26.
41. For Masefield, it would seem – and in keeping with the spirit of a Nativity play – the primary salvation for mankind is to be found in the Incarnation. While the play constantly invokes the imminence of the Crucifixion, its focus is on the sacrifice of Christ, rather than the eternal life and salvation occasioned by his death.
42. Masefield, *The Coming of Christ*, 32.
43. Ibid., 34.
44. Ibid., 35.
45. Ibid., 36.
46. Ibid.
47. Ibid., 36, 37.
48. Ibid., 41.
49. Ibid., 42.
50. Ibid., 42–3.
51. Ibid., 48.
52. Ibid., 56.
53. Ibid., 57.
54. Pickering, *Drama in the Cathedral*, 137–8.
55. Eliot, Editorial, *The Criterion. A Literary Review*, viii. 4 (June 1928): 5.
56. Anonymous critic, *Patriot* 14 June 1928, quoted in Peter Webster, 'George Bell, John Masefield and *The Coming of Christ*: Context and Significance,' in *The Church and Humanity: The Life and Work of George Bell, 1883–1958*, ed. Andrew Chandler (Farnham: Ashgate, 2013), 53–4.
57. Pickering, *Drama in the Cathedral*, 103.
58. Ibid.
59. Speaight, *Drama since 1939*, 35.
60. Phillip Hollingworth, recorded interview with Kenneth Pickering, cited in Pickering, *Drama in the Cathedral*, 197.
61. A.C.H., 'Perplexing Play Brings Some Criticisms', *Kent Messenger*, 6 June 1936.
62. Speaight, *The Christian Theatre* (London: Burns & Oates, 1960), 129.

63. Anne Ridler, 'Introduction' to *Seed of Adam and Other Plays*, by Charles Williams (London: Oxford University Press, 1948), viii.

64. Ibid., vi.

65. Williams, 'Notes for an Address Delivered after a Performance [*Seed of Adam*] at Colchester, October 1937', reprinted in Williams, *Seed of Adam*, 94.

66. Ibid., 95.

67. Ibid.

68. Glen Cavaliero, *Charles Williams: Poet of Theology* (Eugene: Wipf & Stock, 2007), 47.

69. Williams, 'Synopsis for *Seed of Adam*. Written for the Programme', reprinted in Williams, *Seed of Adam*, 93.

70. Williams, *Seed of Adam*, 3.

71. Ibid., 4.

72. Williams includes a note: 'The Hebrew is written phonetically, as for the Sephardi pronunciation . . . The Ashkenazi pronunciation can be used if desired' (ibid., 10).

73. Ibid., 13.

74. Williams, 'Synopsis for *Seed of Adam*', 94.

75. Williams, *Seed of Adam*, 23.

76. Ibid.

77. Grevel Lindop, *Charles Williams: The Third Inkling* (Oxford: Oxford University Press, 2015), 264.

78. Williams, *Seed of Adam*, 4.

79. Ibid., 17.

80. Ibid., 9. Not all have agreed with this assessment; Lindop hails the play's 'wonderfully speakable verse' as one of the reasons why the play can be seen as 'a minor masterpiece' (*Charles Williams*, 265).

81. Cavaliero, *Charles Williams*, 47.

82. This is not to say that there was not an audience for such works: *Seed of Adam* became a relative staple with religious drama societies for some years.

83. To some extent, the play can be read as an initial exploration of the themes that Sayers would develop in her theological work *The Mind of the Maker* (1941), a discussion of the idea of creativity in relation to the doctrine of the Holy Trinity.

84. Reynolds, *Modern English Drama*, 98.

85. Dorothy L. Sayers, *The Zeal of Thy House* (London: Victor Gollancz, 1937), 100.

86. Ibid.

87. Ibid., 106.

88. Ibid.

89. Ibid., 110–11.

90. Ibid., 70.

91. Ibid., 69.

92. Ibid., 50.

93. Ibid., 51.

94. Ibid.

95. Ibid.

96. Crystal Downing, *Writing Performances: The Stages of Dorothy L. Sayers* (London: Palgrave, 2004), 64.

Chapter 5

1. 'He does not know what to do with the drama in our mass civilization unless it be to limit it to imitations of the ancient Japanese Noh plays performed in a friend's drawing room. A new type of drawing-room play indeed!' (Bentley, *The Playwright as Thinker*, 225).

2. Bottomley, *A Stage for Poetry*, 2.

3. Bottomley identifies Gray as 'the only director of a professional theatre who interested himself in what I wanted to do in the theatre' (ibid., 9).

4. Eliot, 'Religious Drama and the Church', *Rep*, 1.6 (October 1934): 4.

5. Ibid.

6. Sidnell, *Dances of Death*, 98. Ultimately, Eliot's Chorus 'does not represent groups, does not sing, dance or even move much but speaks as the abstract voice of the individual against group behaviour'; in the Christian context of the play, it represents 'the Voice of the Church in God' (ibid., 98–9).

7. Sidnell also identifies an admiration for Michel Saint-Denis's Compagnie des Quinze (*Dances of Death*, 49).

8. Sidnell attempts a comprehensive listing of members of the Group between 1933 and 1935; see *Dances of Death*, 270–4.

9. The Group Theatre, quoted in Edward Mendelson, *Early Auden* (London: Faber & Faber, 1981), 266. Mendelson speculates that these early manifestos were 'hammered into shape by Auden but [did] not necessarily [reflect] his ideas' (ibid., 265).

10. Ibid., 266.

11. Mendelson, *Early Auden*, 265.

12. Stephen Spender, 'Poetry and Expressionism', *New Statesman and Nation* 15.368 (12 March 1938): 407.

13. This support of a variety of approaches to verse drama would continue after the war; Ronald Duncan notes that it was Eliot who first contacted Browne on his

behalf in relation to what would become *This Way to the Tomb*. Following the disastrous London run of *Stratton* at the Mercury (largely thanks to a heatwave), he was to learn from Dukes that Eliot had anonymously covered his financial losses out of his own royalties from *The Cocktail Party*. See Ronald Duncan, *How to Make Enemies* (London: Rupert Hart-Davis, 1968), 217–18.

14. Sidnell's study offers the most incisive account of this moment, not to mention a close assessment of the relationship between *The Rock* and *Dance of Death*.

15. Donoghue notes Eliot's 'progress from the easy, exclusive ritual of *Murder in the Cathedral* to the much more subtle drama of Holiness in *The Cocktail Party* and *The Confidential Clerk*' (*Third Voice*, 113).

16. Sidnell, *Dances of Death*, 38.

17. Eliot, *The Use of Poetry and the Use of Criticism. Studies in the Relation of Criticism to Poetry in England* (London: Faber & Faber, 1933), 154.

18. Eliot, 'Poetry and Drama', 82.

19. Eliot, *The Sacred Wood. Essays on Poetry and Criticism* [1920. 2nd edition 1928] (London: Methuen, 1960), 70.

20. Speaight, in Wahl, *Poetic Drama Interviews*, 21.

21. In 1926 and 1927, Eliot published *Sweeney* in two separate fragments, apparently resigned to the impossibility of creating a cohesive drama out of those fragments and equally convinced of their independent merit as poetry.

22. Arnold Bennett, *Journal* (New York: Viking, 1933), 786–7.

23. Eliot later (tentatively) asserted in *The Use of Poetry*: 'poetry begins, I dare say, with a savage beating a drum in a jungle, and it retains that essence of percussion of rhythm' (155).

24. As Schuchard has detailed in *The Last Minstrels*, Yeats's experimentations with notated chanting were hardly 'musical' in the conventional sense and their primary focus was to attempt a contemporary realization of ancient oral traditions. Within that reading, the innate musicality of poetry itself – not musical setting – was the priority.

25. Eliot, 'The Music of Poetry', in *On Poetry and Poets* (London: Faber & Faber, [1957] 1969), 33.

26. Eliot, 'Poetry and Drama', 96. Walter Pater famously identified 'all art' as 'constantly [aspiring] towards the condition of music', and his assertion proved a minor rallying-cry for many modernist artists. See Walter Pater, *The Renaissance: Studies in Art and Poetry. The 1893 Text*, ed. Donald L. Hill (Berkeley: University of California Press, 1980), 106.

27. Eliot, *Sweeney Agonistes. Fragments of an Aristophanic Melodrama* [1932], in *T.S. Eliot: The Complete Poems and Plays, 1909–1950* (New York: Harcourt, Brace & Co., 1958), 85.

28. Elisabeth Wintersteen Schneider, *T.S. Eliot: The Pattern in the Carpet* (Berkeley: University of California Press, 1975), 95–6. The above assessment resonates with similar, necessarily metaphorical assessments of the musicality of Eliot's

poetry – the 'orchestra' in *The Waste Land* or the musical structure and sonority of *The Four Quartets*.

29. W.H. Auden, 'A Review of *Modern Poetic Drama*, by Priscilla Thouless', in *W.H. Auden: Prose and Travel Books in Prose and Verse*, vol. I, ed. Edward Mendelson (Princeton: Princeton University Press, 1996), 70. In 1932, Guthrie had argued for the restoration of music and dance to the contemporary theatre, citing Nigel Playfair's 1920 production of *The Beggar's Opera* as an ideal – and bemoaning the fact that the production had thus far only managed to inspire pale imitations (*Theatre Prospect*, London: Wishart, 1932, 58–61: 70). Auden later collaborated with Brecht on an adaptation of *The Duchess of Malfi* (1946) and translated the songs from *The Caucasian Chalk Circle* and, with Chester Kallman, *The Seven Deadly Sins* (1959) and *The Rise and Fall of the City of Mahagonny* (1976).

30. Christopher Isherwood, 'German Literature in England', *New Republic*, nos. 98–9 (5 April 1939): 255.

31. Ibid.

32. Rupert Doone, quoted in Robert Medley, *Drawn from the Life: A Memoir* (London: Faber & Faber, 1983), 153.

33. Sidnell, *Dances of Death*, 103.

34. Ibid., 151.

35. Eliot, interview with *Glasgow Herald* (27 August 1949), quoted in Browne, *The Making of T.S. Eliot's Plays*, 236.

36. Carol H. Smith justifiably identifies this 'struggle toward unity' as 'the distinguishing characteristic' of Eliot's dramatic career (*T.S. Eliot's Dramatic Theory and Practice. From Sweeney Agonistes to The Elder Statesman*, Princeton: Princeton University Press, 1963, 5).

37. Eliot, 'Poetry and Drama', 87.

38. Ibid.

39. Ibid.

40. Ibid.

41. Ibid., 87–8.

42. Ibid., 88.

43. Eliot, *The Use of Poetry*, 153.

44. Browne, *The Making of T.S. Eliot's Plays*, 8.

45. Eliot, *The Rock* (London: Faber & Faber, 1934), 5.

46. Browne, *The Making of T.S. Eliot's Plays*, 16.

47. Eliot, letter to Martin Shaw, quoted ibid., 13.

48. Browne, *The Making of T.S. Eliot's Plays*, 82.

49. See ibid., 81–3.

50. Eliot, 'The Aims of Poetic Drama', 6.

51. Eliot, 'John Marston' [1932] in *Selected Essays* (London: Faber & Faber, 1951), 229.

Notes

52. Eliot, 'Four Elizabethan Dramatists' [1924], in ibid., 111.

53. Eliot, *Murder in the Cathedral*, in *The Complete Plays of T.S. Eliot* (New York: Harcourt, Brace & World, Inc. 1967), 48–51.

54. Ibid., 52.

55. Speaight, *The Christian Theatre*, 127.

56. Reynolds, *Modern English Drama*, 98.

57. Donoghue, *The Third Voice*, 76.

58. Eliot, 'Poetry and Drama', 81.

59. Eliot, *Murder in the Cathedral*, 47.

60. Browne, *The Making of T.S. Eliot's Plays*, 87.

61. Cole, *Fogie*, 165.

62. Ibid.

63. Ibid., 165.

64. J.M.C. Crum, 'Mr T.S. Eliot's Play', *Canterbury Cathedral Chronicle* XXI (1945), 22–4, quoted in Pickering, *Drama in the Cathedral*, 183.

65. '[T]he director should find ways of bringing these characters into positions in which they can slide almost imperceptibly into concerted speech' (Browne, *The Making of T.S. Eliot's Plays*, 127).

66. Ibid.

67. Eliot, 'Poetry and Drama', 83. David E. Jones similarly argues that the writing demands that the play 'be listened to in a special way, much as one would listen to a small-scale opera, with its arias, duets, quartets, and so on' (Jones, *The Plays of T.S. Eliot* [Toronto: University of Toronto Press, 1965], 121).

68. Eliot, 'Poetry and Drama', 85–6.

69. Auden, 'The Future of English Poetic Drama', in *W.H. Auden and Christopher Isherwood. Plays and Other Dramatic Writings by W.H. Auden, 1928–1938*, ed. Edward Mendelson (Princeton: Princeton University Press, 1988), 521.

70. Auden, 'A Review of *Modern Poetic Drama*', 70. See Mendelson, *Early Auden*, 258.

71. Ibid.

72. Ibid.

73. Mendelson, *Early Auden*, 258.

74. Auden, 'The Future of English Poetic Drama', 521.

75. Mendelson, *Early Auden*, 259–60.

76. Auden, 'The World of Opera', *Secondary Worlds* (London: Faber & Faber, 1968), 116.

77. The first version was written in 1928 and not published until after Auden's death; the second, much-expanded version was published by Eliot in *The Criterion* in 1930. The play was first produced in England at the Cambridge Festival Theatre in 1934, some months after Gray had departed.

78. Sidnell, *Dances of Death*, 63.

79. Auden, *The English Auden: Poems, Essays and Dramatic Writings, 1927–1939*, ed. Mendelson (London: Faber & Faber, 1977), 301.

80. Auden, *The Dance of Death*, in Auden and Isherwood, *Plays and Other Dramatic Writings*, 83.

81. Sidnell, *Dances of Death*, 68.

82. Auden, *The Dance of Death*, 105.

83. Ibid., 83.

84. Ibid.

85. Ibid., 83–4.

86. Ibid., 84.

87. Ibid., 90.

88. Ibid., 91.

89. Ibid., 92.

90. Ibid., 92.

91. Auden, synopsis to *The Dance of Death*, quoted in Sidnell, *Dances of Death*, 84.

92. Auden, *The Dance of Death*, 104.

93. Ibid., 105.

94. Sidnell, *Dances of Death*, 87.

95. Auden, *The Dance of Death*, 107.

96. Mendelson, *Early Auden*, 270.

97. Auden and Isherwood, *The Ascent of F6*, in *Plays and Other Dramatic Writings*, 304.

98. Ibid., 310.

99. Ibid. Sidnell identifies an intriguing influence of *Murder in the Cathedral* on the play, with both works focusing on the individual's attempt 'to save himself and redeem others' (*Dances of Death*, 186).

100. Auden and Isherwood, *The Ascent of F6*, 313.

101. Ibid., 354.

102. E.M. Forster, 'Chormopuloda', *The Listener*, 14 October 1936: 7.

103. Mendelson, *Early Auden*, 286.

104. Isherwood, quoted in ibid.

105. Auden and Isherwood, *The Ascent of F6*, 295.

106. Ibid.

107. Ibid.

108. Sidnell, *Dances of Death*, 341.

109. Ibid., 187.

110. The division of labour in the writing of the play is well-documented: Isherwood wrote most of the plot and the dialogue; Auden wrote Ransom's opening (prose) speech, the dialogue with the mother, the verse dialogue, and the choruses. Both collaborated on the ending(s).

111. Auden and Isherwood, *The Ascent of F6*, 297.

112. Ibid., 346.

113. Sidnell, *Dances of Death*, 203.

114. Auden and Isherwood, *The Ascent of F6*, 344–5.

115. John Maynard Keynes, letter to Auden 6 October 1937, quoted in Sidnell, *Dances of Death*, 241.

116. Auden, in Wahl, *Poetic Drama Interviews*, 103.

117. Mendelson, *Early Auden*, 261.

118. An exception is his radio adaptation, with James Stern, of D.H. Lawrence's 'The Rocking Horse Winner' in 1941.

119. This enthusiasm began early: as Cornwell notes, 'One of the books that Britten chose as prizes at the end of his time at Gresham's School was John Drinkwater's *Collected Plays*' (*Only by Failure*, 225).

120. Soon after their collaboration on *Paul Bunyan*, Britten refused to collaborate with Auden. For a closer overview of Auden's approach to opera and musical collaboration, see Irene Morra, *Twentieth-Century British Authors and the Rise of Opera in Britain* (Aldershot: Ashgate, 2007), 1–10 and 21–44.

121. Auden and Chester Kallman, *The Bassarids*, in *Libretti and Other Dramatic Writings by W.H. Auden, 1939–1973*, ed. Edward Mendelson (Princeton: Princeton University Press, 1993), 276.

122. Auden and Kallman, 'Genesis of a Libretto', in ibid., 247.

123. Auden, 'The World of Opera', 116.

124. Duncan, *How to Make Enemies*, 351.

125. See Morra, *Twentieth-Century British Authors*, 21–44. According to Auden, 'The verbal text of an opera is to be judged, not by the literary quality or lack of it which it may have when read, but by its success or failure in exciting the musical imagination of the composer' ('The World of Opera', 90).

126. Auden and Kallman, *Libretti*, 678.

127. Ibid., 682.

Chapter 6

1. *This Way to the Tomb* transferred to the West End and ran for 300 performances; *A Phoenix Too Frequent* established the immediate popularity of Fry that led (amongst other acknowledgements) to the commission of *The Lady's Not for*

Burning, and a 1950 West End performance of his 1938 religious play *The Boy with A Cart,* originally commissioned for amateur performance in Steyning, West Sussex. Ridler recounts of *The Shadow Factory:* 'The play did go well, and the applause was warm. . . . Beverley Baxter in the *Evening Standard,* who had praised the other two plays [*The Old Man of the Mountains* and *This Way to the Tomb*], was also enthusiastic, saying to his readers 'I am very much afraid you will have to go again to the Mercury Theatre' (Ridler, *Memoirs* [Oxford: The Perpetua Press, 2004], 147).

2. Norman Nicholson, *The Old Man of the Mountains,* rev. edition (London: Faber & Faber, 1950), 28.

3. Ibid., 9.

4. Ibid., 10.

5. Ibid., 83.

6. Ibid.

7. Ibid.

8. Browne likens the verse of Nicholson to that of Bottomley, 'that fine craftsman . . . who has for many years been working away at the problems of the poetic dramatist and laid foundations on which younger men are building' ('The Poet and the Stage', 88).

9. Nicholson, *The Old Man of the Mountains,* 10.

10. Ibid., 11.

11. Ibid.

12. Ibid.

13. Speaight, *Drama Since 1939,* 38.

14. Nicholson, *The Old Man of the Mountains,* 12.

15. Ridler, *The Shadow Factory: A Nativity Play* (London: Faber & Faber, 1946), i.

16. Ibid., 9.

17. Ibid., 12.

18. Ibid., 1.

19. Ibid., 2.

20. Ibid.

21. Ibid., 13.

22. Ibid., 15.

23. Ibid.

24. Ibid., 16.

25. Ibid., 36.

26. Ibid., 41.

27. Ibid., 43.

28. Ibid., 44.

29. Ibid., 47.

30. Ibid., 49.

31. Ibid., 50.

32. Ibid., 55.

33. Ibid., 66.

34. Duncan, *How to Make Enemies*, 154.

35. Ibid., 258.

36. Duncan, *All Men Are Islands: An Autobiography* (London: Rupert Hart-Davis, 1964), 198. Duncan notes that Eliot had refused to publish *The Eagle has Two Heads*, 'as Faber's are interested in your own work and not your adaptations' (*Enemies*, 155).

37. As Duncan notes, he and Pound 'constituted the entire audience' (*All Men Are Islands*, 198).

38. Duncan, *How to Make Enemies*, 272.

39. Duncan, *All Men Are Islands*, 196.

40. Ibid., 132.

41. Duncan, *How to Make Enemies*, 37.

42. Ibid., 81.

43. Ibid., 156.

44. Ibid., 156.

45. Ibid., 157.

46. Ibid., 382.

47. Ibid., 370.

48. Ibid., 371.

49. Ibid.

50. Ibid., 378.

51. Ibid.

52. Ibid., 385.

53. Ibid., 156.

54. Ibid., 386.

55. Ibid.

56. Ibid., 192.

57. Ibid., 192–3.

58. Ibid., 345.

59. 'Eliot and I had tried to make verse in the theatre a pliable vehicle of our contemporary feeling. We had both turned our backs on *Murder in the Cathedral* and *This Way to the Tomb* and set ourselves the task of writing modern plays in which the verse was not decoration upon the theme but simple, unrhetorical and lucid' (ibid., 384–5).

60. Ibid., 23.

61. Duncan, *All Men Are Islands*, 205.

62. Duncan, *How to Make Enemies*, 20.

63. Ibid.

64. Ibid., 35.

65. Duncan, *This Way to the Tomb: A Masque and Anti-masque* (London: Faber & Faber, 1946), 30.

66. Duncan, *How to Make Enemies*, 20.

67. Duncan, 'Introduction' to *Collected Plays* (London: Rupert Hart-Davis, 1971), ix.

68. Ibid., ix.

69. Duncan, *This Way to the Tomb*, 58.

70. Ibid., 96.

71. Leeming, *Poetic Drama*, 103.

72. Duncan, *This Way to the Tomb*, 71.

73. Ibid.

74. Ibid.

75. Duncan, *How to Make Enemies*, 26.

76. Ibid.

77. Duncan, 'Introduction' to *Collected Plays*, x.

78. Duncan, *Obsessed: A Third Volume of Autobiography* (London: Michael Joseph, 1977), 21

79. Ibid.

80. Duncan, *How to Make Enemies*, 385.

81. Lambert, 'Verse Drama', 66.

82. Bentley, *The Playwright as Thinker*, 223.

83. Charles Spencer, 'Awkward Moments with Eliot the Guilty Housemaster', *The Daily Telegraph*, 18 June 1999.

84. Gill Plain, *Literature of the 1940s: War, Postwar and 'Peace'* (Edinburgh: Edinburgh University Press, 2013), 23.

85. Peter Ackroyd, *T.S. Eliot* (London: Penguin, 1993), 308.

86. Eliot, 'John Marston', 229.

Notes

87. Eliot, 'Poetry and Drama', 84–5.

88. Ibid., 85.

89. Ibid., 81.

90. Ibid., 82.

91. Ibid., 82.

92. Eliot, interview in the *Glasgow Herald*, quoted in Browne, *The Making of T.S. Eliot's Plays*, 237.

93. Ibid.

94. Smith, *T.S. Eliot*, 147.

95. Browne, *The Making of T.S. Eliot's Plays*, 237.

96. Speaight, *The Christian Theatre*, 128.

97. Eliot, *The Cocktail Party*, in *The Complete Plays of T.S. Eliot* (New York: Harcourt, Brace and World, Inc. 1967), 123.

98. Ibid., 132.

99. Ibid., 133.

100. Ibid.

101. Ibid.

102. Ibid., 135.

103. Ibid.

104. Eliot, 'The Love Song of J. Alfred Prufrock' [1917], in Eliot, *Complete Poems and Plays*, 3.

105. Eliot, *The Cocktail Party*, 134–5.

106. Speaight, *Christian Theatre*, 128-29.

107. Smith, *T. S. Eliot*, 157-80.

108. Eliot, *The Cocktail Party*, 182.

109. Ibid., 189.

110. Ibid., 188.

111. Smith, *T.S. Eliot*, 173.

112. Eliot, *The Cocktail Party*, 192.

113. Ibid., 212.

114. Ibid., 209.

115. Eliot, 'On Poetry and Drama', 85.

116. Eliot, *The Cocktail Party*, 134.

117. 'One-Eyed Riley' was composed through dictation by Eliot himself, and a notated version was published along with the play.

118. Eliot, *The Cocktail Party*, 137.

119. Ibid., 137.

120. Ibid., 192.

121. Ibid., 203.

122. Ibid.

123. Ibid., 209.

124. Browne, *The Making of T.S. Eliot's Plays*, 233.

125. Eliot, *The Cocktail Party*, 212.

126. Fry, 'Why Verse', 137.

127. Ibid.

128. Ibid.

129. It was first performed at St James's Church in London, then toured.

130. *Punch* review, quoted in Leeming, *Christopher Fry* (Boston: Twayne, 1990), 111.

131. Harold Hobson, quoted in ibid.

132. Philip Roberts, *The Royal Court Theatre and the Modern Stage* (Cambridge: Cambridge University Press, 1999), 74, 75. *Curtmantle*, a historical drama about Henry II and Thomas Becket, was eventually staged by the Royal Shakespeare Company in 1962.

133. Duncan, *How to Make Enemies*, 385.

134. Duncan in William B. Wahl, *Ronald Duncan: Verse Dramatist and Poet Interviewed by William B. Wahl* (Salzburg: Institut Für Englische Sprache und Literatur, 1973), 163–4.

135. Fry, 'Why Verse', 137.

136. Peter Brook, quoted in 'Christopher Fry Remembered – by Hugh Whitemore', The Royal Society of Literature, http://rsliterature.org/fellow/christopher-fry (accessed 14 January 2016).

137. Fry, 'Poetry and the Theatre', *Adam* 19 (1951): 8.

138. Fry, *The Lady's Not for Burning*, in *Plays One* (London: Oberon, 2007), 9.

139. Ibid., 11.

140. Ibid., 13. See also Leeming, *Christopher Fry*, 68.

141. Fry, *The Lady's Not for Burning*, 13.

142. Ibid., 18.

143. Ibid., 19.

144. Ibid., 91.

145. Ibid., 83–4.

146. Ibid., 92.

147. Ibid.

148. Ibid.

149. Fry, 'Why Verse', 137.

150. Eliot's essays formulate a contemporary ideal of modern drama in relation to Shakespeare. They also, however, argue for the necessary transformation of Shakespeare's aesthetic and social achievement into distinctly contemporary terms.

151. Philip Gibbs, *The New Elizabethans* (London: Hutchinson, 1953), 145.

152. Ibid. For a closer reading of the New Elizabethan moment in relation to constructions of national culture, see Irene Morra, 'New Elizabethanism: Origins, Legacies, and the Theatre of Nation' and 'History Play: People, Pageant and the New Shakespearean Age', in *The New Elizabethan Age: Nation, Culture and Modernity after World War II*, eds. Irene Morra and Rob Gossedge (London: I.B. Tauris, 2016), 17–48 and 308–36.

153. Duncan, *How to Make Enemies*, 385.

154. Fry, 'Talking of Henry', *Twentieth Century* 169 (February 1961): 189.

155. Leeming, *Poetic Drama*, 162.

156. Duncan, *How to Make Enemies*, 385.

Chapter 7

1. Dan Rebellato, *1956 and All That: The Making of Modern British Drama* (London: Routledge, 1999), 66.

2. Ibid.

3. Trewin, *Drama in Britain 1951–1964* (London: Longmans, 1965), 9.

4. As Geoffrey Whitworth reflected shortly before his death, in 1951, 'I saw that a National Theatre . . . was no more and no less than a Community Theatre writ large. And for this a democratic background was the first essential, and the creation of a public consciously concerned with the practice of theatre art both for its own sake and as a major factor in the enjoyment of life' (Whitworth, *The Making of a National Theatre*, London: Faber & Faber, 1951, 149).

5. J.L. Styan, *The English Stage: A History of Drama and Performance* (Cambridge: Cambridge University Press, 1996), 397.

6. Aleks Sierz, *Rewriting the Nation: British Theatre Today* (London: Methuen, 2011), 17.

7. Ibid., 4–5.

8. Duncan, 'Introduction' to *Collected Plays*, ix and Duncan, *How to Make Enemies*, 382.

9. Duncan, quoted in Philip Roberts, *The Royal Court Theatre and the Modern Stage*, 114.

10. Trewin, *Drama in Britain 1951–1964*, 57.

11. Rebellato, *1956 and All That*, 4.

12. Pattie, *Modern British Playwriting*, 1.

13. David Ian Rabey, *English Drama Since 1940* (London: Pearson, 2003), 29.

14. John Osborne, *Look Back in Anger* (London: Faber & Faber, 1957).

15. Ibid.

16. Kenneth Allsop, *The Angry Decade: A Survey of the Cultural Revolt of the Nineteen-Fifties* (Wendover: John Goodchild Publishers, 1958), 24.

17. Fry is a notable exception; he did not attend university, and his career began first in teaching, then in drama. In that respect, the development of his career is much closer to that of Bottomley, Masefield and the largely self-educated Drinkwater.

18. Rebellato offers a strong overview of many of the ideologically charged readings that informed and dominated that moment, from Eliot's 'dissociation of sensibility' through to the selective readings of the transformative (and historical) ideal of cultural and literary tradition espoused by Leavis and Richard Hoggart, through to the engagement with those theories by Raymond Williams (Rebellato, *1956 and All That*, 10–36).

19. Sean O'Brien, 'The Poet in Theatre: Verse Drama', in *The Handbook of Creative Writing*, 2nd edition, ed. Stephen Earnshaw (Edinburgh: Edinburgh University Press, 2014), 234.

20. Susan Rusinko, *British Drama, 1950 to the Present: A Critical History* (Boston: Twayne, 1989), 4.

21. George Devine letter to the Earl of Harewood, quoted in Roberts, *The Royal Court Theatre and the Modern Stage*, 37.

22. Ibid.

23. Ibid.

24. Although it had not met with critical success, John Whiting's *Saint's Day* had won first prize in the play competition at the Festival of Britain; in their tendency towards expressionism and existential themes, his plays also anticipated the more absurdist elements that marked many experimental political dramas of the 1970s.

25. Rebellato, *1956 and All That*, 128. See also Jen Harvie, *Staging the UK* (Manchester: Manchester University Press, 2005), for a useful discussion of European-UK interactions in theatre at this time.

26. Most influential to the new drama, perhaps, was the 1956 visit of the Berliner Ensemble to London, which found a particular resonance with the experimental, improvisatory political theatre at Stratford East.

27. For further discussion of Brechtian influences on British theatre, see Janelle Reinelt, *After Brecht: British Epic Theatre* (Ann Arbor: University of Michigan Press, 1994) and Dominic Shellard, *British Theatre Since the War* (New Haven: Yale University Press), 71–80.

Notes

28. Claire Armistead, 'LIFTing the theatre: the London International Festival of Theatre', in *Contemporary British Theatre*, rev. edition, ed. Theodore Shank (London: Macmillan, 1996),152.

29. Sierz, *In-Yer-Face Theatre: British Drama Today* (London: Faber & Faber, 2001), xi.

30. Harvie, *Staging the UK*, 115. See also Christopher McCullough, *Theatre and Europe: 1957–96* (Exeter: Intellect, 1996).

31. Rebellato, *1956 and All That*, 150.

32. Ibid., 151.

33. Osborne, *Look Back in Anger*.

34. Ibid.

35. Bentley, *The Playwright as Thinker*, 225.

36. Noël Coward, diary entry February 1957, in *The Noël Coward Diaries*, 2nd edition, ed. Graham Payn and Sheridan Morley (Boston: Da Capo, 1982), 349.

37. Duncan, quoted in Roberts, *The Royal Court Theatre and the Modern Stage*, 28. Roberts contests this assertion, arguing that it had been Duncan alone who had set up the initial artistic criteria for the Company (ibid., 76).

38. Duncan, 'Artistic Policy of the English Stage Company', in *Ronald Duncan: The Man and the Artist*, ed. Krysia Cairns (Plymouth: University of Plymouth Press, 1998), 114.

39. As Leeming notes, although the Auden-Isherwood plays 'were the nearest precursors to these in England . . . there is almost certainly no direct line of influence, merely an indication that the earlier dramatists were ahead of their time' (*Poetic Drama*, 189).

40. Jane Arden, *Vagina Rex and the Gas Oven* (London: Calder & Boyars, 1971), 11.

41. Micheline Wandor, *Look Back in Gender (Routledge Revivals): Sexuality and the Family in Post-War British Drama* (London: Routledge, 2014), 95.

42. The greater emphasis on the career of Arden rather than on Arden/D'Arcy is here justified by his much more consistent and critical engagement with the theatrical potential of verse on stage.

43. Arden and D'Arcy provide a useful account of the staging and picketing of *The Island of the Mighty* in their respective introductions to the published text. See also Robert Leach, *Partners of the Imagination: The Lives, Art and Struggles of John Arden and Margaretta D'Arcy* (Stoney Stanton: Indigo Dreams, 2012), 175–90.

44. John Arden, 'The Reps and New Plays', *New Theatre Magazine* 1.2 (January 1960): 25.

45. Arden, 'Introductory Note' to *The Workhouse Donkey*, in Arden, *Plays: Two* (London: Methuen, 1994), 4.

46. Arden, 'Correspondence to the Editors', *Encore* 20 (May–June 1959): 42.

47. Arden, 'Telling a True Tale', in *New Theatre Voices of the Fifties and Sixties*, ed. Charles Marowitz, Tom Milne and Owen Hale (London: Methuen, 1981), 125.

48. Arden, 'Preface to John Arden', in Arden, *Plays: Two* (London: Methuen, 1994), xii.

49. Arden, 'Telling a True Tale', in Arden, *Plays: Two*, 125–6.

50. Ibid., 126.

51. Arden, 'The Reps and New Plays', 25.

52. Arden, 'Preface' to *The Island of the Mighty*, Arden and Margaretta D'Arcy (London: Eyre Methuen, 1974), 12.

53. See Frances Gray, *John Arden* (London: Macmillan, 1982), 8.

54. Arden, 'Telling a True Tale', 127.

55. Arden, interview with Elizabeth Hale Winkler, cited in Winkler, *The Function of Song in Contemporary British Drama* (Newark: University of Delaware Press, 1990), 58.

56. Arden, in *The Playwrights Speak*, ed. Walter Wager (London: Longmans, Green, 1967), 211.

57. Irving Wardle, 'Arden Talking about his Way of Writing Plays', *The Observer*, 30 June 1963.

58. Simon Trussler, *John Arden* (New York: Columbia University Press, 1973), 8.

59. The verses for songs tend more towards simple rhymes and images.

60. Arden and D'Arcy, *Friday's Hiding: An Experiment in the Laconic* in Arden/D'Arcy, *Plays: One* (London: Methuen, 1991), 76.

61. Ibid., 77.

62. Arden, 'Verse in the Theatre', *New Theatre Magazine* (April 1961): 202.

63. Arden, 'Preface' to *The Island of the Mighty*, 12.

64. Ibid., 14.

65. Arden and D'Arcy, *The Island of the Mighty*, 234.

66. Ibid., 235.

67. Ibid.

68. Michael Tippett, 'The Birth of an Opera', in Tippett, *Moving into Aquarius* (London: Routledge, 1959), 49.

69. Tippett, 'Love in Opera', in *Michael Tippett, Music of the Angels: Essays and Sketchbooks of Michael Tippett*, ed. Meirion Bowen (London: Eulenberg, 1980), 214.

70. See Morra, *Twentieth-Century British Authors* for a closer discussion of this phenomenon.

71. An account of the exchange is given in detail in Benjamin Britten, *Letters from a Life: The Selected Letters of Benjamin Britten, 1913–1976*, vol. 3, ed. Donald Mitchell, Philip Reed and Mervyn Cooke (London: Faber & Faber, 2004), 330–2.

Notes

72. Lincoln Kirstein, letter to Igor Stravinsky, 23 August 1950, in Stravinsky, *Selected Correspondence*, vol. 1, ed. Robert Craft (New York: Alfred A. Knopf, 1982), 276–7.

73. Tippett, *Those Twentieth-Century Blues: An Autobiography* (London: Hutchinson, 1991), 188.

74. Ibid., 51.

75. Tippett gives a detailed account of his consultations with Eliot over *A Child of our Time* in 'A Child of Our Time: T.S. Eliot and *A Child of Our Time*', in *Michael Tippett, Music of the Angels,* ed. Meirion Bowen, 117–26.

76. Ibid., 189–90.

77. Tippett, 'Love in Opera', 214.

78. Ibid., 'A Child of our Time', 118.

79. Suzanne K. Langer, *Problems of Art* (London, 1957), quoted in Tippett, 'A Child of our Time', 119.

80. Morra, *Twentieth-Century British Authors*, 21.

81. Ibid., 14.

82. Tippett, *Selected Letters of Michael Tippett*, ed. Thomas Schuttenhelm (London: Faber & Faber, 2005), 295.

83. Ibid.

84. Ibid.

85. Ibid., 'The Relationship of Autobiographical Experience to the Created Work of Art', in *Michael Tippett: Music and Literature,* ed. Suzanne Robinson (Aldershot: Ashgate, 2002), 22.

86. Ibid., 'Birth', 49.

87. Ibid., 52.

88. Ibid., 49.

89. Robinson, 'From Agitprop to Parable: A Prolegomenon to *A Child of Our Time*', in *Michael Tippett,* ed. Robinson, 95.

Chapter 8

1. Elaine Aston, *Caryl Churchill* (London: Northcote House, 2nd edition, 2001), 75. See also Roberts, *About Churchill: The Playwright and the Work* (London: Faber & Faber, 2008), 109.

2. Caryl Churchill, *Serious Money* [1987] (London: Methuen, 2002), 106.

3. Ibid., 87.

4. Ibid., 87–8.

5. Ibid., 50.

6. Ibid., 50, 52.

7. Ibid., 58.

8. Ibid., 109.

9. Ibid., 110.

10. Ibid., 59.

11. Ibid., 58.

12. Aston, *Caryl Churchill*, 71.

13. Churchill, 'Preface' to Churchill, *Serious Money*, xxxvii.

14. Churchill, *Serious Money*, 66.

15. Ibid., 17.

16. Ibid., 17–19.

17. Steven Berkoff, *Decadence*, in *Decadence and Other Plays* (London: Faber & Faber, 1989), 33.

18. Ibid., 3.

19. Ibid.

20. Berkoff, *Free Association: An Autobiography* (London: Faber & Faber, 1996), 5.

21. Ibid.

22. Ibid.

23. See ibid., 57.

24. Churchill, *Serious Money*, 110.

25. Berkoff, *Decadence*, 38.

26. Ibid.

27. Berkoff, *Sink the Belgrano!* in *Sink the Belgrano! with Massage Lunch* (London: Faber, 1987), 166.

28. Berkoff, author's note to *East*, in *Decadence and Other Plays*, 43.

29. Berkoff, *Free Association*, 48.

30. Ibid.

31. Ibid.

32. Ibid., 57.

33. Ibid.

34. A notable exception to this tendency is Berkoff's curious verse play, *The Secret Love Life of Ophelia* (2001). Consisting entirely of the recitation of imagined letters between Hamlet and Ophelia, the play is written in a verse that suggests Shakespearean pastiche, its sole revisionism lying in its imagining of a more detailed relationship between the protagonists.

35. Berkoff, *West*, in *Decadence and Other Plays*, 92.

36. Ibid., *East*, 43.

Notes

37. Berkoff, *Greek*, in *Decadence and Other Plays*, 141.

38. Ibid., 153.

39. Berkoff, *Free Association*, 2–3.

40. Ibid., 51.

41. Ibid.

42. Ibid., 4.

43. Ibid., 340.

44. Berkoff, *Greek*, 183.

45. Ibid.

46. Ibid., 145.

47. Berkoff, *Free Association*, 344.

48. Ibid., 388.

49. Ibid., 391.

50. Abercrombie, *An Essay Towards a Theory of Art*, 110–11.

51. Peter Wilson, interview with Ted Hughes. Originally published in the *Tamasha Daily Bulletin* (1971), republished online by Ann Skea, http://ann.skea.com/Persepolis%20Orghast%20interview.html (accessed 14 January 2016).

52. Rosemary Burton, 'Tony Harrison: An Introduction', in *Bloodaxe Critical Anthologies I: Tony Harrison*, ed. Neil Astley (Newcastle upon Tyne: Bloodaxe, 1991), 15.

53. Ibid.

54. Harrison, quoted in ibid., 26.

55. Harrison, *The Labours of Herakles*, in Harrison, *Plays Three* (London: Faber & Faber, 1996).

56. Ibid.

57. Harrison, in Richard Hoggart, 'In Conversation with Tony Harrison', *Bloodaxe Critical Anthologies I*, 42, 45.

58. Harrison, 'Preface' to *Aikin Mata*, reprinted in *Bloodaxe Critical Anthologies I*, 85.

59. The work was commissioned by the Metropolitan Opera, but the composer Jacob Druckman never completed a score.

60. Harrison, 'Introduction' to *The Misanthrope*, in Harrison, *Plays Two*, 5.

61. Harrison, 'Introduction' to *Phaedra Britannica*, in Harrison, *Plays Two*, 136.

62. Ibid., 118.

63. Harrison, in Hoggart, 'In Conversation with Tony Harrison', 43.

64. Harrison, in John Haffenden, 'Interview with Tony Harrison', reprinted in *Bloodaxe Critical Anthologies I*, 246.

65. Ken Worpole, 'Scholarship Boy: The Poetry of Tony Harrison', reprinted in *Bloodaxe Critical Anthologies I*, 66.

66. Harrison, quoted in Burton, 'Tony Harrison: An Introduction', 14.
67. Ibid.
68. Harrison, 'Them and [uz]', in *Collected Poems* (London: Penguin, 2007), 122.
69. Harrison, in Hoggart, 'In Conversation with Tony Harrison', 40.
70. Ibid.
71. Harrison, 'Them and [uz]', 123.
72. Harrison, in Hoggart, 'In Conversation with Tony Harrison', 44.
73. Ibid.
74. Ibid.
75. Harrison, *The Mysteries*, in Harrison, *Plays One* (London: Faber & Faber, 1999), 11.
76. She continues by acknowledging the incorporation of verse within the anti-naturalist political theatre of Arden/D'Arcy, amongst others: 'but the evolution of modern theatrical writing and performance has found a place for verse in drama, where each different use of verse is judged on its own terms and its own merits' (*Poetic Drama*, 205).

Conclusion

1. Dominic Maxwell, review of *King Charles III*, *The Times*, 11 April 2014.
2. Paul Taylor, review of *King Charles III*, *The Independent*, 11 April 2014.
3. Spencer, review of *King Charles III*, *The Daily Telegraph*, 11 April 2014.
4. Sarah Crompton, 'History is the Future', *The Daily Telegraph*, 6 September 2014, http://www.telegraph.co.uk/culture/theatre/theatre-news/11077640/History-is-the-future.html (accessed 15 January 2016).
5. Ibid.
6. Billington, review of *King Charles III*, *The Guardian*, 12 September 2014, http://www.theguardian.com/stage/2014/sep/12/king-charles-iii-review-shakespeare-mike-bartlett-wyndhams-tim-pigott-smith (accessed 15 January 2016).
7. Dominic Cavendish, review of *King Charles III*, *The Daily Telegraph*, 3 October 2014, http://www.telegraph.co.uk/culture/theatre/theatre-reviews/11092427/King-Charles-III-Wyndhams-Theatre-review-attendance-is-compulsory.html (accessed 15 January 2016).
8. Spencer, review of *Charles III*.
9. Mike Bartlett, *King Charles III*, revised edition (London: Nick Hern, 2014), 17, 19.
10. Ibid., 26.
11. Ibid., 50.

Notes

12. Ibid., 51.

13. Ibid., 54.

14. Ibid., 54.

15. Ibid., 52.

16. Ibid., 12.

17. Ibid., 91.

18. Ibid., 97.

19. Ibid., 115.

20. Ibid., 114.

21. Ibid., 116.

22. Ibid., 27.

23. Ibid., 13.

BIBLIOGRAPHY

Abercrombie, Lascelles, 'The Function of Poetry in the Drama (A Paper Read before the English Association of Manchester)', *The Poetry Review* (March 1912): 107–118.

Abercrombie, Lascelles (1922), *An Essay Towards a Theory of Art*, London: Martin Secker.

Abercrombie, Lascelles (1930), *The Poems of Lascelles Abercrombie*, London: Oxford University Press.

Abercrombie, Lascelles (1930), 'Preface', ibid., vi.

Abercrombie, Lascelles (1930), *The Adder*, ibid., 363–82

Abercrombie, Lascelles (1930), *The Staircase*, ibid., 383–400

Abercrombie, Lascelles (1930), *The End of the World*, ibid., 420–50.

Abbott, Claude Colleer (1953), 'Introduction' to Gordon Bottomley, *Poems and Plays*, 9–19, London: Morrison & Gibb.

Abbott, Claude Colleer and Anthony Bertram, eds (1955), *Poet and Painter: Being the Correspondence between Gordon Bottomley and Paul Nash, 1910–1946*, London: Oxford University Press.

Ackroyd, Peter (1993), *T.S. Eliot*, London: Penguin.

Agate, James ([1926] 1969), *A Short View of the English Stage, 1900–1926*, Freeport, NY: Books for Libraries.

Alexander, Neal and James Moran (2013), *Regional Modernisms*, Edinburgh: Edinburgh University Press.

Allsop, Kenneth (1958), *The Angry Decade: A Survey of the Cultural Revolt of the Nineteen-Fifties*, Wendover: John Goodchild Publishers.

Archer, William (1887), 'Drama', in Thomas H. Ward (ed.), *The Reign of Queen Victoria: A Survey of Fifty Years of Progress*. vol. 2, 561, London: Smith & Elder.

Archer, William (1904), *Real Conversations. Recorded by William Archer. With Twelve Portraits*, London: William Heinemann.

Archer, William (1923), *The Old Drama and the New: An Essay in Re-Valuation*. London: William Heinemann.

Arden, Jane (1971), *Vagina Rex and the Gas Oven*, London: Calder & Boyars.

Arden, John (May–June 1959), 'Correspondence to the Editors', *Encore* 20: 42.

Arden, John (January 1960), 'The Reps and New Plays', *New Theatre Magazine* 1.2: 25–6.

Arden, John (1961), 'Verse in the Theatre', *New Theatre Magazine* 2.3: 200–6.

Arden, John (1964), *Three Plays*, New York: Grove.

Arden, John (1974), 'Preface', *The Island of the Mighty. A Play on a Traditional British Theme in Three Parts*, by John Arden and Margaretta D'Arcy, 9–16, London: Eyre Methuen.

Arden, John (1977), *Plays: One*, London: Methuen.

Bibliography

Arden, John (1981), 'Telling a True Tale', in Charles Marowitz, Tom Milne and Owen Hale (eds), *New Theatre Voices of the Fifties and Sixties*, 125–9, London: Methuen, 1981.

Arden, John (1994), *Plays: Two*, London: Methuen.

Arden, John (1994), 'Preface', ibid., ix–xvii.

Arden, John (1994), 'Introductory Note' to *The Workhouse Donkey. A Vulgar Melo-Drama*, ibid., 1–6.

Arden, John and Margaretta D'Arcy (1974), *The Island of the Mighty. A Play on a Traditional British Theme in Three Parts*, London: Eyre Methuen.

Arden, John and Margaretta D'Arcy (1974), 'Preface', ibid., 17–21.

Arden, John and Margaretta D'Arcy (1991), *Plays: One*, London: Methuen.

Arden, John and Margaretta D'Arcy (1991), *Friday's Hiding: An Experiment in the Laconic*, ibid., 61–84.

Armistead, Claire (1996), 'LIFTing the theatre: the London International Festival of Theatre', in Theodore Shank (ed.), *Contemporary British Theatre*, rev. ed., 152–65, London: Macmillan.

Armstrong, William A. ed. (1963), *Experimental Drama*, London: G. Bell & Sons Ltd.

Armstrong, William A. ed. (1963), 'Preface', ibid, 9–14.

Armstrong, William A. ed. (1963), 'The Playwright and His Theatre, 1946–62', ibid, 15–35.

Astley, Neil ed. (1991), *Bloodaxe Critical Anthologies I: Tony Harrison*, Newcastle upon Tyne: Bloodaxe.

Aston, Elaine (2001), *Caryl Churchill*, 2nd ed., London: Northcote House.

Auden, W.H. (1968), *Secondary Worlds*, London: Faber & Faber.

Auden, W.H. (1968), 'The World of Opera', ibid., 85–116.

Auden, W.H. (1996), 'The Group Movement and the Middle Classes', in Edward Mendelson (ed.), *W.H. Auden: Prose and Travel Books in Prose and Verse*, vol. I, 47–54, Princeton: Princeton University Press.

Auden, W.H. (1996), 'A Review of *Modern Poetic Drama*, by Priscilla Thouless', in ibid., 69–70.

Auden, W.H. (1996), 'Selling the Group Theatre', in ibid., 134–5.

Auden, W.H. (1996), 'A Modern Use of Masks: An Apologia', in ibid., 157–8.

Auden, W.H. (2002), 'The Dyer's Hand', in Edward Mendelson (ed.), *W.H. Auden: Prose*, vol. II, 29–31. Princeton: Princeton University Press.

Auden, W.H. (1988), *Paid on Both Sides* [first version] (1928), in W.H. Auden and Christopher Isherwood, Edward Mendelson (eds), *Plays and Other Dramatic Writings by W.H. Auden, 1928–1938*, 3–13, Princeton: Princeton University Press, 1988.

Auden, W.H. (1988), *Paid on Both Sides* [second version] (1928), in ibid., 14–34.

Auden, W.H. (1988), *The Dance of Death*, in ibid., 81–108.

Auden, W.H. (1988), 'The Future of English Poetic Drama', in ibid., 513–33.

Auden, W.H. and Christopher Isherwood (1988), *The Dog Beneath the Skin*, in ibid., 189–292.

Auden, W.H. and Christopher Isherwood (1988), *The Ascent of F6*, in ibid., 293–356.

Auden, W.H. and Christopher Isherwood (1988), *On the Frontier*, in ibid., 357–418.

Auden, W.H. and Chester Kallman (1993), *Elegy for Young Lovers*, in W.H. Auden and Chester Kallman, Edward Mendelson (eds), *Libretti and Other Dramatic Writings by W.H. Auden, 1939-1973*, 189–244, Princeton: Princeton University Press.
Auden, W.H. and Chester Kallman (1993), 'Genesis of a Libretto', in ibid., 245–7.
Auden, W.H. and Chester Kallman (1993), *The Bassarids*, in ibid., 249–313.
Badenhausen, Richard (2004), *T.S. Eliot and the Art of Collaboration*, Cambridge: Cambridge University Press.
Badenhausen, Richard (2004), 'Drama', in Jason Harding (ed.), *T.S. Eliot in Context*, 125–33, Cambridge: Cambridge University Press.
Barker, Harley Granville (1922), *The Exemplary Theatre*, London: Chatto & Windus.
Barker, Harley Granville (1931), 'Preface' to *Little Plays of Saint Francis*, First Series, by Laurence Housman, vii–xv. London: Sidgwick and Jackson, 1931.
Barker, Harley Granville (1937), *On Poetry in Drama*, London: Sidgwick & Jackson.
Barker, Harley Granville (1974), *Prefaces to Shakespeare* [1927–1946], vol. 6., ed. Edward M. Moore, London: B.T. Batsford.
Bartlett, Mike (2014), *King Charles III*, revised edition, London: Nick Hern.
Bax, Clifford (1951), *Some I Knew Well*, London: Phoenix House Ltd.
Bax, Clifford (1951), 'Stephen Phillips. Poetic Dramatist', ibid., 17–29.
Bax, Clifford (1951), 'Gordon Bottomley. Poet and Dramatist', ibid., 36–50.
Bax, Clifford (1951), 'W.B. Yeats. Chameleon of Genius', ibid., 97–104.
Bax, Clifford (1951), 'Call no Man Great', ibid., 115–26.
Beckson, Karl, ed. (1977), *The Memoirs of Arthur Symons. Life and Art in the 1890s*, University Park: Pennsylvania State University Press.
Bennett, Arnold (1933), *Journal*, New York: Viking.
Bentley, Eric (1946), *The Playwright as Thinker: A Study of Drama in Modern Times*, New York: Reynal and Hitchcock, 1946.
Berkoff, Steven (1987) *Sink the Belgrano! with Massage Lunch*. London: Faber & Faber.
Berkoff, Steven (1989), *Decadence and Other Plays*, London: Faber & Faber.
Berkoff, Steven (1989), 'Note' to *Decadence*, ibid., 1–40.
Berkoff, Steven (1989), 'Note' to *East*, ibid., 41–83.
Berkoff, Steven (1989), 'Note' to *Greek*, ibid., 140–83.
Berkoff, Steven (1989), *East* [first performed 1975], ibid.
Berkoff, Steven (1989), *Greek* [first performed 1980], ibid.
Berkoff, Steven (1989), *West* [first performed 1983], ibid.
Berkoff, Steven (1996), *Free Association: An Autobiography*, London: Faber & Faber.
Berkoff, Steven (2001), *The Secret Love Life of Ophelia*, London: Faber & Faber.
Bigold, Melanie (2016), 'English Ballet: A National Art for the New Elizabethan Moment', in Irene Morra and Rob Gossedge (eds), *The New Elizabethan Age: Culture, Society and National Identity after World War II*, 243–64, London: I.B. Tauris.
Binyon, Laurence (1907), *Attila: A Tragedy in Four Acts*, London: John Murray.
Binyon, Laurence (1912), 'The Return to Poetry', *Rhythm* 1.4: 1–2.
Binyon, Laurence (1923), *Arthur: A Tragedy*, London: William Heinemann.
Binyon, Laurence (1927), *Boadicea: A Play in Eight Scenes*, London: Ernest Benn.
Billington, Michael (2007), *State of the Nation: British Theatre Since 1945*, London: Faber & Faber.

Bibliography

Bond, Edward (2013), *Selections from the Notebooks of Edward Bond*, vol. 2, 1980–95, London: Bloomsbury.

Bottomley, Gordon (1929), *Scenes and Plays*, London: Constable & Co.

Bottomley, Gordon (1932), *Lyric Plays*, London: Constable & Co.

Bottomley, Gordon (1932), 'To W.B. Yeats', ibid., v–vi.

Bottomley, Gordon (1932), 'Note', ibid., 120–3.

Bottomley, Gordon (1948), *A Stage for Poetry: My Purposes with my Plays*, Kendal: Titus Wilson & Son Ltd.

Bottomley, Gordon (1953), *Poems and Plays*, London: Morrison & Gibb.

Bottomley, Gordon (1953), *King Lear's Wife* [1915], ibid., 129–63.

Bottomley, Gordon (1953), *Gruach* [1921], ibid., 165–210.

Bridges-Adams, William (1946), *The British Theatre*. 1944. third rev. ed. published for the British Council. London: Longmans Green & Co.

Bridges-Adams, William (1971), *A Bridges-Adam Letter Book*, ed., with a memoir, Robert Speaight, London: Society for Theatre Research.

Bridges, Robert (1901), *The First Part of Nero*, in *The Poetical Works of Robert Bridges*, vol. 3, London: John Murray.

Browne, E. Martin (8 August 1925), 'A Country House Theatre: Mr. John Masefield's Innovation at Boar's Hill, Oxford', *Country Life*: 233–4.

Browne, E. Martin (1947), 'The Poet and the Stage', *The Penguin New Writing* 31: 81–92.

Browne, E. Martin (1952), 'Poetry in the English Theatre', *Proceedings of the Royal Institute of Great Britain* 34: 287–93.

Browne, E. Martin (1953), 'The British Drama League', *Educational Theatre Journal* 5.3: 203–6.

Browne, E. Martin (1966), 'T.S. Eliot in the Theatre: The Director's Memories', in Allen Tate (ed.), *T.S. Eliot: The Man and His Work*, 116–32. New York: Delacorte Press.

Browne, E. Martin (1969), *The Making of T.S. Eliot's Plays*, Cambridge: Cambridge University Press.

Browne, Henzie (1945), *The Pilgrim Story: The Pilgrim Players, 1939–1943. With a Chapter on the Organisation by E. Martin Browne*, London: Frederick Muller.

Browne, Terry (1975), *Playwrights' Theatre: The English Stage Company at the Royal Court*, London: Pitman.

Bullough, Geoffrey (1963), 'Christopher Fry and the "Revolt" Against Eliot', in William A. Armstrong (ed.), *Experimental Drama*, 56–78. London: G. Bell & Sons, Ltd.

Bulwer-Lytton, Edward (1839), *Richelieu. Or, The Conspiracy, A Play in Five Acts*, London: Saunders & Otley.

Burton, Rosemary (1991), 'Tony Harrison: An Introduction', in Neil Astley (ed.), *Bloodaxe Critical Anthologies I: Tony Harrison*, 14–31, Newcastle upon Tyne: Bloodaxe.

Cairns, Krysia (1998), *Ronald Duncan the Man and the Artist*, Exmouth: University of Plymouth.

Cavaliero, Glen (2007), *Charles Williams: Poet of Theology*, Eugene: Wipf & Stock.

Chandler, Andrew ed. (2013), *The Church and Humanity: The Life and Work of George Bell, 1883–1958*, Farnham: Ashgate.

Churchill, Caryl (2002), *Serious Money* [1987], with commentary and notes by Bill Naismith, London: Methuen.

Churchill, Caryl ([1990] 2002), 'Preface' to *Serious Money*, ibid., xxxvii.

Cochrane, Claire (2011), *Twentieth-Century British Theatre: Industry, Art and Empire*, Cambridge: Cambridge University Press.

Cohn, Ruby (1991), *Retreats from Realism in Modern English Drama*, Cambridge: Cambridge University Press.

Cohn, Ruby (2015), *Modern Shakespeare Offshoots*, Princeton: Princeton University Press.

Cole, Marion (1967), *Fogie: The Life of Elsie Fogerty*, London: Peter Davies.

Cook, Judith (1976), *The National Theatre*, London: Harrap.

Cornwell, Paul (2004), *Only by Failure: The Many Faces of the Impossible Life of Terence Gray*, Cambridge: Salt.

Coward, Noël (1982), *The Noël Coward Diaries*, 2nd edition, eds Graham Payn and Sheridan Morley. Boston: Da Capo.

Craig, Sandy (1980), *Dreams and Deconstructions: Alternative Theatre in Britain*, Oxford: Amber Lane Press.

Cross, Robert (2004), *Steven Berkoff and the Theatre of Self-Performance*, Manchester: Manchester University Press.

Cunningham, Valentine (1988), *British Writers of the Thirties*, Oxford: Oxford University Press.

D'Arcy, Margaretta. See Arden, John.

Dane, Clemence (1921), *Will Shakespeare. An Invention in Four Acts*, London: William Heinemann.

Davies, Andrew (1987), *Other Theatres: The Development of Alternative and Experimental Theatre in Britain*, Basingstoke: Macmillan.

Davies, Cecil (2002), *The Adelphi Players: The Theatre of Persons*, London: Routledge.

De Valois, Ninette (1953), *Invitation to the Ballet*, London: John Lane.

De Valois, Ninette (1962), 'Introduction' to *The Ballet in Britain. Eight Oxford Lectures*, ed. Peter Brinson, 1–8, London: Oxford University Press.

De Valois, Ninette (1977), *Step by Step. The Formation of an Establishment*, London: W.H. Allen.

Dean, Basil (1951), 'Introduction' to *Hassan, An Acting Edition prepared and Introduced by Basil Dean with Commentary and Notes by E.R. Wood*, James Elroy Flecker, xi–xxi. London: Heinemann.

Demastes, William W. and Katherine E. Kelly (1996), *British Playwrights, 1880–1956: A Research and Production Sourcebook*, Westport: Greenwood.

Dent, Edward J. (1946), *A Theatre for Everybody: The Story of The Old Vic and Sadler's Wells*, London: T.V. Boardman & Company.

Devine, Brian (2006), *Yeats, the Master of Sound: An Investigation of the Technical and Aural Achievements of W.B. Yeats*, Gerrards Cross: Colin Smythe.

Dolmetsch, Mabel (1958), *Personal Recollections of Arnold Dolmetsch*, New York: Macmillan.

Bibliography

Donoghue, Denis (1959), *The Third Voice: Modern British and American Verse Drama*, Princeton: Princeton University Press.

Downing, Crystal (2004), *Writing Performances: The Stages of Dorothy L. Sayers*, London: Palgrave.

Drakakis, John (1981), *British Radio Drama*, Cambridge: Cambridge University Press.

Drinkwater, John (1918), *Prose Papers*, London: Elkin Mathews.

Drinkwater, John (1925), *Collected Plays*, vol. 1, London: Sidgwick & Jackson.

Drinkwater, John (1925), 'Preface', ibid., v–xiv.

Drinkwater, John (1925), *The Storm* [1915], ibid., 93–112.

Drinkwater, John ([1927] 1929), *The Gentle Art of Theatre-Going*, London: Ernest Benn.

Drinkwater, John (1932), *Discovery: Being the Second Book of an Autobiography*, London: Ernest Benn.

Dukes, Ashley (1928), *The World to Play With*, London: Oxford University Press.

Dukes, Ashley (1942), *The Scene is Changed*, London: Macmillan.

Duncan, Ronald (1946), *This Way to the Tomb: A Masque and Anti-masque*, London: Faber & Faber.

Duncan, Ronald (1964), *All Men Are Islands: An Autobiography*, London: Rupert Hart-Davis.

Duncan, Ronald (1998), 'Artistic Policy of the English Stage Company', in Krysia Cairns (ed.), *Ronald Duncan: The Man and the Artist*, 114. Plymouth: University of Plymouth Press.

Duncan, Ronald (1968), *How to Make Enemies*, London: Rupert Hart-Davis.

Duncan, Ronald (1971), *Collected Plays*, London: Rupert Hart-Davis.

Duncan, Ronald (1971), 'Introduction', ibid., vii–xiii.

Duncan, Ronald (1977), *Obsessed: A Third Volume of Autobiography*, London: Michael Joseph.

Eliot, T.S. ([1920, 2nd edition 1928] 1960), *The Sacred Wood. Essays on Poetry and Criticism*, London: Methuen.

Eliot, T.S. (6 October 1923), 'The Beating of a Drum', *Nation and Athenaeum*: 12.

Eliot, T.S. (1933), *The Use of Poetry and the Use of Criticism. Studies in the Relation of Criticism to Poetry in England*, London: Faber & Faber.

Eliot, T.S. (October 1934), 'Religious Drama and the Church', *Rep* 1.6: 4–5.

Eliot, T.S. (1934), *The Rock*, London: Faber & Faber.

Eliot, T.S. (1949), *The Aims of Poetic Drama*, The Presidential Address to the Poets' Theatre Guild, London: The Poets' Theatre Guild.

Eliot, T.S. (1951), *Selected Essays*, London: Faber & Faber.

Eliot, T.S. (1951), '"Rhetoric" and Poetic Drama' [1919], ibid., 37–42.

Eliot, T.S. (1951), 'Euripides and Professor Murray' [1920], ibid., 59–64.

Eliot, T.S. (1951), 'Swinburne as Poet' [1920], ibid., 323–7.

Eliot, T.S. (1951), 'Four Elizabethan Dramatists' [1924], ibid., 109–17.

Eliot, T.S. (1951), 'Lancelot Andrewes' [1926], ibid., 341–53.

Eliot, T.S. (1951), 'A Dialogue on Dramatic Poetry' [1928], ibid., 43–58.

Eliot, T.S. (1951), 'John Marston' [1934], ibid., 221–36.

Eliot, T.S. (1958), *T.S. Eliot: The Complete Poems and Plays, 1909–1950*, 74–85, New York: Harcourt, Brace & Co.

Eliot, T.S. (1958), 'The Love Song of J. Alfred Prufrock' [1917], ibid., 3–7.

Eliot, T.S. (1958), *Sweeney Agonistes. Fragments of an Aristophanic Melodrama* [1932], ibid., 74–85.

Eliot, T.S. (1967), *The Complete Plays of T.S. Eliot*. New York: Harcourt, Brace & World, Inc.

Eliot, T.S. (1967), *The Cocktail Party* [1949], ibid., 123–213

Eliot, T.S. (1967), *Murder in the Cathedral* [1935], ibid., 9–54.

Eliot, T.S. (1969), *On Poetry and Poets* [1957], London: Faber.

Eliot, T.S. (1969), 'The Music of Poetry' [1942], ibid., 26–38.

Eliot, T.S. (1969), 'Poetry and Drama' [1951 with additional notes, 1957], ibid., 72–88.

Eliot, T.S. (1969), 'The Three Voices of Poetry' [1953], ibid., 89–102,

Ellehauge, Martin (1931), *Striking Figures Among Modern English Dramatists*, Copenhagen: Levin and Munksgaard.

Ellman, Richard (1979), *Yeats: The Man and the Masks*, Oxford: Oxford University Press.

Evans, Gareth Lloyd (1977), *The Language of Modern Drama*, London: Dent.

Farr, Florence (1909), *The Music of Speech*, London: Elkin Matthews.

Ffoulkes, Richard (2002), '"How fine a play was Mrs Lear": The Case for Gordon Bottomley's *King Lear's Wife*', *Shakespeare Survey* 55: 128–38.

Flecker, James Elroy (1951), *Hassan. An Acting Edition prepared and Introduced by Basil Dean with Commentary and Notes by E.R. Wood*, London: Heinemann.

Flecker, James Elroy (1925), *Don Juan*, London: Heinemann.

Frazier, Adrian (1990), *Behind the Scenes: Yeats, Horniman, and the Struggle for the Abbey Theatre*, Berkeley: University of California Press.

Frost, Peter (1982), 'The Rise and Fall of Stephen Phillips', *English Literature in Transition, 1880–1920* 24.4: 25–231.

Fry, Christopher (1951), 'Poetry and the Theatre', *Adam* 19: 2–10.

Fry, Christopher (March 1955), 'Why Verse?' *Vogue*, 136–7.

Fry, Christopher (February 1961), 'Talking of Henry', *Twentieth Century* 169: 186–9.

Fry, Christopher (2007), *Plays One*, London: Oberon.

Fry, Christopher (2007), *The Lady's Not for Burning* [1948], ibid., 92.

Fry, Christopher (2007), *Plays Two*, London: Oberon.

Fry, Christopher (2007), *Plays Three*, London: Oberon.

Gardner, Philip (1973), *Norman Nicholson*, New York: Twayne.

Gibbs, Phillip (1953), *The New Elizabethans*, London: Hutchinson.

Gibson, Wilfrid (March 1912), 'Some Thoughts on the Future of Poetic-Drama', *The Poetry Review* 3: 119–22.

Gibson, Wilfrid (1924), *Kestrel Edge and Other Plays*. London: Macmillan & Co.

Glover, Halcott (1924), *Drama and Mankind: A Vindication and a Challenge*, Boston: Small, Maynard & Co.

Gowda, H.H. Anniah (1963), *The Revival of English Poetic Drama: In the Edwardian and Georgian Periods*, Bangalore: Government Press.

Bibliography

Granville-Barker, Harley. See Barker, Harley Granville.

Gray, Frances (1982), *John Arden*, London: Macmillan.

Gray, Terence (1926), *Dance-Drama: Experiments in the Art of the Theatre*, Cambridge: W. Heffers & Sons Ltd.

Grimbert, Joan Tasker (2013), 'Introduction' to *Tristan and Isolde: A Casebook*, ed. Joan Tasker Grimbert, xiii–cii, London: Routledge.

Guthrie, Tyrone (1932), *Theatre Prospect*, London: Wishart.

Guthrie, Tyrone (1959), *A Life in the Theatre*, New York: McGraw-Hill.

Gwynn, Frederick L. (1951), *Sturge Moore and the Life of Art*, Lawrence: University of Kansas Press.

Haffenden, John (1991), Interview with Tony Harrison, reprinted in Neil Astley (ed.), *Bloodaxe Critical Anthologies I: Tony Harrison*, 227–46. Newcastle upon Tyne: Bloodaxe.

Harding, Jason, ed. (2011), *T.S. Eliot in Context*, Cambridge: Cambridge University Press.

Harrison, Tony (1991), 'Preface' to *Aikin Mata*, reprinted in Neil Astley (ed.), *Bloodaxe Critical Anthologies I: Tony Harrison*, 84–7, Newcastle upon Tyne: Bloodaxe.

Harrison, Tony (1996), *Plays Three*, London: Faber & Faber.

Harrison, Tony (1996), *The Labours of Herakles* [1995], ibid.

Harrison, Tony (1999), *Plays One*, London: Faber & Faber.

Harrison, Tony (1999), *The Mysteries* [1985], ibid., 9–229.

Harrison, Tony (2002), *Plays Two*, London: Faber & Faber.

Harrison, Tony (2002), *The Misanthrope* [1981], ibid., 1–110.

Harrison, Tony (2002), Introduction to *The Misanthrope*, ibid., 3–24.

Harrison, Tony (2002), *Phaedra Britannica* [1981], ibid., 111–207.

Harrison, Tony (2002), 'Introduction' to *Phaedra Britannica*, ibid., 113–37.

Harrison, Tony (2002), 'Introduction' to *The Prince's Play*, ibid., 211–27.

Harrison, Tony (2002), *Plays Four*, London: Faber & Faber.

Harrison, Tony (2004), *Plays Five*, London: Faber & Faber.

Harrison, Tony (2004), *The Trackers of Oxyrhynchus* [1990], ibid.

Harrison, Tony (2007), *Collected Poems*, London: Penguin, 2007.

Harrison, Tony (2007), 'Them and [uz]', ibid., 133–4.

Harvie, Jen (2005), *Staging the UK*, Manchester: Manchester University Press.

Hassall, Christopher (1959), *Edward Marsh, Patron of the Arts: A Biography*, London: Longmans.

Hatcher, John (1995), *Laurence Binyon: Poet, Scholar of East and West*, Oxford: Clarendon.

Hayman, Ronald (1968), *John Arden*, London: Heinemann.

Hinchcliffe, Arnold P. (1977), *Modern Verse Drama*, London: Methuen.

Hobson, Harold (1984), *Theatre in Britain: A Personal View*, Oxford: Phaidon.

Hoggart, Richard (1991), In Conversation with Tony Harrison, reprinted in Neil Astley (ed.), *Bloodaxe Critical Anthologies I: Tony Harrison*, 36–45, Newcastle upon Tyne: Bloodaxe.

Holdsworth, Nadine, ed. (2002), *John McGrath, Naked Thoughts That Roam About: Reflections on Theatre 1958–2001*. London: Hern.

Housman, Laurence (1902), *Bethlehem, a Nativity Play*, New York: Macmillan.

Housman, Laurence (1931), *Little Plays of St Francis*, First Series, London: Sidgwick & Jackson.

Housman, Laurence (1931), 'Author's Preface', ibid., xvii–xix.

Housman, Laurence (1937), *The Unexpected Years*, London: Jonathan Cape.

Housman, Laurence (1950), *Old Testament Plays*, London: Jonathan Cape.

Housman, Laurence and H. Granville Barker (1906), *Prunella, or Love in a Dutch Garden*. London: A.H. Bullen.

Hunt, Albert (1974), *Arden: A Study of His Plays*, London: Eyre Methuen.

Hurd, Michael (1993), *Rutland Boughton and the Glastonbury Festivals*, Oxford: Clarendon.

Innes, Christopher (1992), *Avant Garde Theatre 1892–1992*, London: Routledge.

Innes, Christopher (2002), *Modern British Drama: The Twentieth Century*, Cambridge: Cambridge University Press.

Irving, Laurence (1951), *Henry Irving: The Actor and his World*, London: Faber & Faber.

Isherwood, Christopher (5 April 1939), 'German Literature in England', *New Republic*, nos. 98–9: 255.

Isherwood, Christopher. See also Auden, W.H.

Jessup, Frances (2009), *Christopher Fry: A Dramatic Reassessment of the Fry-Eliot Era of Verse Drama*, Bethesda: Academica.

Jones, David E. (1965), *The Plays of T.S. Eliot*, Toronto: University of Toronto Press.

Kallman, Chester. See Auden, W.H.

Kaplan, Milton Allen (1949), *Radio and Poetry*, New York: Columbia University Press.

Kelly, Mary (1939), *Village Theatre*, London: Thomas Nelson and Sons.

Kennedy, Dennis (1989), *Granville Barker and the Dream of Theatre*, New York: Cambridge University Press.

Kershaw, Baz (1992), *The Politics of Performance: Radical Theatre as Cultural Intervention*, London: Routledge.

Kruger, Loren (1992), *The National Stage: Theatre and Cultural Legitimation in England, France, and America*, Chicago: University of Chicago Press.

Lacey, Stephen (1995), *British Realist Theatre: The New Wave in its Context 1956–1965*, London: Routledge.

Lall, Chaman (1919), 'Shaw, The Show, and the Shawm, or, What's Wrong With the Theatre?' *Coterie* 3: 74–8.

Lambert, J.W. (1954), 'The Verse Drama', in J.C. Trewin (ed.), *Theatre Programme*, 51–72, London: Frederick Muller.

Leach, Robert (2006), *Theatre Workshop: Joan Littlewood and the Making of Modern British Theatre*, Exeter: University of Exeter Press.

Leach, Robert (2012), *Partners of the Imagination: The Lives, Art and Struggles of John Arden and Margaretta D'Arcy*, Stoney Stanton: Indigo Dreams.

Lee-Browne, Martin and Mark Elder (2014), *Delius and His Music*, London: Boydell & Brewer.

Leeming, Glenda (1974), *John Arden*, Harlow: Longmans.

Bibliography

Leeming, Glenda (1989), *Poetic Drama*, London: Macmillan.

Leeming, Glenda (1990), *Christopher Fry*, Boston: Twayne.

Lhombreaud, Roger (1963), *Arthur Symons: A Critical Biography*, London: Unicorn Press.

Lindop, Grevel (2015), *Charles Williams: The Third Inkling*, Oxford: Oxford University Press.

Little, Ruth, and Emily McLaughlin (2007), *The Royal Court Theatre Inside Out*, London: Oberon.

MacCarthy, Desmond (1907), *The Court Theatre*, London: A.H. Bullen.

MacCarthy, Desmond (1932), *Criticism*, London: Putnam.

McCullough, Christopher (1996), *Theatre and Europe: 1957–96*, Exeter: Intellect.

Manchester Literary Club ([1902] 2013), *Papers Manchester Quarterly, 1902: A Journal of Literature and Art*, vol. 28, London: Forgotten Books.

Marks, Duncan (2014), 'We ARE Amused! The Comical Uses and Historical Abuses of Queen Victoria's Infamous Approach "We are Amused"', in Barbara Korte and Doris Lechner (eds), *History and Humour: British and American Perspectives*, 133–50. Bielefeld: transcript Verlag.

Marsh, Edward, ed. (1912), *Georgian Poetry, 1911–1912*, London: The Poetry Bookshop.

Marsh, Edward, ed. (1915), *Georgian Poetry, 1913–1915*, London: The Poetry Bookshop.

Marsh, Edward, ed. (1917), *Georgian Poetry, 1916–1917*, London: The Poetry Bookshop.

Marsh, Edward, ed. (1919), *Georgian Poetry, 1918–1919*, London: The Poetry Bookshop.

Marsh, Edward, ed. (1922), *Georgian Poetry, 1920–1922*, London: The Poetry Bookshop.

Marshall, Norman (1948), *The Other Theatre*, London: John Lehmann.

Masefield, John ([1909] 1927), *Multitude and Solitude*, London: Jonathan Cape.

Masefield, John (1910), *The Tragedy of Nan and Other Plays*, London: Grant Richards.

Masefield, John (1924), *With the Living Voice: An Address*, Cambridge: Cambridge University Press.

Masefield, John (1925), *Verse Plays*, New York: Macmillan.

Masefield, John (1925), 'Introduction', ibid., v–vi.

Masefield, John (1925), *Philip the King*, ibid., 55–102.

Masefield, John (1925), *A King's Daughter* [1923], ibid., 211–313.

Masefield, John (1927), *Tristan and Isolt. A Play in Verse*, London: William Heinemann.

Masefield, John (1928), *The Coming of Christ*, New York: Macmillan.

Masefield, John ([1932] 1933), *Recent Prose*, New York: Macmillan.

Masefield, John (1933), 'John M. Synge', ibid., 163–87.

Masefield, John (1933), 'On Mr. W.B. Yeats', ibid., 193–8.

Masefield, John (1933), 'Play-Writing', ibid., 105–41.

Masefield, John (1933), 'Shakespeare and Spiritual Life', ibid., 225–56.

Masefield, John (1933), *End and Beginning*, New York: Macmillan.

Masefield, John (1952), *So Long to Learn: Chapters of an Autobiography*, London: William Heinemann.

Medley, Robert (1983), *Drawn from the Life: A Memoir*, London: Faber & Faber.

Mendelson, Edward (1981), *Early Auden*, London: Faber & Faber.

Mendelson, Edward, ed. (1977), *The English Auden: Poems, Essays and Dramatic Writings, 1927-1939*, London: Faber & Faber.

Mendelson, Edward, ed. (1996), *W.H. Auden: Prose and Travel Books in Prose and Verse*, vol. I, Princeton: Princeton University Press.

Mendelson, Edward (1999), *Later Auden*, New York: Farrar, Straus & Giroux.

Mendelson, Edward, ed. (2002), *W.H. Auden: Prose*, vol. II, Princeton: Princeton University Press.

Mendelson, Edward, W.H. Auden and Christopher Isherwood, eds (1988), *Plays and Other Dramatic Writings by W.H. Auden, 1928-1938*, Princeton: Princeton University Press.

Mendelson, Edward, W. H. Auden and Chester Kallman, eds (1993), *Libretti and Other Dramatic Writings by W.H. Auden, 1939-1973*, Princeton: Princeton University Press.

Mitchell, Donald, Philip Reed and Mervyn Cooke eds (2004), *Letters from a Life: The Selected Letters of Benjamin Britten, 1913-1976*, vol. 3: 1946-51, London: Faber & Faber.

Monro, Harold (March 1912), 'Dramatic Poetry and Poetic Drama', *The Poetry Review* 3: 131-2.

Monro, Harold (1920), *Some Contemporary Poets*, London: Simpkin, Marshall.

Morgan, Margery M. (1961), *A Drama of Political Man: A Study in the Plays of Harley Granville Barker*, London: Sidgwick & Jackson.

Morra, Irene (2007), *Twentieth-Century British Authors and the Rise of Opera in Britain*, Aldershot: Ashgate.

Morra, Irene (2016), 'New Elizabethanism: Origins, Legacies, and the Theatre of Nation', in Irene Morra and Rob Gossedge (eds), *The New Elizabethan Age: Nation, Culture and Modernity after World War II*, London: I.B. Tauris, 17-48.

Morra, Irene (2016), 'History Play: People, Pageant and the New Shakespearean Age', ibid., 308-36.

Muir, Kenneth (1962), 'Verse and Prose', in J.R. Brown and Bernard Harris (eds), *Contemporary Theatre*, 96-115, London: Edward Arnold.

Murray, Gilbert (1960), *An Unfinished Autobiography*, eds Jean Smith and Arnold Toynbee, London: George Allen & Unwin.

Nicholson, Norman (1950), *The Old Man of the Mountains*, rev. edition, London: Faber & Faber.

Nicoll, Allardyce (1973), *English Drama, 1900-1930: The Beginnings of the Modern Period, Part 2*, Cambridge: Cambridge University Press.

Noble, Peter (1946), *British Theatre*, London: London British Yearbooks.

O'Brien, Sean (2014), 'The Poet in Theatre: Verse Drama', in Stephen Earnshaw (ed.), *The Handbook of Creative Writing*, 2nd edition, 229-35, Edinburgh: Edinburgh University Press.

Bibliography

Osborne, John (1957), *Look Back in Anger*, London: Faber & Faber.

Page, Malcolm (1984), *John Arden*, Boston: Twayne.

Pater, Walter (1980), *The Renaissance: Studies in Art and Poetry. The 1893 Text*, ed. Donald L. Hill, Berkeley: University of California Press.

Pattie, David (2012), *Modern British Playwriting: The 1950s: Voices, Documents, New Interpretations*, London: Methuen.

Peacock, Keith D. (1991), *Radical Stages: Alternative History in Modern British Drama*, Westport: Greenwood.

Peacock, Ronald (1946), *The Poet in the Theatre*, New York: Harcourt, Brace & Co.

Pearson, Hesketh (1950), *The Last Actor-Managers*, London: Methuen.

Phillips, Helen (1991), 'Gordon Bottomley and the Scottish Noh Play', *English Studies 3: Proceedings of the Third Conference on the Literature of Region and Nation*, part 1, eds J.J. Simon and Alain Sinner, 214–33, Luxembourg: Publications du Centre Universitaire de Luxembourg.

Phillips, Stephen (1901), *Herod: A Tragedy*, London: John Lane.

Phillips, Stephen ([1900] 1902) *Paolo and Francesca. A Tragedy in Four Acts*, 10th edition, London: John Lane.

Pickering, Kenneth (2001), *Drama in the Cathedral: A Twentieth-Century Encounter of Church and Stage*, 2nd edition, Colwall, Worcestershire: J. Garnet Miller.

Plain, Gill (2013), *Literature of the 1940s: War, Postwar and 'Peace'*, Edinburgh: Edinburgh University Press.

Poel, William (1913), *Shakespeare in the Theatre*, London: Sidgwick & Jackson.

Rabey, David Ian (2003), *English Drama Since 1940*, London: Longman.

Rebellato, Dan (1999), *1956 and All That: The Making of Modern British Drama*, London: Routledge.

Reinelt, Janelle (1994), *After Brecht: British Epic Theatre*, Ann Arbor: University of Michigan Press.

Reynolds, Ernest (1950), *Modern English Drama: A Survey of the Theatre from 1900*, Greenwood: Greenwood Press.

Ridler, Anne (1946), *The Shadow Factory: A Nativity Play*, London: Faber & Faber.

Ridler, Anne (1948), 'Introduction' to *Seed of Adam and Other Plays*, by Charles Williams, v–x, London: Oxford University Press.

Ridler, Anne (2004), *Memoirs*, Oxford: The Perpetua Press.

Roberts, Philip (1999), *The Royal Court Theatre and the Modern Stage*, Cambridge: Cambridge University Press.

Roberts, Philip (2008), *About Churchill: The Playwright & the Work*, London: Faber & Faber.

Robinson, Suzanne (2002), 'From Agitprop to Parable: A Prolegomenon to *A Child of Our Time*', in Suzanne Robinson (ed.), *Michael Tippett: Music and Literature*, 78–121, Aldershot: Ashgate.

Ross, Robert H. (1965), *The Georgian Revolt 1910–1922: Rise and Fall of a Poetic Ideal*, Carbondale: Southern Illinois University Press.

Rowell, George (1956), *The Victorian Theatre, 1792–1914: A Survey*, London: Oxford University Press.

Rowse, A.L. (1952), *A New Elizabethan Age?* London: Oxford University Press.

Rusinko, Susan (1989), *British Drama, 1950 to the Present: A Critical History*, Boston: Twayne.

Sayers, Dorothy L. (1937), *The Zeal of Thy House*, London: Victor Gollancz.

Schneider, Elisabeth Wintersteen (1975), *T.S. Eliot: The Pattern in the Carpet*, Berkeley: University of California Press.

Schuchard, Ronald (1978), 'W.B. Yeats and the London Theatre Societies, 1901–1904', *Review of English Studies* 116: 415–46.

Schuchard, Ronald (2008), *The Last Minstrels: Yeats and the Revival of the Bardic Arts*, Oxford: Oxford University Press.

Shaw, George Bernard ([1901] 1909), 'Preface' to *The Admirable Bashville; or, Constancy Unrewarded, Being the Novel of Cashel Byron's Profession Done into a Stage Play in Three acts and in Blank Verse with a Note on Modern Prizefighting*, 5–11, New York: Brentano's.

Shaw, George Bernard (2000), 'Preface' to *Mrs Warren's Profession*, in *Plays Pleasant*, George Bernard Shaw, 181–212, London: Penguin.

Shellard, Dominic (1999), *British Theatre since the War*, New Haven: Yale University Press.

Shepherd, Simon and Peter Womack (1996), *English Drama: A Cultural History*, Oxford: Blackwell.

Shields, Ronald A. (1987), 'Noble Poetry, Nobly Spoken: Marjorie Gullan and the Glasgow Nightingales', *Literature in Performance* 7.2: 34–45.

Shields, Ronald A. (1996), 'Voices inside a Poet's Garden: John Masefield's Theatricals at Boar's Hill', *Text and Performance Quarterly* 16.4: 301–20.

Sidnell, Michael J. (1984), *Dances of Death: The Group Theatre of London in the Thirties*, London: Faber & Faber.

Sierz, Aleks (2001), *In-Yer-Face Theatre: British Drama Today*, London: Faber & Faber.

Sierz, Aleks (2011), *Rewriting the Nation: British Theatre Today*, London: Methuen.

Simon, Myron (1975), *The Georgian Poetic*, Berkeley: University of California Press.

Smith, A.C.H. (1972), *Orghast at Persepolis. An Account of the Experiment in Theatre Directed by Peter Brook and Written by Ted Hughes*, London: Eyre Methuen.

Smith, Carol H. (1963), *T.S. Eliot's Dramatic Theory and Practice. From Sweeney Agonistes to The Elder Statesman*, Princeton: Princeton University Press.

Smith, Constance Babington (1978), *John Masefield: A Life*, New York: Macmillan.

Spanos, William V. (1967), *The Christian Tradition in Modern British Verse Drama: The Poetics of Sacramental Time*, foreword by E. Martin Browne, New Brunswick: Rutgers University Press.

Speaight, Robert (1947), *Drama Since 1939*, London: Longmans Green.

Speaight, Robert (1954), *William Poel and the Elizabethan Revival*, London: William Heinemann.

Speaight, Robert (1960), *The Christian Theatre*, London: Burns and Oates.

Spender, Stephen (1938), *Trial of a Judge. A Tragedy in Five Acts*, London: Faber & Faber.

Speaight, Robert (12 March, 1938), 'Poetry and Expressionism', *New Statesman and Nation* 15.368: 407.

Bibliography

Stanford, Derek (1951), *Christopher Fry: An Appreciation*, London: Peter Nevill.

Stanford, Derek (1954), *Christopher Fry*, rev. ed., London: Longmans.

Stravinsky, Igor (1982), *Selected Correspondence*, vol. 1., ed. and with commentaries Robert Craft, New York: Alfred A. Knopf.

Styan, J.L. (1996), *The English Stage: A History of Drama and Performance*, Cambridge: Cambridge University Press.

Sutton, Graham (1925), *Some Contemporary Dramatists*, Port Washington: Kennikat Press.

Symons, Arthur (1903), *Plays, Acting, and Music*, London: Duckworth.

Symons, Arthur (1906), *Studies in Seven Arts*, London: Archibald Constable & Co.

Symons, Arthur (1924), *Tragedies: Volume One*, London: Martin Secker.

Taylor, John Russell (1969), *Anger and After*, London: Methuen.

Tennyson, Alfred Lord (1875), *Queen Mary. A Drama*, New York: Robert M. De Witt.

Tennyson, Alfred Lord ([1884] 1885), *Becket*. London: Macmillan.

Tennyson, Hallam ([1897] 2012), *Alfred, Lord Tennyson: A Memoir*, Cambridge: Cambridge University Press.

Thouless, Priscilla ([1934] 1968), *Modern Poetic Drama*, New York: Books for Libraries Press.

Tippett, Michael (1959), *Moving into Aquarius*, London: Routledge.

Tippett, Michael (1959), 'The Birth of an Opera', ibid., 47–63.

Tippett, Michael (1980), *Michael Tippett, Music of the Angels: Essays and Sketchbooks of Michael Tippett*, ed. Meirion Bowen, London: Eulenberg.

Tippett, Michael (1980), 'A Child of Our Time: T.S. Eliot and *A Child of Our Time*', ibid., 117–26.

Tippett, Michael (1980), 'Love in Opera', ibid., 210–21.

Tippett, Michael (1991), *Those Twentieth-Century Blues: An Autobiography*, London: Hutchinson.

Tippett, Michael (2002), 'The Relationship of Autobiographical Experience to the Created Work of Art', in *Michael Tippett: Music and Literature*, ed. Suzanne Robinson, 20–34, Aldershot: Ashgate, 2002.

Tippett, Michael (2005), *Selected Letters of Michael Tippett*, Ed. Thomas Schuttenhelm, London: Faber & Faber.

Tolley, A.T. (1975), *The Poetry of the Thirties*, London: Victor Gollancz.

Tolley, A.T. (1985), *The Poetry of the Forties in Britain*, Ottawa: Carleton University Press.

Trewin, J.C. (1956), *Verse Drama Since 1800*, Cambridge: Cambridge University Press for the National Book League.

Trewin, J.C. (1963), *The Birmingham Repertory, 1913–1963*, London: Barrie & Rockliff.

Trewin, J.C. (1965), *Drama in Britain, 1951–1964*, London: Longmans.

Trewin, J.C. (1976), *The Edwardian Theatre*, Oxford: Basil Blackwell.

Trussler, Simon (1973), *John Arden*, New York: Columbia University Press.

Trussler, Simon (1994), *The Cambridge Illustrated History of British Theatre*, Cambridge: Cambridge University Press.

Turner, W.J. (1937), 'Music and Words', *New Statesman and Nation* 14: 146–7.

Turner, W.J. (1938), 'Poets and Musicians', *New Statesman and Nation* 16: 347–8.

Wager, Walter, ed. (1967), *The Playwrights Speak*, London: Longmans, Green.

Wahl, William B. (1973), *A Lone Wolf Howling: The Thematic Content of Ronald Duncan's Plays*, Salzburg: Institut Für Englische Sprache und Literatur.

Wahl, William B. (1973), *Ronald Duncan: Verse Dramatist and Poet Interviewed by William B. Wahl*, Salzburg: Institut Für Englische Sprache und Literatur.

Wahl, William B. (1976), *Poetic Drama Interviews. Robert Speaight, E. Martin Browne and W.H. Auden*, Salzburg: Institut Für Englische Sprache und Literatur.

Wandor, Micheline (2014), *Look Back in Gender (Routledge Revivals): Sexuality and the Family in Post-War British Drama*, London: Routledge.

Weales, Gerald Clifford (1961), *Religion in Modern English Drama*, Philadelphia: University of Pennsylvania Press.

Webster, Augusta (1879), *Disguises; a Drama*, London: C. Kegan Paul.

Webster, Peter (2013), 'George Bell, John Masefield and *The Coming of Christ*: Context and Significance', in Andrew Chandler (ed.), *The Church and Humanity: The Life and Work of George Bell, 1883–1958*, 47–58, Farnham: Ashgate.

Welland, Dennis (1963), 'Some Post-War Experiments in Poetic Drama', in William A. Armstrong (ed.), *Experimental Drama*, 36–55, London: G. Bell & Sons, Ltd.

Wetmore, Kevin J. (2008), '"Avenge me!" Ghosts in English Renaissance and *Kabuki* Revenge Dramas', in Kevin J. Wetmore (ed.), *Revenge Drama in European Renaissance and Japanese Theatre: From Hamlet to Madame Butterfly*, 75–90, New York: Palgrave Macmillan.

Whitehead, Kate (1989), *The Third Programme: A Literary History*, Oxford: Clarendon.

Whittington-Egan, Richard (2006), *Stephen Phillips: A Biography*, High Wycombe: Rivendale Press.

Whitworth, Geoffrey. *The Making of a National Theatre*. London: Faber, 1951.

Wike, Jonathan, ed. (1994), *John Arden and Margaretta D'Arcy: A Casebook*, London: Garland.

Williams, Charles (1936), *Thomas Cranmer of Canterbury*, London: Oxford University Press.

Williams, Charles (1948), *Seed of Adam and Other Plays*. London: Oxford University Press.

Williams, Charles (1948), *Seed of Adam: A Nativity Play* [1936]. ibid., 1–24.

Williams, Charles (1948), synopsis for *Seed of Adam*, written for the programme [1936], reprinted ibid., 93–4.

Williams, Charles (1948), notes for an address delivered after a performance [*Seed of Adam*] at Colchester, October 1937, reprinted ibid., 94–5.

Williams, Charles (1963), *Collected Plays*, London: Oxford University Press.

Williams, Raymond (1971), *Drama from Ibsen to Brecht* [1968], London: Chatto & Windus.

Winkler, Elizabeth Hale (1990), *The Function of Song in Contemporary British Drama*, Newark: University of Delaware Press.

Wood, E.R. (1951), Commentary and Notes to *Hassan, An Acting Edition prepared and Introduced by Basil Dean with Commentary and Notes by E.R. Wood*, by James Elroy Flecker, 89–102. London: Heinemann.

Bibliography

Woodfield, James (2015), *English Theatre in Transition, 1881–1914*, London: Routledge.

Worpole, Ken (1991), 'Scholarship Boy: The Poetry of Tony Harrison', reprinted in Neil Astley (ed.), *Bloodaxe Critical Anthologies I: Tony Harrison*, 61–74, Newcastle upon Tyne: Bloodaxe.

Worth, Katharine J. (1972), *Revolutions in Modern Drama*, London: G. Bell & Sons.

Worthen, W.B. (1992), *Modern Drama and the Rhetoric of Theater*, Berkeley: University of California Press.

Worthen, W.B. (2010), *Drama: Between Poetry and Performance*, Malden: Wiley-Blackwell.

Yeats, W.B. (1923), *Plays and Controversies*, London: Macmillan.

Yeats, W.B. (1989), *Prefaces and Introductions. The Collected Works of W.B. Yeats*, vol. VI, Ed. William H. O'Donnell, New York: Macmillan.

Yeats, W.B. (2001), *The Plays. The Collected Works of W.B. Yeats*, vol. II, eds David R. Clark and Rosalind E. Clark, New York: Scribner.

Yeats, W.B. (2001), 'The First Performance of *At the Hawk's Well*', in ibid., 689–92.

Yeats, W.B. (2003), *The Irish Dramatic Movement. The Collected Works of W.B. Yeats*, vol. VIIII, ed. Mary FitzGerald and Richard J. Finneran, New York: Scribner.

Yeats, W.B. (2003), '*Beltaine*: February 1900 – Plans and Methods', in ibid., 152–5.

Yeats, W.B. (2003), '*Samhain*: 1906 – Literature and the Living Voice', in ibid., 94–107.

Yeats, W.B. (2003), 'A People's Theatre: A Letter to Lady Gregory', in ibid., 124–34.

INDEX

Index

Index

Index